# Deep Mexico
# Silent Mexico

PUBLIC WORLDS

Dilip Gaonkar and Benjamin Lee, Series Editors

C L A U D I O   L O M N I T Z

# Deep Mexico

## Silent Mexico

*An Anthropology*

*of Nationalism*

PUBLIC WORLDS, VOLUME 9

UNIVERSITY OF MINNESOTA PRESS

MINNEAPOLIS   LONDON

Every effort was made to obtain permission to reproduce the illustrations in this book. If any proper acknowledgment has not been made, we encourage copyright holders to notify us.

The University of Minnesota Press gratefully acknowledges permission to reprint the following. An earlier version of chapter 1 appeared as "Nationalism as a Practical System: A Critique of Benedict Anderson's Theory of Nationalism from a Spanish American Perspective," in *The Other Mirror: Grand Theory through the Lens of Latin America,* edited by Miguel Angel Centeno and Fernando López-Alves (Princeton, N.J.: Princeton University Press, 2000), 329–59; copyright 2000 Princeton University Press, reprinted by permission of Princeton University Press. An earlier version of chapter 3 appeared as "Modes of Citizenship in Mexico," *Public Culture* 11, no. 1 (1999): 269–93; copyright 1999 Duke University Press. An earlier version of chapter 4 appeared as "Passion and Banality in Mexican History: The Presidential Persona," in *The Collective and the Public in Latin America: Cultural Identities and Political Order,* edited by Luis Roniger and Tamar Herzog (London: Sussex Academic Press, 2000), 238–56; copyright 2000 Sussex Academic Press. An earlier version of chapter 5 appeared as "Fissures in Contemporary Mexican Nationalism," *Public Culture* 9, no. 1 (1997): 55–68; copyright 1997 Duke University Press. An earlier version of chapter 7 appeared as "Ritual, Rumor, and Corruption in the Constitution of Polity in Mexico," *Journal of Latin American Anthropology* 1, no. 1 (1995): 20–47; copyright 1995 American Anthropological Association, reprinted by permission of American Anthropological Association, Arlington, Virginia. An earlier version of chapter 10 appeared as "An Intellectual's Stock in the Factory of Mexican Ruins: Enrique Krauze's 'Biography of Power,'" *American Journal of Sociology* 103, no. 4 (1998): 1052–65; copyright 1998 by the University of Chicago, all rights reserved.

Published by the University of Minnesota Press
111 Third Avenue South, Suite 290
Minneapolis, MN 55401-2520
http://www.upress.umn.edu

Library of Congress Cataloging-in-Publication Data
Lomnitz-Adler, Claudio.
    Deep Mexico, silent Mexico : an anthropology of nationalism / Claudio Lomnitz.
        p.    cm. — (Public worlds ; v. 9)
    Includes bibliographical references and index.
    ISBN 0-8166-3289-8 (HC : alk. paper) — ISBN 0-8166-3290-1 (PB : alk. paper)
        1. Nationalism—Mexico.   2. Group identity—Mexico.   3. Mexico—Politics
    and government.    4. Anderson, Benedict R. O'G. (Benedict Richard O'Gorman),
    1936– Imagined communities.   5. Intellectuals—Mexico—History.   I. Title.
    II. Series.
        JC311 .L743 2001
        320.972—dc21
                                                                                        2001002740

Printed in the United States of America on acid-free paper
The University of Minnesota is an equal-opportunity educator and employer.

12  11  10  09  08  07  06  05  04  03  02  01        10  9  8  7  6  5  4  3  2  1

*This book is dedicated*

*to the memory of*

*Jorge Simón Lomnitz (1954–93)*

# Contents

*Part III  Knowing the Nation*

# Acknowledgments

To me, this book is like a "cabinet of curiosities," a showcase for a whole extended family of subjects that were first washed upon my shore by the tide of a previous book, *Exits from the Labyrinth*. The essays that I have included here were written between 1993 and 2000, and they were crafted in an environment of intellectual engagement and friendship that is too rich and diverse to acknowledge properly. There are, however, a few ongoing conversations, a few influences and instances of friends coming to my aid that I cannot omit.

Over the past five years I have benefited tremendously from the criticism, example, friendship, and support of my colleagues and students in the departments of History and Anthropology at the University of Chicago. As an anthropologist, I am drawn to the peripheral, to the curiosities and details of human sociability. Friedrich Katz has brought me back to the great current of world events, and in the process has also taught me much of what I know about Mexican history. He has been my closest colleague these past years.

The friendship, conversation, and example of Fernando Escalante, Robin Derby, Roger Bartra, Beatriz Jaguaribe, Néstor García Canclini, Andrew Apter, Eric Fassin, Manuela Carneiro da Cunha, Juan Pérez, Liz Henschell, Marshall Sahlins, Ricardo Pozas, Ilan Semo, Arjun Appadurai, Martin Riesebrodt, Tom Cummins, Francisco Valdés, Fred Myers, Annette Weiner, and Guillermo de la Peña sustained and inspired me more than I can say. Some of the particulars in one or another essay benefited from the advice of Tamar Herzog, Steve Pincus, Carlos Forment, and Cristóbal Aljovín. The late Galo Gómez was the courageous friend who helped me go through with the original publication of chapter 10 in Mexico.

I am especially indebted to Dilip Gaonkar for encouraging me to write this book. The *Public Culture* collective, whose meetings I have attended regularly over the past years, has also inspired me in many ways. The manuscript as a whole gained from the careful and critical engagement of Roger Rouse and Eric Van Young. I am greatly in debt to these exemplary readers.

A number of students who have worked closely with me over the past years have been an influence. I am especially grateful to Ev Meade, Chris Boyer, Dimitra Doukas, Paul Ross, Heather Levy, Daniel Resendez, Matthew Karush, and Katherine Bliss. More generally, I am indebted to the students of the Latin American History Workshop at Chicago. Finally, my editors at Minnesota, Robin Moir, David Thorstad, and, especially, Carrie Mullen, put up with this increasingly grumpy writer and cajoled him into writing a better work.

The essays in this book were also written under a very different influence, a tide that rose and fell with the pull of the dark moon of my brother Jorge's death, and of the glowing delight of my family, and especially of my children, Enrique and Elisa, and my wife, Elena Climent. Conversations with Elena have been formative in the deepest sense, and her work as an artist is a source of constant inspiration.

# Introduction

*The Balcony of the Republic*

There is a class of intellectuals who have the delightful privilege of constantly keeping their readers company—writers who take down their impressions of the significant events of a community and supply it with a steady stream of commentary. The role of these intellectuals is something like that of a village priest, consecrating significant events, offering advice and sympathy, proffering benedictions, and even threatening the unbelievers with excommunication. Their lives are like a book that opens onto their community.

Perhaps because it is, at heart, a Catholic and provincial society, Mexico has always had a special preference for these chroniclers, and they have thrived even in today's mass society. Carlos María Bustamante, Guillermo Prieto, and Ignacio Manuel Altamirano were figures of this sort in the nineteenth century, as was Salvador Novo in the decades following the Mexican Revolution. Currently, writers such as Carlos Monsiváis, Héctor Aguilar Camín, Enrique Krauze, and Elena Poniatowska fall into this category. Even intellectuals who have kept a greater distance from the bustle of the day to day, such as the late Octavio Paz, or Carlos Fuentes, descend from their lofty heights, like bishops going to a confirmation, when it comes to consecrating the truly important events: the 1968 student movement, the earthquake of 1985, or the Zapatista revolt of 1994. The *cronista* accompanies the community, guides it through its dilemmas, consoles it in its grief, and shares in its triumph. Mimesis with the people is such that this intellectual is a natural representative of the nation.

How different this is from my own situation! I left a job at El Colegio de México in 1988 and came to work in the United States not as an exile, but voluntarily. Although I go back to Mexico constantly, and sometimes for long periods, and although I have access to the comings and goings of Mexican politics and its cultural affairs, my position is reminiscent of that of an infirm uncle who keeps to his quarters, and who only makes an occasional appearance.

These confusing feelings of access and isolation, of accompanying the nation's tribulations from afar, reflect the circumstances and conditions in which this book was written. The position of chronicler can only be attained through immersion in the day to day of that great city that is Mexico City, the place that Porfirio Díaz recognized long ago as "the balcony of the republic." In an authoritarian country, public opinion and national sentiment were both concentrated and represented in the national capital. The values of the provinces and foreign values both were realized there, and they were made to radiate from there to the entire nation. My generation is the first in which a few members of Mexico's intelligentsia have chosen to forsake Mexico City for another balcony, which is the American academy.

In the past, Mexican intellectuals used the experiences of Mexicans in the United States as grist for the nationalist mill. As the Mexican-American folklorist José Limón has shown, Mexican intellectuals have decried the conditions of their fellow countrymen in the United States, and used their condition to further political projects in Mexico. What they have rarely done is acknowledge the Mexican-American vantage point as the source of new critical perspectives.[1]

In my years in the United States I have often thought of my experiences in relation to those of Mexican migrant workers, to their ties to home villages and to the ways in which their lives are lived and justified in the United States. I do not mean to make too much of this comparison, as I am not especially interested in Mexican-American identity politics, nor do I seek a new group to represent now that I have "abandoned" Mexico. On the contrary, what I share with many Mexican migrants is their emotional and material investment in Mexico, the sense that the migratory experience can be used for setting past situations right, and the ambivalent realization that the difficulties of the migratory process have changed us. The nature of our investments, the sources of our frustrations on the home front, the specific qualities of our transformations in the United States are different, no doubt. I do not mean to use the hardship of the peasant migrant to make my own cause more noble, nor am I about to raise a class-action suit on their behalf. I cannot speak for them.

I am, rather, interested in the ways in which immigration to the United States offers a critical perspective on Mexico and on the United States. My current position in the American academy and my experience in Mexico afford, I believe, a vista of its own, a vantage point that is mounted neither on the balcony of Mexican public opinion nor on the well-greased machine of American expertise, though it leans on both. My concern is to understand the social conditions in which national distinctions emerge.

## Depth and Silence

It is common knowledge that nationalism involves an appeal to origins. The Frontier Society, the Melding of Two Races, the Chosen People of God, the Children of Revolution—these myths appeal to the historical "depth" of nations, a depth that finds material expression in the land itself. As in Australian aboriginal "dreamings," ties to ancestors are encrusted in the landscape, and contemporaries inhabit the outer surface of that amalgam between a land and a people that is the nation. Stories of origins are required for spreading feelings of kinship in a heterogeneous and unconnected population.

Images of a nation's rootedness are also used to displace or ignore particular claims.[2] In nineteenth-century Spanish America, for instance, national symbols tended to be chosen from nature: the quetzal (bird) of Guatemala, the copihue and araucaria (plants) of Chile, the Argentine pampa, the Popocatepetl and Ixtaccihuatl (mountains) of Mexico, and so on. Alongside the exaltation of the land came the idealization of the remote indigenous past: of unconquerable chieftains such as Caupolicán, Cuauhtémoc, and Túpac Amaru, and indigenous achievements in astronomy, urban design, and engineering. Both natural and historical images were mobilized for the exclusion of the opinions and immediate interests of large portions of the population who, it was felt, needed to be civilized, educated, racially improved, or even, in some cases, exterminated. Appeals to the "depth" of the nation have been a staple in the packaging of modernizing projects, calling potential dissenters to order in the name of a shared trajectory. In national societies, "depth" and "silence" are mutually implicated.

This relationship between depth and silence reveals a national secret, which is that democracy, popular sovereignty, and a rational governmental administration are never fully attainable. The national state is always involved in the work of shaping public opinion with the aid of rigid systems of discipline and exclusion. This is because the connections between the state, the people, and the territory are anything but harmonious and stable. States are shaped in processes of expansion and conquest, or else in processes of decolonization. In either case, diverse peoples, sometimes unrelated to each other, are subjects of the same state.

The movements involved in claiming popular and territorial sovereignty thus require arrangements between peoples who do not necessarily identify with one another, and who may have only tenuous and indirect links. In extreme situations, this can lead to civil war and territorial fragmentation, but even in milder cases the segmentation of "the nation" has profound political and cultural consequences, including the exacerbated use of nationalism. Moreover, the shape of a territory is never perfectly attuned to the traditional habitat of a people, even in cases when such relations between a people and a territory can credibly be made. Territories need to be claimed, boundaries need to be enforced, and so they are dependent not only on the national community, but also on its neighbors. In short, neither a people nor its connections to a state and territory are stable facts. Instead, these relationships need constantly to be shaped and reshaped.

In this, Mexico is not an exception, but rather an extreme. Like all other nations, Mexico came into being as the result of world-historical conditions that were beyond the control of its inhabitants and, although the viability of Mexico as a polity was common sense for locals and foreigners alike at the time of independence, the size of the territory, its lack of economic integration, the diversity of its people, and the desirability of its resources to foreign powers all conspired to make nationality a desired achievement more than a well-established fact.

In the era of independence, national consciousness was uniform neither in its contents nor in its extension. Even as late as 1950, Octavio Paz prefaced his book on Mexican national culture warning that his analysis did not apply to all inhabitants of Mexico, but only to that segment of the population that was conscious of being Mexican, which he saw as a minority.[3] Today it may be difficult to find a Mexican who is not aware of being Mexican, but the contexts in which nationality is pertinent, and its symbolic and practical referents, still vary substantially. Nationality is neither an accomplished fact nor an established essence; it is, rather, the moving horizon that actors point to when they need to appeal to the connections between the people and the polity, when they discuss rights and obligations, or try to justify or reject modernization and social change. National filiation is therefore used in order to hammer out a consensual, or hegemonic, arrangement; it involves cajoling and purchasing, exhibits of strength and coercion. Depth and silence are the Siamese twins of national state formation.

## National Distinction: Theory and History of National Spaces

The national ideal of popular sovereignty can never be fully accomplished. It is instead like a receding horizon, a point of reference that is used to organize relationships between the people and the state in processes of modernization that can never be contained by national borders. As a result, the national space is constantly changing. Isolated communities are integrated into the national public sphere, while newly pauperized classes are marginalized from it; power brokers rise and fall; foreign interests are successfully reigned in and subsequently escape governmental control. In short, the development of a national space is a historical process. Abstract generalization, theorization with no historical referent, is difficult given the current state of our comparative knowledge, and yet theorization is required to make adequate descriptions of that great abstraction that is "national space."[4] A theoretically inclined history is thus useful at this particular junction.

But we need historically sensitive theories just as much. Nations are at once aspects of an international order and the product of local processes of state formation. As a result, their position in the international order itself shapes the ways in which theories are written and understood.[5] There is an inherent tendency for standards to emerge between nations. The culture of the state, the form and contents of its programs and of its organization, are often the brainchild of transnational communities of specialists. However, this does not relieve us from having to understand systems of national distinction in their singularity; for social theories as they are developed and deployed in practice are aspects of this system of distinction too. There is thus a polyphony, a bizarre range of harmonics, in any social explanation or body of theory, because, for the most part, these explanations resonate differently when they are sounded in the scientific or artistic vanguards than when they are brought into national contexts as policy or as social criticism. History thus helps understand the range of theories, as well as their polyphony, slippage, or movement.

Nationalism, which is a way of framing communitarian relations, itself develops in relation to other communitarian forms, including families, villages, and religious communities. The ways in which nationalism relates to these various communities depend on the ways in which the national territory is tied together, economically, politically, and culturally. Moreover, in order to disseminate nationalism, it has to be shaped into signs and told; it has to be tied to sites of local memory in effective ways. Finally, the very uses to which nationalism is put, the projects that it shapes and promotes, the internal distinctions that it facilitates, and its uses in dealing with what is foreign, vary.

This is why students of globalization do not cease to insist on the fact that globalization is not mere homogenization, and that "its" effects are locally differentiated. Nonetheless, making this point in the abstract is much easier than showing it at work—the very persistence of the disclaimer on the part of students of "globalization" attests to this. This is because the study of the conditions in which nations are produced involves a historical sociology of state formation; it cannot bypass the particular.

## Grounded

Mexican social sciences are as much a part of the international horizon as any other science. Mexican authors do not hesitate to borrow from the works of foreign colleagues, and they participate actively in international discussions and publications. There is a sense, however, in which they are entirely encompassed by national history, for the very justification of Mexico's scientific establishment has been tied to national development, to the formation of a national conscience, and to addressing the kind of issues that Andrés Molina Enríquez called "Great National Problems."[6] It is fair to capitalize this expression because it names the fetish of Mexican social science. Social sciences are supposed to respond to Great National Problems, when in fact it is the social sciences that have named and given form to those problems in the collective imagination.

Mexican fetishism of Great National Problems occupies a position analogous to the fetishism of the "Western tradition" and of "Rationality" in the United States. Historians of curricular development in American universities have shown how and why schools in the United States decided to incorporate their own tradition within a narrative of "the West."[7] Universities were designed as neoclassical palaces or else as imitations of the great English universities, an architecture that proclaimed the desire to emulate empire while spurring republican pride, to appropriate the grandeur of both Greece and Britain. The United States has liked to think of itself as the westernmost portion of "the West," a place that inherited all that was reasonable and open-minded of English liberalism, and yet was unfettered by an aristocracy or by a degraded mass of "commoners." Today, in the United States, economics and much of political science and sociology are dominated by theories in which the habits of American consumers, of American voters, and of foreign-policy makers are presented as paragons of rationality. The collective habits of the world's Great Power can be nothing short of "rational." Just as Mexican social scientists have named and shaped Great National Problems, so too have American economists given form to an allegedly universal rationality.

For those who share in this spirit, the historical sciences are quaint and old-fashioned disciplines that are still devoted to the study of the particular. No grand theories of general applicability can come forth from their stubbornly idiographic methods. They can never add up to anything, though they may deserve to be modestly supported, since they can readily provide those tedious facts that are still needed to avoid entirely confusing Bolivia with Brazil.

Consonant with these imperial pulsations, non-Western areas became a special branch of knowledge, subordinated to the universalizing interests of "the West." Thus, the mores and intellectual traditions of Latin America have been called "non-Western," despite the fact that they have as much of a claim to Europe as does the United States. Older or weaker empires, as Arjun Appadurai has pointed out, have been associated with intriguing and vastly simplified characteristics that were useful for sharpening the self-image of the West: the Mediterranean stood for honor and shame, India for caste, China for filial piety and minute women's footwear . . .[8] Latin America provided proud and superstitious men, beautiful señoritas, venal tyrants, and whimsical revolutions.[9] How can widely useful ideas emerge in areas that are dominated by particular complexes of traits that are so clearly bounded in scope and limited in vision? The category of the non-Western is the category of the particular; it is not a suitable place from which to think through either human universals or events of world-historical significance.

In Mexico, narratives that identify the habits of the Mexican people as paradigms of rationality, and therefore as universally applicable, have had little success. The country has been hyperconscious of its backward condition for at least 150 years. Moreover, it has had to deal with a layered history of imperialist depictions: in the nineteenth and early twentieth centuries, Mexicans could not be made into the paragon of rationality because they were racially inferior; later on, the Mexican people were portrayed as traditionalists, as fatalists whose rational capabilities, though no longer biologically deniable, were no less blinded by superstition. Today Mexico is routinely labeled a "developing nation." Because it is allegedly not yet developed, it is not in a position to speak for humanity at large. Not surprisingly, then, Mexican faculties have concentrated on contributions to the resolution of the nation's problems. These need to be dealt with first; universality will come later.

As in the American case, the architecture of Mexico's principal universities reflects these aspirations. Modernism, with its characteristic combination of state-of-the-art technology, abstracted traditional motifs, and the subordination of the whole to modern usage, provided the ideal vehicle. The National University is a paradigmatic instance: research and teaching facilities are laid out in a plan that is reminiscent of pre-Columbian urban design, while the whole was developed with the most modern materials and techniques available.

The definition of the Great National Problems and of their resolution thus involves incorporation to a "civilizational horizon" that transcends Mexico's borders: the language of science and of the arts is recognized as a universal language, and so the process of developing a national conscience or of contributing to national development involves building an infrastructure that is oriented to learning and disseminating works created on the outside.[10] Thus, Mexican modernism takes an inward turn, both because of the effort to translate and appropriate foreign innovations and because of the obsession with making internal conditions more favorable for progress.

Given this self-centeredness, and given the ethnocentrism involved in imperial universalism, it is not surprising that there are considerable difficulties in getting whatever originality there has been in Mexican social and scientific thought recognized as innovative outside of Mexico's borders, because whereas the thinking of American authors is usually inscribed in a universalizing language (even in cases when its significance is parochial), in Mexico contributions that might be of general utility are subsumed into the language of the particular, of the national.

This state of affairs produces an interesting complex regarding the hidden contributions of Mexican culture to universal civilization. Thus, Mexicans sometimes mutter that the inventor of color television was Mexican; that Thomas Edison was half Mexican; that Walt Disney stole characters from Mexican composer Cri-Cri; and that historian Edmundo O'Gorman's ideas concerning the invention of America went unacknowledged by the school devoted to "invented traditions." In short, we have the whole complex that Katherine Verdery described among Romanian intellectuals as "protochronism," that is to say the doctrine that struggles to rescue a series of national figures who had prefigured well-known "Western" developments from an imperial conspiracy that has confined them to oblivion.[11]

The conditions for protochronism are produced by asymmetries of power between the scientific establishments of Mexico and Europe or the United States. However, they are also the result of the way in which Mexico's knowledge establishment has been justified. In order to engage public interest in Mexico, in order to attract funds, and so on, one must engage the Great National Problems. This means that thinkers who recycle works and ideas produced abroad and apply them to the national conscience can enjoy an undeserved (though entirely local) reputation, and it also means that thinkers who have had a contribution to make to the broader civilizational horizon can go underacknowledged, especially when the country does not have the capacity to absorb the work to its full potential.

I have myself worked for many years under the strain of these tensions, desiring to contribute to the discussion of Mexico's particular problems, while holding to the conviction that any real engagement with particularity requires a degree of critical thought, a kind of thought that knows no national frontiers. My work has therefore tended to inhabit a margin: a bit too theoretically inclined for most Mexican social scientists, a bit too engaged with Mexican political quandaries for most of my American colleagues. However, this situation, which is not so very singular, also affords, I think, a certain kind of engaged critique, a kind of theoretical particularism that is well suited to the study of the national form. It is a form of "grounded theory" in both senses of this term: grounded because it works through a vast and dense set of facts, and grounded because it has to confront, and hopefully to transgress, an order of confinement.

*Road Map*

This is a book of essays. It came to life as a volume when my friend and colleague Guillermo de la Peña suggested that I publish a volume in Mexico with a collection of essays that had appeared only in English. I followed Guillermo's advice and put together a volume that appeared in 1999 under the title *Modernidad indiana: nación y mediación en México*. As I prepared that work, however, I realized that my general project of these last years, which has been to develop a historical sociology of Mexican national space, was not far from completion and I spent an additional eighteen months writing the essays that were required. This book reproduces five of the nine essays included in *Modernidad indiana* (the earliest was written in 1993), and adds to them seven newer essays that mark the end of a long project (the last was completed in the first months of 2000).

The book is divided into three parts. Part I, "Making the Nation," is composed of five essays. Taken together, these chapters provide a historical and theoretical framework for understanding Mexican nationalism and national identity as a process that began with colonization. The essays in this section generally take a very historical broad sweep.

Chapter 1 is a critical appraisal of Benedict Anderson's theory of nationalism, written from the vantage point of Spanish America. I show that the relationship between nationalism, secularism, and social hierarchy diverges somewhat from Anderson's proposition. This leads both to amendments to Anderson's theory and to a discussion of the political usage of nationalism in Mexico and Spanish America. Chapter 2 extends the discussion of communitarian ideologies initiated in the discussion of Benedict Anderson by exploring competing versions of Mexican nationalism, and also other historically powerful communitarian forms that are pertinent for understanding the appeal and limits of any nationalist project in Mexico. Both chapters are wide-ranging historical essays that explore the *longue durée.*

Chapter 3, by contrast, focuses on the transformation of Mexican citizenship during the nineteenth and early twentieth centuries. Here I seek to historicize Roberto DaMatta's ideas regarding the cultural logic of hierarchy and citizenship in Latin America. As in the essay on Benedict Anderson's theory, I complement a cultural reading (in this case of citizenship) with an emphasis on the political field in which the cultural construction of citizenship develops. In the process, I argue against the view that imagines the development of citizenship and democracy in Mexico as a process that had an early and very brief golden age during the Restored Republic (1867–76), only to fall during the *porfiriato* (especially after 1884), and then to begin a heroic recovery in the aftermath of 1968. I show that the prominence of discourses of citizenship and of civic virtue in the first two-thirds of the nineteenth century is related to the political instability of the country, and that the exalted language of citizenship that was popular in this period declined not so much as a result of dictatorial repression as because of the alliances among the political class that modernization and economic growth made possible. The history of Mexican democratization thus appears in a somewhat less heroic light than in the triumphal narratives of contemporary democrats.

Chapter 4 complements the discussion of the political consolidation of the Mexican state by focusing on the development of the image of the national president as a fetish of sovereignty. In particular, this essay explores the relationship between religion, race, and images of sovereignty, and it shows the ways in which power was secularized, and the law and economic modernization were indigenized during the nineteenth century and into the Mexican Revolution (1910–20).

The final chapter of Part I is devoted to the contemporary crisis of Mexican nationalism, and it can be read as an alternative introduction to this book (as a complement to this Introduction). In the last two decades, innovations in the organization of transnational capital have provoked profound changes in Mexico, changes that include a reorientation of the national economy, the dismemberment of the revolutionary state, and increasing class polarization. As a result, there is a chronic crisis concerning the relationship between nationalism and modernization. This essay explores this changing relationship and discusses the strain on Mexican nationalism in the contemporary moment. It thus spells out the context in which the essays of this book were written, which is the long period known as Mexico's "transition to democracy."

Commentators such as Paul Krugman of the *New York Times* have crowed that the historic Mexican election of July 2, 2000, should be chalked up to the North American Free Trade Agreement (NAFTA) and globalization, and that the neoliberal presidents who presided over this transition (de la Madrid, Salinas, and Zedillo) were in fact the well-meaning democrats that they always claimed to be.[12] However, it was Mexican authoritarianism, not Mexican democracy, that led Mexico into the General Agreement on Tariffs and Trade (GATT) and NAFTA in the first place. The full power of Mexico's revolutionary state was needed to preside over the sea change in the economy that finally buried revolutionary nationalism, which is why the transition to democracy was so protracted. Now that the change in economic models was an accomplished fact, Mexicans were allowed to choose their president freely from among three candidates who had strikingly similar platforms, and the economists who imposed their models on Mexico could claim to have given birth to democracy.[13]

Part II, "Geographies of the Public Sphere," is dedicated to the cultural geography of the national space, and it is composed of three chapters. The first, Chapter 6, deals with the contexts in which national identity and xenophobia emerge. It introduces one of the central motifs of Mexican nationalism, which is that the nation cannot contain capitalism and economic modernization, much of which comes from abroad. The chapter proposes a rudimentary topography of "contact zones" in which national identity emerges as a significant political resource.

Chapter 7 argues that ritual, rumor, and corruption have historically been the critical mechanisms for the constitution of national public opinion in Mexico. This is because class divisions are so significant that broad sectors of the population are systematically excluded from the bourgeois public sphere. The chapter then develops elements of a spatial approach to the study of the public sphere.

Chapter 8 is about "centrality" and "marginality." Instead of seeing these categories as stable properties of places, they are best understood as metaphors that are used for the development of internal idioms of distinction that are then deployed to link fractions of communities across the national space. This essay, like chapter 12, uses the case of the anthropologically famous village of Tepoztlán to develop a perspective on this matter. As a locality, Tepoztlán has usually been constructed by outsiders and government officials as "peripheral," but local inhabitants have deployed within their town the same binary oppositions that they have been subjected to. The essay explores the politics of these juxtapositions. Thus, the three chapters of Part II study, first, the geography of national identity production, second, the cultural geography of the public sphere, and finally, the geography of national distinction.

Part III, "Knowing the Nation," is about the different ways of producing public knowledge within and about the nation. Chapter 9 uses Michel Foucault's concept of governmentality to argue that, because of the tribulations of Mexico's development as a weak nation in the international order, intellectuals who sought to speak for the nation on the basis of statistics and population studies have had limited success. Alongside these "governmental intellectuals," national sentiment has been expressed by others, who claim to be close to social movements and revolutions.

Chapter 10 is a polemical essay on the effects of the current privatization of culture, by way of a critique of the work of Enrique Krauze. This essay, originally published in English in 1998, generated a heated polemic in Mexico. I have included the piece in this volume despite its polemical character for two reasons: first, because it deals with the role of history and historians as nation builders and as nationalist intellectuals and is thus of a piece with the preceding chapter on the interpretation of the sentiments of the nation and with my work on the history of anthropology; and second, because this is an instance in which analysis and politics come together—both the writing of the essay and the reactions that it generated in Mexico are related to the "balcony" from which it was written.

Chapter 11 complements this polemical piece by analyzing the historical role of anthropology in shaping Mexican nationalism and, conversely, the role that nationalism has had in shaping Mexican anthropology. It is written as a scholarly piece, whereas the preceding chapter is written as a polemical review, but both develop aspects of the same argument regarding the preponderant role that nationalism has played in shaping Mexican social thought.

The final chapter of the book is a critique of Guillermo Bonfil's notion of a "deep Mexico," a concept that I substitute with a "silent Mexico." The chapter proposes a geography of silence by way of the study of local intellectuals. I show that the mechanisms that intellectuals use to justify their authority to represent their communities provide valuable clues for understanding the geography of Mexican democracy, a geography that is deeply segmented along class and regional lines.

Taken together, the twelve chapters in this book are a historical and theoretical exploration of Mexican national space, by way of an analysis of nationalism, the public sphere, and knowledge production. They are offered both as cultural criticism and as a scholarly contribution to our understanding of these phenomena.

# PART I

## Making the

## Nation

# 1

## Nationalism as a Practical System: Benedict Anderson's Theory of Nationalism from the Vantage Point of Spanish America

Benedict Anderson's *Imagined Communities* has probably been the single most influential work on nationalism of the past two decades. Written with clarity and flair, Anderson's book explains nationalism as a specific form of communitarianism whose cultural conditions of possibility were determined by the development of communications media (print capitalism) and colonial statecraft (especially state ritual and state ethnography—for instance, bureaucratic "pilgrimages," censuses, and maps).

Seen in this light, nationalisms are historically recent creations, and yet terribly successful at shaping subjectivity. In fact, it is nationalism's power to form subjects that truly arrests Anderson's attention: "[patriotic deaths] bring us abruptly face to face with the central problem posed by nationalism: what makes the shrunken imaginings of recent history (scarcely more than two centuries) generate such colossal sacrifices?" (1994; 7). This concern with subject-formation and identity is consonant with Anderson's principal innovation, which is to treat nationalism not as an ideology, but rather as a hegemonic, commonsensical, and tacitly shared cultural construct.

For Anderson, nationalism is a kind of cultural successor to the universalism of premodern (European) religion. Thus, although he locates the birth of nationalism in the late eighteenth and early nineteenth centuries, the preconditions for its emergence occur much earlier, with Europe's expansion in the sixteenth century. In Anderson's view, European expansion created the image of plural and independent lines of civilizational development, and this pluralism or relativism was eventually transformed into a kind of secular historicism in which individuated collectivities—"nations"—competed with each other.

One of the most surprising turns in Anderson's brief book is that he claims that nationalism developed first in the colonial world, and spread from there back to Europe. Despite the fact that religious universalism is first shaken in sixteenth-century Europe, the formation of a system of equal, independent, secular, and progressive collectivities occurs first in America, and almost three centuries after the decline of religious universalism. This move caught Latin Americanist historians off balance, for the historiography of independence up to then was dominated by treatises on the intellectual influences of Europe—of liberalism, of the Enlightenment—on American independence. Rarely did the Latin American specialist dare to claim much originality for these movements, let alone to suggest that nationalism itself had been invented in Spanish America and subsequently exported to Europe.

For his insistence on the singularity of colonial conditions alone, Latin Americanists are collectively in Anderson's debt. However, despite this boon to a profession that often aches to claim singularity for itself, developments in the Latin American field were slow to turn in Anderson's direction, with significant works using Anderson as a point of inspiration appearing practically ten years after the book was first published.

The slothful reaction to Anderson by Latin American historians and anthropologists has been owing not only to the usual reaction of the subfield's antibodies against brash foreign intruders who do not respect the regnant doxa. It is also the result of considerable difficulty in grappling with the relationship between the book's general thesis on nationalism (which is often inspiring) and the fact that Anderson's view of American independence is incorrect in a number of particulars.

My aim in this chapter is to carry out a comprehensive critique of *Imagined Communities*, by which I mean a critique that interrogates both the conceptual and the historical theses. I shall do so by way of a close study of nationalism in the Spanish-American republics, and in Mexico particularly. Because this area is, according to Anderson's formulation, the birthplace of modern nationalism, it is a key to his general thesis. On the other hand, the fertility of Anderson's masterful book is such that criticizing its central thesis requires developing an alternative perspective, the seeds of which are also presented here.

*Review of the Historical Thesis*

In order to understand Anderson's account of the birth of Spanish-American nationalism and independence, we must be clear first on what exactly he is trying to explain:

> [T]he aggressiveness of Madrid and the spirit of liberalism, while central to any understanding of the impulse of resistance in the Spanish Americas, do not in themselves explain why entities like Chile, Venezuela, and Mexico turned out to be emotionally plausible and politically viable, nor why San Martín should decree that certain aborigines be identified by the neological "Peruvians." Nor, ultimately, do they account for the real sacrifices made. . . . This willingness to sacrifice on the part of comfortable classes is food for thought. (52)

At stake, then, is the explanation of what makes a country "emotionally plausible" and "politically viable" from an internal perspective. In addition, there are issues concerning identity and sacrifice: why do Indians become Peruvians, and why do privileged Creoles lay their lives down for national independence? Anderson's explanation of why this is so proceeds along three separate lines.

First, in Spanish America, colonial administrative practices divided Creoles from Peninsulars by reserving the highest offices of the empire for the latter, thereby fostering a sense of resentment and identity among the former. Second, the fact that Creole bureaucrats were constrained to serve only in their administrative units of origin meant that they collectively shared an image of these provinces as their political territory. The bureaucratic pilgrimage through colonial administrative space allowed for the conflation of Creole national identity with a specific *patria*, or fatherland.

Anderson recognizes, however, that these two factors were present before the rise of Spanish-American nationalisms at the end of the eighteenth century, and he feels that they were insufficient to produce true nationalism. The third, and indispensable, factor was the rise of print capitalism and, especially, of newspapers. These papers allowed for the formation of an idea of "empty time" that was to be occupied by the secular process of development between parallel and competing nations:

> [W]e have seen that the very conception of the newspaper implies the refraction of even "world events" into a specific imagined world of vernacular readers; and also how important to that imagined community is an idea of steady, solid simultaneity through time. Such a simultaneity the immense stretch of the Spanish-American Empire, and the isolation of its

component parts, made difficult to imagine. Mexican creoles might learn months later of developments in Buenos Aires, but it would be through Mexican newspapers, not those of the Rio de la Plata; and the event would appear as "similar to" rather than "part of" events in Mexico.

In this sense, the "failure" of the Spanish American experience to generate a permanent Spanish-America-wide nationalism reflects the general level of development of capitalism and technology in the late eighteenth century and the "local" backwardness of Spanish capitalism and technology in relation to the administrative stretch of the empire. (63)

Thus, because they emerge so early, Spanish-American nationalisms exhibit an oddity, which is that linguistic identification does not coincide with the territorial consciousness of Creole bureaucrats and newspaper readers, thus allowing for the emergence of both a series of individual nationalisms and for Pan-Spanish-American quasi-national identity. In most later (European and Asian) cases, linguistic identity would play a more central and defining role:

What the eye is to the lover—that particular, ordinary eye he or she is born with—language—whatever language history has made his or her mother-tongue—is to the patriot. Through that language, encountered at mother's knee and parted with only at the grave, pasts are restored, fellowships are imagined, and futures dreamed. (154)[1]

In short, Anderson explains the rise of Spanish-American nationalisms (Chilean, Peruvian, Bolivian) as the result of (a) a general distinction between Creoles and Peninsulars, (b) a Creole political-territorial imaginary that was shaped by the provincial character of the careers of Creole officialdom, and (c) a consciousness of national specificity that was shaped by newspapers that were at once provincial and conscious of parallel states. Once these early Creole nationalisms succeeded in forging sovereign states, they became models for other nations.[2]

## Definitions

In order to decide whether this theory of the rise of nationalism is an acceptable account, we need to understand precisely what Anderson means by *nationalism*, and whether his definition corresponds in a useful way to the historical phenomena that are being explained.

For Anderson, the nation "is an imagined political community—and imagined as both inherently limited and sovereign" (6). "Nationalism" is the adherence to and identification with such a community. Although the emphasis on the "imaginary" quality of national communities is redundant—all communities are imaginary constructs—Anderson's emphasis on nationalism's imaginary quality is meant to signal that nations are not face-to-face communities, and therefore involve a characteristic form of abstraction.[3] The imaginary quality of the national community is also underlined for a political purpose, for Anderson is critical of nationalism and so is intent on showing its historical contingency and its "invented" nature.

Understanding the "community" half of Anderson's definition is, perhaps, not as simple a matter, because community has a specific and limited connotation for the author: "[the nation] is imagined as community because, regardless of the actual inequality and exploitation that may prevail in each, the nation is always conceived as a deep comradeship. Ultimately it is this *fraternity* that makes it possible, over the past two centuries, for so many millions of people, not so much to kill, as willingly to die for such limited meanings" (7; my emphasis).

This association between nationalism and sacrifice is consonant with Anderson's guiding preoccupation at the time he wrote this book, which was the troubling fact that socialist countries were fighting nationalist wars, showing that nationalism could provide a kind of comradery that ran deeper than the solidarities of shared class interest. This led Anderson to investigate nationalism's secret potency, its capacity to generate personal sacrifice. Correspondingly, the question of sacrifice is, for Anderson, the telltale sign of nationalism, a fact that leads him to view nationalism as a substitute for religious community. Let us pause to consider this definition before moving on to Anderson's historical thesis on the genesis of nationalism.

The first difficulty that must be faced is that Anderson's definition of nation does not always coincide with the historical usage of the term, even in the place and time that Anderson identifies as the site of its invention (i.e., Spanish America, ca. 1760–1830; Anderson 1994, 65).

The subtleties in the usage of the term *nación* can perhaps be introduced through an example. In 1784, Don Joaquín Velásquez de León, director of Mexico City's School of Mining, writes in *La Gazeta de México* that

> I said in my letter of the year 71 that the Machine that is called of fire was easy to use and to conserve; but one year later, that is in 72; the Excellent mister Don Jorge Juan, *honor and ornament of our Nation* in all sciences and mathematics, devoted himself to building that Machine in the Royal Seminary of Nobles of Madrid. (September 8, p. 13; my emphasis)

In this instance, Velásquez, who is writing to a predominantly Creole audience in the context of a debate with Father J. Antonio Alzate, a famous Creole scientist and protonationalist, writes of Jorge Juan that he is "an honor to our nation." The ambiguity of this formulation helps us understand the process of transformation that the semantic field of the term *nation* was undergoing.

In the early eighteenth century, *nación* was defined *strictu sensu* as "the collection of inhabitants of a province, country, or kingdom."[4] This definition is already quite ambiguous. New Spain, for example, was a province (or several provinces), a country (or several countries), and a kingdom, just as Castile was a kingdom that encompassed several provinces and countries. Thus, returning to our example, the Castilian scientist Jorge Juan might not be of the same *nación* as most of the readers of the *Gazeta de Mexico*. However, two further ambiguities in fact make this identification possible.

First, the term *nacional* referred to "that which is characteristic of or originates from a nation." Thus, Mexican Creoles could be of the Spanish nation because they had their roots in Spain, were characteristic (*propios*) of Spain, and so on.

A second ambiguity of the semantic field of *nación* stems from the movement of administrative reforms that Spain's enlightened despots set in motion around the middle of the eighteenth century (the "Bourbon Reforms"). Among other things, there was a concerted effort to streamline the territorial organization of the empire, doing away with the idea of the Spanish Empire as being composed of a series of kingdoms and substituting this notion with that of a unified empire.

Thus, from the viewpoint of Spain's colonies of the late eighteenth century, the term *nación* could be used to pit *peninsulares* against Americans, as Anderson has suggested. However, it could also be used to emphasize the extension of national identity by way of lines of descent and thus be made into a synonym of *blood* or *caste* and thereby provide a rationale for internal divisions within colonial societies. Finally, the concept of *nación* could be used as a sign of panimperial identity.

Moreover, if the referent of the term *nación* was ambiguous with respect to its connection to territory and to bloodlines, it also had complex connections to sovereignty, and this was particularly so in the Americas. So, for instance, if someone took the "bloodline" definition of *nación*, they might point to the varying *fueros* (inviolable legal privileges) attached to the Spanish and Indian republics as separate estates. If, on the other hand, they identified *nación* with a kingdom or province, they could cite the *fueros* enjoyed by its nobility and its citizens. It is important to note that in both of these cases, sovereignty is not absolute or popular sovereignty, but rather a limited form of sovereignty comparable to that of *pater potestas* or to arenas of individual sovereignty granted by the doctrine of free will.[5]

Thus, whereas Anderson's definition of nationhood involves a sense of the sovereignty of a state over a territory, the Spanish definition vacillated between an increasingly unified but nonetheless ambiguous territorial definition and a definition around descent. Both of these forms involved specific *fueros*, in other words, access to limited forms of sovereignty.

It is pertinent to note that this notion survived the American independence movements, for example, in the usage of the term *Indian nations* to refer to nomadic tribes in northern Mexico, or in the ambiguous referents of the term *república*.[6]

Because of the ambiguity in the ties between *nation* and *blood*, Spanish usage of the term *nación* could be distinguished from a second term, *patria* (or fatherland), in such a way that a single land could be the *patria* of more than one *nación*. This was, indeed, the case in most of the Americas, which were conceived as plurinational *patrias*. This tense coexistence between a discourse of loyalty to the land and one of filiation through descent is visible in colonial political symbolism.[7] Common loyalty to the land was a concept that was available in Spanish political discourse at least since the sixteenth century but it was nonetheless not directly assimilable to the notion of "nation." This ambiguity is at the basis of the category of "Creole" itself, which, as a number of historians have shown, emerged in the mid-sixteenth century, but maintained an ambiguous relationship to Spanishness throughout the colonial period.[8]

The move to associate nation with common subjection to the king was promoted by Charles III, who sought to diminish differences of caste in favor of a broad and homogenized category of "subjects." Thus a tendential identification between *nation* and *sovereignty* was being built up by absolutist monarchs, a fact that makes San Martín's dictum that so claimed Anderson's attention ("in the future the aborigines shall not be called Indians or natives; they are children and citizens of Peru and they shall be known as Peruvians" [Anderson 1994: 49–50]) less of a Creole invention than Anderson supposed.[9]

A second significant problem for applying Anderson's definition to the Latin American case is that belonging to an imagined national community does not necessarily imply "deep horizontal comradery." The idea of nation was originally tied to that of lineage; members of a nation could be linked by vertical ties of loyalty as much as by horizontal ties of equality.

This is most obviously relevant when considering the way in which age and sex enter the picture of national identity. Women and children could and can very much identify with their nations even though they are usually not their nation's representative subjects. Similarly, a master and a servant could be part of the same nation without having to construct this tie as a horizontal link based on fraternity.[10]

This is a fundamental point for Spanish-American nationalism in the nineteenth century, when corporations such as indigenous communities, haciendas, and guilds were even more salient than they are today. Nonetheless, the point also has broader significance. Jürgen Habermas (1991) pointed out that the bourgeois public sphere in eighteenth century northern Europe (which was tied inextricably to the development of nationalism) was made up ideally of private citizens. Nonetheless, the citizen's "private sphere" encompassed his family, making the citizen at once an equal to other citizens (Anderson's "fraternal bond") and the head of a household in which he might be the only full citizen. It would be a mistake, however, to presuppose that nationalism was embraced only by the citizen and not by his wife and children.

In more general terms, the horizontal relationship of comradery that Anderson wants to make the exclusive trait of the national community occurred in societies with corporations, and the symbolism of encompassment between citizens and these corporations is critical to understanding the nation's capacity to generate personal sacrifices. Nationalists have fought battles to protect "their" women, to gain land for "their" villages, to defend "their" towns. It is just as true, however, that women, servants, family members, and, more generally, the members of corporate communities or republics could send "their" citizens to war. In other words, citizens could represent various corporate bodies to the state, and they could represent the power of the state in these corporate bodies.

In Spanish America the complexities of these relationships of encompassment (between the national state, citizen, and various corporations) have been widely recognized in analyses of conflicts between various liberal and conservative factions in the nineteenth century, and in the role of local communities in the wars of independence themselves.[11] The relationship between the modern ideal of sovereignty and citizenship and the legitimate claims of the corporations is indeed a central theme in nineteenth and twentieth-century Latin American history.

The third, and final, difficulty with Anderson's definition of nationalism is his insistence on sacrifice as its quintessential symptom. The image of nationalism as causing a lemming-like impulse to sacrifice because of its appeal to community is as misleading as the idea that nationalism is necessarily a communal ideology of "deep horizontal comradery"; for, in order to comprehend what nationalism is and has been about, one must place it in its context of use. The capacity to generate personal sacrifice in the name of the nation is usually not a simple function of communitarian imaginings of comradery. Ideological appeals to nationhood are most often coupled with the coercive, moral, or economic force of other social relationships, including the appeal to the defense of hearth and home, or the economic or coercive pressure of a local community, or the coercive apparatus of the state itself.

Moreover, there are plenty of examples of nationalism spreading mostly as a currency that allows a local community or subject to interpellate a state office in order to make claims based on rights of citizenship.[12] It is misleading to privilege sacrifice in the study of nationalism, because the spread of this ideology is more often associated with the formulation of various sorts of claims vis-à-vis the state or toward actors from other communities.

In sum, I have raised three objections to Anderson's definition of nation and nationalism: first, the definition does not always correspond to historical usage; second, Anderson's emphasis on horizontal comradery covers only certain aspects of nationalism, ignoring the fact that nationalism always involves articulating discourses of fraternity with hierarchical relationships, a fact that allows for the formulation of different kinds of national imaginaries; third, Anderson makes sacrifice appear as a consequence of the national communitarian imagining, when it is most often the result of the subject's position in a web of relationships, some of which are characterized by coercion, while others have a moral appeal that is not directly that of nationalism.

## Toward an Alternative Perspective

In one of his most brilliant moments, Anderson suggests that nationalism should not be analyzed as a species of "ideology" but rather as a cultural construct that has affinity with "kinship" or "religion" (1994, 5). Anderson's selection of "deep horizontal comradery" as the defining element of nationalism is his attempt to give meaning to this proposition. The essence of nationalism for Anderson is that it provides an idiom of identity and brotherhood around a progressive polity ("the nation"). Following Victor Turner, Anderson looks for the production of this fraternity in moments of *communitas* such as state pilgrimages. He also explores the conditions of possibility of national identity, arguing that nationalism depends on a secular understanding of time as "empty" and of the world as being made up of nations whose progress unfolds simultaneously and differentially through this empty time.

Thus, for Anderson, the compelling aspect of nationalism is its promise of fraternity, and this is, I believe, the most fundamental problem of the definition.

I suggested earlier that nationalism is an idiom that articulates citizens to a number of communities, ranging from family, to corporate groups, to villages and towns, to the national state. The connections between these communities are often themselves the substance of nationalist discourse and struggle. It follows that the imagery that is used to build national sentiment cannot so readily be reduced to the brotherhood among citizens.

In order to define the nature of nationalist imaginings, we must ask questions such as: When and how is nationalism invoked in a man's relationship with his wife? How is it deployed in the dealings between a small-town schoolteacher and his villagers, or between an Indian cacique and a president? For, in all of these cases, the ideology of fraternity invoked by Anderson is being used to articulate hierarchies into the polity. The protection of the nation then becomes the protection of the family, or of the village, or of the race.

My first amendment to Anderson's theory is thus that nationalism does not ideologically form a single fraternal community, because it systematically distinguishes full citizens from part citizens or strong citizens from weak ones (e.g., children, women, Indians, the ignorant). Because these distinctions are by nature heterogeneous, we cannot conclude that nationalism's power stems primarily from the fraternal bond that it promises to all citizens. The fraternal bond is critical, but so are what one might call the *bonds of dependence* that are intrinsically a part of any nationalism.

This leads to a second, though minor and derivative, amendment. The pride of place that Anderson gives to sacrifice in his view of nationalism is misleading, for if we accept that the national community is not strictly about equality and fraternity, but rather about an idiom for articulating ties of dependence to the state through citizenship (fraternity), then the defense of the fraternal bond becomes one possible symptom of nationalism among several others.

In other words, the power of nationalism is as evident in the gesture of a *Niño héroe* who wraps himself in the flag and dies for his country as it is in the gesture of the peasant who invokes his citizenship when petitioning for land, or the small-town notable who claims that his villagers and himself descend from Aztec ancestors when he petitions for a school. In fact, nationalism can even be deployed by a peasant who resists induction into the army. Finally, the very nature of patriotic sacrifice is easily misconstrued if we do not pay close attention to the bonds of dependence that are central to the national community—for citizens enlisted to go die in World War I not only because of their fraternal ties with other volunteers or conscripts, but also because their families might reject them if they did not, or their communities might reject their families, and so on.

In short, instead of saying, as Anderson does, that the nation is a community "because, regardless of the actual inequality and exploitation that may prevail in each, the nation is always conceived as a deep comradeship," I define the nation as a community that is conceived of as deep comradeship among full citizens, each of whom is a potential broker between the national state and weak, embryonic, or part citizens whom he or she can construe as dependents.

This brings us to a final question concerning the concept of nationalism, which regards the relationship between the analytic definition of nationalism and actual usage of the terms *nation* or *nationalism*. Although my revised definition would still exclude any form of ethnic identification that did not strive for some degree of political sovereignty, I believe that it has a greater capacity to include and distinguish between historical varieties of nationalism. For instance, the ambiguity between a racial and a political-territorial definition of *nación* that I cited earlier for the late-eighteenth-century Spanish world is a reflection of a specific moment in nation building that should not simply be called "prenational," because it involves a territorially finite state and a sovereign people, even though it tolerated significant differences between stations and even estates. Similarly, the peasant who has never seen a map or aided a census taker, and who has no notion of why, say, "Germany" and "Guadalajara" are incommensurate categories, can still be a nationalist because he makes an appeal as a Mexican, or because he comes home to his wife late and drunk on the night of September 15 (Mexican Independence Day).

### Revised General Historical Thesis

The fundamental thing about nationalism is that it is a productive discourse that allows subjects to rework various connections between social institutions, including, prominently, the relationship between state institutions and other social organizational forms. As such, the power of nationalism lies not so much in its hold on the souls of individuals (though this is not insignificant) as in the fact that it provides interactive frames in which the relationship between state institutions and various and diverse social relationships (family relationships, the organization of work, the definition of forms of property, and the regulation of public space) can be negotiated. Thus, one could write a history of nationalism that would have two bookends: one in which societies were not sufficiently dynamic and states were insufficiently potent for nationalism to emerge as a useful space of negotiation and contention, and another in which states are no longer sufficiently potent and complex to be the key actors in the process of regulating what Michel Foucault called "biopower," that is, the power to administer a "population" and to regulate its habits. Capitalism traverses this history from end to end. It is therefore misleading to begin the history of nationalism at the end of the eighteenth century, and not at the beginning of the sixteenth century.

Instead of positing the notion that nationalism emerged first in the Americas around the time of independence, with the rise of print capitalism, and that it is therefore scarcely two hundred years old, the Spanish and Spanish-American cases suggest that nationalism developed in stages, beginning with European colonization in the sixteenth century or perhaps in the *Reconquista*. In fact, nationalisms developed along different, though interrelated, tracks, such that, as in the analogy between nationalism and kinship, one might locate diverse nationalist systems.

I shall outline what this alternative perspective reveals for the Spanish-American case. I will argue for several moments in the development of nationalism, each of which involved a distinct interconnection between fraternity and dependency. This reinterpretation of the history of Spanish-American nationalism leads me identify theoretical mistakes in Anderson's general argument, including (1) false conclusions concerning the historical connections between "racism" and nationalism, as well as between language and nationalism; (2) a misleading emphasis on the idiom of fraternity as the only available language of national identity; (3) an incorrect or successional view of the relationship between religion and nationalism (nationalism, for Anderson, replaces the universalistic claims of religion, yet Spanish nationalism was in fact based on the national appropriation of the true faith).

*First Moment in Spanish National Formation: Colonization*

A fundamental error in Anderson's account of the history of nationalism is his insistence on associating it with secularization. In the case of Spain, whose formation as a nation is certainly one of the earliest, the opposite is the case: national consciousness emerges as an offshoot of religious expansionism. I cite from Anderson once again to clarify what is at stake:

> In the course of the sixteenth century, Europe's "discovery" of grandiose civilizations hitherto only dimly rumored—in China, Japan, Southeast Asia, and the Indian subcontinent—or completely unknown—Aztec Mexico and Incan Peru—suggested an irremediable human pluralism. Most of these civilizations had developed quite separate from the known history of Europe, Christendom, Antiquity, indeed man: their genealogies lay outside of and were unassimilable to Eden. (Only homogeneous, empty time would offer them accommodation.) (69)

This point of view is perhaps a true reflection of the ways in which expansion was assimilated in England and the Netherlands, but it was not the cultural form that expansion took in Spain (or in Spain's strongest early competitor: the Ottoman Empire).[13] On the contrary, both the Spanish *Reconquista* and subsequent expansion into Africa and to America were narrated very much in the framework of what Anderson describes in shorthand as "Eden."

It is well known that Columbus and other explorers speculated on their proximity specifically to Eden, and to other biblical sites, when they reached the New World. That they attributed their success to God's design is evident in the ways in which they christened the land: islands and mainland being named alternatively for royal and for spiritual sponsors (Isla Juana, Filipinas, and Fernandina alternating with San Salvador, Veracruz, Santo Domingo, etc.). Neither was this identity between conquest and the broader teleology of Christendom abandoned once colonization set in.

Franciscan missionaries interpreted their evangelizing mission in Mexico in terms that were consonant with the messianic scholastic philosopher Joachim de Fiore (see Phelan 1970); the priest Mendieta, an apologist of Hernán Cortés, derived many a moral from the marvelous fact that Cortés had been born in the same year as Martin Luther, the one to work for God in extending the true faith, the other to work for the devil.[14] In fact, the whole of the conquistador's "discourse of the marvelous" was evenly peppered with elements of popular literature (Marco Polo, Mandeville, Virgil, chivalry novels) and with biblical stories. One might argue, contrary to Anderson, that the success of Charles V gave new life and plausibility to a narrative of Eden that had been much weaker in the days of Mandeville and Marco Polo, when the idea of taking Jerusalem and of achieving the Universal Catholic Monarchy was beyond any realistic expectation.

But even after Spanish expansionism was waning, by the 1570s, the relationship between the true faith and the ways of local heathens was still told as part of the Christian eschatology, as is obvious both in narratives of indigenous intellectuals such as Felipe Guamán Poma de Ayala and in those of seventeenth-century Creole patriots, such as Mexico's Carlos de Sigüenza y Góngora. Both of these argued (in different ways) that the Aztecs and the Incas had been evangelized before the arrival of the Spaniards, and had subsequently been led astray by the devil, only to be brought back into the fold by an alliance between the remaining loyal Indians (such as the Texcocans or the Tlaxcalans in Mexico, or Guamán Poma's own family in Peru) and the Spaniards. The significance of this point for the history of Creole patriotism has been extensively argued by both David Brading and Jacques Lafaye.

Not only was Spanish expansion told as part of Christian eschatology, but the social organization of the state that was being built during this expansion innovatively identified the church and church history with a national idea. The earliest formulation of this occurred in the days of the Spanish *Reconquista*, with the legal codification of so-called blood purity *(limpieza de sangre)*. Certificates of blood purity, guaranteeing that the holder was an old Christian, were necessary in order to hold office, to enter the church, or to enter certain guilds. Although the holders of these certificates were not identified as "Spaniards," but rather as "Old Christians," they were thought of as a community of blood and of belief that had privileged access to the state.

This nationalization of the church became much more significant with expansion to America. The whole of the first chapter of the *Laws of the Indies* is in fact devoted to justifying Spanish expansion to the Indies as a divine grace extended to the king so that he might bring the true faith to those lands. Moreover, holding political office or belonging to the privileged classes is also seen in relation to faithfulness to the church, as is evident in a law that threatens any nobleman or holder of office with the loss of all privileges if he takes the name of God in vain (libro 1, título 1, ley 25).

Leaning heavily on these formulas, the concept of "Spanish" was created as a legal category of identity in order to organize political life in the Indies. Spanish authority involved moral and religious tutelage over other social categories of persons, including "Indians," "blacks," "mulattos," and "mestizos," and also served as a category differentiated from other European "foreigners" *(extranjeros)*. For example, law 66, chapter 3, book 3 of the *Laws of the Indies* (first written in 1558) grants "the Viceroys of Peru the faculty to entrust [*encomendar*] any Indians that may be unoccupied [*indios que hubiere vacos*] during their time of arrival to those provinces, or any that may become unoccupied, to the Spaniards [*españoles*] living in them . . . so that they may have them, enjoy their tribute, and give them the good treatment that is mandated in our laws."

Similarly, another law (1608) orders that "Of the people in aid that the Viceroy might send from New Spain to the Philippines, he not allow in any way that mestizos or mulattos go or be admitted, because of the inconveniences that have occurred" (book 3, title 4, law 15). Law 14, title 5, book 3 orders that arms builders cannot teach their art to Indians; title 10, law 7 of the same book prohibits military captains from naming slaves as standard-bearers in the army, while law 12 (1643) of the same book and title orders army officials not to give "mulattos, dark ones [*morenos*], mestizos" the job of soldier. Book 3, title 15, law 33 orders that the wives of the members of the Audiencia (high court) hear Mass in a specific part of the chapel in the company of their families, civil authorities, or women of rank "and not Indian women, black women, or mulatas." On the other hand, the king ordered that when viceroys and judges named a "protector of Indians" (a kind of free lawyer for Indians), "they should not elect mestizos, because this is important for their defense, and otherwise the Indians can suffer injuries and prejudice" (book 6, title 6, law 7); in other words, Spaniards, not mestizos, are the best and most appropriate defenders of Indians. Examples can be multiplied.[15]

In short, a concept of "Spanish" emerged quickly for the colonization of the Americas, and Spaniards were expected to take up a position of spiritual, civil, and military leadership. The notion of Spanishness was formally and legally understood as a question of descent, and it therefore included "Creoles," even though contexts of differentiation and discrimination between American-born Spaniards and Peninsulars did exist from the mid-sixteenth century onward.[16] This process of differentiation was predicated not on blood, but rather on ideas concerning the influence of the land on the character, makeup, and physiognomy of those born in the Indies.[17] The term *criollo* had, in fact, a derogatory slant, in that it tended to assimilate American-born Spaniards with other American-born castes, such as slaves or mestizos (Lavallé 1993, 20). Thus patriotism (in the sense of exaltation of the land of birth) became central to the Creoles, because it was through a vindication of the true worth of the land that they could fully claim the inheritance of their blood.[18] This tension between a nationalism based on community of descent, and a patriotism based on a clear, delimited idea of "Spain" (as opposed both to the Indies and to other

European holdings of the Spanish monarch), would remain important in Spain and in the Americas even after independence.[19]

The degree to which Spaniards, Spanishness, and the Spanish language were identified with the true faith and with civilization comes through in the text of the following law (1550):

> Having made a close examination concerning whether the mysteries of our Holy Catholic Faith can be properly explained in even in the most perfect language of the Indians, it has been recognized that this is not possible without incurring great dissonances and imperfections . . . So, having resolved that it would be best to introduce the Castilian language, we order that teachers be made available to Indians who wish voluntarily to learn, and we have thought that these may be the *sacristanes*.

In short, the Spanish language was not seen in the colonies as merely a convenient and profane vernacular, but rather as a language that was closer to God.[20] Language thus reflected the process of *nationalization of the church*, which lies at the center of the history of Spanish (and Spanish-American) nationalisms, a point of departure that is at the opposite end of the spectrum posited by Anderson, who imagined that secularization was in every case at the root of nationalism.

The civil leadership of Spaniards over Indians and others is laid out in a number of laws and practices, including in laws concerning the layout of Spanish towns and streets; in the superiority of Spanish courts to Indian courts (Indian magistrates could jail mestizos or blacks, but not Spaniards); and, more fundamentally, in that the laws of Castile served as the blueprint for those of the Indies and for every other realm in the Spanish domain (book 2, title 1, law 2 [1530]: "That the Laws of Castile be kept in any matter not decided in those of the Indies"). In sum, the concept of *español*, as a community of blood, associated with a religion, a language, a civilization, and a territory, emerged rather quickly in the course of the sixteenth century.

### Second Moment of Spanish Nationalism: Decline in the European Theater

The first moment of Spanish national construction was, then, quite different in spirit and content from that posited by Anderson; Spanishness was built out of an idea of a privileged connection to the church, Spaniards were a chosen people, led by monarchs that had been singled out by the pope with the title of "Catholic." As Old Christians, they were the true keepers of the faith and therefore the only viable political, moral, and

Figure 1.1. *Nuestra Señora de Guadalupe, patrona de la Nueva España*, anonymous eighteenth-century painting. Collection of the Museum of the Basilica of Guadalupe. In this painting, Guadalupe, patroness of Mexico, is bridging Europe and New Spain. For Hidalgo, that bridge crumbled with the Napoleonic invasion of Spain, and divine grace, embodied in this apparition, is rooted entirely in Mexican soil.

Figure 1.2. *La virgen de Guadalupe escudo de salud contra la epidemía del Matlazahuatl de 1736–1738*, anonymous engraving, 1743. Collection of the Museum of the Basilica of Guadalupe. Here the patroness of Mexico is protecting the city's inhabitants against the plague.

economic elite.[21] The conquistadores were thus instantly a kind of nobility in the Indies and "Spaniards" were the dominant caste. In short, Spanish nationality was built on religious militancy: descent and language all rolled into a notion of a national calling to spiritual tutelage in the Americas and throughout the world.

The Spanish language in the Indies was not simply an arbitrary tongue among others, it was the suitable language in which to communicate the mysteries of the Catholic faith. Even today in Mexico, *hablar en cristiano* ("to speak in Christian") is synonymous with speaking in Spanish. Similarly, the Spanish bloodline—for Spanishness usually included American-born Spaniards—had a special destiny with regard to the true faith. Relativism was not at the origin of Spanish nationalism, nor did the discovery of the Indies dislocate Christian eschatology in any fundamental way. "Eden," as Anderson calls it, was maintained as the framework for histories that explained and situated Aztecs, Incas, and the rest of them.[22]

Spain's precocious consolidation as a state allowed for the rise of a form of national consciousness that was distinct from the relativist vocation of Britain and the Netherlands, whose entry to the game of (early) modern state and empire as underdogs made them fertile ground for the development of liberalism and, eventually, of truly modern forms of nationalism that are more akin to those described by Anderson.[23]

On the other hand, Spain's rapid decadence in the European theater both consolidated and exacerbated national consciousness in peculiar ways. Horst Pietschmann (1996, 18–24) has summarized the development of Spanish economic thinking of the late sixteenth and seventeenth centuries, arguing that the administrative reforms of the Bourbons in the eighteenth century were not a simple importation of French administrative ideas, but rather that they combined the latter with a native body of economic and administrative theories and projects devoted to finding remedies for the economic decline of Spain. Among these, Pietschmann's summary and discussion of the influential work of Luis Ortiz (1558) is pertinent for my argument here.

Ortiz argued that Spain was poor because it only exported raw materials and then reimported them in the form of manufactured goods. The Spaniards' disdain for manual labor contributed to the underdevelopment of industry, as did the progressive depopulation of the countryside. As a partial remedy, Ortiz urged that laws enhance the prestige of manual labor: "these should be extended even to the extreme that the state force all young men (including the nobles) to learn a trade, with the penalty that they would otherwise lose their nationality" (Pietschmann 1996, 19).

These recommendations, and others like them, become a staple of seventeenth-century economic projects and studies, call for the strengthening of the Crown, for the peopling of the country, and for leveling some differences between the various stations. Such recommendations are conceived as a matter of national interest and, in Ortiz's case, proposed penalties for failure to comply include loss of nationality.

Three points concerning this intellectual tradition are pertinent for understanding the history of nationalism in the Spanish world: first, a national consciousness was exacerbated by the perception of Spain's increasing backwardness vis-à-vis its competitors; second, the solutions that were proposed (policies concerning trade, population, education, work, administrative rationalization, etc.) also called systematically for a diminution of regional differences and policy reforms that involved conceptualizing a people in a finite territory, under a more streamlined and tendentially more equalizing administration; third, the idea of relative decline and of competition involved a keen sense of "empty time" (that is, of secular competition between states progressing through time) before the advent of "print capitalism," a fact that is obvious not only in the economic literature, but in all manner of military and commercial policy.

There is in fact some confusion in Anderson's analysis of empty time. Following Walter Benjamin, Anderson defines homogeneous or empty time as "an idea . . . in which simultaneity is, as it were, transverse, cross-time, marked not by prefiguring and fulfillment, but by temporal coincidence" (1991, 24). The novel and the newspaper are artifacts that popularize this conception of time, in that their protagonists can act independently of one another and still have a meaningful relationship to each other only because the characters belong to the same society and are being connected in the mind of the same reader.

The question that this analysis poses to a historian of the Iberian world is whether the novel and the newspaper were the first cultural artifacts that frame events and acts in "empty time." The answer is that they were not.

Government policy making in the Spanish world was running on empty time long before the industrialization of print media, and elites, Creole and Spanish, were well aware of this. Plans and programs for streamlining administration, disciplining the workforce, rationalizing tariffs, and improving transportation systems were discussed and predicated on the recognition of the parallel and simultaneous development of the great European powers. Moreover, these discussions were widely known and debated, as Pietschmann reminds us: "[I]deas concerning the economic troubles of the country had a truly wide audience [in the late sixteenth and seventeenth centuries], since the majority of their projects were printed, and we even find their ideas repeatedly in the works of writers like Cervantes" (1996, 23). Thus, competition between states, and a consciousness of relative decline, were required to promote and justify programs of economic and administrative reform. As a result, this mode of imagining time had long been available to the elites, and cannot of itself explain the rise of Spanish-American nationalism, although it does suggest an earlier sort of Spanish collective consciousness.[24]

A final citation from Pietschmann, who is my principal authority in this matter, summarizes my point concerning this second phase: "[T]ogether with the affirmation of the Catholic religion (the Spanish Enlightenment was qualified as being specifically Christian, and it had its reformist current in Jansenism), we find also the patriotism of the Enlightened thinkers, a fact that differentiates them from the cosmopolitanism of Enlightenment thinkers in France and other European countries. This patriotism, that gave the Spanish Enlightenment a strongly political character, was expressed in the desire that Spain reconquer its earlier economic florescence and its political position as a power of the first order" (1996, 25).

In the eighteenth century, under the Bourbons, the discussions of the prior century and a half were reanimated, and they generated a series of administrative reforms. These reforms were, once again, built on the patriotic and national conscience that had developed since the Conquest, a conscience that simultaneously produced a clearly delimited image of "Spain" as a land, and of "Spaniards" as a nation (even though there was no isomorphism between the nation and Spain).[25]

As an example of the Spanish imagined community that was being constructed through these reforms, I offer the following vignette, taken from the *Gazeta de México* (November 3, 1784), describing the celebration of the birth of royal twins and the signing of a peace treaty with France and the United States in Madrid: "Rarely shall there be a motive for greater complacency, nor more worthy of the jubilation of the *Spaniards*, than the happy birth of the two twin infantes, and the conclusion of a peace so advantageous to the *national interests*" (my emphasis).

Having identified both the subjects of the ritual as Spaniards and the interests being served by the twin birth and by the peace treaty as "national," the *Gazeta de México* goes on to narrate the public festivities that marked the event, especially the content of a series of allegorical floats (*carros alegóricos*):

1st Float: Atlantis Holding the Sky
The first float is preceded by drums, trumpets, pages, heralds, and eight couples of both sexes, six of artisans, one of farmers *[hortelanos]*, and one of field hands *[labradores]*, each with the instrument of its profession. They are followed by the orchestra and immediately thereafter by a super float, pulled like the rest by six horses, in which the statue of Atlantis, characterized with several mottos, holds the sky. Our August Monarch Charles III holds with his heroic virtues and happy government the *Spanish* Monarchy. The love of the *Spaniards* venerates in its glorious Monarch the Princes and the Royal Family, so worthy also of the love that is bestowed to them by *the Nation*.

Here we have, in an officially sanctioned bulletin published in Mexico City, the portrayal of a Spanish nation—a nation, represented by farmers, agricultural workers, and artisans, protected by a national monarch, who holds up the sky over their heads like Atlas. Both the monarchy and the people are called "Spanish" here, and the publication of this in Mexico is clearly meant to make this national celebration inclusive at the very least to a Creole audience. Yet the territory of "Spain" is clearly limited in the ritual, in a way that diverges from the inclusive term *nación*:

5th Float: Spain Jubilant because of the Birth of the Infantes
The last float . . . is preceded by eight couples on horseback, armed with lance and shield. Then two pages, and nine couples that indicate the different provinces of Spain, whose costumes they wear. They are accompanied by an orchestra, to which they respond with dances of their respective provinces.

The description of a series of allegories portraying Spain goes on in detail and is summed up in the following analysis:

The interpretation of this float is easy. Spain is represented in the greatest surge of its happiness as a result of the birth of the two SERENE INFANTES, by [newly signed peace], by its products, by its main rivers, by its Sciences, Arts, Navy, Commerce, and Agriculture, all of which is fomented by our august sovereign, facilitating for this illustrious Nation the abundance and opulence that is promised by its fertile soil and the constancy of its loyal and energetic inhabitants.

In short, a clear image of Spain, represented by a modern idea of the public good (with great prominence given to arts and industry, natural resources, and the customs of the various folk), is present in this state ritual.

At the same time, the inclusiveness of the category of "Nation" appears to be a bit broader than the Spanish territory that is so clearly delimited, because it includes the readers of the *Gazeta de México*, who are fully expected to share in the joy of the occasion. Around the time of this festivity, Charles III would try to implement administrative reforms that would more clearly make the territorial image of Spain inclusive of the Indies in a way that paralleled the inclusive potential of the concept of the Spanish nation.

### Third Moment: Bourbon Reforms and Independence

The high point of this reformist movement, in the late eighteenth century under Charles III, involved trying to make Spain and its colonies into a closed economic space, with a relatively streamlined administration, an active financial and economic policy, a decentralized administration and army. This imperial unity was known as the *Cuerpo unido de Nación* (Unified body of nation; Pietschmann 1996, 302), and its administrative organization was clearly the precursor of the state organizations that were generated with independence.

Interestingly, however, these reforms were promoted not only as a response to a feeling of backwardness and of nostalgia for past national glories, but also to face the political threats posed both by the British navy and the American Revolution. The former threat in particular made the decentralization of administration an important strategy for the fortification of the empire. This system of decentralization and administrative rationalization also involved promoting a view of industry and of public interest that is significant in the formation of a modern form of nationalism, based on individual property, a skilled and well-policed workforce, and a bourgeois public sphere.

Two divergent tendencies are produced with these administrative, religious, and educational reforms. On the one hand, the formation of the idea of a Gran España, made up of Iberia and the Indies together, with a population of subjects tending toward greater internal homogenization under increasingly bourgeois forms of political identity; on the other, the consolidation of the various administrative units—the viceroyalties and the new "intendancies"—as viable state units, each with its own internal financial administration and permanent army.

These contradictory tendencies are in fact intimately related: on the one hand, the administrative consolidation of transatlantic political units was the only logical means to shape a strong Gran España; on the other,

Figure 1.3. *Ex-voto giving thanks to the virgin of Guadalupe for a successful medical operation,* anonymous, 1960. Reformers of the eighteenth century were convinced that divine protection and interjection were not in conflict with modernization and modern technologies. This has been a persistent theme in Mexican nationalism. In this ex-voto of 1960, the Virgin of Guadalupe's light shines in the operating room.

the very process of consolidating their viability made independence all the easier to imagine. Alexander von Humboldt's voyage and writings on Spanish America are a good example of this conundrum. Whereas in the *Laws of the Indies,* which is a compilation made in 1680, printed materials about the Indies were banned from those lands, and foreigners were outlawed from going beyond the ports of the Indies, Humboldt received a royal commission to travel there, and authorities were asked to give him all of their statistics and any information he might find useful. Humboldt's publications on the political economy of the Indies followed the spirit of the Bourbon reforms, as well as German cameralist administrative theory, by treating each principal administrative unit (mainly viceroyalties) as a coherent whole, with a population, an economy, a map, and so on.

The administrative consolidation of viceroyalties, intendancies, and other political units was occurring not as a ploy to keep Creoles boxed into their administrative units, but rather to strengthen the general state of the empire, and to give each segment a greater capacity to respond to a political crisis. From the seventeenth century on, the armada from Spain had to struggle to make successful voyages to the Americas, and there were moments when the armada was entirely incapable of managing Spanish-American trade. Greater administrative and military autonomy would provide another line of imperial defense.

Thus, at the same time that the "political viability" and the "emotional plausibility" of the viceroyalties were strengthened politically by the new system of intendancies and ideologically through a new emphasis on the public good through industry and education, so too was the notion of a truly panimperial identity closer at hand than ever before.

These contradictory tendencies are in evidence at the time of independence: first, in the parallels between the American War of Independence and the "war of independence" of Spain against the French invaders; second, in the fact that the liberal Constitution of Cádiz (1812) defined "Spaniards" as all of the people who were born in the Spanish territories, with no differences made between Iberia and the Indies.

*Fourth Moment: The Rocky Road to Modern Nationalism (Mexico 1810–29)*

In Latin America, the road to national modernity was particularly cumbersome. This was owing to the early date of independence movements, a fact that resulted not so much from the force of nationalist feeling in the region as from the decadence of Spain in the European forum.[26] As a result of this, the new countries faced stiff internal and foreign-relations problems, and it is in the context of these problems that a functioning nationalism developed.

The fourth moment in the evolution of Spanish-American nationalism can best be understood as one in which the dynamics of independent postcolonial statehood forced deep ideological changes, including a sharp change in who was considered a national and who a foreigner, a redefinition of the extension of the fraternal bond through the idea of citizenship, and of the relationship between religion and nationality and between race and nation.

This process of radical transformation occurred alongside the emergence of a new form of popular politics, in which social movements cut across the boundaries of villages and castes, regions and guilds. The Spanish-American revolutions may seem "socially thin" to some contemporary observers (Anderson 1991, 49), but they were by far the most "dense" social and political movements that Spanish America had had since the Conquest. In this section, I explore the dynamics of these

Figure 1.4. *Salve Reina de la América Latina*, by Gonzalo Carrasco (1859–1936), n.d. Collection of the Museum of the Basilica of Guadalupe. Guadalupe here is the patroness of Spanish-American sovereignty. This image also underscores Mexico's presumptive role at the head of the Spanish-American confederation.

transformations through a discussion of certain key events in early independent Mexico (1810–29). As Anthony Pagden has shown, Creole patriotism was predicated on Spanish political philosophy. In the Iberian world, sovereignty was granted by God to the people, who in turn ceded it to the monarch. It is therefore not surprising that the early fathers of

Mexican independence, Hidalgo and Morelos, who were secular priests, claimed to be fighting for the sake of religion. Here, for instance, is a formulation by Morelos:

> Know that when kings go missing, Sovereignty resides only in the Nation; know also that every nation is free and is authorized to form the class of government that it chooses and not to be the slave of another; know also (for you undoubtedly have heard tell of this) that we are so far from heresy that our struggle comes down to defending and protecting in all of its rights our holy religion, which is the aim of our sights, and to extend the cult of Our Lady the Virgin Mary. (Morelos 1812, 199)

Morelos and Hidalgo accused the Spaniards of betraying their true Christian mission and using Christianity as a subterfuge for the exploitation of the Americans.[27] To uphold the true Christian faith was also to drive out all Spaniards who had milked the Mexicans of their native wealth and who had driven them to abjection.

These early movements failed. Morelos and Hidalgo were executed, and although their followers continued the fight, independence was not to be achieved under the leadership of this particular ideological wing. Instead, an alliance was captained by Agustín Iturbide, who had been a loyalist army officer and who enjoyed the backing of a sizable fraction of New Spain's elite. Iturbide's Plan de Iguala gave Spaniards ample guarantees of full inclusion in the new republic.

The backers of Morelos (including *pardos*, Indian village communities, local artisans and merchants) were led by Vicente Guerrero and backed a political program that would eventually gel into what Peter Guardino has called "popular federalism" (1996, 120–27; 179–86). The popular radicals of the 1820s were interested in lowering taxes and broad electoral enfranchisement. They favored the formation of municipal boundaries and institutions that would help villagers defend their lands, gave free rein to anti-Spanish sentiment, and sought to implement a liberal system modeled on that of the United States. The elite of this group came to be associated with the Freemasons of the rite of York, and they supported a movement to expel the Spaniards from Mexico.

In 1828 a *yorquino*-backed coup led to the looting of the market of the Parián in Mexico City, where wealthy Spanish merchants had their shops, and the expulsion of the Spaniards from Mexico followed shortly after.[28] Thus Mexican nationalism went from excluding Spaniards in the early independence movement, to including them at independence, to excluding them again, all in a very short lapse of time.

The very violence of the ideological transformation of early Mexican nationalism suggests that a general or abstract "nationalism" does not help in understanding the specifics of its contents or its dynamics of propagation. In fact, just as the notion of "kinship" is an abstraction of such a general level that it can obfuscate the nature of the practices that are being summed up in the category, so too can we say that Anderson's culturalist reading of nationalism is to such a degree general and abstract that it fails to clarify the politics of community production.

The specific formulations of the nature of the nation and of who was included and who was excluded underwent dramatic shifts that cannot be attributed to changes in consciousness gained by new maps or censuses (Humboldt was still the main source that people drew on in this period). Nor do these shifts respond to an intensification of travel or of the strength of bureaucratic networks across the territory. The formation of Mexican nationalism can be understood in relation to the political conditions of its production. These conditions were determined as much by the new nation's position in an international order as by the fact that it did not have a national ruling class.

This latter point requires elaboration. At the time of independence, Spanish-American countries did not have a Creole bourgeoisie that could serve as a national dominant class. Domestic regional economies were not well articulated to each other; much of the transatlantic merchant elite was Spanish; mining capital often required foreign partnerships. Thus the Creole elite was a regional elite, and not a national bourgeoisie. Only two institutions could conceivably serve to articulate the national space: the church and the military. The military, however, was not a unified body, because it was led precisely by regional caudillos, many of whom controlled their own militias. The church, on the other hand, articulated the national space in terms of credit to some extent, and also ideologically, but it could not serve as a national dominant class.

In this context, uniting regional leaders into national factions was necessary. In the early years after Mexico's independence, Freemasonry had this role.[29] It was through Masonry that regional elites forged interregional networks that could prefigure the national bureaucracy after independence.

When independence was attained, much of Mexico's political elite belonged to Masonic lodges organized in the Scottish rite. These elites were well disposed to Britain and, indeed, Great Britain was the first great power to recognize Mexico. Not surprisingly, George Ward, who was Britain's first ambassador to Mexico, was able to reap numerous economic and political concessions from the government of Mexico's first president, Guadalupe Victoria—so much so that when U.S. ambassador Joel Poinsett arrived on the scene in 1825, he saw gaining some of the terrain that the United States had already ceded to the British as his most formidable task.[30] Poinsett makes a sustained effort to build a pro-American party to counter British influence in Mexico. Part of Poinsett's well-calibered strategy included aid in the organization of Masonic lodges to counter those affiliated to the Scottish rite, and he attached these Masons to the rite of York (chartered by the lodge in Philadelphia). These two Masonic organizations would function as "political parties" in this early period.[31]

Both the Scottish and the Yorkish Masons tried to monopolize as many government posts as they could. As the competition between the *escoseses* and the *yorquinos* became embittered, the "American cause" (of York) begins to identify the Masons of the Scottish rite with imperialist European interests, especially with Spanish interests. This allowed the *yorquinos* to distract attention from the US–British rivalry, and it promised to yield juicy dividends to *yorquinos* in the form of Spanish property, because the Spaniards were still the most prosperous sector of Mexico's population.

The *escoseses*, for their part, because they were losing the contest for national power, denounced the role of Joel Poinsett as a foreigner creating the party of *yorquinos* and the very existence of "secret societies."

Thus, it is in the competition between two secret societies for full control over the apparatus of the state that two critical aspects of Mexican nationalism get consolidated: nationalism as an excluding ideology (even as a xenophobic ideology)—seen both in the move to expel the Spaniards and in the move to expel Poinsett; and nationalism as an ideology that makes *public* access to the state bureaucracy a cornerstone of its ideology. These aspects of nationalism reinforce one another because neither of the two Masonic parties can afford the luxury of identifying entirely with foreign interests (because each needs to attack a different foreign power— the *yorquinos* want to attack British and Spanish interests, the *escoseses* are opposed to U.S. interests), and neither can openly admit that it merely wishes to control the bureaucratic apparatus.

Finally, the links between religion and nationalism should not be taken as constant. Although early Mexican patriotism was identified with a superior loyalty to the Catholic faith, and Mexican nationalists vehemently excluded other faiths from the national order, both the British and the Americans coincide in their interest in propagating freedom of religion. Consequently, some degree of religious tolerance was necessary to maintain trade with England and the United States, and the polarization of the political spectrum ended up producing a Jacobin camp that was absent in the early postindependent period.

Eventually, church properties would be to Jacobins what Spanish properties had been to *yorquinos* in 1829: a source of wealth that could be the spoils for political expansion in a period of little economic growth.

In this fashion, Mexico consolidated a national state with a nationalism built on three principles: the defense against foreigners, the defense of open political parties instead of secret societies (and of an understanding of the state as a normative order rather than as a governing class), and the (uneven) extension of the benefits of nationalism to popular levels (whether through the abolition of tribute, of guild restrictions, of church tithes, of distribution of national lands, the distribution of spoils from the Spaniards, the distribution of goods of new technologies). These three pillars are in part the unintended result of the contest of the secret societies, supported by two imperialist states, for control over the state apparatus. These secret societies, in turn, functioned thanks to the cleavages of economic and political interests that cut across national lines or that did not reach "up" to the national level at all. In short, the bases of communitarian feeling, criteria of inclusion and exclusion in the nation, the imagination of a territory, and the very conceptualization of national fraternity were shaped in the political fray.

*Conclusion*

The cultural density of the phenomenon of nationalism lies in the politics of its production and deployment. Nationalism combines the use of transnationally generated formulas, ranging from legal formulations to state pageantry, with a politics that is inextricably local. A dense or thick description of nationalism is therefore a necessary step for understanding its cultural characteristics.

The Spanish-American and Mexican cases present a significant historical problem for Anderson's conceptualization because in Spain national construction began with an appropriation of the church, and not with a relativization of "Eden." Spanish was seen as a modern form of Latin, and therefore was more appropriate for communicating the faith than indigenous languages. In a related vein, "race" was central to early modern Spanish nationalism, insofar as descent from Old Christians was seen as a sign of a historical tie to the faith, a sign that gave its owners control over the bureaucratic apparatus of both church and state.

Moreover, the concept of "empty time" was present in the Spanish world long before print capitalism, beginning with the decline of empire and Spain's failure to attain a universal monarchy. Thus, Spanish economic thought formulated the notion of a national economy beginning in the mid-sixteenth century. The administrative constructs that allowed for the imaginings of a people tied to a territory can be dated back to the sixteenth century, when both colonial expansion and the defense of the empire against European powers led to the consolidation of the notion of "Spain" and of "Spaniards." As Spain continued to decline in the European forum, state reforms tended to target political middlemen in an attempt to substitute regional political classes with a bureaucracy, to consolidate an idea of a national territory, and to shape a Greater Spanish Nation made up of subjects that tended increasingly toward an internal uniformity vis-à-vis the Crown.

Finally, independence itself, as Anderson recognized, was not the product of cultural nationalism, but rather of the decline of Spain's capacity to run its overseas territories. As a result, much of the specific content of modern nationalist ideology, such as the notion that politics should be public, or that religion should not be a criterion for choosing a trading partner, or that a Spaniard is not a Mexican even if he sympathizes with the Mexican cause, was the cultural product of independence, and not its precondition.

On the theoretical front, the Latin American case leads me to modify Anderson's definition of nationalism in order to stress both fraternal ties and bonds of dependence in the imagined community. It is in the articulation between citizenship and nationality that various nationalisms derive their power. As a result, sacrifice is not the quintessential feature of nationalism, but rather one of a number of possible signs and manifestations.

In addition, because Anderson's ideas concerning the necessity of cultural relativism as a precondition for nationalism are incorrect, it follows that his theoretical emphasis on the centrality of language over race in nationalism can also be questioned. In the case of Spain, at least, "racial" identity (in the sense of a bloodline) was coupled with linguistic identity for the formation of an opposition between "Spaniards" and "Indians," and it was descent from Old Christians who had fought holy wars that made Spaniards a chosen people.

Like kinship and religion, nationalism has come in various strands. In the early modern period, we must distinguish between the nationalism of a chosen people, such as that of Spain, and the defensive nationalism of the British or the Dutch, who created nationalist ideals in order to affirm their right to maintain and sanctify their own traditions. Both of these forms contrast with the highly unstable nationalist fomulations of early postcolonial Spanish America. Nationalism's family tree reaches back to the very birth of the modern world, and ideas of political community that have emerged since then are both more and less than a cultural successor of the religious community.

# 2

## Communitarian Ideologies and Nationalism

*This chapter, first published in 1993, is the earliest of the essays in this book. It was written for a wide audience, with the aim of providing very general historical parameters for the study of Mexican communitarian ideologies.*

The territory now known as Mexico has always been occupied by diverse human groups that speak different languages and have significant variations in belief and customs. Mexican nationality is not a historically transcendent entity. On the contrary, it is the historical product of the peoples who have inhabited those lands. The goal of this chapter is to identify communitarian ideologies that have played salient roles in the formation and transformation of national ideology in Mexico.

Today it is common to assert that nationalism is a communitarian fiction. However, the nation is a kind of community that coexists with others, either as a complementary form or as a competing form of community, and strategies for identifying the communitarian ideologies that are pertinent for the study of nationality are a matter that requires attention. Max Weber defined communal relations as a type of social relationship wherein action is "based on the subjective feeling of the parties, whether affectual or traditional, that they belong together."[1] Thus all communal relations, including family relations, are based on subjective feeling and on fictions regarding the social whole, and who "we" are.

In this chapter, I analyze communitarian ideologies by identifying the goods that each community marks as inalienable. This strategy is based on Annette Weiner's discussion of exchange. In contrast to classical (Maussian) models of exchange, which inspected the role of the reciprocal exchange of goods for building ties of solidarity, Weiner focused on the goods that people decide that they cannot exchange: inalienable goods.[2] In so doing, she showed that reciprocal exchanges not only assert solidarity; they also shape systems of social differentiation. The objects that are exchanged in relations of reciprocity also underline by omission or by implication the resources that will not be exchanged. The relationship between the various things that each exchange partner withholds and keeps out of circulation objectifies a system of social differentiation.

This idea is useful for describing how communitarian ideologies are constructed. The totalizing visions that underlie communitarian relationships are always based on definitions of goods or rights that are common and inalienable to all. The relationships of differentiation that are later constructed within and between communities are defined with reference to the series of goods that are inalienable to the group.

In our case, examining the nation's inalienable goods clarifies how Mexicanness has been formed. National feelings are presented as inherited "primordial loyalties." One is born and dies with them and they are passed on: children must also inherit them. This characteristic of nationality—its ideology of transcendence—can be grasped by studying the communitarian goods and rights that are considered inalienable because they embody the material transcendence of the community. My aim in this chapter is to use the inalienable communitarian possessions to identify the principal types of communitarian ideologies that facilitated or blocked the formation of the feeling of Mexican nationality.

## The Aztecs

The Aztecs are not an obligatory starting point for the analysis of Mexican communitarian ideologies. I begin with them for four reasons: (1) understanding the communitarian ideologies of pre-Hispanic states helps us to visualize the full gamut of ideological sources of modern Mexican nationalism; (2) some features of pre-Hispanic communitarian ideologies have persisted, albeit in a very transformed way; (3) many Mexican nationalist movements have tried to take up the political forms of ancient Mexico;

and (4) ancient Nahua notions correspond at many points with those of other Mesoamerican groups. My aim in considering the Aztecs is not to affirm the precepts of traditional Mexican nationalism, which always saw the grandeur of the Aztec city as the founding moment of Mexican nationality. Rather, it is to understand the nature of Aztec communitarianism so that we may better identify its potential for modern nationalist thought.

When discussing Aztec notions of community, it is necessary to consider kinship, territory, cultural formulations of subordination and domination, and ideas about civilization and barbarism.

In the Aztec period, indigenous states' areas of influence did not correspond to the limits of a single linguistic or territorial community. The great cities of Tenochtitlán, Texcoco, and Azcapotzalco housed migrants from many areas, including speakers of various languages. The great *tlatoani* of Tenochtitlán was the lord not only of the Nahuatl speakers of Tenochtitlán, but also of Otomis, Mazahuas, Zapotecs, and many others, some of whom had been forcibly brought to the city as slaves, while others were migrants, members of guilds, and merchants. Pre-Hispanic states were thus not meant to represent a cultural community in the contemporary sense of the term, although communitarian ideas certainly existed. These notions developed around a discourse of kinship (that is, of alliance and descent) between living and dead people, as well as between kin groups and land.

The cornerstone of the sense of community in the Aztec period was the institution of the *calpulli*. The communitarian ideology of the *calpulli* was manifested in a series of inalienable goods and rights: (1) the land of the *calpulli* belonged to a lineage, not an individual, so individuals could even sell themselves as slaves but they could not freely dispose of *calpulli* lands; (2) the lineage and land were sponsored by a deity (*calpulteotl*), and the link with that deity could not be broken by individual will; (3) the *calpulli*'s links with other *calpultin* were manifested and symbolized in kinship links among their chiefs and among the gods in the cycle of suns, a myth that legitimated the preeminence of a single people (the Aztecs) and their tutelary god over en entire era.[3] This series of kinship relationships was also used to claim Aztec filiation with the Toltec line, which was the source of civilization, and was also seen as an inalienable legacy.

In this sense, in the pre-Hispanic period the "national" question did not depend on "ethnicity" as we understand it; nationality did not depend on membership in the same linguistic, racial, or cultural group. The important thing was to belong to one of a set of landed communities. Belonging to these communities determined a relationship to a series of inalienable goods summed up in the different dimensions of the *calpulli*: common land and a kinship idiom tying all members of a *calpulli* together, filiation with a local deity (*calpulteotl*), and a received set of alliances between *calpultin* (expressed in genealogical form between families of chiefs and between their tutelary gods). These relationships were expressed very powerfully in the words that (according to Fray Bernardino de Sahagún) Aztec priests directed to the Franciscans who came to convert them:

> They [our progenitors] taught us,
> all their ways of worship,
> their ways of revering [the gods].
> Thus, before them we bring earth to our mouths [we swear],
> so do we bleed,
> we pay our debts,
> we burn incense,
> we offer sacrifices.
> They [our progenitors] said:
> that they, the gods, are for whom one lives,
> that they deserved us.
> How? Where? When it was still night.
> And they [our ancestors] said:
> that they give us
> our sustenance, our food,
> everything one drinks, one eats,
> that which is our flesh, maize, beans,
> amaranth, chía.
> They are who we ask for
> water, rain,
> which is why the things of the land are produced.[4]

This vision of community also helps us to understand certain features of the Aztecs' characteristic sense of human life. These features are expressed in the ideologies of sacrifice and slavery. When an individual was captured in war, he was taken by the hair on the crown of his head. This act represented the appropriation of his *tonalli*, his vital force, and the separation of that vital force from the captive's original community.[5]

Thus, sacrifice and slavery were one nation's or community's way of liberating and expending the human energy and vitality that had been separated from another nation or community. This strengthened the alliance between the appropriating nation and the different gods that shaped its political field. Sacrifice and slavery were interpreted as an affirmation of the greater cosmology—the period or reigning sun in which it was thought that they were living—through the expansion of some communities at the expense of others.

In this sense, although the *calpulli* was the primordial communitarian unit, there was also a level of social identification related to the Aztec state. The feelings of belonging to this greater political unit were built on a number of relationships. We have already mentioned the importance of the system of kinship alliance between nobles. Marriage between nobles was so important in the ideological construction of the empire that is almost impossible to imagine this system without polygamy, because Aztec lords formed alliances with subordinated peoples by accepting their noble-women in marriage.[6]

These kinship networks among allied, subordinated communities and imperial centers also had an ideological counterpart in religion. Here, the Aztecs' tutelary god, Huitzilopochtli, ruled the era—the "Fifth Sun"—as a whole. Thus, the *calpultin's* communitarian worship could also find a subordinate place in a religious cosmology that included and favored the empire, with the Aztecs' Huitzilopochtli presiding over the whole era.

Imperial society also had mechanisms for attracting individuals who did not come as slaves or victims. Aztec expansion depended on military and commercial domination. In turn, this domination required powerful armies, and the Aztecs permitted non-Aztecs to join them and rise in rank through battlefield accomplishments. In this way, the Aztec empire developed mechanisms for absorbing and assimilating individuals even though they did not belong to their primordial community of origin.[7]

In conclusion, one can say that in pre-Hispanic society there was a vision of the human individual as an energy that had a value in itself. This energy (figured in the *tonalli*) had to be linked to a series of inalienable possessions that every qualified individual inherited. He or she had to be linked to a piece of land, to a kin group, to a configuration of tutelary gods, and to the political state. The Aztecs' imperial policies were to some degree oriented to channeling these various communal loyalties toward them through a complex system of alliances and threats. They also had the capacity to absorb individuals into the group in return for services rendered, especially on the battlefield. Basically, one can say that, in the Aztec period, belonging to a landed community that was figured as a kindred was the only truly honored way of life, and to be separated from that state of community, the ancient Nahua was destined to serve or to die.

## The Colonial Period

Notions of community in colonial society can also be explored through an analysis of the inalienable possessions that each attributed to itself. New Spain was a caste society that recognized different types of communities that maintained hierarchical relationships with each other. I shall briefly review indigenous, Spanish, and mestizo communitarian ideologies.

Indigenous communities partially maintained some of the *calpulli*'s communal attributes: the community remained legally and officially landed through its "primordial titles," which were decrees from a Spanish monarch that granted a series of lands and goods to a village, sometimes in recognition of tribute paid or to confirm lands that had belonged to those villages in antiquity.

Clearly, one of the colonial indigenous community's inalienable goods was land, despite the fact that communal lands could be rented for long periods or lost through illicit sales. Correspondingly, the primordial titles were converted into almost sacred documents guarded by the most venerable elders and displayed only in special occasions. Knowledge of the content of those titles was a central theme of local oral traditions.

As in pre-Columbian times, this collective relationship with the land was reflected at the ritual, religious, and political levels. Thus, indigenous communities instituted their own offices—*alcaldes, jueces, gobernadores, mandones,* and *alguaciles*—that circulated, in theory at least, among the village *principales,* the descendants of the old indigenous nobility. This political organization of the indigenous community had the double purpose of guarding village interests, imparting local justice, and responding to Spanish demands on the community, including tribute, the organization of labor groups, and the enforcement of Christian worship.

A good part of the territorial, political, and religious organization of indigenous communities also tended to coincide with kin groups in the mode of the *calpulli,* but in general the indigenous quarters and communities of the colonial period were not direct continuations of the *calpultin.* In the first decades after the Conquest, many of the indigenous quarters (*barrios*) that were organized were in fact *calpultin.* However, this correspondence often broke down because of the enormous Indian mortality throughout the sixteenth century and the population movements that responded to new Spanish economic demands. Moreover, to resolve the difficulties in controlling the dispersed indigenous population, the Spanish "concentrated" it in larger population centers (above all in the late sixteenth and early seventeenth centuries). Still, although the physical continuity between *calpulli* and indigenous barrio was generally imperfect, it did reproduce the tendency to organize kinship relationships on the level of the barrio and the community. The indigenous barrios of the colonial period were generally composed of two or three great patrilineages. Even more important, as James Lockhart has shown, colonial indigenous jurisdictions tended to coincide with the pre-Columbian units (*altepetl*), in such a way that the combination of barrios formed a single political community.

On the ritual plane, each village adopted one or several saints, and the Christian tradition of revelation articulated with the shamanism of pre-Columbian peoples. This permitted personalized relationships between saints and individuals (and, by association, between saints and the groups to which individuals belonged). Thus, the indigenous communitarian spirit maintained inalienable links with land, family, and gods, albeit in a transformed way.

In addition to all this, colonial indigenous communities were nations in a racial sense, and this radically differentiated colonial indigenous nationality from pre-Columbian nationalities. Like the *calpulli*, each community identified its limits on the basis of a relationship with a series of inalienable objects—the land, an oral tradition about the land, a series of political relationships within communities, and a series of relationships between communities and deities. However, it is also clear that in the colonial period this form of constituting community was exclusive to Indians and that *Indian* was a "racial" and a legal category of persons: legally, Indians were those people who could aspire to belong to an Indian republic and who were obligated to render tribute, labor, and obedience to the Spaniards. Racially, they were descendants of the original settlers.[8]

Thus, although the indigenous colonial community's internal world partially resembled and perpetuated the *calpulli*'s characteristics, the colonial criteria of inclusion diverged widely from those of the pre-Hispanic period. This is because, instead of belonging to a world composed of dominating and dominated peoples (who remained connected through relationships of kinship, political alliance, and social mobility), all indigenous communities found themselves subordinated to a caste with which they could not easily meld; that is, as a group, indigenous communities formed a caste or subordinated nationality in a social hierarchy that sought to maintain stable distinctions, however unsuccessfully.

On the other hand, the relationship between indigenous individuals and their community also changed. After evangelization, Indians were thought to be subjects with free will, who would be judged by the moral choices made by each person. In part because of this, Indians who separated themselves from their communities were no longer simply a mass of energy that could be appropiated by another group through sacrifice or servitude. On the contrary, Indians separated from their primordial titles, their chiefs, and their village patron saint could continue having an individualized relationship with the saints and carry on with their lives in a world of incipient social classes. In that world, individual energy was liberated in forming one's family and in searching for wages, leisure, vices, and ceremonies of social groups that had no inalienable possessions aside from their souls and the color of their skins.

For these dislocated Indians, the only available sources of collective identity were those created by the racial (or racist) organization of the regime and by the experience of shared living in an urban quarter, mining community, hacienda household, or in a factory or port. On the other hand, the inalienability of the soul allowed these Indians to receive the sacraments of the church and to choose their spouses without strict racial determination. The ideology of free matrimonial choice was especially respected by the clergy in the first half of the colonial period (see Seed 1988), but even in the late colonial period, the only serious obstacle to interracial marriage was parental opposition. For this reason, marriages between members of the same class (even though not of the same lineage or color) or between prosperous people of color and poor whites were common.[9]

Among these new mestizo groups, two new factors in the process of social identification began to assert themselves: money and Hispanic acculturation. These were interrelated in terms of their role in constructing ideas about community, so I treat them jointly. The Spaniards of the colonial period had a genealogical concept of the nation: its members were descended from the same blood. The ideological role of "blood" in Spain is subtle and at the same time crucial for understanding how Mexican nationality was formed.

The importance of "blood" in the Spanish regime dates to the *Reconquista* of Spain (immediately before the discovery of America), when there were movements to separate "Old Christians" from Jewish and Moorish converts. This was part of a broader tendency in Spain to nationalize the Catholic church and to make Spaniards the defending knights of the faith (as well as the principal beneficiaries of the faith's expansion). Thus, beginning in the fourteenth century, "certificates of blood purity" were required for joining the clergy, holding public office, or belonging to certain guilds. These certificates were intended to show that a individual descended from many generations of Christians. The concept is of special anthropological interest because it linked two important features of "honor": (1) the individual's *reliability* (above all with regard to religion, but it was assumed that this loyalty extended to other spheres—loyalty to friends and bravery in defending the group, the family, and one's own honor), and (2) the *chastity* of the women of the group. Because honor was measured through the blood, biological paternity and maternity were critical, thus reinforcing the links between honor, control over virginity, and women's sexual fidelity after marriage.

The notion that "blood" predicted and reflected an individual's reliability became the basis for the Spanish idea of "nation," understood as a people that emanated from the same blood. Belonging to a similar lineage or to a common nation was important in a number of contexts; however, Spanish ideas of character, honor, and right also admitted the possibility of assimilation, and sometimes emphasized the effects of the milieu on inheritance.

The idea of *patria*, or "homeland," recognized the importance of the place where one was born and raised. This is the original sense of the word *Creole*, which comes from the verb *criar*, to rear or raise. When a black slave was born in Veracruz, it was said that he or she was a "Veracruz Creole." For this reason, people of Spanish nationality born in Mexico were sometimes known as "Creoles" (of Mexico).

The importance given to land complicates the scheme of identity through blood and honor. Being born and growing up in a certain place influenced the development of the individual. Thus, for example, there were Spaniards who commented on the "degeneration" of heredity that took place in America: after two generations a green pepper became a chili pepper, and a Spanish worker had Creole sons who became lazy bums.[10] This New World influence was not always conceived in terms of acculturation (i.e., learning); above all, it was thought of in terms of the physical influences that emanated from different places' climatic and chemical qualities. Air, humidity, heat, cold, and drinking water all affected the development of human qualities just as one's heredity did. Consequently, there were widely opposed appreciations of the nature or effects of any particular land: one of the important points in the dispute between Creoles and Iberians was the relative nobility or ignominy of American versus Iberian lands. In sum, land and blood were central components of the person and, by extension, of the nation in Spanish ideology.

The third important factor in the conception of the social group was acculturation through learning. Here the word *ladino* provides a useful key. This word was used to denote a person of a barbarous or pagan nation that had been at least partly civilized. For example, it was said that an Indian was *ladino* when he or she had a good grasp of Spanish. The same usage applied to slaves: recently arrived Africans were *bozales, bozales torpes* (clumsy *bozales*), or *bozalones*, but those who now spoke Spanish and knew local customs were *ladinos*.[11] A *ladino* slave was worth more money than a *bozal*, and a *ladino* Indian was considered more qualified to assume public office in a *república de indios* than a nonacculturated one. A *ladino* slave was also more dangerous than a *bozal*, because the term was most often used to refer to Moorish slaves.[12]

On the other hand, it is indispensable to note the ambivalence felt toward acculturation or "ladinization"; Jews and Muslims were considered members of especially dangerous nations because they were *ladinos*; that is, they could imitate Spaniards and subvert their order from within. This was why Jews and Moors were prohibited from entering the New World— even if they were converts. The meaning of *ladino* as an able but truculent, two-faced person has survived into our times. It is the main meaning that this word has today, but in the past it was part of a far more complex semantic field.

With these considerations in mind, we can now reconsider the Indians who separated themselves from their communities and whose only inalienable possessions were their souls and skin color. We have said that these individuals could aspire to a place within a new community through money and skills. In light of the concepts of free will, blood, homeland, and ladinization, we can better understand these people's strategies and alternatives.

First, although Indian émigrés no longer had inalienable ties to land through primordial titles, oral traditions, and so on, they did have ties to a more abstract "homeland": they were "Indians." Second, through their participation in the market economy, some of these migrants could learn Spanish ways. Thus they had certain advantages over the monolingual village Indian (although here it is crucial to remember the ambivalence toward ladinization: these Indians were at once superior to and more dangerous than those still tied to their villages). Third, if a man managed to make a little money, he could invest in the transgenerational path of honor, for example, by marrying a mestiza or Creole ("improving the race") and by acquiring possessions with which he could assert a certain honor. Successful Indians who separated from their local communities could begin to identify with a larger homeland and aspire to win a small measure of honor and progress.

The problems of Creole collective identities were simpler in some sense. When Creoles identified or were identified as a group (which they often did not), they were distinguished from Peninsulars not by "nationality," but rather by the influences of their respective homelands. This occasionally served to discriminate against some of them in the fields of business, matrimony, religion, the army, and the bureaucracy. Because of this, one cannot speak of Creole nationalism (against the Spaniards), but of Creole patriotism: an ideology that extolled the benign influence Mexico, Peru, and other countries. On the other hand, beyond European nationals born in Mexico, this Creole patriotism also found support among ladinoized Indians who no longer belonged to an indigenous community and for whom a highly valued homeland could be important.

Finally, it is interesting to note African slaves' position with respect to these issues of homeland, nationality, and community. Unlike Indians, slaves had no inalienable possessions; all their goods were alienated. Moreover, the very legitimation for slavery was to undo peoples who resisted evangelization. In principle, slaves were captives of "just wars" against unbelievers who refused even to listen to the missionaries. In this context, it was legitimate to take slaves and oblige them to receive Christian instruction in hopes that they would go on to a better world after passing through all the sufferings of a life dedicated to servitude. Thus, unlike the Indians, slaves were not redeemable as a nation, but only as individuals, and this only after the bitterness of slavery. Because of this, black communities were regularly watched or flatly banned: the association of more than two blacks and all corporate bodies except the military companies of Pardos y Morenos of the eighteenth century and religious sodalities were prohibited, and even sodalities were illegal at times because of their subversive potential.[13]

However, there was an important contradiction with respect to the collective nature of slaves: despite all the efforts against the formation of a slave society parallel to indigenous society, slaves were brought from Africa and nowhere else precisely because they could not be confused with either Europeans or Indians. Undoubtedly, this confluence of factors helps us understand the fear that the idea of Afro-American kingdoms inspired in Spaniards. However, the tendency to form Afro-Mexican collectivities was limited to the groups of maroons who succeeded in establishing themselves in coastal areas. Meanwhile, most slaves were marrying free people and contributing to the formation of the colonial *plebe* that constituted the popular classes in cities, mines, and ports.

These considerations about indigenous, Creole, and black nationality and patriotism are fundamental for understanding the development of

Mexican nationality properly speaking. Before passing to that topic, however, it is important to mention one unintentional political effect of the colonial regime. It is clear from all the evidence that the predominant ideological, legal, and economic system in the colonial period helped forge a multinational society in which different "national" groups could share interests in their homelands. One must add to this, however, that the colonial political system in itself helped to produce images of political sovereignty that people were trying to emulate after independence: in the colonial period, Mexico City was the seat of a viceroyalty presided over by a viceroy, who conceived of himself as the king's alter ego. His court was composed of nobles, the high clergy, learned men, merchants, and miners. The viceroy was ultimately responsible for all branches of government—administrative, ecclesiastical, and military. The existence of this pinnacle of state power in New Spain undoubtedly helped the Creoles and their various allies to imagine a new state with its capital in Mexico City, ruled by Mexican patriots and not by Iberians.

## Nationality after Independence

One of the central ideological problems of the independence period was how to transform Creole patriotism into a new nationalism that could include social groups that had been born in Mexico but did not belong to the "Hispano-Mexican race."

This was a practical question even before it became a theoretical one: how to give the homeland enough stature so that patriotic concerns would eclipse class and caste questions. At a purely logical level there were only two solutions to this problem: the first was to redefine the ideas of nation and nationality so that belonging to a common homeland determined and defined belonging to the nation; the second was to maintain the multinational system with a European elite, but in a context where everyone benefited from the fact that this elite was as attached and loyal to the same homeland as the Indians and blacks. On a practical level, there were obviously different, extremely complex ways of blending these two options, which need to be explained. Regardless of which option was adopted, any independence ideology had to have a common patriotic basis; it was much simpler to share a love for the homeland than to agree on the characteristics of the nation.

Because of this, the first formulations of Mexico's sacred and inalienable goods were very directly linked with symbols of the (home)land: its "sacred soil," the central mesa's deep blue skies, the Aztec eagle, the volcanos, the silver extracted from the homeland's "belly," and the pyramids and other grandeurs of the pre-Hispanic indigenous cultures, the material remains of which now formed part of the land and gave the landscape its own name: Mexico, not New Spain.

This set of symbols, which were of the homeland and not strictly national, had first been developed by Creole patriots beginning in the late sixteenth century. By the time of independence, these symbols had already become part of a well-known repertoire: the artworks that extolled the products and landscapes of the New World, the presentation of pre-Columbian civilizations as parallel to those of Greek and Roman classical antiquity, the assertion of Mexican Christianity's legitimacy and autonomy through the cult of the Virgin of Guadalupe, the search for a pre-Hispanic Christianity in such figures as Quetzalcoatl, and so on.[14]

The novelty of independence patriotism in the face of this Creole tradition was that, given the Mexican state, one could proceed to grant official status to these symbols. Thus, Hidalgo flew the standard of the Virgin of Guadalupe; José María Morelos used a flag with an eagle on a nopal cactus and the inscription "VVM" (¡Viva la Virgen María!); Iturbide also adopted the Aztec eagle (albeit with a crown), and in 1821 he formed the Order of Guadalupe for soldiers, insurgents, teachers, and distinguished clergymen. The first coins were minted with figures of the Aztec eagle. From 1821 to 1853, various national anthems were composed until the patriotic song of González Bocanegra was adopted. One cannot say that it is nationalistic: it is almost exclusively about the importance of sacrificing for the homeland, and its most representative stanza is the one that proclaims, "No longer shall the blood of your sons / be spilled in contention between brothers / only may he who insults your sacred name / encounter the steel in your hands."

However, the speed with which the sacred signs and objects of the homeland were formed did not have such a simple counterpart in the way the nation was defined. In fact, the national question properly speaking has been polemical ever since.

The ways in which the homeland was identified with the nation were evolving in interesting ways. In the first years of independence, one of the legacies uniformly claimed for the nation was the Catholic religion. This nationalization of the church can be partially understood as an extension of the appropriation of the faith that was the ideological cornerstone of Spanish imperialism. The church was considered a fundamental and inalienable legacy of the Mexican nation in all the principal laws and documents of the early independence period, from the appropiation of the

Virgin of Guadalupe by Father Hidalgo to the political programs of Morelos, Iturbide, and the 1824 constitution. The Seven Laws (1835) stipulated that Mexicans had the obligation to profess the Catholic religion, and not even the anticlerical laws promoted by José María Luis Mora in 1833 undermined the official status of Catholicism. The essentialized link between the nation and religion was not broken until the 1857 constitution, and the process of denationalizing religion was never fully achieved.

On the other hand, regardless of the support that nationality could find in religion, the difficulty in defining the nation was reflected in the fluctuating ways in which citizenship was defined. Although there was a more or less uniform movement to make ties to the homeland the definitive criterion of nationality, the definition of which individuals were citizens properly speaking was much more restricted. Thus, for example, in the Seven Laws—which were valid from 1835 until the Reform laws—only men of legal age with an annual income more than one hundred pesos could vote. In 1846, these men were also required to know how to read and write. In order to be a congressional deputy, one needed a minimal annual income of 1,500 pesos, to be a senator, 2,000, and to be president, 4,000.

Thus nationalist ideology in the first half of the nineteenth century permitted the de facto retention of colonial social hierarchies: distinction through money could strengthen systems of discrimination by "race" given the fact that the majority of Indians and other people of color were poor.

However, there were also great differences between the system established after independence, which favored the rich, and the explicitly caste-based system of the colonial period. One of the central differences is that supposedly belonging to a common nation (defined on the basis of a common homeland) made it possible for peasant villages and other poor contingents to make their political claims in terms of citizens' rights and not in terms of the subordinated complementarity of caste. But this transformation could also mean the loss of certain special rights for subaltern groups, above all Indians. The ideological, legal, and physical assault on communal village lands and other indigenous community institutions such as hospitals, public political offices, schools, and the management of community chests began in the first years of independence. The counterparts to this assault were the indigenist movements that sought to identify the nation with the indigenous race. These early *indigenista* movements expressed themselves in national political spheres through such figures as the congressional deputy Rodríguez Puebla, who in the first congresses fought to keep indigenous community institutions (except tribute) intact.

This political position was contrary to the central precept of liberalism, however, which was becoming the dominant ideology of the independence movement. An *indigenismo* that attempted to maintain and strengthen indigenous communities within a pluriracial national order threatened to divide the nation. Don José María Luis Mora summed up the liberal stance toward this *indigenismo*:

> The real reason for this opposition was that the new arrangement of public instruction was in open conflict with Mr. Rodríguez Puebla's desires, goals, and objectives with respect to the destiny of the remains of the *Aztec race* that still exist in Mexico. This gentleman, who pretends to belong to the said race, is one of the country's notables because of his good moral and political qualities; in theory, his is the party of *progress* and personally he is a *yorkino*; but, unlike the men who labor in this together, Mr. Rodríguez does not limit his scope to winning liberty, but extends it to exalting the Aztec race, and therefore his first objective is to maintain it in society with its own existence. To that end he has supported and continues to support the Indians' ancient civil and religious privileges, the status quo of the goods that they possessed in community, the poorhouses intended to attend to them, and the college in which they exclusively received their education; in a word, without an explicit confession, his principles, goals, and objectives tend to visibly establish a *purely Indian system*.
>
> The Farías administration, like all the ones that preceded it, thought differently; it was persuaded that the existence of different races in the same society was and had to be an eternal principle of discord. Not only did he [Farías] ignore these distinctions of past years that were proscribed in constitutional law, but he applied all his efforts toward forcing the fusion of the Aztec race with the general masses; thus he did not recognize the distinction between *Indians* and non-*Indians* in government acts, but instead he replaced it with that between the *poor* and the *rich*, extending to all the benefits of society.[15]

The conflict over the place of indigenous communities in the new national society did not end with these squabbles in the country's high political spheres: above all, it translated into regional conflicts in which indigenous groups sought to construct their own national autonomies. These movements were called "caste wars" by the nation's political classes, but they must also be understood as national movements in the sense that they sought congruency among indigenous nations, management of territory, and appropiation of religion.

Many Indians' nostalgia for their own states, a land with one blood under the rule of their own wise men and the mantle of an indigenous Christianity, translated into social movements at various points in the eighteenth, nineteenth, and even twentieth centuries. For example, during the famous "caste war" of Yucatán, the Indians had their capital in Chan-Santa Cruz and constructed their leadership around a cross that spoke directly to the priests who directed the rebellious Indian movement. Among other, structurally similar, movements were those that took place in the Chiapas highlands (1868), the Yaqui desert of Sonora (1885–1909), the Huasteca of San Luis Potosí (1888), and the coastal Mixteca region (1911). There were also a number of nonviolent movements of this type, some of them allied with now urbanized classes. In the very capital of the country, there are currently pro-Nahuatl groups of mixed social origins that seek the return of Moctezuma's headdress and the installation of a new indigenous empire.

On the other hand, given the fact that nineteenth-century liberalism was against upholding a "multiracial" nation, racist ideas that had existed since the colonial period could persist and become increasingly pernicious.

The ideologist who most influenced educated racist thought in Mexico was Herbert Spencer, who believed in the fundamental importance of social evolution and in the inheritance of acquired characteristics. This combination of doctrines, applied to Mexico, led to the conclusion that the Indians had been subsidized by the colonial state for centuries, and that the negative characteristics that had been acquired would continue to plague national evolution if the proportion of fit individuals (Europeans) did not increase.[16]

On the other hand, Spanish forms still dominated racist thought in Mexico even after the importation of northern European ideas. According to the dominant ideologies of the colonial period, the indigenous race was inferior to the Spanish race, but it was also redeemable through Christian faith and procreation with Spaniards. There was a well-known formula according to which the child of a Spaniard and an Indian was a *mestizo*; the child of a mestizo and a Spaniard was a *castizo*; and the child of a *castizo* and a Spaniard was a Spaniard; that is, an individual's indigenous origins could be "erased" through a couple generations of intermarriage with Europeans.

This is why, in the colonial period, racial identity was manipulated: birth certificates were altered so that children could be classified as Creoles and not as some inferior caste; mestizos bought access to indigenous communities; rights to dress as Spaniards, ride horses, and bear arms were conceded to certain Indians. With independence, the definitions and legal guarantees of caste were abandoned, the slaves were freed, and indigenous tribute as well as racial classifications in baptismal certificates were prohibited. However, the manipulation of racial identity continued, above all in the struggle for status. Only in this way can we understand why Porfirio Díaz powdered his face white and why politicians and rich men with dark skin had an exaggerated preference for white wives.

On the other hand, after independence, the ideas of granting the mestizo a certain racial dignity and of making the mestizo into a national race began to gain currency. In the beginning, this tendency was limited simply to recognizing the greatness of both the indigenous and the Spanish sources of nationality. However, this recognition of the central importance of *mestizaje* for Mexican nationality could not be easily translated into an ideology in which the mestizo was equal to the Mexican, for two reasons: liberalism's attempt to rid the definition of *nation* of any links with race and the ever-greater influence of pseudoscientific racist thought.

Thus, the liberalism of Juárez and his generation—which had great political and intellectual figures of indigenous origin—was completely distinct from the *indigenismo* of Rodríguez Puebla. Whereas Rodríguez sought to maintain indigenous communities within a pluralistic national framework, Juárez showed that Indians were perfectly capable of "ascending" to the Europeans' cultural level if given the opportunity and resources. Juárez's generation of liberals sought to redeem the Indians by giving them access to the goods of citizenship: education, universal rights, and equality.

Juárez sought to form a nationality composed of a citizenry (defined by common birth in a homeland) that had a truer equality of access to state protection and representation. One can say that, in the 1857 constitution, the nation had three inalienable legacies: national territory, state sovereignty, and a set of inviolable individual rights. This is also why liberals of this generation broke the privileged link that the church had maintained with Mexican nationality until then: they no longer needed a national church to legitimize the country because the freedom and equality of Mexicans under the rule of law and in the framework of the homeland were sufficient. On the other hand, the dark-skinned Juárez was himself living proof that these ideals were attainable.

It was easier to denationalize the church, however, than it was to construct a national citizenry. The laws promoted by Juárez helped erode the indigenous communities that had mantained the *calpulli*'s transformed communitarian legacy, but the proletarianized masses continued to be principally dark-skinned and under the economic yoke of foreigners.

The majority of Mexico's poor continued to be excluded from the benefits of nationality (citizens' equality, public education, and the right of representation in the state) because the national bureaucracy's resources were meager and, worse yet, those resources were primarily utilized for paving the way for capitalist investment. For this reason, in the nineteenth century the term *Indian* gained a new acceptance, fusing racial and class factors: for the urban middle and upper classes, any poor peasant was an "Indian"; that is, the category "Indian" came to mean those who were not complete citizens.

This also explains why Spencer's racist thought gained some influence in official circles. Social Darwinism permitted certain official groups to blame the victims for the negative results of postindependence social development: Mexico had not attained the social level of the United States because of the Indians' negative influence. The only way to achieve political evolution was by importing Europeans and dominating Indians through education or, in more recalcitrant cases, crueler disciplinary forms: in this period, indigenous slavery was revived and massacres of Indians were perpetrated in Sonora and Yucatán.

The power and class struggles of this period also became a national struggle in some sectors because the progress achieved by Porfirio Díaz was largely based on concessions to foreign capital, and the social sectors that were negatively affected by those concessions allied themselves with political groups that had been excluded from the monopoly that Don Porfirio's group exercised over the bureaucratic apparatus. These alliances gave rise to the revolution.

## The Redefinition of Nationality in the Revolution

From the point of view of nationality, the Mexican Revolution was a watershed at least as important as the Juárez reforms. Here I focus on two features, the revaluation of the mestizo as quintessentially national and the redefinition of the inalienable goods of the nation. As already mentioned, the placement of the mestizo as a central personage has a history that began with independence, but the revolution broke ties with two doctrines that had inhibited the adoption of the mestizo as the national race. On the one hand, Juárez's classical liberalism was complemented with a protectionist state that was willing to take special measures and dispositions for specific national groups such as Indians, peasants, and workers. On the other hand, the racist ideas of social Darwinism were overturned.

These two ruptures were complementary and went hand in hand. The most important figure in the battle against pseudoscientific racism was

Manuel Gamio, who is frequently considered the "father" of Mexican anthropology because of his role in the construction of revolutionary nationalism. Gamio relied on the authority of his teacher, Franz Boas, in claiming both the equality of all races and the validity of all cultures. Based on this, Gamio developed an *indigenismo* that dignified Mexican Indian features and blood, thereby paving the way for the mestizo to emerge as the protagonist of national history.

The principal ideologists of Mexican nationalism (Luis Cabrera, Andrés Molina Enríquez, Manuel Gamio) imagined the mestizo as the product of a Spanish father and an indigenous mother. This very particular formula had a twofold importance. First, it made the Spanish Conquest the origin of the national race and culture. This point of origin was fertile for the production of a national mythology, a task that captured the attention of prominent artists and intellectuals, including Diego Rivera, Samuel Ramos, and Octavio Paz. Second, and even more important, the identification of the European with the male and the feminization of the Indian fit well with the formulation of a nationalism that was at once modernizing and protectionist.

We can better understand this by analyzing Andrés Molina Enríquez's close discussion of the matter (1909), which was influential in the formulation of revolutionary nationalism. According to Molina, who leaned on Darwin, and on Mexican luminaries such as Vicente Riva Palacio and Francisco Pimentel, for crucial aspects of his argument, "[t]he mestizo element, formed by the cross of the Spanish element and the indigenous element, is not a new race, it is the indigenous race, defined as the totality of indigenous races of our land, modified by Spanish blood."[17] Mestizos were thus a fortified version of the indigenous race,[18] and the modifications brought about by this mixture of Spanish and Indian races would, eventually, create a population that would finally be capable of holding its own against the United States.[19]

In Molina, as in practically every pro-mestizo nationalist, the Spanish race came to Mexico through men, and the indigenous element was associated with the feminine. This was true both literally (the mestizo was imagined, in his origin, as the child of a Spanish man and an Indian woman) and more abstractly, in the characteristics of each race. "If the white races can be considered superior to the Indian races because of the greater efficacy of their *action* (which is a logical consequence of their superior evolution), the indigenous races can be considered superior to the white races because of their greater *resistance* (which is a consequence of their higher degree of selection)."[20] Action, which is highly masculine in this context, and resistance, which is feminine, are thereby embodied in the Spaniard and the Indian, respectively. The combination of action and resistance in the body of the mestizo is powerful, for it combines the best qualities of each race, but with the Indian element, that is, the maternal element, predominating. The results are destined to lead the nation to success against foreign aggression and neocolonial exploitation.

Mestizo nationalism thus implicitly supported the creation of a protectionist and modernizing state. It was to be a modernizing state because the mestizo, like his European father, had a propensity for action, for history. It was protectionist because the mestizo sought to protect his maternal legacy from exploitation by Europeans, who felt no loyalty whatsoever to the land or to the Indian, and whom Molina Enríquez saw as the dominant class that needed to be assimilated or pushed out.

The nationalization of the mestizo also represented a break with some features of laissez-faire liberalism and introduced a new version of the national patrimony. There was no longer the notion that progress and modernity emanated simply from free-market forces and respect for the rights of man; instead, there emerged the idea that progress could only occur under the jealous protection of a nationalist state.

Thus, in addition to guaranteeing citizens' rights, the sanctity of democratic institutions, and national sovereignty, the 1917 constitution claims the state's right to permit or prohibit the free action of foreigners in the country and to watch over the public interest. The latter includes public education, labor conditions, the right to expropriate any land for reasons of public utility, the regulation of foreign investment and of the amount of land that can be legally possessed, preferential contracting of Mexicans over foreigners, and so on. This constitution explicitly states that all the land of Mexico is an inalienable possession of the nation that may be bought and sold but can always be returned to public use when so needed.

Under the watchful eye of the postrevolutionary state, a regime that fostered class-based corporations as an integral portion of a one-party system, Mexico went from being predominantly rural and agricultural to having an urban majority, and the population grew from about 20 million in 1950 to about 80 million in 1990. This urbanization and the generally growing complexity of national society began to complicate the management of state representation through the "sectors" of the ruling party and the policies of the one-party state. At the same time, the mechanisms of state bureaucratic administration could not avoid the country's bankruptcy in 1982, which meant that foreign economic demands had to be attended to.

A chain of reforms that began under President Miguel de la Madrid has tended to revive some features of the nineteenth-century liberal model, including the redefinition of what constitutes the inalienable wealth of the nation: a decline of the so-called social rights of the revolution and greater emphasis on individual rights. For this reason, nationalists of the old school have compared the sale of state enterprises and the privatization of the *ejido* with the sale of the family jewels. The legal and economic changes carried out since 1982 represent a profound transformation in the very definition of the nation and of the things and relationships that belong to it.

The contemporary nationalist discourse appears to be reverting to the patriotic formulas of the nineteenth century: it is long on praising the *patria* and past glories of our "millennial culture," but it is very short on defining what the nation and its legacy currently are. There have only been two historical moments when the relationship between homeland and nation has been congruently and explicitly defined. The first was the universalist liberalism promoted by Benito Juárez, when the nation was separated from its bonds with race and the church. This was tremendously influential in national history, although it was never realized as a practical project. The second moment was revolutionary nationalism, which is internally more contradictory than Juárez's formula because it adopted some elements of democratic liberalism at the same time that it constructed a corporativist and protectionist state. This model tied nationality to race and "mestizo" culture, and it adopted a modernizing, protectionist, corporativist, one-party regime.

The current regime has been abandoning the now rusty or fossilized precepts of revolutionary nationalism, but it has been slow to embrace Juárez's universalist liberalism because unpopular economic reforms have required a strong, authoritarian state like those that arose from the revolution. On the other hand, universalist liberalism was a more potent ideology in the hands of Juárez because he was proving with his own flesh that Indians could gain access to the benefits of civilization that were in the hands of an economic elite that did not identify with the bulk of the population. For all these reasons, the current regime has needed revolutionary nationalism even to destroy the regime that created it.

Current tastes reflect weariness with the epic visions of revolutionary nationalism: today the intimate world of Frida Kahlo is of greater interest than the epic grandiloquence of Diego Rivera; even when they distill nationalism, as with the narratives of Poniatowska or Monsiváis, intimate chronicles are consumed with more interest than the comprehensive national epics of a Carlos Fuentes. This situation is symptomatic of the crisis of old nationalism: the longing for community and an inheritance continues, but the state definitions of those communities are almost as weak as they were in the nineteenth century.

## Conclusion

The development of the communitarian ideologies that I have tracked in this chapter permits us to systematize certain considerations with respect to the future. As this is a moment of profound changes in the national question, it appears to me to be pertinent to conclude with some ideas in this regard, even if they are not necessarily novel. I hope at least that the foregoing discussion permits us to understand the known options with greater clarity.

Currently there are at least three logical alternatives for national ideology insofar as it is manifested in the definition of inalienable goods: The first option is to consolidate democracy in the way desired by Juárez's generation. This option would mean giving priority to the inalienable rights defended by Juárez, including human rights and democratic representation. The second option is to reanimate revolutionary nationalism. This option would mean maintaining the "tutelage of the state" over some goods considered central to nationality and the public interest, such as land, the subsoil, the communications industries, and educational and cultural services, and industries. This option could keep mestizo nationalism unscathed but it has the problem of being championed principally by the leftist opposition, which also needs to sustain the value of democracy "in the style of Juárez" to win power. For that reason, it would have to design a kind of state that does not fall into the same antidemocratic vices that revolutionary nationalism fell into when it was in power. The concrete way in which revolutionary nationalism mixes with liberal ideals has always been a central problem for this kind of nationalism, and, if this ideology returns to power, it will again have to confront this problem.

The third option is less clearly delineated but would have to try to build a social democracy based on a recodification of human rights. This formula would differ from the second because it would not depend on a racial metaphor ("the mestizo") to define nationality, but would center its efforts in defining the rights of persons: it would not put "the nation" ahead of the rights of persons, and therefore it would distance itself from the populist and authoritarian formulas that have predominated in Mexico. On the other hand, this option separates itself from liberalism and "neoliberalism" because it seeks to broaden the definition of the human right to defend certain general social interests against the "natural" tendencies of the market (for example, defending child nutrition or the right to inhabit unpolluted spaces).

This direction also entails a recodification of civil society. This new civil society would rid itself of the sectorial organization that developed under revolutionary statism, and it would create new forms of state protection for the new human rights. The principal ideological adversary of this option will be the current nationalist mythology. This mythology tends to demand a state with tutelage over the entire national interest and includes many of the prior bases for the definition of national communities, such as the reification of nationality in racial terms. Also, behind this lies the proposition that the state's central role is to direct the "modernizing" process. It will be necessary to impose limits on the reign of the ideology of modernization, to avoid modernizing at any cost.

It appears to me that the third path is the only really desirable and viable one in the long run. But to move in that direction, one must be ready to question both revolutionary nationalism and neoliberalism. It will also be necessary to create images of nationality and modernity that are separate from the teleology of the muralists and the "Fathers of the Country."

# 3

## Modes of Mexican Citizenship

One of the first cultural accounts of citizenship in Latin America was Roberto DaMatta's effort to understand the specificity of Brazilian national culture. DaMatta identified the coexistence of two broad discourses in Brazilian urban society, and he called them the discourse of the home and the discourse of the street.[1] According to his description, the discourse that he called "of the home" is a hierarchical and familial register, where the subjects are "persons" in the Maussian sense, that is, they assume specific, differentiated, and complementary social roles. The discourse "of the street," by contrast, is the discourse of liberal citizenship: subjects are individuals who are meant to be equal to one another and equal before the law.

The interesting twist in DaMatta's analysis regards the relationship between these two discourses, a relationship that he synthesizes with the Brazilian adage "For my friends, everything; for my enemies, the law."[2] For DaMatta, Brazilian society can be described as having "citizenship" as a degraded baseline, or zero degree, of relationship, a fact that is visible in the day-to-day management of social relations.

Specifically, DaMatta focuses on an urban ritual that he called the "Voçe sabe com quem esta falando?" (Do you know who you are talking to?), a phrase that is used to interrupt the universal application of a rule, that is, to interrupt what he calls the discourse of the street, in order to gain exceptional status and to rise above the degradation reserved for all nobodies. Thus, for instance, a lady cuts in front of a line to enter a parking lot; the attendant protests and points to the line, but she says "Do you know who you are talking to? I am the wife of so and so, member of the cabinet," and so on.

A similar dynamic has characterized modern Mexican citizenship. For instance, it has long been noted that in Mexico much of the censorship of the press has been "self-censorship," and not direct governmental censorship.[3] Speaking to a journalist about this phenomenon, he remarked that much of this self-censorship resulted from the fact that journalists, like all members of Mexican middle classes, depend to an unpredictable degree on their social relations. Reliance on personal relations generates a kind of sociability that avoids open attacks, except when corporate interests are involved. Thus, the censorship of the press is in part also a product of the overall dynamics of DaMatta's degraded citizenship.

The logic that DaMatta outlined for understanding the degradation of Brazilian citizenship could easily be used to guide an ethnography of civic culture and sociability in Mexico. The ease of application stems from similarities at both the cultural and structural levels: familial idioms used to shape a "discourse of the home" have common Iberian elements in these two countries, the result not only of related concepts and ideas of family and friendship, but also similar colonial discourses for the social whole.

In this chapter, I develop a historical discussion of the cultural dynamics of Mexican citizenship. I begin with a series of vignettes that explore what the application of DaMatta's perspective to Mexico might reveal. I argue that the notion that citizenship is the baseline, or zero degree, of relationship needs to be complemented by a historical view of changes in the definition and political salience of citizenship. Without such a perspective on the changing definition of citizenship, a critical aspect of the politics of citizenship is lost. The bulk of this chapter is devoted to interpreting the dynamics of citizenship in modern Mexico, as it developed in the nineteenth and twentieth centuries and argues against narratives of Mexican modernity that tell contemporary history as a simple "transition to democracy."

## Cultural Logic and History

Mexico City is a place of elaborate politeness, a quality that is epitomized by the people whose job is to mediate (for instance, secretaries and waiters), but that is generally visible in the socialization of children and in the existence of elaborate registers of obsequiousness, attentiveness, and respect. All of these registers disappear in the anonymity of the crowd, however, where people will push, pull, shove, pinch, cut in front of you, and so on. There is no social contract for the crowd; there are only gentleman's pacts among persons. Drivers in Mexico City, for instance, tend to drive with their eyes pointed straight ahead and cast slightly downward, much like a waiter's. This way they need not make concessions and can drive with presocial Hobbesian rules: don't give away an inch. If, however, the driver's eye wanders even just a little, it may catch another driver's eye, who gently and smilingly asks to be let into the flow of traffic. At this point, the world of personal relations often takes hold of the driver who had been trying to keep things anonymous, and he may gallantly let the other car through.

This dynamic contrasts with the culture of societies that have strong civic traditions, in which citizenship is the place where the social pact is manifested (making a queue being a sacrosanct rite of citizenship in a place like England, for instance), but where personal relationships do not extend as far out. Thus, a British traveler to Mexico may be scandalized at the greedy and impolitic attitude of the people on the street, whereas a Mexican will complain that no plea or personal interjection was ever able to move an English bureaucrat to sympathy.

What are the mechanisms of socialization into this form of courtesy? Access to an alleged right, or to a governmental service, in Mexico is very often not universal. Education, for instance, is meant to be available to all, but it is often difficult to register a child in a nearby school, or to get into a school at all; public medicine exists, but it is always insufficient; moving through Mexico City traffic in an orderly fashion is often made difficult by the overuse of public space. In short, Mexico has never had a state that was strong enough to provide services universally. In this context, corruption and other market mechanisms easily emerge as selection criteria: if you pay money, the bureaucrat will see you first. The system has also generated forms of sociability that help shape a practical orientation that is well suited to the discretionary power that scarcity gives to bureaucrats and other gatekeepers. One notable example of this is summed up in the very Mexican proverb "Whoever gets mad first, loses" ("El que se enoja, pierde").

According to this principle, a wise person shall never explode out of exasperation, because he or she can only lose by such an outburst. A service provider will only clam up when faced with an angry user and, since the service is a scarce resource, he or she will use politeness as a selection criterion.

Socialization into politeness, patience, and self-censorship thus has at least two significant social conditions. The first is a strong reliance on personal relations in order to activate, operate, and rely on any bureaucratic apparatus; the second is the reliance on personal relations to achieve positions in society. Both of these conditions would appear to support DaMatta's claim that citizenship is the zero degree of relationship.

There is, however, a difficulty in the argument that can be exposed by focusing closely on the implications of the saying "For my friends, everything; for my enemies, the law." The saying is clearly a model for political action, yet it contains significant ambiguities in the proposed categories ("friends," "enemies," "law," and "everything"), particularly if the saying is a recipe for a bureaucrat or a member of the political class. In many, if not most, situations, a bureaucrat will be dealing with neither personal friends nor personal enemies, but principally with people to whom he or she is unrelated and initially indifferent. The saying is useful, however, because some of these people will not receive the full service that the gatekeeper controls, whereas others will. Thus, an initially undifferentiated public needs to be shaped into "friends" and "enemies." Money (bribes) and prior personal connections are two routes to receiving exceptional treatment (as "friends"), but patience and politeness may at least keep you in the game, whereas a breach of politeness or an outburst of anger will in all likelihood place you in the "enemy" camp. The application of "the law" as a criterion of exclusion in each of these cases is simply the use of bureaucratic procedure as a fundamental mechanism of exclusion.

We have, then, a logic that favors the development of personal relations, the elaboration of forms of obsequiousness and politeness, the cultural routinization of bribery, and the use of bureaucratic rules and procedure as mechanisms of exclusion. This logic is undergirded by structural conditions, of which I have stressed two: a relatively weak state, and a large poor population. Because these conditions have existed throughout Mexican history, one might expect that bribery, politeness, and a highly developed system of informal relationships have been equally constant practices, and that they have been elaborated according to cultural idioms that apply a "discourse of the home" in order to create distinctions between potential users of a service. This is true at a general level.

However, although the cultural logic that we have outlined shows that citizenship is a degraded category, it also gives a false sense of continuity and constancy. We noted that the category of "friends" and "enemies" can be constructed in the very process of applying a bureaucratic rule, and that most of the population that is being classified in this way is initially indifferent to the bureaucrat. But the definition of the pool that the bu-reaucrat is acting on is not determined by the cultural logic of social dis-tance from the bureaucrat or gatekeeper. In other words, the gatekeeper is not actually ruling over a preselected group of friends and enemies, but is instead culturally constructing "friends" and "enemies" out of a pool of people who are preselected not by him, but by their theoretical relation-ship to a right.

As a result, although it is correct to say that—given a bureaucrat, a set of rules, and a pool of citizens—citizenship shall be the zero degree of relationship that needs to be complemented by a prior personal claim, by a bribe, or by sympathy, the baseline of citizenship is not determined by this cultural logic, and it varies historically in important ways. These variations are not trivial, for they define the potential pool of users of a service that is being offered, an issue that also has critical significance for a *longue-durée* history of cultural forms of sociability in connection to citizen-ship. A comprehensive view of modern Mexican citizenship therefore re-quires an interpretation of the relationship between legal and institutional definitions of citizenship and its cultural elaboration in social interaction. I shall attempt to sketch key elements of such a comprehensive view.

## Early Republicanism and the Rise of the Ideal Citizen

The debates of Mexico's Junta Instituyente between independence (1821) and the publication of the first federal constitution (1824) gave little sus-tained attention to citizenship. Laws about who was a Mexican national and who was a Mexican citizen were vaguely inclusive, with attention lav-ished only on the question of patriotic inclusion or exclusion and very little said about the qualities and characteristics of the citizen. Neverthe-less, the process of independence had a critical role in shaping a field for a politics of citizenship.

For instance, Miguel Hidalgo, father of Mexican independence, pro-claimed the emancipation of slaves, the end to all forms of tribute and taxation that were targeted to Indians and "castes," and the end of certain guilds' monopolies over specific activities.[4] Of course, Hidalgo's revolt failed, but his move to create a broad base for citizenship and to level differences between castes was preserved by leaders of subsequent move-ments. For example, Ignacio López Rayón's (also failed) project of a Mexican constitution (1811) also abolished slavery (article 24) and stated that "[w]hoever is to be born after the happy independence of our nation will find no obstacle other than his personal defects. No opposition can stem from the class of his lineage; the same shall be observed with regard to those who represent the rank of captain and above, or who render any special service to the country" (article 25). The only fundamental exclusionary clause in this constitution, as in all early Mexican constitutions until that of 1857, regards the role of religion: "The Catholic religion shall be the only one, with no tolerance for any other" (article 1).

In addition to a common movement to broaden the base of citizenship such that lineage and race were abolished as (explicit) criteria of inclusion or exclusion, early proclamations and constitutions did tend to specify that only Mexicans—and often only Mexicans who had not betrayed the nation—could hold public positions (articles 27 and 28 of López Rayón's constitutional project).[5] Thus, from the very beginning, the idea was to create an ample citizenry and a social hierarchy based on merit: "The American people, forgotten by some, pitied by others, and disdained by the majority, shall appear with the splendor and dignity that it has earned through the unique fashion in which it has broken the chains of despotism. Cowardice and slothfulness shall be the only causes of infamy for the citizen, and the temple of honor shall open its doors indiscriminately to merit and virtue" (article 38).[6]

Despite the general identification between early Mexican nationalism and the extension of citizenship rights in such a way as to include (former) slaves, Indians, and castes, there were a number of ambiguities and differences regarding the meaning of this extension. Article 16 of the Mexican empire's first provisional legal code, for instance, states, tellingly, that "[t]he various classes of the state shall be preserved with their respective distinction, but without prejudice to public employment, which is common to all citizens. Virtues, services, talents, and capability are the only medium for achieving public employment of any kind".[7] On the other hand, the federal constitution of 1824 does not even specify who is to be considered a citizen. Instead, it leaves to the individual states of the federation the definition of who shall be allowed to vote for their representatives in Congress (article 9), and the selection of the president and vice president was left to Congress. Thus citizenship was to be determined by regional elites in conjunction with whomsoever they felt they needed to pay attention to, and access to federal power was mediated by a Congress that represented these citizens.

It is worth noting that most of the distinctions between who was a Mexican citizen and who was merely a Mexican national are similar to the formulation found in the Spanish liberal constitution that was promulgated in Cádiz in 1812. Some of the early independent constitutions are a bit harsher than that of Cádiz on matters of religion (e.g., Father Morelos's Apatzingán constitution sanctioned the Holy Office—that is, the Inquisition—and it upheld heresy and apostasy as crimes that led to loss of citizenship). In one matter, however, the constitution of Cádiz narrows citizenship beyond what is explicit in the earliest Mexican constitutions: debtors, domestic servants, vagrants, the unemployed, and the illiterate all forfeited their rights as citizens (article 25). This move was not explicitly embraced in the first Mexican constitutional projects, but neither was it entirely avoided: Iturbide's Plan de Iguala, which was the first effective political charter of independent Mexico, specified that until a constitution was formed, Mexico would operate according to the laws of the Spanish Cortes. The federal constitution of 1824 left the door open for these mechanisms of exclusion by delegating the decision regarding who would be a citizen to the individual states. Finally, the centralist and conservative legal code of 1836 reasserted the points of exclusion of Cádiz and added much greater restrictions; the rights of citizenship were suspended for all minors, domestic servants, criminals, and illiterates, they were lost definitively to all traitors and debtors to the public coffers. All citizens had to have an annual income of one hundred pesos, and substantially more if they wanted to be elected to office.

In short, early Mexican constitutions displayed tensions between the elimination of criteria of caste and of slavery in order to create a broadly based nationality and the restriction of access to public office and to the public sphere to independent male property holders who could read and write. The category "citizen" was (and still is) not identical to that of "national" in legal discourse, though the two were tellingly conflated in political discourse: in fact, the relationship between the two was one of hierarchical encompassment. The Mexican citizen had the capacity to encompass Mexican nationals and to represent the whole of the nation in public.

### Inclusion and Exclusion in the Era of National Vulnerability

At first glance, these early citizenship laws developed in a contested field in which the pressure to broaden the basis of citizenship coexisted with pressures to maintain political control in the hands of local notables.

Historian François Xavier Guerra has argued that the urban patricians who had controlled the bureaucratic apparatus during the colonial period usually kept control over government despite these changes, relying on their power to materially control local election processes.[8] However, Florencia Mallon has shown that in the unstable context of mid-nineteenth-century Mexico, the need to mobilize popular constituencies, and the space that was available for spontaneous popular mobilization, led to the development of forms of liberalism that catered to popular groups.[9] It was in part the challenge that universal citizenship at times posed to these local patricians and chieftains that fanned the development of a negative discourse about "the masses" in nineteenth-century Mexico: *la chusma, el populacho, la canalla, la plebe*, and other epithets portrayed masses as both dangerous and insufficiently civilized to manage political life.

Alongside damning images of the *plebe*, a series of positive words referred to popular classes who were seen as ordered and civilized: *el pueblo, los ciudadanos, la gente buena*. To a large degree, the difference between positive and negative portrayals of the *pueblo* corresponded to whether the people in question were acting as dependents or whether they were difficult to control. Like the difference between the lumpenproletariat and the proletariat, the distinction between a *canalla* and a *ciudadano* was that the latter was a notable, or at least depended on the same system as the notables who made the distinction, whereas the former had only loose connections of dependency to "good society." In political speeches of the nineteenth century, for instance, there are differences drawn between a lower class that might be described as "abject" and as an obstacle to progress, but that is also perceived as unthreatening and in need of state protection, and a lower class that is potentially or in fact violent and dangerous to civilization.

In a chronicle of his voyage to the United States, published in 1834, Lorenzo de Zavala, a liberal from Yucatán who had been governor of the state of Mexico, congressman, and apologist for the U.S. colonization of Texas, asks his readers to

> [c]ompare the moral condition of the people of the United States with that of one or two or our [federated] states and you will understand the true reason why it is impossible for us to raise our institutions to the level of our neighbor's, *especially in certain states*. In the state of Mexico and in that of Yucatán, which are the ones that I know best, of the 1,200,000 inhabitants of the former and the seven hundred thousand inhabitants of the latter, there is a proportion of, at the most, one in twenty [who know how to read and write]. [Of these,] two-fifths do not know arithmetic, three-fifths do not even know the meaning of the words *geography, history, astronomy*, etc., and four-fifths do not know what the Bible is . . . To this we must add that at least one-third of the inhabitants of Yucatán do not speak Spanish, and

one-fifth of the state of Mexico is in the same condition. Those who do not take into account the degree of civilization of the masses when they *make institutions for the people are either highly ignorant or extremely perverse.*[10]

Thus, the native population in particular was at the bottom of the heap, and in need of elevation. A similar sentiment is echoed three decades later, after the French intervention, when the 1857 constitution was reinstated. There, in a session in Congress, representative Julio Zárate presented a proposal to prohibit private jails in haciendas and, more generally, to outlaw all punishment that was meted out in these private institutions. He described the conditions of the Indian in the following terms:

> In the states of Mexico, Puebla, Tlaxcala, Guerrero, and Querétaro, where the bulk of the indigenous population is concentrated, there is slavery, there is abjection, there is misery sustained by the great landowners. And this abject condition comprises close to 4 million men.
>
> It has been eleven years since the constitution was ratified: private trials were prohibited; flogging and other degrading punishments were abolished; and authorities were given the right to establish jails for crimes . . . nonetheless, there are jails in the haciendas and stocks where the workers are sunk, and the foreman gives lashes to the Indians, and debts are passed from father to son, creating slavery, a succession of sold generations (February 15, 1868).[11]

This view of the proto-citizen who needed to be elevated to true citizenship through state protection, miscegenation, or education, and whose condition was abject but not directly threatening to true and effective citizens, contrasts with other portrayals of popular folk who are more difficult to redeem and more menacing. I will offer two examples from the same congressional sessions that I have just cited.

On January 9, 1868, representative Jesús López brought to Congress a proposed law to banish bullfighting. This initiative was one of several attempts to locate the causes of incivility and to transform the habits of a people who would not conform to the ideal of citizenship that the constitution granted them:

> The benefits of a democratic constitution, which raise the Mexican from the condition of slavery to the rank of the citizen, announce that Mexico marches toward greatness under the auspices of liberty. In contrast to this, as an obstacle that blocks Mexico's march toward prosperity, there exists in each community a place that symbolizes barbarism . . .

Moreover:

> If we descend, sir, from these philosophical and moral considerations to search for material transcendental evils in society, we shall be confronted by the degradation of that class that, because of its ignorance, is called the lowliest class [clase ínfima], and that has been indelibly inoculated with a propensity to bloody acts . . . This class, which has been disinherited from the benefits of enlightenment, does not know the goodness of virtue except by the harm it receives for being criminal; in it the noble sentiments that inhere in the human heart degenerate, because the government and the clergy, publicists and speakers try to show them in abstract the matters of religion and of politics that their uncultivated intelligence cannot comprehend. All the while, the attractions of vice and the emotions that are produced by certain spectacles excite and move their passions. Since it is not possible to establish schools everywhere where this class can be well taught, remove at least those other [schools] where they learn evil, where the sight of blood easily fosters the savage instincts to which they have, by nature, a propensity. If we want good citizens, if we want brave soldiers who are animated in combat and humane in triumph, prohibit spectacles that inflate sentiments and that dull [embrutecen] reason.[12]

Readers would be incorrect, too, to think that the dangerous "lowliest" classes referred to here are strictly urban and that all rural Indians were thought to be safe for state or hacendado patronage. Rebellious Indians, usually labeled "savages," were known to be highly dangerous. Thus, for instance, in his campaign against Indian rebels and a few remaining pro-Hapsburg imperialists in Yucatán (1868), President Juárez asked Congress to suspend a series of individual guarantees in Yucatán in order to carry out a military campaign there. One of the suspended rights was article 5 of the constitution, which reads: "No one can be forced to render personal services without a fair retribution and without their full consent. The law cannot authorize any contract that has as its object the loss or irrevocable sacrifice of a man's liberty." In other words, slavery and corvée labor were authorized for the duration of the Yucatecan campaign, which was fought principally against the Indians.[13]

Thus, a discourse of the sort that DaMatta called "discourse of the street," that is, an egalitarian and universalistic discourse of citizenship, could be applied to the "good pueblo." At the same time, the fact that in some nineteenth-century constitutions servants were not allowed to vote because they were dependents, and therefore did not have control over their will, was indicative of the fact that most of the good pueblo was made up of a kind of citizenry that was guarded not so much by the constitutional rights of individuals as by the claims that loyalty and dependency had on the conscience of Christian patriarchs.

Nevertheless, the image of a good *pueblo* was not simply that of the dependent masses either, because these could be figured as a harmonious and progressive collectivity or (as we have seen) as abject slaves. In order to comprehend ideological dynamics within this field better, two further elements need to be introduced: the nation's position in a world of competing predatory powers, and the question of national unity.

A sharp consciousness of national decline and of uncontrollable dangers for the nation can be found among Mexican political men almost from the time of the toppling of Iturbide (1822). References to decline and to danger abound both in the press and in discussions in Congress. For instance, Deputy Hernández Chico claimed that the nation's situation was "deplorable" because of lack of public funds (June 14, 1824).[14] On June 12 of that same year, Deputy Cañedo warned of the need to guard against a full civil war, in light of secessionist movements in the state of Jalisco. The image of the republic being split apart by rival factions is almost always seen as the cause of this decline or imminent disaster, as in the case of a speech read in Congress by the minister of war against a pro-Iturbide uprising in Jalisco on June 8, 1824:

> Yes, sir, there are vehement indications that these two generals are plotting against the republic, that they desire its ruin, that it is they who move those implacable assassins that afflict the states of Puebla and Mexico, they who propagate that deadly division, that confrontation between parties, they who are behind the conspirators who cause our unease and who make life so difficult.

This feeling of pending or actual disaster caused by lack of union increased and became pervasive in political discourse as the country indeed became unstable, economically ruinous, and subjected to humiliations by foreign powers.

In a remarkably frank, but not entirely extraordinary, "civic oration" proffered on the anniversary of independence in the city of Durango in 1841, Licenciado Jesús Arellano recapped the history of political divisions and fraternal struggle in the following terms:

> Let's go back in time to September 27, 1821 . . . That day, my fellow citizens, the very day of our greatest fortune, also initiates the era of our greatest woes. It is from that day that a horrible discord began to exert its

deadly influence. Unleashed from the abysmal depths where it resides, it flung itself furiously in the midst of our newly born society and destroyed it in its crib . . . There in the shadows of that frightful darkness we can hear the roar of the monster that spilled in Padilla the blood of General Iturbide: the blood of the hero who finished the work of Hidalgo and Morelos. There, too, you can hear the horrible cry of that malicious and treacherous spirit that sold the life of the great [benemérito] and innocent General Guerrero to the firing squad.[15]

The heroes who had initiated the revolution (Hidalgo, Allende, Aldama, Morelos) had all been martyred by Spaniards, but the two who actually achieved independence (Iturbide and Guerrero) were both murdered by fractious Mexicans. This was to stand symbolically in a position analogous to original sin: Mexicans are denied their entry to national happiness because of their internal vices and divisions:

Woe is you, unfortunate Mexico! Woe is you because, not having yet fully entered the age of infancy, you decline in a precocious decrepitude that brings you close to the grave! Woe is you because you are like the female of those venomous insects that thrive in our climate, and of whom it is said that it gives birth to its children only to be eaten by them![16]

Decline was caused by personal ambition and folly among leaders and would-be leaders of government, so much so that Arellano begins his remarkable speech distancing himself from any sort of political activity:

I have not yet traveled—and God spare me from ever taking—the murky paths of the politics that dominate us, of that science whose principles are the whim of those who profess it, where the most obvious truths are put in doubt, and where he who is best at cheating and who is best at disguising his deceptions is considered wise.[17]

The ultimate results of vice, selfishness, and ambition have been the ruination of Mexico, its decline, its inability to reap the benefits of freedom and independence. For some speakers, these vices were typical of one party: monarchical interests of conservatives, for instance; or Catholic fanaticism that led to blocking the doors to colonization from northern Europe and the United States; or to federalist folly in delegating too much power and autonomy to states. For all, they reflected a lack of virtue and the fall of public morality. To quote again from Arellano: "We must acknowledge that our vices have grown and that public morality is every day extenuated, that our country has been a constant prey of ambition, of jealousy, of fratricidal tendencies, of atrocious vendettas, of insatiable usury, of fanaticism and superstition, of ineptitude and perversity, and of clumsy and inhumane mandarins."[18]

In sum, it is mistaken to imagine that, in its origins, the discourse of citizenship was in any simple way about settling a "zero degree of relationship." On the contrary, early legal codes had quite significant strictures regarding who could be a citizen. These restrictions readily allowed for the emergence of one specific discourse about the good and the bad *pueblo*: good *pueblo* was the *pueblo* that was obedient, the portion of Mexican nationals who allowed themselves peacefully to be represented by Mexican citizens; bad *pueblo* was the *pueblo* that was not governed by the class of local notables, and this included rebellious Indians (like those cited in Yucatán or in Durango) as much as the feared *clases ínfimas* that were not assimilable through public education.

At the same time, the tendency to conflate nationality and citizenship, at least as a utopian idea, existed from the very beginning, and this allowed for another kind of distinction between good and bad citizens. This distinction focused on "petty tyrants." Some of these were perceived, particularly after the constitution of 1857, as local caciques or hacendados who kept Indians in a slavelike position and separated from their rights as Mexicans, as was the case in the speech, cited earlier, against jails in haciendas. Others, and this was particularly prevalent in the earlier period, were tyrants in their selfish appropriation of what was public.

This latter form of dividing between virtuous and vicious elites readily allowed for the consolidation of a discourse of messianism around a virtuous caudillo, as is illustrated in another patriotic speech, pronounced on September 11, 1842 (anniversary of the triumph against the Spanish invasion of 1829) in the city of Orizaba:

> The political regeneration of Anahuac [Mexico] was reserved ab initio to a singular Veracruzano: an entrepreneurial genius, an animated soldier, a keen statesman, a profound politician, or, in sum, to Santa Anna the great, who, like another Alcides and Tesco, will purify the precious ground of the Aztecs and rid it of that disgusting and criminal riffraff *[canalla]* of tyrants of all species and conditions.[19]

In short, the political field around the definition of citizenship involved three kinds of distinctions: one between a *pueblo* that would be encompassed by a group of notables and a *pueblo* that would not; another between selfish and false citizens who sought private gain from their public position as citizens and those who equated citizenship with public service and sacrifice; and a third between citizens who strived to open the way for the extension of citizenship rights and those who blocked them in order to enhance their own tyrannical authority.

In some contexts, these views could be articulated to one another; for example, the situation of the "bad *pueblo*" was compared to that of a young woman who was not under the tutelage of a man, it was fodder for "seduction" by bandits or by factious aspiring politicians. In other words, the bad *pueblo* was fodder for the vicious politician, as much as it was the principal challenge for enlightened liberal governments who sought to expand public education, eliminate the obscurantist influence of the church, prohibit bullfights, cockfights, and other forms of barbaric diversions, and so on.

The description of citizenship as a zero degree of relationship is misleading, then, because it emphasizes only one aspect of the phenomenon, which is the fact that familial discourses have always been used to supersede the universalism of the legal order. Moreover, the notion of the citizen as the baseline of all political relationships is historically incorrect, because in the early national period it was clearly a sign of distinction to be a citizen, and even after the constitution of 1857 and the revolutionary constitution of 1917, it still excluded minors and women. Having established this general point, let us return to our evolutionary panorama of the development of citizenship in Mexico.

## The Demise of Early Liberal Citizenship

The first truly liberal constitution of Mexico (1857) develops an inclusive and relatively unproblematic identification between citizenship and nationality: in order to be a citizen, all that one needed was to be a Mexican over eighteen (if one was married, over twenty-one if one was not), and to earn an honest living (article 34). Simplicity, however, is sometimes misleading.

Because in theory everyone was a citizen if they were of age (the article does not even specify that one needed to be male to be a citizen, though this apparently went without saying, because female suffrage was not to be allowed for another hundred years), the constitution and the congresses that met after its ratification were very much concerned with giving moral shape to the citizen.

Fernando Escalante ends his pathbreaking book on politics and citizenship in Mexico in the nineteenth century arguing that "[t]here were no citizens because there were no individuals. Security, business, and politics were collective affairs. But never, or only very rarely, could they be resolved by a general formula that was at once efficacious, convincing, and presentable."[20] His book demonstrates that there was a high degree of pragmatic accord between liberals and conservatives on the matter of laws and institutions not being applicable in a systematic fashion because consolidating state power was more fundamental and urgent, and neither group could adequately resolve the contradiction between creating an effective and exclusive group of citizens and the actual politics of inclusion and exclusion demanded by the society's numerous corporations.

Despite this pragmatic agreement regarding the priority that consolidating state power had over citizenship rights, the ideal of citizenship was about as obsessively pervasive in Mexican political discourse as was the rejection of politics as a site of vice. Part of this obsession was a result of the fact that, until Juárez's triumph over Maximilian in 1867, political instability and economic decline raised fears that Mexico could be swallowed up by foreign powers or split apart by internal rifts. Collective mobilization seemed the only way forward, and there is a sense in which Mexican history between independence and the French intervention (1821–67) can be seen as a process of increasing polarization. In the end, it was this process, in conjunction with emerging capitalist development and the construction of the first railroads in the 1870s, that allowed the first successful centralized governments of Juárez and, especially, of Díaz, to operate.

Escalante has argued convincingly that the old idea, championed by Cosío Villegas, that Juárez's restored republic was a genuine experiment in liberal democracy is simply wrong, and that the consolidation of the central state under Juárez and Lerdo needed to sidestep the legal order and to create informal networks of power as much as the Díaz dictatorship that followed it.

I have no space here to go into detail concerning the evolution of citizenship under the Díaz regime (1876–1910), but a few remarks are necessary. First, the achievement of governmental stability and material progress pushed earlier recurrent obsession over citizenship into the background. A plausible hypothesis is that a strong unified state and the concomitant process of economic growth led by foreign investment was a more valued goal for the political classes than citizenship. In fact, the earlier fixation on citizenship was in large part the result of the fact that regional elites needed to appeal to altruistic patriotism in order to try to hold the state together; once the state could hold its own, this motivation disappeared.[21] A discourse on "order and progress" quickly superseded earlier emphasis on citizenship and the universal application of laws as the only way to progress, and a strong state that could guarantee foreign investment was the key to that progress.

Thus, during the Porfirian dictatorship, it was the state, and its power to arrange space and to regiment an order, that was the subject of political ritual and myth; the masses, it was hoped, might eventually catch up to progress or—if they opposed the national state, as the Yaqui, Apache, and Maya Indians did—be eliminated. In short, whereas the law and the citizen were the ultimate fetishes of the era of national instability,[22] progress, urban boulevards, railroads, and the mounted police (*rurales*) were the key fetishes of a Porfirian era that upheld the state as the promoter of that progress, and the vehicle for the ultimate improvement of Mexico's abject rural masses.[23]

## Contemporary Transformations

If this were the end of the story, however, how could we come to terms with the fact that in the 1930s Samuel Ramos, the famous founder of a philosophy about the Mexican as a social subject, identified the *pelado*, that is, the subject who had been considered beyond the pale of citizenship since independence, as the quintessential Mexican? Ramos argued that Mexican national character was marked by a collective inferiority complex. This inferiority complex was exemplified in the attitude of the *pelado* (urban scoundrel), who is so wounded by the other's gaze that he replies to it aggressively with the challenge of "¿Qué me ves?" (What are you looking at?).[24] Thus, where the driver of our earlier Mexico City example seeks anonymity in order to act like a wolf, but becomes a gentleman with eye contact, the *pelado* rejects eye contact with a threat of violence. But whereas the nineteenth-century politician would not have hesitated in identifying the true citizen with the (unconstantly) amiable driver and the *pelado* as an enemy of all good society and an individual lacking in love and respect for his *patria*, postrevolutionary intellectuals such as Ramos made the urban rabble into the Ur-Mexicans. Why the change?

Before the revolutionary constitution of 1917, Mexican citizens had individual rights, but very few social rights. The right of education existed in theory but, as historical studies of education have shown (Vaughan 1994), public education during the *porfiriato* was controlled to a large extent by urban notables, a fact that was reflected in extremely low literacy rates. Moreover, as I mentioned earlier, the right to vote was often nullified by the machinery of local bosses, who controlled voting as a matter of routine.

The 1917 constitution and the regimes following the revolution changed this in several significant ways. First, under the leadership of José

Vasconcelos in the 1920s, and in an effort to wrench the formation of citizens from the hands of the church, public education went on a crusade to reach out to the popular classes. This effort was successful to a significant degree, and schools were built even in remote agrarian communities. Second, the 1917 constitution established the right of access to land for agricultural workers. The land, according to this constitution, belonged to the nation, as did the subsoil and territorial waters. Citizens had rights to portions of that national wealth under certain conditions. Third, the 1917 constitution specified a series of worker's rights, including minimum wages, the prohibition of child labor, the prohibition of debt peonage, maximum working hours, and the like. Thus, being a citizen promised rights of access to certain forms of protection against the predatory practices of capitalists, who, significantly, were often identified as foreign in constitutional debates.

Identifying members of the urban rabble as the prototypical Mexicans was, in this context, consonant with the state's expansive project. The modal citizen should, indeed, be the affable and reasonable member of the middle classes—and Ramos's portrayal of the *pelado* was in no way laudatory; however, Mexico's backwardness and the challenge of its present made it useful to identify the typical subject as being off center from that ideal.

At the same time, the revolutionary state, like the Porfirian state, did not concern itself so much with producing citizens. Instead, the goal was to create and to harness corporate groups and sectors into the state apparatus. Although presidents Obregón and Calles upheld the ideal of the private farmer in the 1920s and thought it a much more desirable goal than that of the communitarian peasant, the task of building up the state was more important to them than building up the citizen.

The principal shift between the Porfirian and the postrevolutionary state is that the latter consolidated a political idiom of inclusive corporativism that could be used to complement the Porfirian (but still current and useful) theme of the enlightened and progressive state. By the time President Cárdenas nationalized the oil industry (1938), political discourse in the Mexican press by and large lacked any reference to the ideal citizen and portrayed, instead, a harmonious interconnection between popular classes under the protection of the revolutionary state.

In short, early republican obsession with citizenship was primarily owing to the extreme vulnerability of Mexico's central state. It was not produced by an existing equality among citizens, but rather by existing divisions among the elites and by the pressure of popular groups. As soon as a central state was consolidated, citizenship went from being seen as an urgent and supreme ideal to being a long-term goal that could be achieved only after the enlightened, scientific state had done its job. This perspective was, in its turn, transformed by the postrevolutionary state, which complemented it with the organization of the *pueblo* into corporations that were regulated and protected by the state.

These broad shifts have had their corresponding counterparts in the history of the private sphere. The private sphere of citizens in Mexico has never been very fully guaranteed. In the early republican period, liberals identified corporate forms of property as a central obstacle to citizenship: specifically, they targeted the property of Indian communities and of the church. However, the expropriation of both communal and ecclesiastical corporate holdings in 1856 did not lead to the desired end, which was to create a propertied citizenry, but instead to even greater concentration of landed wealth in the hands of an oligarchy. As a result, wide layers of the population lacked a secure base of privacy and lived either as dependents or as members of communities whose rights could only be defended collectively.

After the 1910 revolution, the state sought to protect individuals from slavelike dependence on the oligarchy, but the relations of production that it fostered were equally problematic from the point of view of the consolidation of a private sphere. Agrarian reform failed to build a Lockean citizenry in the countryside because *ejidatarios* (land grantees) are not legal owners of their land. Moreover, they depend on local governmental support for many aspects of production, and so are feeble participants in the construction of a bourgeois public sphere. Similarly, the numerous indigent peoples of Mexico lack a secure private sphere, as ethnographies of the "informal economy" have amply attested: people working in the informal sector lead lives that are largely outside of the law. As a result, they need to negotiate with state institutions in order to keep tapping into illegal sources of electricity, to keep vending in restricted zones, to keep living in property that is not formally theirs, and so on.[25]

Thus, although incorporation into a modern sector was one of the critical goals of postrevolutionary governments, the modalities of incorporation retained significant sectors of the population that not only did not benefit from access to a private sphere that was immune from governmental intervention, but in fact depended on governmental intervention in order to eke out a living in a legally insecure environment. Of the three sectors that made up Mexico's state party, two—the peasant sector and the popular sector—had no sacrosanct private sphere from which to criticize the state, and therefore no protected basis for liberal citizenship.

This situation complicates the vision of citizenship as a debased category, for it is through claims of citizenship that the peasantry and the informal sector have negotiated with the postrevolutionary state—exchanging votes and participation in revolutionary national discourse for access to lands, credits, electricity, or urban services. At the same time, this citizenship belongs to a faceless mass, not to a collection of private individuals. The *pelado* who, in Ramos's account, felt wounded by the mere gaze of the erstwhile modal citizen, and who asserted his right to nationality by his involvement in revolutionary violence, is harnessed back into nationality not through patron–client ties to private elites, but through a series of exchanges with state agencies through which he receives the status of massified citizen.

Let me illustrate what the shape of official citizenry was like in the era of single-party rule. In the 1988 presidential campaign of the Partido Revolucionario Institucional (PRI), which was in many respects the last traditional PRI campaign, public rallies and events were divided into several types.[26] There were, first, events targeted to specific portions of the party's tripartite sectorial organization (peasant sector, labor sector, and popular sector); second, there were meetings with regional and national groups of experts, who organized problem-focused discussions with the candidate and an audience (CEPES [Centros de Estudios Políticos y Sociales] and IEPES [Instituto de Estudios Políticos y Sociales], both of the PRI); third, there were massive public rallies that were meant to show the party's muscle by uniting the whole *pueblo* in a single square; and finally (this was an innovation for the 1988 campaign), there were talk-show–like events where the candidate fielded questions from callers who were not identified as members of a party sector.

The image of the nation as it was generated in the massive public rallies was that of a corporate organism. Like public displays of the social whole since the colonial period, the public of these rallies was divided internally by sectors, each of which signaled its corporate presence with electoral paraphernalia (sheets painted with the candidate's name and the name of the supporting sector; flags, T-shirts, tags, or hats that had the candidate's initials and those of the party or sector), but also with a certain uniformity of look: peasants in their hats and sandals, railroad workers in their blue hats, schoolteachers in their modest, lower-middle-class garb, and so on.

Alongside this hierarchical and organic image of the nation as being made up of complementary, unequal, and interdependent masses, however, campaign rituals also presented certain modal images of the citizenry.

This is apparent in the use of dress in the various rallies, for although the presidential candidate dressed up as member of the sector that he was visiting (as a rancher when in a rally of the peasant sector, as a well-dressed worker in a rally of the labor sector, or in a suit in a discussion with experts), the relationship between "the suit" and other costumes is not one of equality. Rather, the suit is the highest formal garb, the one that the candidate will use on a daily basis when he is in the presidency, and the one that he has daily used as a government official prior to becoming a presidential candidate. The suit is the modal uniform of the public sphere. Public sessions devoted to the discussion of regional and national problems are attended almost exclusively by suits, even when their inhabitants are representing interests associated with labor or agriculture. Thus, the image of the citizen with a voice stands in contrast to the massified citizen.

This situation has been identified by Mexican democrats as a lack of a civil society, and these same democrats have been building a narrative of Mexican democracy that has the heyday of the corporate party (the 1940s and 1950s) as the historical low point in Mexican citizenship. According to this view, the corporate state effectively funneled Mexican society into its mass party until the 1960s, when certain groups, especially middle-class groups—but also some peasants and urban poor—no longer found a comfortable spot in the state's mechanisms of representation and resource management, producing the 1968 student movement.[27]

The violent suppression of this movement, and the expansion of state intervention in the economy in the 1970s, gave a second wind to the corporatist state. However, an unencompassable civil society would keep growing during this period and would reemerge politically in the mid-1980s, when the state's fiscal crisis weakened its hold on society. This situation has been leading inexorably to the end of the one-party system and the rise of Mexican democracy.

During the period of state party rule, political classes in Mexico had a pretty clear mission, which was to tap into resources by mediating between state institutions and local constituencies. It was in this period that a clever politician coined the phrase "vivir fuera del presupuesto es vivir en el error" (to live outside of the state budget is to live in error). The expansion of the state for several decades was a process of always incorporating political middlemen as new social movements emerged. Thus, in the 1970s and 1980s, positions were created for leaders of squatters' movements, for leaders of urban gangs, for student movement leaders, for teachers' movement leaders, and others.

The fiscal crisis of the state that began in 1982 severely limited its possibility of engaging in this co-optive strategy, and so the numbers of nongovernmental organizations in active service rose dramatically, as did opposition parties. There has undoubtedly been an intensification of citizen activity in this period, with vast numbers of people rejecting massified corporate forms of political participation that are no longer providing real benefits, and strong voter participation as well as a huge increase in participation in political rallies, demonstrations, and the like. The press, too, has broken with the unspoken rule of preserving the figure of the national president from direct attack, and its criticism of government has become much louder.

At the same time, however, the fact that many political leaders and mediators are now living outside of the fiscal budget may also mean that a new form of massified citizenship is being constructed. The economic costs of democracy and democratization are so far very high in Mexico, and a lot of money is going to all political parties, as well as to running electoral processes. Elections and electoral processes have become a source of revenue in their own right, and the jockeying between party leaderships could become divorced from the ever-growing needs of the country's poorest, particularly because the middle and proletarian classes are now large enough to sustain such an apparatus. This situation is illustrated in the fact that today, although there is undoubtedly more democracy in Mexico than at any time in recent memory, the extent of urban insecurity, the numbers of fences and walls, and the presence of the military and of private security guards are also the highest in recent memory.

At this juncture, as in the postrevolutionary years in which Ramos was writing, there is an increasing number of people who are unprotected by relations of private patronage, unprotected by the state, and who have insufficient private possessions to participate as reliable citizens. On the other hand, as in the unstable years of the early and mid-nineteenth century, there is an increasingly large class of lumpenpoliticians who seek to funnel the "bad *pueblo*" into "factious" movements. And the passage from unruly anonymity to amicable personal contact may become more strained as the capacity to claim that "whoever gets mad first, loses" itself loses credibility.

*Conclusion*

DaMatta's analysis of the relationship between liberal and Catholic-hierarchical discourses in the negotiation of citizenship is a useful entry point for the description of debased forms of citizenship as they have existed in Iberoamerica. However, his strategy is best suited to highlight the micropolitics of access to state institutions and does not clarify the specific ways in which citizenship is filled and emptied of contents. It therefore misses an important dimension of the culture of citizenship, including how, when, and by whom it is politicized.

In this chapter, I have presented a rough outline of the politics surrounding citizenship in modern Mexico. I argued that there have been two periods when discussions of citizenship have been truly central to political discourse. The first period, which I analyzed in some detail, is the era of political instability and economic decline that followed Mexican independence; the second is the contemporary, post-1982 debt crisis period of privatization and the end of single-party hegemony. The view that I developed suggests that the intensity of discussions surrounding citizenship in the first five decades after independence reflected both the complex politics of including or excluding popular classes from the political field and the fact that national unity seemed unattainable by any means other than through unity among citizens, and violence against traitors (be these indigenous groups or fractious "tyrants" with their clientele of *canallas*). In other words, citizenship was continually invoked as the foremost need of the nation at a time when the country had no effective central state, a declining economy, and was threatened both by imperial powers and by internal regional dissidents.

Beginning with President Juárez, but especially under Díaz, the national state was consolidated and a national economy was shaped thanks to the state's capacity to guarantee foreign investment and national sovereignty. As a result, the "bad *pueblo*" was slowly neutralized and substituted only by the growth and expansion of what I have called the "abject *pueblo*," or the people who were not fit for citizenship (not knowing how to read or write, not speaking Spanish, or living in conditions of servitude that effectively precluded full participation as independent citizens). In the process, the national obsession with citizenship diminished even as the celebration and fetishization of the state as the depositary of rationality, order, and progress grew. The combination of national consolidation, rapid modernization, and the extension of a degraded form of citizenship to the vast majority is part of the backdrop of the Mexican Revolution of 1910.

The constitutional order that emerged from the revolution allowed Mexicans access to a series of benefits, including land and protection against employers. Nevertheless, the postrevolutionary order did not achieve the liberal goal of turning the majority of the population into property holders. In fact, the fragility of the private sphere for large sections of the population has been one of the constants in modern Mexican history. As a result, the revolutionary state combined the Porfirian cult of enlightened, state-led progress with an organicist construction of the people.

This revolution gave citizenship another kind of valence. Instead of attacking communal lands and trying to transform every Mexican into a private owner, postrevolutionary governments gave out land and protection as forms of citizenship, but they retained ultimate control over those resources. As a result, citizenship in the postrevolutionary era (up to the mid- or late 1980s) can be thought of in part as massified and sectorialized, because peasants and workers of the so-called informal sector received benefits on the force of their citizenship, and yet lacked independence from the state. Thus, the debased citizen that DaMatta speaks of is different in the prerevolutionary and the postrevolutionary periods, because, in the latter, "nobodies" could make claims for state benefits on the basis of their collective identity as part of a revolutionary *pueblo*, whereas in the former they could not.

Part of the current difficulty in Mexican citizenship is that social critics acknowledge that state paternalism and control over production led to unacceptably undemocratic forms of rule and, indeed, to policies that led to the bankruptcy of the country. However, at least the 1917 constitution envisaged parceling out some benefits to people by virtue of the fact that they were citizens. The contraction of the state has produced massive social movements and a very strong push around democratization and the category of the citizen, but the current emphasis on electoral rights risks emptying the category of its social contents once again, and, given the fact that Mexico still has a large mass of poor people with little legal private property or stable and legally sanctioned work, and given too that Mexico's state is still incapable of extending rights universally, we may yet see the reemergence a pernicious dialectic between the good *pueblo* and the bad *pueblo*.

# 4

## Passion and Banality in Mexican History:

## The Presidential Persona

In Mexico, theories about national destiny have often eclipsed broader concerns with human history. Development in Mexico has been national development, history has been national history, and theories of history have been theories of national history. This phenomenon is not caused by isolation. It is instead the result of a pervasive peripheral cosmopolitanism, of an acute conscience of wanting to catch up, to reach "the level" of the great world powers.

The need to explain the dynamics of national history stems from the national project's failure to deliver its promise, its failure to free Mexico from subservience and to make the nation an equal of every great nation. Curiously, however, theories of Mexican history do not usually begin by inspecting the impact of national independence on the sense of disjointedness that generates national self-obsession. Instead, they always want to reach further back in an attempt to forge a national subject who can then be liberated through the sovereignty of a national community.

My argument in this chapter takes an alternative route. Ideally, sovereignty may indeed coincide with the liberation of the national subject, but this has never been a realistic expectation. Instead, real sovereignty, independence as it has actually existed, has generated a dynamic of cultural production that shapes Mexican obsessions with national teleology because it creates a systematic divide between national ideology and actual power relations. This chasm is especially evident in the state's tense relationship to modernization and to the broad project of cultural modernity.

All national states can be threatened by modernization. After all, capitalist development has thrived on the inability of states fully to encompass the economies of their people. The technical, social-organizational, and cultural innovations that are linked to industrial growth (i.e., "modernization") can threaten both the interests and the technical basis of state power. Cultural modernity, too, is an expansive project that has challenged specific state institutions by shaping and upholding a series of rights around the category of the citizen, by insisting on a degree of autonomy for artistic and scientific production, and by fostering a "public sphere" from which state policies and institutions can be evaluated and criticized.

In Mexico, the state's active role in propitiating and channeling development and modernization has depended on institutional forms that often contradict democratic ideals of citizenship, freedom of expression, artistic and scientific autonomy, and other ideals of cultural modernity. This fact is manifested in the resilience of the category "ancien régime" in Mexican political and historical texts. Eighteenth-century modernizing reforms introduced by the Bourbons are correctly cast against a classical ancien régime, which is described as corporatist and premodern; but corporatism, the ownership of political office, and the primary importance of personal negotiation with a sovereign did not die with these reforms. Historian François Xavier Guerra discusses the 1910 Mexican Revolution against the backdrop of a still-crumbling "ancien régime," despite the fact that Porfirio Díaz was indisputably a modernizing dictator and that Mexico had been independent for nearly ninety years when the revolution broke out.[1] Even today, political writers have resurrected the ancien régime label, but this time to refer to the postrevolutionary one-party system that is in the process of collapsing.

The persistence of the epithet "ancien régime" is a manifestation of the perceived divide between the national ideal, wherein the law has universal extension and application, and real state power, which is seen as making decisions on a self-serving and ad hoc basis. This chasm has been the declared cause of revolutions and reforms. However, reforms have failed to redress the gulf between the real and the normative order, modern and traditional "hybrids" proliferate, and this process usually ends up being interpreted as a manifestation of the resilience of a national culture. The cycle of nationalist angst is thereby closed, because the failure of modernizing projects is itself used to construct the national subject that is meant to be liberated by the national state, and by the next set of reforms.

I have argued that the limitations of various modern projects in Mexico have reflected the highly segmented quality of the public sphere there. This segmentation can be properly understood through a geography of mediations. My research agenda has been to develop such a geography by focusing both on agents of mediation, such as intellectuals and politicians, and on the public enactment of national unity and articulation in political ritual. In this chapter I will focus on the secular process through which the ideal of national sovereignty was incarnated; I mean the shaping of the public persona of the president of the republic. I will argue that the rocky process by which presidential power became routinized affords a glimpse of the way in which the state has brokered Mexico's modernity.

## First Time as Farce?

Disturbed perceptions of the disjunction between the central tenets of national ideology and actual political practice are visible in Mexico as early as the independence movement itself. For instance, José María Luis Mora, a man who worked tirelessly and to a large extent unsuccessfully at creating the persona of the liberal citizen, complained that his contemporaries believed that "[t]he constitution and the laws are here to place limits on a power that already existed and was invested with omnimodal power, and not that they are here to create and form that power."[2] In other words, the presidency after independence saw its power as preceding the rules and laws of the constitution, which might limit it in some ways, but not shape it ex nihilo. State power was not born of a formal social contract, but the nation allegedly was.

Despite the persistence of this ideological disjunction, liberal theories regarding social contract, political representation, and citizenship flourished. This fact can be understood in part as a mimetic strategy for the state's survival: the adoption of the great powers' own idiom of statehood was necessary for navigating a weak state in international waters. The temptation to cloak local struggles for national power in a language that enjoyed a degree of international prestige, a temptation that was provoked at once by imperial pressures and by the strategic utility of foreign ideas for internal self-legitimation, produced political habits that have been described since the early moments of Mexican national independence and up until the present day as a grotesque penchant for imitation—imitation not only of liberal ideals, but of every kind of glorious foreign practice. I quote again from Mora:

> The men who arrogantly claim that "constitutions are sheets of paper that have no value other than that which the government wishes to give them" are deluded. That expression which was in some way tolerable coming from the hero of Marring, of Jena, and of Austerlitz, from the man who saved France a thousand times and led its armies victoriously into Russia, has been repeated not far from us by pygmies without merit, service, or prestige.[3]

Here, Mexican politicians are tiny Africans, aping Europeans in their banana republic. But, as historian Fernando Escalante has demonstrated, the citizen that was meant to monitor these politicians was an equally fictitious character, because the power of the state was never sufficient to defend the property and the rights of Mexicans who enjoyed formal citizenship.[4] In this context, the office of the presidency became a vehicle for imagining sovereignty, and presidents built their authority by shaping and embodying these images.

### Excommunication and "Primary Process" since Independence

Once Miguel Hidalgo's (1810) movement for independence had ravaged several towns of the Bajío region, the bishop of Michoacán and erstwhile friend of Hidalgo, Manuel Abad y Queipo, decreed the excommunication of the priest and of his followers.[5] This act, and some of the insurgent clergy's reactions, set the tone for later metaphors of national unity and apostasy.

The bishop began his edict with a citation from Luke—"Every kingdom that is divided into factions shall be destroyed and ruined"—and then proceeded to review the ravages of the wars in French Saint-Domingue (Haiti), which were caused, he reminded his flock, by the revolution in the metropole. The result of that revolt was not only the assassination of all Europeans and Creoles, but also the destruction of four-fifths of the island's black and mulatto population and a legacy of perpetual hatred between blacks and mulattos. No good could come from a false division between Europeans and Americans.

Abad then expressed particular chagrin regarding the fact that the call of disloyalty and arms came from a priest, Miguel Hidalgo of the parish of Dolores, who not only killed and injured Europeans and used his robes to "seduce a portion of innocent laborers," but also,

[i]nsulting the faith and our sovereign, Ferdinand VII, painted on his banner the image of our august patroness, our Lady of Guadalupe, and wrote the following inscription: "Long Live the Faith. Long Live Our Holiest Mother of Guadalupe. Long Live Ferdinand VII. Long Live America, and Death to Bad Government."[6]

Abad y Queipo subsequently excommunicated Hidalgo and threatened to do the same to any person who persisted in fighting on Hidalgo's side or in aiding him in any way.

This edict, which was soon endorsed by the archbishop of Mexico, caused great indignation and rage with Hidalgo, Morelos, and other members of the insurgent clergy. Hidalgo made a formal reply, in which he swore his loyalty to the Catholic faith: "I have never doubted any of its truths, I have always been intimately convinced of the infallibility of its dogmas."[7] Hidalgo then vehemently deplored his excommunication as a partisan act: "Open your eyes, Americans. Do not allow yourselves to be seduced by our enemies: they are not Catholics, except to politic; their god is money, and their acts have our oppression as their only object."[8] He then called for the establishment of a representative parliament that,

> *having as its principal object to maintain our holy religion,* will promote benign laws [*leyes suaves*], useful and well suited to the circumstances of each *pueblo.* They shall then govern with the tenderness of parents, they shall treat us as brothers, banish poverty, moderate the devastation of the kingdom and the extraction of its moneys, foment the arts, liven up industry, . . . and, after a few years, our inhabitants shall enjoy all of the delicacies that the Sovereign Author of nature has spilled on this vast continent.[9]

In sum, Hidalgo warns against the use of the true faith for the enrichment of foreign oppressors. He identifies national sovereignty with rule of the Catholic faith, a rule that is to be paternalistic in that it shall recognize the specific needs and circumstances of each *pueblo,* and he imagines a nation guided by a single true faith that will quickly become a kind of Christian paradise in which poverty is eradicated by the fraternal sentiment and benign intentions that exist between true coreligionists. Thus Hidalgo performed a kind of counterexcommunication of European imperialists who used Catholicism in order to "seduce" those whom they sought to oppress and exploit.

Hidalgo's position found concrete juridical expression in the edicts of his follower, the priest José María Morelos. In his first edict abolishing slavery and Indian tribute (1810), Morelos proclaimed that "[a]ny American who owes money to a European is not obliged to pay it. If, on the contrary, it is the European who owes, he shall rigorously pay his debt to the American." Moreover, "[e]very prisoner shall be set free with the knowledge that if he commits the same crime or any other that contradicts a man's honesty, he shall be punished."[10]

These laws portrayed "Europeans" as usuriously living off of "Americans," such that there was no possible American debt to the Europeans that had not been handsomely paid for beforehand, and that the judgment of crimes under the Spanish regime was systematically unfair. In sum, the counterexcommunication of the Spanish clergy by Hidalgo and Morelos fuses the national ideal with a Christian utopia. Paternalistic beneficence and brotherhood would be achieved in an independent Mexico ruled by true Catholics, instead of by oppressors who used Catholicism to pursue their unchristian aims: the extraction of money and the oppression of a nation.

Morelos's political spirit would perdure because the defense of nationals against foreign extortion and the dispensation of Christian justice proved impossible to achieve after independence. Thus, Hidalgo's image of sovereignty as the Christian administration of plenty remained a utopia, and Mexican governments after independence were just as subject to the politics of religious appropriation/excommunication as their Spanish predecessors.

A similar formulation of national ideals can be found a hundred years after Hidalgo's cry in Dolores, issuing from the pen of that foremost ideologue of the Mexican Revolution, Luis Cabrera, who blasted the official celebration of the centenary of independence just two months prior to the first revolutionary outburst of November 20, 1910:

> The celebration of our glories and the commemoration of our heroes is a cult, but those who suffer and work cannot arrive together at the altar of the fatherland with those who dominate and benefit because they do not share the same religion. Just as the Christian's plea to pardon all debts cannot fit in the same prayer as the Jew's plea for daily bread exacted from profits, neither can there be a unified homage to our fathers by those with an insatiable thirst for power and by the noble desire for justice that moves the hearts of the *pueblo* that suffers and works.[11]

This significant, indeed foundational, strain of Mexican nationalism therefore sees the national state as the ideal medium for achieving a Christian community. In fact, however, the standards for sovereignty that were set by Hidalgo, whereby poverty would be banished "in just a few years," or by Morelos's declaration of a clean slate for all, would be impossible to uphold. They were ill suited to serve as the basis for consolidating a huge territory peopled by a weakly integrated nation that gained its independence at a moment of intense imperial competition.

## Dead Presidents

The consolidation of a central authority has been a complex problem in Mexican history, for although such an authority existed during the colonial era in the figure of the king and his surrogate, the viceroy, establishing a central state and authority after independence proved to be highly problematic.

Monarchical solutions to this quandary were consonant with the ideology of Mexican independence, which leaned heavily on traditional Spanish legal thought to legitimate itself. The dream of a smooth transition between the colonial and the independent order was simply not to be. On one side, radical insurgents were not keen to see the precolonial status quo upheld to such a perfect degree. On another, Spain did not immediately relinquish its claims over the new Mexican empire and attempted to reestablish a foothold on the continent for ten more years, sufficient time for an anti-Spanish sentiment that had been growing along with the construction of Mexican nationalism to become virulent. Moreover, the United States was clearly and loudly opposed to the establishment of a monarchy in Mexico.[12] As a result, monarchists were forced to set their hearts on acquiring a European monarch with the simultaneous backing of all or most European powers, a solution that was tried and failed in the 1860s. Thus the early fractures among the nascent national elite were connected ab initio to the contest between the United States, France, Spain, and Britain.

It was not until 1867, after the French departed and Maximilian was shot, that Mexico finally earned its "right" to exist as a nation. Until that time, no strong central state had existed, and the country's sovereignty was severely limited. In the words of a Porfirian commentator,

[before the wars of intervention] being a foreigner came to mean being the natural-born master of all Mexicans. It was enough, as a few of the exceptionally rare honest diplomats acknowledged, for a foreigner to be imprisoned for three days on poor behavior or intrigue for that person to become a creditor for fifty or one hundred thousand pesos to the Mexican national budget as a result of a diplomatic agreement.[13]

The state had become the guarantor of foreign interests against its own people. The bullet that killed Maximilian effectively ended the possibility of ever establishing a European-backed monarchy, while making a highly visible international statement about the sovereignty of Mexico and of its laws. Until that time, Mexico had been routinely "Africanized" in foreign eyes.

In the years between 1821 and 1867, Mexican leaders had tried a series of strategies for constructing central power, combining varying forms of messianism, aspects of monarchic power, republicanism, and liberalism, in a large number of short-lived presidencies. Given the nonexistence of a successful hegemonic block among early postindependence elites, and given a number of foreign pressures that were not fully comprehended by these elites until half the country's territory had been lost, the difficulty in constructing an image of national sovereignty and authority in the office of the president became a major cultural challenge; for whereas political ritual and the stability of office in the colonial period reveal a clear-cut ideology of dependency—that is, of a combination of subordination, complementarity, and mutual *reliance*—this sense of reliance and encompassment between the centers of empire and Mexico was decidedly shaken, and sometimes completely shattered, after independence.

The difficulty in shaping presidential power was increased, too, by the weakness, and at times nonexistence, of modern political parties. Political organization around the time of independence flowed to a large extent through Masonic lodges. In the early independence period, there was only one Masonic rite, the Scottish rite, which had been imported by Mexico's representatives at the Cortes of Cádiz in 1812. A second lodge, of York, was established in Mexico by the first U.S. ambassador, Joel Poinsett, with the explicit aim of consolidating a federalist, republican, and more Jacobin organization into Mexico's political arena. In neither case, however, were these lodges open to public scrutiny, as political parties are, and political power was taken in the name of ideologies, such as federalism, centralism, liberalism, or conservatism, with no party structure to back them.

As a result, the construction of the persona of the president as the personification of sovereignty was both important and highly problematic. It involved creating an image that could rise above and reconcile a regionally fragmented society, an image that could also be manipulated in order to seduce or to frighten off imperial power—contradictory uses that are surely part of the famous distance between the *país real* and the *país legal*. I shall explore three significant strategies in the evolution of the presidential persona: the strategy of the martyr, the strategy of the exemplary citizen, and the strategy of the modernizer. In discussing selected aspects of these three presidential repertoires, I hope to clarify one aspect of the distance between legal forms and actual political practice.

## An Arm and a Leg

The salience of martyrdom in politics has often been noted in popular commentary in Mexico. Mexico has a large pantheon of national leaders who were shot or martyred, including Hidalgo, Morelos, Allende, Aldama, Iturbide, Guerrero, Mina, Matamoros, Maximilian, Madero, Villa, Carranza, Obregón, and Zapata, to name only the most prominent ones. The first martyrs of independence were Hidalgo, Allende, Aldama, and Santa María, whose heads were severed by Spanish authorities and displayed in the four corners of the Alhóndiga de Granaditas, where Hidalgo's army had massacred a number of Spaniards and Creoles. Many other leaders of independence were also executed in later periods.

When it came to insurgent priests, Spanish authorities tried to degrade the leaders before and after execution. The subjects were defrocked in ecclesiastical courts and then turned over to the civil authorities, who dictated their sentences. In cases where military officers had to take justice into their own hands, some officers "reconciled their duties as Christians with their obligations as soldiers" by undressing the rebel priest, shooting him, and then redressing him with his robes for burial.[14] Despite these and other degradations, these dead became the martyred "fathers" of the nation.

The use of messianic imagery was significant on two levels: it was a way of identifying the presidential body with the land, and it cast the people as being collectively in debt to the caudillo for his sacrifices. The relationship to kingly ideology is clear. Because Mexico was unable to enshrine its own king, in whom a positive relationship between personal welfare and national welfare could be state dogma ("The King and the Land are One"), its national leaders had to create this relationship negatively, through sacrifice. Thus, it was through personal sacrifice that the president could attempt to convince people of his capacity to represent the entire nation.

The most successful example of a president who relied primarily on this strategy for fashioning his persona was Antonio López de Santa Anna, who dominated Mexican politics during the first half of the nineteenth century. Santa Anna was called to the presidency eleven times, alternatively as a liberal, a conservative, and a moderate. Ideological purity was clearly not the way to establish oneself as a durable alternative for the presidency in early nineteenth-century Mexico. Instead, historian John Lynch observes that Santa Anna saw himself as a preserver of order, not as an ideologically inconsistent opportunist: "The fault [according to Santa Anna] lay with the political parties, which divided Mexico and created a need for reconciliation" (1992, 336).

Above the political fray between parties, nothing remained in the rhetoric of the period but the fatherland (patria) itself, and so Santa Anna cultivated his reputation as a war hero. He led the defense against the Spanish in 1829, his leg was amputated after wounds acquired in the "Pastry War" against the French in 1839 (offsetting, somewhat, his humiliating defeat in Texas), and he organized the defense against the U.S. invasion at a time of political disarray.

In 1842, Santa Anna was once again called to power, and at that point he attempted to build the rudiments of a political geography that would have him at its center. He had a luxurious municipal theater built (the Teatro Santa Anna), with a statue of himself in front of it. A solemn and much-attended ceremony was enacted to inaugurate a third monument, which was a mausoleum in which his left leg was reinterred.

The significance of Santa Anna's leg—a limb that linked him to Hidalgo, Morelos, and all the dead heroes whose love for the patria at that point was the only ideology capable of unifying the country—is best appreciated in Santa Anna's own words:

> The infamous words the messenger read me are repeated here: "The majority of Congress openly favor the Paredes revolution . . . The rioters imprisoned President Canalizo and extended their aversion to the president, Santa Anna. They tore down a bronze bust erected in his honor in the Plaza del Mercado. They stripped his name from the Santa Anna Theater, substituting for it the National Theater. Furthermore, they have taken his amputated foot from the cemetery of Santa Paula and proceeded to drag it through the streets to the sounds of savage laughter and regaling . . ." I interrupted the narrator, exclaiming savagely, "Stop! I don't wish to hear any more! Almighty God! A member of my body, lost in the service of my country, dragged from the funeral urn, broken into bits to be made sport of in such a barbaric manner!" In that moment of grief and frenzy, I decided to leave my native country, object of my dreams and of my disillusions, for all time.[15]

Given Mexico's ideological rifts, the difficulties in creating a national center in the face of internal divisions and international pressure, the only

Figure 4.1. *Viceroy don Juan Vicente Güemes Pacheco y Padilla, segundo Conde de Revillagigedo,* anonymous painter, eighteenth century. Oil on canvas, 52 × 41. Collection of Banco Nacional de México. This is a usual representation of a viceroy's arrival in New Spain. The viceroy is assisted on one side by the power of arms, and on the other by the power of justice, the same two powers that caudillos claimed for themselves when they claimed to stand above all parties.

Figure 4.2. *Imagen de Jura con retrato de Fernando VII*, anonymous painter, nineteenth century. Oil on canvas, 140 × 98 cm. Collection of Museo Regional de Guadalajara. The message on the painting reads: "Beloved Fernando, Spain and the Indies placed on your head this [image of the crown]"; the bottom reads, "This lion, which is the Spanish nation, will never let go from its clutches the two worlds of Ferdinand VII." The representation of the king is strikingly similar to portraits of Iturbide and Santa Anna.

Figure 4.3. Santa Anna as president.

good president could be a selfless one. The dead insurgents became examples of this ideal, and the earliest viable examples of the presidential persona were built around the figure of the martyr—presidents who did not receive salaries, who sacrificed their families, who abandoned their family fortune, who gave up their health for their country.

Santa Anna lost his leg and it became the focus of contention. Álvaro Obregón, caudillo of the Mexican Revolution, president from 1920 to 1924, reelected for office in 1928, and murdered on the day of his election, lost an arm in the battle of Celaya against Pancho Villa. This arm was preserved in alcohol and it became the centerpiece of a monument built in his name by the man who created the Partido Revolucionario Institucional that ruled the country for seventy-one years. Obregón's martyrdom was thus used to funnel charisma into a bureaucracy that has insistently called itself revolutionary.

Two less well known and curious stories are the ends met by the bodies of Guadalupe Victoria and of General Francisco (Pancho) Villa. Guadalupe Victoria, Mexico's first president, died in 1842. During the U.S. invasion of Mexico in 1848, American soldiers violated the tomb where his mummy and preserved innards were kept. According to one hagiographer, two U.S. soldiers drank the alcohol in which Victoria's innards were preserved and died—the remains of Guadalupe Victoria were still powerful in the struggle for sovereignty. In 1862, just before the French invasion, Victoria's remains were transferred to Puebla by General Alejandro García, and they were placed at the foot of the Angel of Independence in Mexico City by President Calles in the 1920s.[16]

U.S. patriots apparently also had a bone to pick (so to speak) with Pancho Villa, whose tomb was desecrated and whose head allegedly ended up in the Skull and Bones Society at Yale University, a secret society of which George Bush was a member.[17] It would appear that Villa, who was initially portrayed by the U.S. media as a great popular hero and then demonized as the bandit who had the gall of invading Columbus, New Mexico, and getting away with it, became the object of "scientific interest" by patriots in the United States, while Villa's invasion of Columbus is still a source of pleasure for Mexican *revanchistes.*

The politics around these remains reveals the degree to which the nation's inalienable possessions have been vulnerable to foreign appropriation, as well as to internal desecration. It suggests that martyrdom has been fundamentally linked to an often unworkable ideal of sovereignty in modern Mexico. Sovereignty, that ideal location where all Mexicans are created equal, has been a place that only the dead can inhabit, which is why we sometimes fight over their remains.[18]

## Unconventional Conventionalists, or the Fetishism of the Law

It fell to Benito Juárez to create the first strong image of the presidency as an *institution* of power that was truly above the fray, and his strategy was to present himself as a complex embodiment of the meeting between the nation and the law. As an Indian, Juárez could stand for the nation; as an impenetrable magistrate and keeper of the law, he attempted to create an image of the presidency as being above ambitious self-aggrandizement.[19] Francisco Bulnes provides a biting creole perspective on Juárez's distinct public image:

> Juárez had a distinctively Indian temperament; he had the calm of an obelisk—that reserved nature that slavery promotes to the state of comatoseness in the coldly resigned races. He was characterized by the secular silence of the vanquished who know that every word that is not the miasma of degradation is punished, by that indifference that apparently allows no seduction but that exasperates . . . Juárez did not make speeches; he did not write books, use the press, or write letters; he did not have intimate conversation, nor did he have *esprit*, an element that makes thought penetrating, like perfume. Nor was he subtle or expressive in his gestures, his movement, or his gaze. His only language was official, severe, sober, irreproachable, fastidious, unbearable. His only posture that of a judge hearing a case. His only expression the absence of all expression. The physical and moral appearance of Juárez was not that of the apostle, or the martyr, or the statesman; it was instead that of a god in a *teocalli*, inexpressive on the humid and reddish rock of sacrifices.[20]

Juárez created a lasting image of what the relationship of the president to the nation should be: he had no need of the kind of martyrdom that Santa Anna utilized because his race already proved his links to the land. Nor, as Bulnes says, was he an apostle, in that his role was to *remind* Mexicans and foreigners of the rule of the law. The result appears at first as an impossible combination: the legalistic bureaucrat as national fetish.

Juárez's construction of the presidential persona as the embodiment of the law depended on a racial element for its success. Mexican presidents who belonged to the local aristocracy could only achieve full identification with the land through the theater of messianism and martyrdom. Juárez, on the other hand, relied on the mythology of the Aztec past that was important in Mexican nationalism as a way of establishing a credible relationship to the land without relying on messianism. When he relied on biblical imagery, Juárez usually turned to Moses, the lawgiver and liberator, and not to Jesus and the martyrs. This was because Juárez's challenge was not to demonstrate loyalty to the land, but rather to show that he could "rise above his race." The law resolved this problem to some extent. The Indian, who indisputably was connected to the land, could identify so fully with the law that he would become faceless: a national fetish of the law, an idol in a *teocalli*, as Bulnes says. This contrasts with the role of the law in the persona of the messianic president, whose attitudes in this regard were usually inspired by Napoleon.

Juárez was aided in this project by the fact that he presided over the definitive defeat of European powers, the execution of a prestigious European monarch, the defeat of the clergy, and an alliance with the United States. He succeeded in identifying himself with the land not through the greatness of his individual acts (as Bulnes would have liked), but rather through his sober image as the inexorable instrument of the law.

After Juárez, two alternative images of that national fetish that is the president had been rudimentarily established: the president as messianic leader—overflowing with personality, ideologically inconsistent, and abandoning his fortune for the sake of the nation—and the expressionless leader who claims the rule of law in the name of the nation. The fact that the two could not easily be combined is evident in a satirical verse directed to León de la Barra, interim president of Mexico after General Díaz's fall in 1910:

| | |
|---|---|
| El gobernar con el frac | Governing with a tuxedo |
| y ser presidente blanco | Being a white president |
| es tan sólo un pasaporte | Is only just a passport |
| de destierro limpio y franco.[21] | To certain banishment. |

One could use a tuxedo like Juárez if it underlined a fusion between the Indian and the law, but if one were white and sought to be president, one could not take on the persona of the bourgeois or the bureaucrat; instead, one needed the force of arms and a messianic language.

After Juárez, the image of saving the law in the name of the nation became a powerful way of claiming the presidency and of shaping the presidential persona, and this despite the fact that Juárez's self-serving use of the law was no different from either his predecessors nor his successors.[22] During the Mexican Revolution, Madero revolted against Díaz in the name

Figure 4.4. *Tlahuicole,* by Manuel Vilar. Collection of Museo Nacional de Arte; photograph by Agustín Estrada. This exemplar of *indigenista* art from the time of Juárez has the Indian embody the classical ideal of strength and beauty. The discrepancy between the potential of the Indian race in its moments of sovereignty and its degeneration, caused by foreign subjugation, was implicit in the representation itself.

Figure 4.5. *Indios carboneros y labradores de la vecindad de México*, lithograph by Carlos Nebel (1850). This representation of contemporary Indians is characteristic of the period and contrasts with the ideal embodied in *Tlahuicole*.

of the 1857 constitution and he was punctilious in setting himself up as a law-abiding citizen. In fact, Madero combined the messianic image with that of the law provider in his "apostle of democracy" persona. Carranza's army called itself the "Constitutionalist Army" when it organized against the usurper Huerta; Villa and Zapata called themselves "Conventionalists" and claimed to be fighting Carranza out of respect for the resolutions of the Aguascalientes Convention. Finally, and perhaps most important, Mexico's dominant party, established in 1929, saw itself as the institutionalized heir of the revolution, which was interpreted as the fount of national *comunitas* whose spirit was embodied in the constitution of 1917. In each of these cases, including Juárez's, the nationalization of the law was a way to construct a viable presidential authority whose actual policies often had no more than a casual or after-the-fact relationship to the law.

*Inventos del hombre blanco: Modernization and Presidential Fetishism*

I have outlined two ways in which the president's persona was shaped: the messianic strategy and the indigenized-legalist strategy. These alternatives were developed at different moments, though both are components

Figure 4.6. *President Juárez,* anonymous engraving autographed by President Juárez. Juárez, the Indian who studied law and who made Europe pay for its intervention by ordering Maximilian's execution in conformity with that law, is the modern reconciliation between the idealized pre-Hispanic Indian and the promise held out by national sovereignty. Juárez's identity as a civilian demonstrates the potential of Mexican society to back this ideal, while simultaneously affirming that national liberation would not be attained by "caste wars."

IGNACIO M. ALTAMIRANO.

Figure 4.7. *Altamirano, the Indian Orator,* anonymous engraving published in Evans (1870). Ignacio Manuel Altamirano was, on the cultural plane, a symbol quite similar to Juárez. The Indian body clothed in European high culture was a reclamation of what had been due to the Indian race. It was a consequence of sovereignty and became its fitting symbol.

of contemporary Mexican "presidentialism." The messianic strategy was the first successful option because there was no way that the presidency could feign ideological consistency in the first half of the nineteenth century. The fetishization of the law occurred in conjunction with the consolidation of Mexico's position in the international system and as a result of the polarization of the country to a degree that only one party could conceivably emerge as the victor.

The third strategy that I will discuss concerns the nationalization of modernization as a presidential strategy. According to historian Edmundo O'Gorman:

Figure 4.8. *Presidente Benito Juárez*, by Hermenegildo Bulstos. Collection of the Senado de la República (Mexico). This contemporary portrait of a green-eyed Juárez hangs today in Mexico's Senate. The *mestizaje* of Juárez is here embodied in the whitening of his face, a strategy that made sense while Juárez lived.

[In the early and mid-nineteenth century] [w]e have two theses corresponding to two tendencies [the liberal and the conservative tendency], which struggle against each other because of their respective aims and because they are founded on two different visions of the direction of history. However, these two theses end up postulating the same thing, to wit, they both wish to acquire the prosperity of the United States without abandoning

Figure 4.9a. *Caballero Águila*. Sculpture from the Mexican pavilion of the Exposición Iberoamericana de Sevilla (1929). These twin statues, adorning Mexico's contribution to the Ibero-american Exhibition in Seville, make the Spanish and Indian nobles equivalents. Mestizo power is the logical consequence of this vision.

Figure 4.9b. *Un caballero español del siglo XVI.* Sculpture from the Mexican pavilion of the Exposición Iberoamericana de Sevilla (1929).

traditional ways of being, because these were judged to be the very essence of the nation. Both currents wanted the benefits of modernity, but neither wanted modernity itself.[23]

In other words, the contest for modernization (material and technological progress) was a high aim of the national struggle that was claimed by all factions, while cultural modernity was, in different ways, rejected. This tendency was clearly expressed at the turn of the twentieth century—when the contest between liberals and conservatives had been transcended—in *arielismo*, an ideology that posited the spiritual superiority of Latin America over the United States and envisioned modernizing Latin American countries without absorbing the spiritual debasement created by the all-pervasive materialism that was attributed to U.S. society.

Although Enrique Rodó's *Ariel* ties Latin spirituality to a Hellenic inheritance, the fundamental tenet of *arielismo* (greater spirituality that is nonetheless compatible with selective modernization) has multiple manifestations, some of which are present even today in the form of *indigenismo*, and in nationalistic forms of socialism. Taken at this level of generality, *arielismo* presupposed a certain cosmopolitanism and a high degree of education (at least at the level of the elites), combined with the maintenance of hierarchical and paternalistic relationships within society. The cosmopolitanism and spiritual education of the elite were required, in fact, in order to guarantee a well-reasoned selection of modern implements and practices to import. In other words, *arielismo* was an ideology that was well adapted to the circumstances of Mexican political and intellectual elites from the end of the nineteenth century to the end of the era of import substitution industrialization (1982), because it cast Mexicans as consumers of modern products that retained an unaltered "spiritual" essence, an essence that was embodied in specific—unmodern—relations at the level of family organization, clientelism, corporate organization, and so on.

Moreover, *arielismo, indigenismo*, and other avatars of this posture implicitly fostered a defensive cultural role for the state and its statesmen: to guard Latin societies against the base materialism of U.S. society. Given this mediating position, the state was meant to be savvy about the consumption of modern products. Its knowledge was derived from the humanistic education of its leaders and the spirituality of communal relations in Latin America. This mediating position allowed the appropriation of modernization as part of the presidential manna. "Los inventos del hombre blanco" (the white man's inventions) were a third critical prop in creating a stable view of sovereignty and of presidential power in the history of ideological uncertainty.

In the early nineteenth century, there are relatively few examples of this political usage of modernization by the presidential figure. One partial exception is the use of statistics, to show that, morally, Mexico City was the equal of Paris, with lower percentages of prostitutes, higher educational levels, and other illusions.[24] Early efforts were usually cultural rather than technological—Santa Anna's choice to build a theater as his most public work is an example. However, these never had the nationalist power of the later technological imports.

The image of the state presiding over or introducing some major technological innovation or material benefit has been critical to the construction of the persona of the president since Porfirio Díaz's regime (1876–1910), whose introduction of the railroad did much to lend verisimilitude to Díaz's studied resemblance of Kaiser Wilhelm. Recent examples of the nationalization of modernization include the construction of the Mexico City subway under President Díaz Ordaz (1964–70), the construction of the National University's modernist campus and the development of Acapulco under Miguel Alemán (1946–52), the development of Cuernavaca under Calles (1929–34), the construction of the Pan American Highway and the nationalization of the oil industry under Cárdenas (1934–40), and the electrification of the Mexican countryside under Echeverría (1970–76).

The identification of the president with modernization has at times been used against the more racialist images of the presidency as the embodiment of national law and of the nation's martyrs. This has especially been the case in times of great economic growth, when presidents usually show ideological eclecticism. The father of this eclectic style is Porfirio Díaz, who nonetheless concentrated in his persona much of the two earlier components of Mexican presidentialism (identity as racially Mexican, and identity as war hero). Díaz's unparalleled personal success in combining all three strands of the presidential persona seems to have received divine sanction: the day of his namesake, San Porfirio, coincided with Mexican Independence Day; the birth of the hero and of the nation were thus celebrated on the same day.

This almost ideal overlap between a modernizing image (gained only by presiding over the country in a moment of economic growth) and an image of personal sacrifice and racial legitimacy has only rarely coincided since. To a certain degree, Álvaro Obregón (1920–24) had it: his pickled arm, which was blown off at the Battle of Celaya, linked him to the earth,

Figure 4.10. *Excursión al puente de Metlac,* photograph by C. B. Waite (early 1900s). Feats of engineering, such as the bridge over the ravine of Metlac, became emblematic of Porfirio Díaz and his accomplishments as president.

while his modernizing policies eventually gave him popularity with Mexico's industrial classes. Arguably Lázaro Cárdenas (1934–40) also had a credible mix of these ingredients. At any rate, since World War II, with peace in the land and sustained economic growth for a couple of decades, the image of the modernizing president became more and more significant.

Moreover, with the exhaustion of models of industrialization organized around the national market through import substitution industrialization, variants of *arielismo* as an official ideology have become increasingly untenable. Therefore, modernizing presidents since the 1982 debt crisis have gambled everything on a successful bid to be like the United States—materialism and all. As a result, the Mexican presidential image has suffered greatly, especially to the extent that presidents have failed to achieve the promised goal.

*Conclusion*

The idea of sovereignty was firmly entrenched in New Spain before independence, but it became an elusive ideal afterwards. The source of this insecurity was the weakness of Mexico's position in the contest between imperial powers and Mexico's internal economic and cultural fragmentation, a situation that made the construction of a central power difficult.

Although the uncertainty of sovereignty was most keenly felt in the periods between 1821 and 1867 and between 1910 and 1939, the cultural dynamics that were unleashed by these uncertainties have been relevant for the whole of Mexico's independent history.

The three strategies for constructing the presidential figure that I have discussed originate and culminate in different moments—all three were routinized into the presidential office in the postrevolutionary era.

Figure 4.11. *General Porfirio Díaz, presidente de la República para el período 1877–1880*, Gustavo Casasola Collection. Díaz as a war hero—a representation reminiscent of Santa Anna's self-fashioning strategy.

Figure 4.12. *A Painting Lesson,* El hijo del Ahuizote, July 31, 1887; Benson Collection, University of Texas. A newspaper portrays the young President Díaz modeling himself after Juárez. The virtues associated with Juárez are civilian (constitutionalism, civism, respect for the law, firm principles, intelligence, patriotism) and Indian (abnegation, modesty, constancy, discretion, and honesty). Díaz the war hero had to copy some of these.

Figure 4.13. *Arc of Triumph Erected in Honor of Porfirio Díaz.* Here militarism, indigenism, and modernization are rolled into one: the construction of the arc is a feat of engineering and architecture, a sign of the wealth produced by modernization, a nod toward Europe, and an identification of Díaz as a savior, a soldier, and an Indian.

Nonetheless, representing the nation internally while maintaining an adequate external facade has been a chronic difficulty. The importance of the nation's self-presentation to the external world, and the conflicts between the state's needs in this regard and its connections to internal social groups, led to the invention of a state theater that was often divorced from the quotidian practices of state rule.

As a result of this structural problem, moments of governmental self-presentation before foreign powers have been vulnerable targets of public protest, as occurred during Díaz's centenary independence celebrations in 1910, before the Olympic Games in 1968, and on the day of the inauguration of the North American Free Trade Agreement (NAFTA) on January 1, 1994. Clashes between communitarian revivals of the ideal of sovereignty and stiff and self-serving international presentations of the state have often been understood by analysts as manifestations of what Victor Turner

(1974) called "primary process" in his classical essay on Hidalgo's revolt. These are moments in which the original idea of sovereignty as a moment in which the Mexican nation would be free to construct its own destiny and to live in fraternal bliss are revived. Nevertheless, these moments of communitarianism are always betrayed because the popular ideal of sovereignty has been a structural impossibility for Mexico. As a result, Mexican history generates a characteristic combination of passion and banality, with long periods of modernizing innovation being perceived, despite their novelty, as facade or farce, and short bursts of unrealizable communitarian nationalisms as the manifestations of the true feelings of the nation. The martyrs that are generated in these moments of primary process are subsequently harnessed and appeals to their image are routinely made by aspiring presidents and used as the blueprint by which to build a more stable political geography.

At the same time, this very strategy of constructing a national center by brokering modernity through the presidential office, and by nationalizing it through the cult of martyrs and through the racialization of the law, is what has helped generate a national self-obsession. This obsession was fostered to a large degree by the aspiration of liberals and conservatives, of *arielistas* and *indigenistas*, to modernize selectively and to attain the promised modernity within a national framework. *Arielista* cosmopolitanism, the cosmopolitanism of the statesman as the nation's official international taster, is at the heart of the preponderance of the nation as an intellectual object in Mexico. This cosmopolitanism, which sometimes conceives of itself as provincial, has forged sagas of national history that reach to the Aztecs or to the Conquest for an understanding of the qualities and properties of the Mexican nation, but it is Mexico's persistent dismodernity that generates this form of self-knowledge.

# 5

## Fissures in Contemporary Mexican Nationalism

Mexicans have been tormented with recurring modernizing fantasies and aspirations ever since independence. Dreams of the nation wrestling with the angel of progress have been especially haunting in moments of profound social change, such as those that are transpiring in Mexico today.

Worrisome symptoms of epochal cultural and social transformation first came to the attention of the reading public in the mid-1980s. At that time, many a social diagnostician thought that Mexico had contracted "postmodernity" and that its twisted historical trajectory might at last have brought it to that vanguard that ends all vanguards (albeit in a disheveled state). Nevertheless, this notion was soon corrected by Roger Bartra (1987) who, having carefully analyzed Mexico's symptoms, came to the sobering conclusion that, although indeed strange things were happening regarding modernity in Mexico, these might more aptly be described as a particular form of dismodernity or, more playfully, as "dis-mothernism": a mixture of a quite postmodern *desmadre* (chaos) and continuing aspirations to an unachieved modernity.

Unsatisfied with this state of affairs, Mexico's political parties and the press soon made the issue of modernity into their central theme. In the political realm, for instance, democracy has received obsessive attention. It has become a hegemonic ideology, bringing together all parties, including such unlikely democrats as Mexico's longtime state party (the PRI) and Mexico's traditional left. In the sphere of scientific and academic production, the government has implemented draconian measures for modernization, doggedly promoting standards of production and productivity that are meant to put Mexican science in line with an "international standard." Finally, in the economic realm, the idea of competing in global markets has gained enormous authority, and it has served to justify the transformation of state enterprises that were run on a redistributive ideology of "national interest" and "social justice" into privately owned, competitive, and, yes, "modern" businesses.

The confluence of all of these changes and themes of public discussion reflects, undoubtedly, the fact that Mexico entered yet a new phase of dismodernity in the past two decades. The 1982 debt crisis dealt a terrible blow to the regime of state-fostered national development, and the economic arrangement that has emerged provoked an intense struggle for supremacy between diverse modernizing formulas. Those involved in this contest continuously make appeals to various idealized national audiences, but those audiences have themselves changed.

In this chapter, I explore one aspect of this transformation, which is the relationship between national culture and modernity. Specifically, I discuss the ways in which national identity has changed from being a tool for achieving modernity to being a marker of dismodernity and a form of protest against the most recent reorganization of capitalist production. In the process, both the substance and the social implications of nationalism have been deeply transformed.

## *The Telltale* Naco

One phenomenon that helps to capture the changed relationship between nationality, cultural modernity and modernization is the way in which the connotations of the term *naco* have changed in the past decades. Until sometime in the mid-1970s, the term *naco*, which is allegedly a contraction of *Totonaco*, was used as a slur against Indians or, more generally, against peasants or anyone who stood for the provincial backwardness that Mexico was trying so hard to emerge out of. In the 1950s, Carlos Fuentes described the *naco*'s counterparts as "little Mexican girls . . . blonde, sheathed in black and sure they were giving international tone to the saddest unhappiest flea-bitten land in the world."[1] The *naco*, then, was the uncultured and uncouth Indian who could only be redeemed through an international culture.

In the past twenty years, however, the connotations of *naco* began breaking out of their rustic confinement to such a degree that *naquismo* came to be recognized as a characteristically *urban* aesthetic. Similar processes have occurred elsewhere in Latin America, with terms such as *cholo* in Peru and Bolivia, and *mono* in Ecuador. Resonating with the imagery of colonial *castas*, the aesthetics of the *naco* denote impurity, hybridity, and bricolage, but, above all, the more recent usage of *naco* designates a special kind of kitsch.

The *naco's* kitsch is considered vulgar because it incorporates aspirations to progress and the material culture of modernity in imperfect and partial ways. We recognize a form of kitsch here because the *naco* is supposed to feel moved by his own modernized image. So, for example, the *naca* is moved by the sofas in her living room and she seeks to preserve their modernizing impact by coating them with plastic.

It is worth noting, however, that in defining *naco* in this new sense, the category can no longer be confined or reduced to a single social sector or class, because the kitsch of modernization affects upper classes quite noticeably, and I have in mind not only such outstanding *naco* monuments as former Mexico City Chief of Police Arturo Durazo's weekend house that is known as "The Parthenon," but also many of the attitudes of Mexico's bourgeoisie, whose self-conscious fantasies are easily perceived in the domestic architecture of any rich post-1960 neighborhood.

The category of *naco* as modern kitsch is thus directly connected to an idiom of distinction that appears to have lost its moorings in the indigenous and peasant world: it now targets that whole sector of society that silently sheds a tear of delight while witnessing its own modernity. And it is this self-consciousness, this unnaturalness of the modern, that explains the persistence of a (derogatory) Indian brand, for, like the colonial Indians, today's *nacos* have not fully internalized their redemption; they are therefore unreliable moderns in the same way that Indians were unreliable Christians, and so the whole country is dyed with Indianness.

In addition to marking a kind of kitsch, the epithet *naco* also connotes a certain lack of distinction, or at least a lack of hierarchy, between "high culture" and its popular imitations. Specifically, *naco* can be used to designate an overassimilation of television and of the world of capitalist commodities. It is an assimilation of the imitation with no special regard for the original. For example, foreign-sounding names such as "Velvet," "Christianson," and "Yuri" have proliferated in the past decades. One unusual but telling example is "Madeinusa," a name that was inspired by the label "Made in USA" and that is used in Panama. Broadly speaking, these names come from comic books, magazines, and soap operas, and they are rejected by anti-*naco* sectors, who are increasingly inclined to use names from the Spanish Siglo de Oro (e.g., Rodrigo, María Fernanda) or from the Aztec and Maya pantheons (e.g., Cuauhtémoc, Itzamnah, Xicoténcatl).

This latter group sees the former as *nacos*, but one could also argue that the distinction is rather one between closet *nacos* (modernizers who are nevertheless worried about erasing historical distinctions between high and low, foreign and national culture) and open or "popular" *nacos*, who couldn't care less. This is recognized playfully by some in the distinction between "Art-Naqueau," which is a more elite *naco*, and "Nac-Art," which is based on commercial North American culture, a distinction that flags an elitization of history. Whereas the popular *naco* breaks with the weight of tradition (the mother is called Petra, the daughter is named Velvet), traditionalists try to appropriate History with its Rodrigos and Cuauhtémocs. Thus we can distinguish between *nacos* who try to affiliate to the modern via the great national or Western narratives, and those who erase history and simply luxuriate in modernization.

The popular *naco's* move toward the diminution of the weight of national and Western history brings some problems to those non- or closet *nacos* who depend to some degree on those histories. For example, in politics certain new populist styles have debunked long-standing political forms in Latin America. In La Paz, Bolivia, a highly "cholified" city, "El compadre Mendoza" and his sidekick, "La Cholita Remedios," DJs of a popular radio station, have won important political posts. In Ecuador, former president Abdala Bucaram identified simultaneously with Batman, Jesus, and Hitler, while in Brasília, Mexico City, Buenos Aires, and Lima presidents and ministers have protagonized intense melodramas— confrontations between spouses, rivalries between brothers, love affairs between cabinet members—that generate sympathies and antipathies that threaten to overshadow the significance of the great narratives of national power. Thus the new vulgarity is at times a threat to traditional political forms, just as it can threaten traditional mechanisms of class distinction, reducing the old elite to ever-narrower and culturally obsolete circles of "oligarchs."

These threats to civilization are complemented by a growing horror toward the masses, a situation that is attributable to the combined effects of the lack of respect for "distinction" involved in the new *naquismo* and the tremendous growth of urban unemployment and crime. The fear of looting and of armed robbery has a counterpoint at the level of distinction: fear of proletarianization and of blending in with the "vulgar classes."

Political scientists are scandalized by a new "lumpenpolitics," closet *nacos* are scandalized by open *nacos*, and the ghost of the Indian haunts America once more, not as a redeemed Indian, but as an irredeemable Indian.

The emergence of new forms of distinction that are evident in the transformation of the category of *naco*, in its change from a discriminatory term aimed at peasants to a (low-status) aesthetics of modernity that is arguably applicable to the vast majority of the urban population, is symptomatic of a process of deep cultural change in Mexican national space.

Until recently, nationality had been a mechanism for modernization. This identification emerged as early as the wars of independence, when ideologues such as Carlos María Bustamante placed the blame for the economic backwardness of Mexico at the feet of Spanish colonialism, and progress was neatly associated with national sovereignty and freedom. Moreover, the identification between nationality and cultural modernity was strongly fortified in the aftermath of the 1910–20 revolution, when the state intervened actively to shape a lay, modern citizenry out of Mexico's agrarian classes. This process was to be achieved through education and economic redistribution, through "land and books," as one *agrarista* from Michoacán put it.[2] The result of this would be, according to president Lázaro Cárdenas's well-known formulation, not to Indianize Mexico, but to transform Indians into Mexicans.

Accordingly, the old usage of *naco* marked peasants and other traditional peoples and practices as "Indian," that is, as not yet fully Mexican. The new usage, contrarily, marks Mexicans on the whole as not fully at home in modernity. Nationality and national culture are no longer the vehicle of modernity; they are the lingering mark of dismodernity.

*Understanding the Background: Modernity and Citizenship under Import Substitution Industrialization and in the Neoliberal Era*

The crisis of nationalism in the current era has to be understood against the backdrop of Mexico's regime of import substitution industrialization (ISI), which lasted roughly from 1940 to 1982. That era of intense modernization developed under the aegis of a one-party system that was ideologically founded on revolutionary nationalism. The public sphere was largely centered in Mexico City, where institutional spaces were carved out for intellectuals to interpret "national sentiment" on the basis of highly ritualized political manifestations by social groups that had little direct access to the media of national representation and debate.[3]

This whole system of ritualized mobilizations, segmented spheres of political discussion, and intellectuals with privileged access to the media was complemented by the uncontested power of arbitration and intervention of the national president, who became a much-sanctified figure.

In this respect, the one-party regime that was at the height of power during ISI can be seen as a refashioning of the colonial system of political representation, when the viceroy was the highest arbitrator and political expressions were channeled into the ritual life of various corporations. One major difference between the two systems, however, was that there was only a very incipient public sphere in the colonial period: the press was stringently controlled and void of all political commentary, the university had no autonomy, there was no national parliament, and the Inquisition still stood as a symbol of state vigilance over belief and expression. Moreover, the colonial system was premodern in that it was doggedly determined to prevent the separation between public morality, science, and art.

On the other hand, neither can it be said that national society in the postrevolutionary era was unflinchingly modern, for although there was a public sphere in the Habermasian sense, the forums for discussion and the citizens that they included were a very restricted proportion of the population.

Moreover, although Mexico had effectively achieved a separation between church and state by 1930, it had not achieved a separation between politics, science, and art. Instead, both art and science were fostered under the patriarchal umbrella of the protectionist state, and were ultimately confined by it. Scientific production in Mexico has thrived disproportionately at its public universities, especially the national university, which until recently produced about 70 percent of Mexico's scientific output. On the other hand, policy making in Mexican state institutions has not always held scientific production at the forefront of its preoccupations: education has been too deeply associated with state-fostered mobility, and sound scientific policies have at times been eschewed in favor of using the educational apparatus as a mechanism of redistribution. A similar sort of argument can be made for state policies in financing the arts. Few Mexican intellectuals have escaped the ensuing ambivalence toward the revolutionary state.

At the regional level, until the 1970s Mexican culture was constituted out of a dialectic between the capital, which was both the center of national power and the paradigmatic center of modernity, and various sorts of provinces. Incorporation to modernity meant incorporation to state institutions, especially schools, and knowledge and culture found their climax in Mexico City. This led to a simplified view of the provinces as a homogeneous bedrock of tradition and backwardness, a feeling that is summed up in the famous maxim: "Fuera de México, todo es Cuauhtitlán" (Outside of Mexico City, there is nothing but Cuauhtitláns).

In fact, however, Mexican regions were spatially fragmented into a complex system of localities and classes with concomitantly rich idioms of distinction between them—I have called the ways of life of these spatially fragmented classes "intimate cultures."[4] Abstractly stated, regional cultures were made up of combinations of agrarian and industrial classes. The agrarian classes comprised peasant villagers, day laborers, cowboys, and ranchers, and each of these had regional peculiarities and various degrees of prominence in each region. On the other hand, the period of ISI was also a time of accelerated urban growth and of migration from rural settings to cities, giving cities a strong presence of peasant folk, many of whom returned to their villages at least for fiesta days and became active transformers of village social life as well.

The entry into a new phase in social and cultural history can be traced to several sources, including (1) urbanization and new industrial poles of development outside of Mexico City—most notably on or near the U.S. border; (2) the consolidation of television and the telephone in the national space (which can be dated to around 1970); and (3) the 1982 debt crisis and the corresponding end of the regime of import substitution industrialization and of models for self-sustained growth. These changes radically altered the regional organization of production—including cultural production—as well as the government's place in the modernizing project.

The reduction of the role of the state in the economy led to governmental attempts to divest from its former role in science, education, and art: public universities found their budgets strangled; Televisa, the private television giant, stepped up its role in "high culture," filling part of the void that the government was leaving behind by building a major modern-art museum, consolidating its cultural TV channel, and creating strong links with one of Mexico's two main "intellectual groups."[5]

On the other hand, because of the government's will to maintain party hegemony and the social system's acknowledged reliance on both higher education and research, the government found that it could not afford simply to abandon its ties to intellectuals, and so it developed new forms of patronage for restricted groups of artists and scientists. Thus, state divestment left most intellectuals dependent on Televisa and other corporate investors, or on highly exclusive and specially targeted governmental scholarship programs. The status of scientists and artists as social groups was undermined. In this way, intellectuals benefited from some decentralization and a bit more autonomy of cultural production from the state, at the cost of impoverishment and reduction of the size of the community of cultural producers, and a significant takeover of this area by private monopolies.

At the level of regional cultures, rural localities became less tied to their historical regions. Increasing dependence on industrial commodities, and agile modes of communication (the telephone and TV), have substantially simplified what had until now been spatially quite intricate nested hierarchies of productively and commercially interdependent localities, and television plus the urban experience have served to instate a more standardized idiom of distinction in the regions. This latter aspect sometimes provokes a feeling of homogenization and of cultural loss: the increased social role of industrialized commodities, standardized and publicized by a monopolized medium (TV).

In sum, in the era of ISI, Mexico was made up of a complex and differentiated set of cultural regions. The state had a pivotal role in fostering industrialization and in creating the institutional framework for a national citizenry, and these two processes were intimately related. The state as educator, as employer, as provider of social security, of agricultural credits, or of housing subsidies was the main modernizing agent. Becoming a fully fledged citizen, unencumbered by conflicting loyalties to native communities, was thus a sign of modernity.

In the past few decades, however, the mass media has created forms of transregional communication that circumvent governmental institutions and that transcend their unifying power. For example, since Carlos Salinas's presidential campaign (1988), television stars were used as a main draw to attain public attendance at his rallies. On the other hand, the withdrawal of the state as a primary employer, and its constrained sponsorship of intellectuals, artists, and journalists, serve to sever the identity that had existed between citizenship and modernity. More recently, opposition parties such as the Partido de la Revolución Democrática (PRD) have used television and movie stars as successful candidates for congress.

## Consumption, Recycling, and the Resilience of National Identity

Given this general context, forms of consumption have become perhaps the single most important signs of the modern, and recycling is one of the main signs and idioms of distinction. It is useful to distinguish between strategies of staggered distribution that are designed to underline degrees of separation from the holy grail of the so-called international standard or fashion, and recycling proper, which involves transforming the use of a standardized item (appropriation, resistance, or affirmation of difference).

In the first category, we have as examples the distribution of films, which is spatially ordered in such a way that the films that mark higher status are screened in the United States first, then in fancier Mexico City theaters and in a few provincial capitals, and finally in the popular cinemas. It is also evident in the phenomenon of "dumping" in the fashion industry—where prestigious brands are mimicked with cheap imitations—or in software, where piracy prevails and few people own manuals to their (often slightly outdated or virus-infected) programs. On the whole, the distribution of brand names and goods places Mexicans slightly off the cutting edge of international consumption.

In contrast to this form of staggered distribution, recycling involves improvisation: using generic instruments for fixing the big brand names or, more drastically, using products for entirely different aims than they were designed for: plastic bags as plant pots, a broken-down refrigerator as a trunk for storage, and so on. The prevalence of both of these forms of distribution and recycling invades the whole country with a sense of second-classness. This feeling is menacing to most political elites, including aspiring oppositional groups, and they correspondingly develop forms of distinction that stand against Americanization and turn either to Europe or inward (to the hacendado, to the urban notable, to the Aztec lord) for inspiration. In this way, various local and national elites can obviate a destiny of becoming a middle-class periphery of Houston.

In Spanish, there is a saying: "Más vale cabeza de ratón que cola de león" (I'd rather be the head of a mouse than the tail of a lion). People who are interested in asserting leadership need to construct themselves as being at the head of a community with a degree of sovereignty; they cannot simply be the lower-middle cog in a system of distinction that has its capital in some corporate headquarters in Atlanta, and this situation reinforces the legitimacy of state-protected monopolies and political prerogatives that Mexican elites, and to some extent Mexican citizens, have always had in their country, thereby pitting nationalism against a globalizing form of modernization.

This same problem can also be gleaned from another angle. One characteristic of Mexico's modernity has been the persistent reproduction of vast social classes that are not fully incorporated into modern forms of work: the resilience of the peasantry, the ubiquitous presence of personal servants for the middle and upper classes, the vast urban class of "semi-employed." Political control over these sectors, whose direct dependence on specific capitalists has often been unstable, was until recently achieved through corruption.

Corruption worked in two important ways: first, specific state institutions were appropriated by individuals who took charge of dispensing resources and repressing dissenters; second, corruption tended to reinforce or create a corporate structure both because it involved consolidating access to work via the mediation of a political leader, and because political leaders legitimated their position to superiors and subordinates by way of various political rituals that involved some redistribution. Thus, modern Mexico prolonged the baroque tradition of popular representation in a spatially intricate fiesta system.

In the current moment, however, this system has undergone serious strains. The retrenchment of government has begun to erode the communitarian framework that was ultimately the referent of these various rituals. For example, local village factions used to strive for gaining the PRI nomination to their municipal presidencies. The fact that the struggle occurred within a single party signified that local village factions acknowledged the encompassment of the village as a whole by both the state governor and the national president (both of whom always belonged to the PRI). This tacit recognition of encompassment helped consolidate an idiom of village unity that was expressed in the inclusiveness of village fiestas.

The contraction of national government has meant giving up some party control over this hierarchy, and it will certainly mean giving most of it up in the near future. Village factions today are often funneled into separate political parties. This multipartisanship may well strain some of the communitarian ideologies and rituals in national space. For example, when the late Fidel Velázquez, perennial leader of the officialist confederation of unions called the CTM (Confederación de Trabajadores Mexicanos), announced that, for the first time, the CTM would not carry out a Labor Day parade on May 1, 1995, unions and people sympathizing with the opposition participated in a—now uncontrolled—demonstration, that was widely interpreted as a rift between state and nation.

Thus the incapacity of the new state to funnel employment, and its concomitant difficulty in securing key ritual spaces, added to the severity of the current economic crisis, creating an image of a state that is controlled by and used for the benefit of a thin and unpopular Americanizing elite that is overlain on a popular, Mexican nation. This image is unquestionably new (although it has historical precedents) and threatening. Corruption today appears as a more individualistic phenomenon than it was in the past: instead of being a system that had the president at its apex and worked smoothly down from there, today higher officials are seen as plunderers who do not share with a broad base of supporters. The connection between corruption and corporate ritual is not as pervasive now as it was in the ISI period, leading to an image of a schism between people and state. Whereas the image of the pyramid was a root metaphor for Mexican society in the period of ISI, today the elite is often portrayed as a technocratic crust that is increasingly out of touch with society.[6]

In sum, the two logics of distribution—staggered distribution and recycling—both tend to reaffirm the incorporation of Mexico into a system of distinction that has its capital in the United States. However, this same fact generates two forms of nationalism to counter it; one comes from the recyclers and the other from all manner of political leaders. Recyclers affirm difference from the international market simply by existing. Politicians need to affirm national difference in order to place themselves at the apex of the various levels of an imagined national community.

On the other hand, the capacity of political leaders to portray themselves as sitting at the apex of a cultural and political community has been seriously eroded by transformation in the economic system, whose contraction has led to democratization and to a reduction of state sponsorship of communitarian rituals. As a result, the pyramidal imagery that was typical of revolutionary nationalism has been replaced by various images of the political elite as a free-floating crust of predators. This makes their identification with the nation problematic.

*Nationalism and the International Standard*

So far I have described a situation in which demands for the extension of the benefits of modernization and modernity have expanded to all levels of the regional system, while contradictions have emerged between these desires (whose pulsating vitality is evident in the ebullience of *naco* aesthetics) and the very limited response from state institutions that have been retreating from their roles as providers. In this context, there is much ambivalence regarding the so-called international standard: free trade means producing for an international market and competing internationally, so that any Mexican product, sports hero, artist, or scientist who can compete internationally risks being transformed into a metonym of Mexico's idealized place in a commoditized world of equals. Thus the "international standard" achieves a status akin to that of truth for science: competing internationally is the ultimate legitimation.[7]

On the other hand, much of the country's population, which grew and developed under the systemic logic of import substitution cannot easily reach this standard, and this population seeks the protection of the state against the global market, while it asserts the value of local cultural forms, traditions, and products. There is thus a cultural dialectic between acceptance and rejection of globalization that is obvious in the ambivalent position of *naquismo*: enthusiasm for modernity and a (sometimes involuntary) assertion of the individual's eccentricity.

From a spatial perspective, this dialectic implies a change in the places and contexts in which nationalism is deployed. Whereas nationalism under ISI was the hegemonic idiom of the state, an idiom that was appealed to in negotiating local political demands but that was less relevant in the day-to-day reality of production and consumption, nationalism emerges today as a quotidian question that is deployed in connection to issues of work and of consumption. Whereas under ISI there was only one dominant form of nationalism, and it was predicated on the teachings of the Mexican Revolution and had the national state, personified in the president of the republic, as its ultimate locus, today there are two forms of nationalism, one that sees reaching full modernization and the rule of the international standard as the ultimate patriotic end, and another that insists on the intrinsic superiority of local products and traditions and that sees the neoliberal state as having traded its patriotic legacy for a bowl of U.S.-made porridge.

The first form of nationalism requires a credible bid to enter a North American economic community in order to survive. The feasibility of this today is questionable because of both Mexico's economic crisis and a nationalist backlash against NAFTA and against Mexican migrants in the United States. The second form of nationalism has not yet devised a political formula that can simultaneously work in a contested democratic field and provide the kind of state protection that revolutionary nationalism once offered.

## Conclusion

The transformation in the logic of capital accumulation and in the role of the state in the economy has had a counterpoint at the level of cultural production in national space. Changes at this level include (1) a reduction of the cultural independence of provincial and Mexico City upper classes and a standardization of idioms of distinction through mass consumption; (2) a contraction of state sponsorship of science and art and a concomitant growth in the control over those sectors by a couple of industrial groups; (3) a relative decline of Mexico City as the uncontested center of national modernity; (4) a new battle over the contents of nationalism that spills into the ways in which transformations in the system of production and in consumption habits are embraced or rejected; (5) a breakdown in the regional chain of corruption and controlled political ritual that has transformed the images with which the government is portrayed from a pyramidal metaphor to various images of parasitism; and (6) a division between those who recycle without regard to the status definitions of mass consumption and those who do their utmost to be in the first cycles of consumption.

All of this adds up to a serious crisis in the politics of nationalism. Under the protectionist revolutionary state, nationalism and modernity came in the same package; today nationalism can serve as a counter to globalization. However, the hopes of using the state effectively as an alternative route to modernity have not been renovated with ideas that make it seem more viable than the model that was already tried and exhausted or than failed attempts to foster socialism in one (dismodern) state. On the other hand, neoliberal politicians have not succeeded in reformulating Mexican nationalism in a way that preserves the sense that the nation has its own internal system of value production. As a result, the opposition between state and nation, between a "deep Mexico" and a commercial, international, and superficially modernizing elite, emerges as a common image of the national situation.

Politically, these dialectics of nationalism and national culture do not hold positive promise. Mexico is currently condemned to continue being a nation-state for a while, given the United States' ever more militant resolve to patrol its borders and control immigration. As long as current aspirations to modernity go unquestioned and unanalyzed, and as long as new formulas for state intervention in a modernizing project are not invented, the future looms darkly, one of economic decline and unresolvable political divisions.

The spatial analysis of the cultural dialectics of modernity/dismodernity that I have presented here is a necessary step for envisioning alternatives, and could be particularly useful on two levels: in the elaboration of possible alternative narratives for the nation that are in line with its best real possibilities; and in understanding the cultural implications of the geography of modernity, thereby helping to specify the sorts of social and political demands that are truly relevant in the reformulation of political programs, beyond our current ideological bankruptcy.

# PART II

# Geographies of
# the Public Sphere

# 6

## Nationalism's Dirty Linen:
## "Contact Zones" and the Topography
## of National Identity

The production of knowledge, the narrative strategies, and the psychology of colonial and postcolonial relations have been the topic of a body of writing that has come to be known in the anglophone world as "postcolonial theory." Within this broad field, there is an area of sociological inquiry that is of central importance, which is the systemic aspect of national identity production. Until recently, nationalist narratives were predominant, and they portrayed national identity and national consciousness as processes of "self-awakening." National identity was portrayed as emerging out of a dialectic that was internal to the national community.

In the past couple of decades, this approach has itself been shown to be an instrument of national identity production. Instead of looking for the secret of national identity within the "soul" or "spirit" of each nation, contemporary analysts have looked at the history of nationalism as an aspect of transnational relations. Local innovations to nationalist imagery, discourse, and technique are communicated between politicians, experts, and intellectuals the world over, in a complex history that leads to the standardization of various strands of nationalism. This history implicates scientific theories and measurements, narrative strategies in fiction and nonfiction, and aesthetic solutions to shaping the national image in art, architecture, and urban planning.[1]

National identity has thus been shown to be fashioned in transnational networks of specialists, intellectuals, and politicians, many of whom proceed to cover their tracks and to tell their tales as if they were strictly local inventions. Moreover, the denial of interdependency between nations has been shown to have a variety of political uses. Thus, intellectuals from colonized areas have criticized the ways in which their countries' material and intellectual contributions have been appropriated by the great powers, whose nationalism is thus easily identified with "rationality" and "civilization." The nationalism of weak nations is, as a result, in constant need of self-assertion, and it tends to mirror the nationalism of the great powers by claiming independent or prior invention of civilization for itself.[2]

The shift from internal accounts of the origins of national identity to accounts that understand nationalism as a cultural product that is generated in a web of transnational connections is thus of great consequence. Nevertheless, this development has not yet provided all of the elements that are required for a systematic account of the contexts in which national identity actually emerges. Nationalism, as Benedict Anderson argued, is not a coherent ideology, but rather a broad cultural frame in which a variety of contradictory claims are made.[3] We know that states put forth their proposals for a national image and implement them in schools, museums, and public squares, but at which points, in which social relations, is national identity pertinent, underlined, or referred to by other actors?

It is quite easy to produce lists of disparate contexts and relationships in which national identity "naturally" emerges: in the exclusion of an upwardly mobile urban Aymara teenager from an afternoon social by her "white" Bolivian classmates; in the negotiation of a business deal in broken English; or in the film that features an exotic woman who is made to represent the bounties of her country to potential foreign investors . . . The list of identity-producing social relationships is limitless, and placing its diverse items in the frame of a broader political economy is a challenge. I seek here to put order in the various sorts of contexts in which national identity "naturally" emerges. The matter is of some importance to the general project of this book, which is to understand the conditions for the production of "Mexico" as a polity, as national identity, and as national culture.

These conditions have often been precarious.[4] Like many peripheral nations, Mexico emerged as the result of the collapse of an empire more than because of an overwhelming popular desire for national independence. Nationalism was thus not widely shared at the time of the national revolutions. Moreover, like most Spanish-American countries, Mexico achieved statehood long before its territory was bound together in a "national market" or by a "national bourgeoisie." As a result, the territorial consolidation of the country was a long, conflict-ridden process involving secessions, annexations, civil wars, and foreign interventions. National consolidation came half a century after independence, and was still called into question on several later occasions. As a result, understanding the process of identity formation in Mexico is both a historical and a sociological challenge. It is a historical challenge because it has been such an uneven and differentiated process. It is sociologically demanding because identities are always relational; the specification of the relationships that generate national identity implies a sociology of national identity.

The case is thus a paradigmatic context for what I have called "grounded theory": the confrontation of a historical and a political problem that requires sociological innovation. The theoretical requirement here is constrained by the historical object (Mexico), an object that is generally believed to be provincial. The knowledge that stems from that which is provincial is usually thought to be parochial and prosaic. As opposed to England, France, Germany, or the United States, the Latin American countries have generally not been held up to be the cradle of anything in particular that is of world-historical significance.[5] Moreover, even Latin America's status as "Western" or "non-Western" is ambiguous, and it thus falls short in providing a radical sense of alterity for Europeans. Thus, the continent has not usually been cast in the role that "the Orient," Africa, or Oceania have played in the Western imaginary—at least it has not often done so for the past couple of centuries. Mexico and Latin America have much more often been portrayed by Europeans and Americans as "backward" than as radically different.[6]

On a theoretical plane the, continent would thus appear to be destined to play Sancho Panza to the North Atlantic's Don Quixote: not a radical other, but rather a common, backward, and yet pragmatic and resourceful companion. An inferior with a point of view. A repository of customs and relations past, where universalizing theories that were built to explain world-historical phenomena are constantly applied, and yet are often too high and disengaged from immediate interest. Even now, when the very notion of a historical vanguard has been so thoroughly questioned, the social thought emerging from these provinces is somewhat cumbersome when it is put to work elsewhere, usually requiring further extension and translation. "Grounded theory" is a kind of theory that flies more like a chicken than a hawk.

My aim in this chapter is to propose a simple generative principle for national identity production in peripheral postcolonial societies. From this general principle I derive four classes of social dynamics that generate particular frames of identity production. Each of these is discussed and illustrated with historical examples from Mexico.

## National Identity in the World System (Sancho's Version)

Weak national communities adrift in the international system constantly run the risk of indecent exposure, of involuntarily revealing the tenuous connections between national imagery and everyday practice. Quite simply, a country's weakness in the international system undermines the basic tenets of modern nationalism and thereby calls national identity into question. These basic principles are, first, that the national state is a vehicle for the modernization of a people that shares a set of values and traditions; second, that this process of modernization chiefly serves the interests of national community and not those of foreigners; and third, that nationalism is a sign of progressive modernity and not of backwardness. The peripheral postcolonial condition poses constant challenges to the most fundamental dogmas of nationalism. This is my general structural principle.

To this we should add one general historical principle, which is that peripheral nations generally develop in a forcefield that is shaped by two contradictory impulses: the desire to appropriate for the nation the power and might of the empires that they have broken away from, and the impulse to shape modern national communities based on an idealized bond of fraternity between citizens. These two impulses can be thought of as a tension between liberalism and ("internal") colonialism, a tension that is heightened by weakness in the international arena. Maintaining the system of internal differences inherited from the colonial world, the hierarchical differences of race, sex, and ethnicity that are used to organize exploitation can be seen as antagonistic to the ideal of the nation—a charge that can be levied not only by the lower classes of the country, but also by foreigners, who can use the charge to raise their own claims. It is in relation to these principles that one can develop a sociology and a topography of the frames of identity production in which national identity is generated.

## National Identity

Our subject is the interactions that generate an awareness of differences of ascription among actors, contacts between actors who identify as "national" in contrast to others who are portrayed as "foreign." This specification is necessary because many contacts between persons, or between persons and objects that represent other persons, are not marked in this way, even when differences in nationality exist.

The ongoing implementation of "neoliberal" policies in Mexico, for example, has led some people to "foreignize" the government officials who have furthered these policies. From their point of view, neoliberal officials are serving the interests of U.S.-controlled institutions such as the International Monetary Fund and the World Bank, and they are following teachings of their equally American professors at Harvard, Chicago, Stanford, or MIT. When this powerful movement of reform began, however, there were a number of intellectuals and politicians who had been calling for a "return" to the liberal policies of Benito Juárez and Sebastián Lerdo de Tejada, Mexican national heroes of the nineteenth century. The same set of policies and relationships were "indigenized" by some and marked "foreign" by others. Thus "neoliberalism" in Mexico is an ideological tendency that involves questions of national identity for some, and not for others. For a cultural contact to be considered under the definition that interests us here, it must serve to construct a difference in national identity between actors.

*Frames of Contact*

The concept of "contact frame" refers to the relational contexts in which national identity production occurs. We can identify classes or types of such contexts from the dynamics of nation building and transnational interactions that can be isolated on the analytic plane. Contact frames are thus the minimal analytic units of a vast topography of national identity. For example, there is an entire class of contact frames that is produced by the logic of commodity production and consumption under capitalism, which is an international system that national communities can never completely encompass or regulate: a shop that sells foreign goods in La Paz, Bolivia, is called "Miamicito" (and so provides a frame that marks both the foreignness of its wares and the nationality of its customers); during the 1970s, the Latin American left referred to Coca-Cola as "the sewage" (*las aguas negras*) of Yankee imperialism, and thereby framed its distribution and consumption as so many episodes in the national struggle. We shall identify several such classes of contact frames.

## "Contact Zones" and the Topography of National Identity

In traditional geography there is a distinction between the concept of "zone" (an internally homogeneous space) and "region" (the functional integration of different kinds of zones). I shall call an internally homogeneous class of contact frames a *contact zone*. Contact zones are integrated into a broader "region" of national identity production that includes a zone of state institutions that define rights and obligations for citizens and produce images and narratives of nationality, and zones of local and class identity production that are equally critical.[7] Thus contact zones are part of the "region" of national identity production which is the national space, complete with the cultural production of the state and the internal idioms of distinction that give shape to national culture. These national spaces are, in their turn, part of a global system of identity production. A typology of zones of contact like the one we are proposing here thus forms part of a broader project, which can be conceived of as a topography of national identity.

In this chapter I distinguish among four classes of frames of contact in the topography of national identity. They are generated by (1) the material culture of capitalism; (2) the ideological tension between tradition and modernity that is necessary to the founding of nation-states; (3) the entropy of modernization, which is intrinsic to the development process; and (4) the international field of ideas and models of civilization, science, and development that forms part of what could be called the civilizing horizon of nation-states. I now describe each of these frames of contact using Mexican examples in order to understand how the contact frame challenges the stability of national regimes.

### International Business and Imported Material Culture

The four types of contact zones that I discuss are abstractly related to an intrinsic quality of nation-states: they are political communities within a world system of communities, but they are part of an economy that cannot be contained by national borders. This quality of nation-states means that economic modernization (and its agents) can generate spaces of national identification and confrontation. This is especially the case in "peripheral" nations, for which technological innovation and capital often come from abroad. In these contexts especially, consuming commodities or adopting productive techniques of foreign origin can be understood in relation to national identity.

For example, if we look at the history of Mexico, a number of anti-foreign manifestations have centered on commerce: anti-Spanish sentiment in the first republic led to the sacking of Mexico City's Parián Market in 1828. This in turn preceded the expulsion of the Spaniards, who only eight years earlier had been proclaimed to be fellow Mexicans by the triumphant leaders of independence. Some of the most acutely xenophobic movements in Mexican history associate foreigners' supposedly pernicious influence with their position as businessmen. This was true of the anti-Chinese movements in Sonora during the revolution and of journalists' complaints against itinerant commerce by Jews and Arabs in Mexico City during the 1930s. Moreover, there are numerous occasions when the products themselves have been seen as transporting a pernicious foreign influence. Thus, much of the activity of the interior ministry's censorship commissions in the 1950s and 1960s was geared to this. For years these commissions were in charge of censoring comics, films, and other products of mass culture when it was judged that they conspired against basic Mexican values. In other words, anti-Spanish, anti-Semitic, anti-Chinese, and anti-American discourses have been constructed around the space of commerce and imported material culture.[8]

This is significant because the causes of each of these xenophobic movements were in fact different from each other. The anti-Spanish movement at the dawn of the republican era was related to the competition between England and the United States for political hegemony in Mexico and to power struggles between local parties; the anti-Chinese riots were spurred on by members of regional political elites who saw the Chinese as easy targets; the identification of itinerant commerce as "foreign" in the 1920s and 1930s was a strategy to diminish an activity that affected established businesses. Despite these different motivations, however, the identification of foreign businessmen and products as a danger to national integrity is a viable political argument because they do not conform to Mexican national customs and interests.

In the 1920s and 1930s, the Mexican press emphasized that the trade in narcotics in Mexico's northern states was in the hands of foreigners: Chinese, Americans, and Russians. Vice was being brought in from abroad. During the Díaz Ordaz presidency in the 1960s, an attempt was made to restrict the importation of films and records that promoted the hippies' "effeminate decadence." Díaz Ordaz's crusade against American pop culture went hand in hand with his repression of a number of middle-class social movements. More recently, a proposal before Congress sought to ban the cartoon show *Beavis and Butthead* from Mexican television because it perverted the nation's values, especially as regards proper adolescent behavior.[9]

International business constantly produces national identity because businessmen can be credibly portrayed as furthering foreign or private interests at the expense of the national community. Also, the exogenous material culture of modernization can be perceived as corrupting morals or subverting the ruling forms of cultural distinction that can easily be nationalized. Thus, the fact that national communities do not successfully encompass and control the national economy generates a zone of contact that is manifested in an open-ended number of contact frames. In each of these frames, a social actor identifies a product or an agent as "foreign" and as opposed to the "national" collective interest. This way of framing the national interest usually advances more particular interests that are unnamed and fused into the national collective.

## The Tension between Tradition and Modernity

The second type of contact zone arises from the very logic of nationalism as an ideological construct. It is known that, in different ways, nationalism depends on ideological constructs that tie "tradition" to "modernity." This dependency is necessary because modern nation-states are supposed to be vehicles for the modernization of collectivities (nations) that are, in their turn, defined in a genealogical relation to a "tradition."[10] This ideal relationship can be precarious, however, especially in the case of weaker nations. When national tradition is perceived to be divorced from or opposed to modernization, a contact zone emerges.

In Mexico, postindependence nationalism appropriated the pre-Hispanic world in a way analogous to the European appropriation of classical antiquity, but with a twist. The Aztecs were the forerunners of independent Mexico; the colonial period was a parenthesis that served to bring Christianity and certain traits of civilization, but it also barbarously degraded the condition of the indigenous peoples. Therefore, in principle, the glorification of the pre-Hispanic past did not imply claims on behalf of the contemporaneous Indians because their habits and condition were seen to be the result of colonial degradation. Thus, in the early postindependent era, modernization could readily be made to trample over indigenous traditions without challenging national identity. The same was not true, however, with respect to the preservation of Catholicism and of a number of the mores of the Spanish colonial world.

Thus, modernization in the first half of the nineteenth century produced deep rifts between national versions, one of which sought to preserve the Catholic and Hispanicist traditions, while the other sought to found nationality squarely on liberal principles, and was fervently anti-Spanish and anticlerical. These two national versions even honored two distinct heroes of independence and two different dates for national independence.[11] Each side accused the other of lack of patriotism and of collusion with foreign interests.

This situation changed with the end of the civil wars that followed the French intervention (1867), a peace that involved a pragmatic arrangement between liberal and conservative factions under a universally acknowledged liberal hegemony. The peace also allowed Mexico to make a concerted effort to gain international respect and to attract foreign investment. This involved displaying the individuality of its culture to foreigners, an aim that was more readily achieved with tequila than with whiskey and with indigenous *huipils* before manufactured shirts. Since that time, the official construction of tradition necessarily visited certain features of Mexico's rural and artisan life, not only the pre-Columbian past.

At the same time, the relationship that the state was trying to create between tradition and modernity continued to hold. In some cases, the existence of a "Mexican tradition" made it possible for Mexico to claim a particular modernity, but it never denied the nation-state's fundamental and eternal aspiration: modernity and modernization.[12] Therefore, the great official points of pride could not and still cannot reside principally in the world called "traditional": the modern must be granted a privileged place in the national utopia. Thus, some of the crown jewels of Mexican state nationalism have been President Santa Anna's theater, Emperor Maximilian's boulevards, Don Porfirio's trains, Lázaro Cárdenas's nationalized petroleum industry, Miguel Alemán's Acapulco and the National University campus, López Mateos's National Museum of Anthropology, Díaz Ordaz's subway and Olympics, and Echeverría's highways, Cancún, and nationalized industries. Of these examples, the National Museum of Anthropology is exemplary in that it combines traditional aesthetics with an avant-garde architecture that relies heavily on state-of-the-art technology. In this formulation, tradition is like the country's spiritual dimension, which is incorporated as an aesthetic into a unique modernity that is the country's present and, above all, its future.

However, Mexico's position as a relatively poor country in the international order threatened the ideal relationship that nationalism constructs between tradition and modernity, making it into a fissure where zones of transnational contact could endanger that very nationalism.

Tourists, travelers, scientists, and other inquisitive foreigners have generally tended to turn toward the traditional sector, and yet the state's capacity to get visitors to appreciate the alleged connection between the traditional and the modern has always been limited. For example, Eric Zolov describes the history of the hippie movement in Mexico as a case of cultural production in the context of transnational communication. Among his sources, Zolov cites the *People's Guide to Mexico* travel guide, which began to be published in the 1960s especially for countercultural tourists. In its heyday, this book served to orient the hippie to countercultural pilgrimage centers and to avoid friction with official Mexico. In a passage dedicated to the problems that hippies suffer when they cross the border, for example, the guide points out that, to beat the system, "we look like small town teachers or college students from the early Sixties [when we cross] . . . The border officials love it."[13]

In this case, the foreign visitor is disguising herself as the Mexican government's ideal of an American visitor, a clean-cut student or teacher eager to visit the Mexico that the government was interested in exhibiting. Once this tourist crossed the border, however, she presumably removed her bra, put the beads back on, and then moved across the national territory with greater interest in Mexico's "backward" areas and more suspicion of its "progressive" sector than was desirable.

The contact frames that tourism and scientific study open up between the traditional and modern worlds had their first problematic moments long before the hippie movement. The U.S. and European travelers who came to Mexico in the 1920s, 1930s, and 1940s frequently felt more attracted to the rural, indigenous world than to the modern, urban one, which generally was less modern than their own cities. However, at that time the attraction that the foreign intellectual felt for the indigenous world went hand in hand with the state's own renewed interest in identifying with that world: the Mexican Revolution had reconfigured the ties between the indigenous and modern worlds in some respects. Also, even many official Mexican *indigenistas* of the period frequently sought inspiration for the modern in the indigenous.[14] On the other hand, as the revolutionary order became more routinized and Mexico entered a modernizing era with ever more tenuous ties to the agrarian and popular world of the revolution, the relationship with the traditional world became more propagandistic, and foreign visitors' and intellectuals' lack of interest in modern Mexico could become irritating.

The countercultural hippie movement was the most conflictive moment in the recent history of this contact zone because it coincided with a phase of national development spurred by a strong, closed state that wanted to transform the country's position on the international scene. While President Díaz Ordaz sought to show the world a Mexico that was capable of hosting the Olympics—a Mexico with a recently inaugurated subway system, an Olympic village built expressly for the event, and an architecturally impressive new gym, pool, and stadium—a number of people who rejected the labor and very idea of progress looked for mushrooms in Huautla, walked around in peasant sandals, and changed the very image of Mexican youth.

The contact zone that inverts the hierarchy of tradition and modernity also touches the history of anthropology. This discipline's fieldwork methodology made middle- and upper-class Mexicans and foreigners privilege the peasant over the local schoolteacher or the village merchant. Anthropological fieldwork gave cultural authority to people who in their own regions had been disdained or even silenced for their supposed backwardness, a practice that would be repeated and reinforced by travelers who were attracted to Mexico's indigenous people and peasantry.

The search for the authentic, in both science and travel, sometimes inverted the scale of prestige; by showing little interest in Mexico's modern sector, travelers interested in authenticity exposed its lack of distinctiveness. The sector that was paraded internally as the vanguard and latest cry of modernity was old hat to the foreigner. By revealing that the country was not on the cutting edge of modernity and by nonetheless exalting its traditional sector, foreign visitors and scientists could destabilize the ideal relationship between tradition and modernity that is so essential to all nationalism. Thus foreigners in the traditional world generate a contact zone that produces nationalist reactions.

The famous educator José Vasconcelos discussed the politics of this contact zone in his autobiography, in which he describes his childhood on the Mexico–U.S. border. Vasconcelos recounts that, as a Mexican child who crossed into the United States every day to go to school, he was impressed by the fact that the U.S. school textbooks shared his sympathy with Mexican Indians and rejected the Spaniards. As an adult, however, Vasconcelos viewed the love that Americans professed for the Mexican Indian as a thinly veiled desire to replace the Mexican Creole with an American. By denying the ties between Mexico's modernizing elite and its indigenous traditions, the country was defenseless against U.S. imperialism.[15] Other active agents in this contact zone do not necessarily seek to strengthen an imperial center against Mexico's government and official culture. However, these agents can create doubts about the government's efficacy or even the legitimacy of its modernizing goals.

## The Disorder of Modernization

Modernization, as we have seen repeatedly, is critical to the legitimation of the national state. When modernization destroys an aspect of the status quo that can be claimed as a national tradition, a contact zone emerges in which the modernizing agent is assimilated with "foreignness." When traditional sectors of the country are portrayed by foreigners as more accomplished than the modern sector, or as being in an unhealthy competition with it, a contact zone emerges. There is yet a third related source of national identity production, which is the entropy of modernization. Our third type of contact zone is generated by the difficulties that nationalists face when the disorder that is produced by modernization is exposed. In order to understand the contours of this contact zone, we need to review the place that modernizing projects have in the cultural production of the state.

The culture that states produce has diverse purposes. On one hand is what Arjun Appadurai has called the "ethnographic state."[16] This is the form of state cultural production that describes the national population— which is the alleged subject of the state—by manufacturing censuses, questionnaires, histories, and statistics. Alongside the ethnographic state is the "modernizing state"—the form of official cultural production that seeks to lay out the task of development. Once "the population" is described, the ethnographic state's scales and measures serve to define lacks or scarcities such as "poverty," "illiteracy," and "unhealthy conditions," as well as a series of growth- and progress-oriented measures that define the efficacy of governments.[17]

Together with these two aspects of state cultural production is a third, which is the production of the country's image for both international and domestic consumption. This includes cultural production for attracting tourism, international sports events, international congresses, national museums, television stations, and schools. All institutions that are presented as national dedicate at least some effort to shaping or conforming to the national image. A fundamental difficulty for this third aspect of state cultural production is that the national image is not at all easy to manage.

Erving Goffman's theatrical metaphor of "front stage" and "backstage" describes the relationship between a subject's public presentation and what he or she wants to hide or protect.[18] The state production of nationalism seeks to construct spaces where the official image of the national takes material form and can be displayed to insiders and outsiders; that is, states seek to create a "front stage" (public) image characterized by an ideal combination of modern and traditional components. They usually seek to show a booming country that marches inexorably toward progress and modernity.

However, the very creation of this public image leaves disorder in its wake: the history of tourism is the supreme example of this. In Mexico, Cuernavaca was probably the first modern tourist destination, developed during the 1920s and 1930s. Cuernavaca's main attraction was its stupendous climate, its proximity to Mexico City, and the fact that both the nation's *jefe supremo*, Don Plutarco Elías Calles, and the U.S. ambassador, Dwight Morrow, built residences there. This attracted both the Mexican political class and an important contingent of American retirees. In addition to the climate was the Casino de la Selva, which offered distractions to tourists who might otherwise get bored by the quaint and the picturesque. However, the casino was also seen as a bad influence on the population, presenting an undesirable image of Mexico as a place where foreigners could shed the moral strictures they faced in their own countries. Reflecting on this, President Lázaro Cárdenas judged that the casino created undesirable frames of contact: a form of tourism based on the promotion of public vices.

The "ugly" side of tourism is not easy to root out, however, and around tourist centers the differences between foreign tourists and national workers in terms of their consumption and purchasing power became apparent. Therefore, beginning with Acapulco and continuing with Cancún, Ixtapa, and others, the cities constructed for tourism are "twin cities": a "front stage" coast and hotel zone is exposed to the tourist, and "backstage" zones combine poverty, prostitution, and so on. This relationship between the presentable side and its hidden consequences makes a number of politically volatile frames of contact possible. For example, in her work on prostitution in Mexico City during the 1920s and 1930s, Katherine Bliss describes the discussion that took place in the capital city government about the creation of a red-light district near the La Merced market. The neighbors organized to protest against the project. Among their arguments was that the red-light district should not be authorized because it would be located on the route between the Mexico City international airport and downtown, and so would be one of the first images that visitors would have of the city.[19]

In the same way that a housewife tries to make sure that her visitors stay in the parlor and do not see the mess in the bedrooms or kitchen, the government, tourist industry, and a good number of patriots seek to display an image of order and cleanliness to foreigners, and the strain involved in these efforts easily turns into a political liability. In a 1910 essay titled "Los dos patriotismos" (The two patriotisms), Luis Cabrera, who would be one of the principal ideologues of the Mexican Revolution, described how the Porfirian elite organized a spectacular celebration of the independence centennial for the benefit mainly of foreign investors. The festivities were so concerned with managing the national image that when a ragged group of women workers organized their own celebratory march, it was brutally dispersed by the police. The national image is difficult to control, not only because it is difficult to keep the ragged workers from the view of the investors, but also because the very occasion of a national show is a tempting occasion for union leaders to display them. A better-known example of a similar political context is the violence of the Mexican '68, which was tied to upholding the national image during the Olympics. Indeed, President Díaz Ordaz and the antistudent social sectors spoke insistently of evil foreign influences that goaded the innocent Mexican student: only a foreigner would seek to sully Mexico's public image before the world.

Other cases, such as the border cities of northern Mexico, present the same problem in a more routine fashion. These cities are all part of bicephalous urban sets often called "twins," though if they are twins they are clearly of the fraternal kind, because, even though they develop in tandem with one another, they are not identical: one part of the urban zone is located in the United States and the other in Mexico. The relationship between the Mexican and U.S. parts of the urban border zone has not been symmetrical, but rather symbiotic, and in many senses the cities on the Mexican side have generally been a "backstage" for the U.S. cities. The Mexican border town's prosperity has depended on abortion clinics, divorce lawyers, judges, bars, prostitutes, sweatshops, garbage dumps, and so on. The fact that Mexican cities constitute the backstage of U.S. cities threatens nationalism's foundational credo: modernity is for the nation's own benefit and not for foreign outsiders.

The frames of contact created by the entropy of modernization can generate extreme nationalist reactions. This was the case in Cuba, where the image of Havana as a brothel was an important motivation for many revolutionaries to rise against the Batista regime. In the case of Mexico's northern border, the very concept of a "border zone," which for many years occupied a marginal position with respect to the rest of the country, was supposed to resolve the contradictions of this contact zone. The inhabitants of that liminal zone were said to have a dubious sense of belonging or even of loyalty to the country, a fact that was reflected in their impure *pocho* language, zoot-suit clothing, and other marks of cultural impurity. Controlling the "border zone" proved to be impossible for the Mexican government, however, and the incorporation of ever-greater proportions of Mexico into the "backstage" of U.S. economic interests has been an inexorable process. Peasant villages from all over the country have been turned into the seasonal equivalent of dormitory communities whose inhabitants travel to work in inferior conditions, as "illegal migrants," in the United States, while *maquiladora* assembly plants can now set up shop on any portion of the territory. Cultural impurity can no longer be contained at the border, and the dark side of modernization is harder to hide than ever.

## The Scientific Horizon as a Contact Frame

The final type of contact exists because nation-states are supposed to march *together* toward progress. Without this ideal, there would be no obsession with national history, because modern history as we know it is only understood in terms of the dogma of progress. The universal importance that all nation-states attribute to progress implies that there is always a civilizing horizon or vanguard of progress on the international level. This civilizing horizon is identified in terms of technological development, scientific advances, and the techniques used to govern the population. The civilizing horizon serves to measure a country's individual progress as well as different countries' relative progress. The parameters used tend to be produced in countries with robust cultural and scientific infrastructures. Therefore, science, art, and fashion can destabilize the nation's dominant models.

The recent work of Alexandra Stern on Mexican eugenics provides a good example of the ways in which scientific development constitutes a zone of contact.[20] Between 1920 and 1950, a number of medical doctors and anthropologists participated in international eugenics congresses, read international journals in that discipline, and formulated ideas about the Mexican racial and genetic inheritance. Their work served two ends: on the one hand, it strengthened the "mestizophilic" Mexican Revolution's antiracist arguments; on the other hand, it tended to characterize Mexico's various poor populations (from rural Indians to urban workers) as comparatively deficient. Eugenics' racial relativism (each race was supposed to be adapted to a specific environment and so was in some respects superior, and in others inferior, to the rest) and its simultaneous characterization of the Mexican majority in terms of a series of relative lacks offered hope for eventual equality between Mexico and European peoples. It also offered ample justification for a kind of "internal colonialism." Eugenics offered a way to objectify and quantify differences between poor Mexicans and ideal norms represented by the elite. This in turn permitted the state's development mission to be defined, while the poor national majority could remain scientifically devalued. At the same time, the potential uses of race science to undercut the imagined potential of Mexico's "halfbreed" race is well known and was always a potential liability for the nationalists.

The introduction of new ideas and theories always presents challenges and opportunities to governments and to processes of national identity formation. The ideas of "scientific socialism" allowed opposition movements like the guerrilla movement led by Genaro Vázquez in southern Mexico in the 1960s to refer to the Mexican government as the "disgovernment" and to propose a series of demands to the state in name not only of Marx and Lenin, but also in that of the heroes of national independence. The monetarist ideas of the Chicago school of economics allowed a group of technicians to take control of the Mexican state, accuse the previous governing elite of backwardness, and describe the Mexican state as "obese." The scientific ideas of Darwin, Freud, and Marx were at the center of a schism in the Mexican educational establishment in the 1920s and 1930s, and they were used to rethink nationality. The Lamarckian notion that acquired characteristics are inherited led some members of the Porfirian elite to advocate an aggressive policy of European immigration before reforming the Indian through education.

Each of these movements has had implications for national identity and the precepts of nationalism. The scientific contact frame produced by the international civilizing horizon destabilizes dominant formulas of nationality and good government; it presents growth opportunities for certain sectors and threatens others.

### Reflections on the Four Types of Contact Zones

I have identified four types of contact zones. All are related to the nexus between modernization and nationalism as it develops in weak or peripheral nations. In the first case, there is a contact zone created by the instances in which foreign business concerns or imports unsettle local arrangements or mores. This is a zone that may appear whenever there are technological innovations, changes in the intensity of foreign investment, or internal political factionalism that can profit from assimilating economic competitors to foreignness.

The second and third types of contact zones are produced by the difficulties that weak nations have in managing the national image. The second emerges as a result of the comparative weakness of these nation's modern sector. This situation allows foreigners or opponents to the dominant nationalist scheme to attribute greater value to the "backward" than to the "modern" sector, and even to portray the modern sector as antagonistic to tradition, and therefore as failing to develop a true or successful nationalism. The third type of contact zones emerges as a result of the difficulty that these same governments face in controlling the modernization process, and in successfully sweeping the adverse aspects of modernization under the carpet.

The fourth type of contact zone is produced by the instability that is generated by the (international) civilizing horizon. This contact zone, which is produced through the mediation of scientists, professionals, and artists, can destabilize the national image by portraying it as old-fashioned and out of tune with modernization. Conversely, nationalists can try to reject a development in these fields by portraying it as alien to the national interest, to the national aesthetic, or to custom. Like each of the other contact zones, this fourth type lends itself to shrewd political usage and can respond equally to internal factionalism and to important changes emerging from abroad.

I have extended Mary Louise Pratt's term *contact zone* to refer to transnational spaces of national identity formation.[21] As we have seen, however, the concept of "zone" implies a geography of regions: a zone is a kind of place within a system of functionally related places. What position do these contact zones occupy in a broader geography? The frames of contact that we have analyzed are relationships that emerge from the tension between the nation-state as a certain type of political and cultural community and the fact that modernization neither begins nor ends in such a community. This fact is problematic for nationalism because nation-states are erected as forms of social organization for coordinating modernization: zones of contact with the transnational dimension of capitalism and progress can therefore call into question some of the basic precepts of any particular nationalism. Moreover, the very process of shaping and extending nationalism opens a country up to foreign interests and forms of consumption that can undermine the nationalism that made room for them.

This is the case with frames of contact that open up because of the relationship that nationalism postulates between tradition and modernity. This relationship existed because each country forms part of an international system and so must attain a sense of specificity. Moreover, in the case of postcolonial or backward countries, national singularity is more readily built out of their traditional sectors than their modern sectors. In the Mexican case, it has proved easier to construct a national singularity on the basis of *pulque*, folk dancing, woven *serapes*, and beef tacos than on the basis of whiskey, rock 'n' roll, tuxedos, and French cuisine, even when the latter may also be local products. At the same time, the identification of the nation's soul with the traditional world and its body with the modern world is an unstable formulation because the world called "traditional" persists as underdevelopment and in a series of relationships of domination that are generally understood to be continuous with colonial domination. Foreigners pursue their own relationships with those modern and traditional worlds, creating a zone of contact that can challenge nationalist narratives.

In addition, I showed that the scenic presentation of national achievements mobilizes resources that can in turn spoil the presentation. Just as Brasília, the model city of Brazilian modernity, provided the material conditions for the growth of shantytowns that could never embody the supreme rationality of nationality, so were all the great tourist projects and grand international macroprojects born with their own dirty twins. On the other hand, even the most avant-garde example of national modernity ages, thus creating new challenges to national identity and the state.[22]

In each of these cases, contact zones frame relationships in which the logic of national development clashes with the transnational logic of modernization, and they exist because the production and consumption of commodities is a transnational process, because people can cross national borders for work or recreation, and because there is an international horizon of scientific and technological progress. Therefore, contact zones are border areas between the logic of the nation-state and capitalist progress that exist within the national space.

## Conclusion

I conclude with some thoughts on the implications that these frames of contact have for the construction of internal frontiers between social groups in the national framework. It is clear enough that frames of contact created by commercial and tourist relationships, labor migration, and scientific and artistic production produce instability in the internal forms of social distinction. This instability is reflected both in fashion cycles and in the reconfiguration and reproduction of social classes.

For example, when the Mexican state assigned itself the task of modernizing, national elites immediately took on the cosmopolitan role par excellence: they were the official agents of foreign contact because their patriotism, their resources, and their educated taste gave them greater access to the civilizing horizon. Thus, the "comprador elites" of Mexico's nineteenth century inhabited a contact zone that ideally served to discriminate between the aspects of modernity that were desirable and those that were undesirable to the nation. Their maturity and special role gave them license to fashions and affectations that they would then try to bar from general consumption in their countries. Only a strong cultural elite could design the ticket that a weak and backward country needed to be allowed into the "concert of nations."

However, Mexican elites have not always been able to maintain a privileged position in the area of foreign contacts. The migrant who manages to become the owner of an auto-repair shop in Los Angeles can return to his village with more money, prestige, and knowledge of the modern than the old political boss there. An Indian from Zinacantán, Chiapas, may converse more extensively and gain more information from an American anthropologist than the mestizo rancher who oppresses him. Moreover, the spectacular growth of the middle class in the second half of the twentieth century also made the political brokerage of the "civilizing horizon" increasingly difficult to sustain. Thus, neither the government nor the political class has full control over the national image.

Here, it seems to me, is a key to understanding the internal dynamic of the frontiers of social distinction, and even of violence. A social movement that can cast doubts on the national image may become the object of state violence. At times, violence explodes when a group whose members had been designated as part of the nation's traditional residue prefers to shape its own separate political community and paths to progress. Violence also erupts when the state insists on controlling spaces where there is little possibility of establishing the ideal order in a permanent fashion but where the ideal order must nonetheless be asserted. This is the case of violence against itinerant commerce or against illegal housing settlements. It is also occasionally deployed against social movements that governments cannot assimilate as properly national because they conspire against the country's public image. This is the case of much of the repression against youth subcultures.

We cannot conclude from these examples, however, that patrolling the national image is only the concern of the government, of political classes, or of other elites, for these same contact zones are also used to denounce sectors of these very elites as strangers to the national community. Thus, elite-directed attempts to change mores and social practice can be targeted and ridiculed as Americanized, Francophile, Jewish, or Oriental. Attempts to professionalize the state bureaucracy have at times been portrayed as "technocratic" reforms, and therefore as Americanizing. Criticism of new forms of consumption, such as fast-food chains or brand fetishism, are other common examples.

On the political plane, the Porfirian cultural elite, the *científicos* who had such a key historical role in shaping Mexico's national image, was portrayed by Mexico's revolutionaries as foreign. Marxist parties during the Cold War portrayed the Mexican government as a pawn of U.S. interests. Harvard-trained President Carlos Salinas was often compared to the national traitor Santa Anna after the fall of the peso in 1995. These denunciations are thus used both in the construction of difference and in the organization of political opposition.

Nation builders try to fashion the national image the same way that people build a house. Starting with the most modern materials and designs at their disposal, they want to have diverse, functionally and hierarchically organized interior spaces, including spaces for exhibition to whoever comes in from outside. All this is ideally governed by the political equivalent of a paterfamilias who seeks the entire family's orderly modernization and regulates contacts between his home and the outside world. However, national architecture and space do not have the stability of a house and the government lacks a patriarch's security because the nation's internal order is always warped by transformations in the conditions of production, consumption, and communication. Therefore, nationalism's dirty linen can be exposed by the exploited stepdaughter, the disinherited son, or the affronted mother if there is a window—a contact frame—that permits them to do so. This relative openness and permeability of national space becomes a dynamic factor in the production of fashions and distinctions, but it is also the root of xenophobia and violence.

# 7

## Ritual, Rumor, and Corruption

## in the Formation of Mexican Polities

This chapter provides a perspective on the connections between ritual and polity in Mexico. Evidently, constructing even the roughest map of this relationship is a daunting task, both empirically and conceptually. Nevertheless, as the number of historical and anthropological studies of ritual and politics grows, so too does the need to construct various organizing perspectives.[1] I shall propose such a vantage point here by exploring the historical connections between various sorts of rituals and the development of a nationally articulated public sphere. My ultimate goal is to clarify the connection between political ritual and the constitution of political communities in the national space.

In order to carry out this aim, I propose a line of historical and spatial inquiry that is driven by a set of methodological and theoretical innovations that may be summarized as follows. First, I hypothesize a complex relationship between the existence of areas of free political discussion and the centrality of political ritual as an arena where political decisions are negotiated and enacted. At any given local level, the relationship between public discussion and ritual is negative: ritual substitutes for discussion and vice versa. However, when one sees the relationship in an integrated national space, the relationship can be complementary: localized political rituals become the stuff from which a (restricted) nationally relevant public sphere derives its legitimacy. Second, I propose a few characteristics of the geography of public spheres (in the plural), emphasizing the fact that civic discussion in Mexico has been segmented along class and regional lines, and that the consolidation of national public opinion has always been an problematic affair. Third, I posit that the creation of a national public sphere in this spatially segmented field of opinion and discussion involves creating mechanisms for privileged interpretations of a diffuse "popular will." I therefore explore the relationship between political ritual, rumor, and the dramatization of political interests. Finally, I argue that there is a general relationship between political ritual and localized appropriations of state institutions (corruption). The expansion of state institutions is historically linked to the conflicting demands of antagonistic local groups, a factor that strengthens the importance of ritual, of festivities, and of the redistributive actions that are associated with them. As a result, there is a connection between footing the bill of these rituals and the ways in which state institutions are appropriated. The inception and growth of state institutions involves the production of ritual, so the patrons of these rituals have a degree of control over the local branches of those institutions.

## Locating Public Spheres

François Xavier Guerra has painted a portrait of Mexico's nineteenth century in which he maintains that Mexico's traditional political and social organization was left without a political ideology and program to support it after independence. Without the monarchy, the nation's regions, its political bosses and clients, its corporate indigenous communities, hacendados, and retainers had to create or accommodate to a system of political representation that was in theory based on equal individual rights.[2]

Thus an idealized national community was shaped by an elite made up of military leaders, hacendados, miners, merchants, and intellectuals whose discussions occurred in institutional forums provided by Freemasonry, by the development of a commercial press, by a few urban literary and scientific institutes, and in salons and social gatherings (tertulias). This elite was the national public opinion that mattered, and its ideas and ideals were formally nationalized in institutions such as Congress, the supreme court, and the national presidency.

As a result, there was considerable distance between what occurred in the national public sphere that was shaped by the opinion of these men of substance and the way in which popular interests were actually interpreted and dealt with by the government. For example, Porfirio Díaz maintained a remarkable, continuous, private correspondence with all of his governors and some *jefes políticos* and local notables. In this correspondence, regional issues were frankly discussed, instructions were received, and suggestions were provided. Governors would, in their turn, meet with representatives of what Guerra calls the principal "collective actors" of their regions: representatives of villages, *jefes políticos*, heads of elite families of hacendados, merchants, and miners, and they would engage in closed-door discussions that paralleled those that had been carried out with Díaz. Finally, these leaders would institute the new policies.

Thus, public opinion was constructed almost exclusively by elites, and there was no open national or regional forum for civic discussion during the *porfiriato* (or, a fortiori, in any of the previous regimes). On the other hand, the various collective actors whose leaders were brought together in closed-door discussions also had their own local forms and forums of communication, some of which involved free public discussion and some of which did not, and the criteria of inclusion in these forums were also diverse and not always based on citizenship. This is why it is necessary to speak of public *spheres* (in the plural).

## Overview of Mexican Public Spheres

Mexican cities in the preindustrial age had as their main collective actors local urban elites (merchants, miners, hacendados, church authorities, civil and military authorities), artisanal guilds, and petty merchants, Indian community members, and an urban rabble that at times acted collectively but had no official corporate status. In rural areas, major relevant collective actors for this early period included textile workers and miners, inhabitants of haciendas and of ranches, and inhabitants of peasant communities. Most of these collectivities were organized in the religious plane in *cofradías* (sodalities for the cult of saints) and were also visible as collectivities in the period's best-attended events, such as bullfights, the *entrada* of a viceroy, archbishop, *alcalde mayor*, or priest, or major religious festivities.[3]

Participation in these *cofradías* provided occasions to discuss the internal affairs of the collective actors. This is probably the cause of the occasional conflicts that emerged between local authorities and slave and black *cofradías*, and of colonial regulations regarding the place and time when these brotherhoods could meet.[4] The organization around the cult of each collective actor's patron saint also allowed discussion and expression of collective interests within each of those groups.

Colonial society offered no political arena in which discussions could be publicized and broadened, so each group depended on the crown's justice. Direct arbitration, added to investigative political reporting (climaxing in the famous *visitas*), was crucial. Newspapers, which were introduced in the 1720s, did not become a forum for public discussion until the late eighteenth century, and then discussions were limited to scientific and technical questions. For the most part, newspapers provided short information briefs on the ritual life of the city, glorifying the political life of the colony (for years, each issue of the *Gaceta de México* began with a short biographical note on a past viceroy or archbishop), and occasionally announcing major international events (battles won in Europe, ships coming in and out of Veracruz and Acapulco).

In short, collectivities were represented in the ritual life of the kingdom but their problems were not examined in a national forum of public opinion. Instead, collectivities relied on the crown's justice and on its respect for acquired and traditional rights and prerogatives (*usos y costumbres*) or, at best, on some discussion and debate of these rights in the town council.

Each of these corporate groups was made up of networks of families, friends, neighbors, patrons, clients, and allies. These networks have generally not been characterized in communicative terms by free dialogue and discussion.

Elite families, for example, have been known to gather hundreds of members in family rituals and to construct complex webs of communication within these large groups. Yet, most of these familial decisions and debates could not be said to occur democratically because members do not confer in an unrestricted fashion. Instead, discussion occurs in a hierarchical framework: women and men argue in different ways and places, and there are rules of seniority and significant status differentials between major power holders and weaker family members, who are systematically inhibited from participating in discussion. Thus there is a rich ritual life in elite families, where the results of complex negotiations, alliances, and decisions are displayed, but these do not add up to an "open" forum of public discussion. Instead, familial ritual and communicative practice are more akin as a decision-making process to what Habermas called "representative publicity," that is, public representation of the whole on the basis of hierarchical status, and not as the result of free internal discussion.[5]

The same conclusion applies to the typically smaller kindred of peasants, workers, artisans, and small merchants: we see significant familial rituals, strong channels of information, and opinions coming from all members of the family, but only limited intrafamilial discussion by members as equals. Instead, information and opinions are weighed by powerful family members who make up their minds and impose their decisions.[6]

Of the main agrarian collective actors (hacienda and ranch dwellers, mine and *obraje* textile workers, and peasant communities), only peasant villages developed institutionalized local public spheres. Unions were prohibited in haciendas, factories, and mines, and the fact that hacienda workers often lived on the land of the owners limited open discussion between members of those collectivities. Instead, discussion was informal, with no forum to focus collectively on a single issue and to sound out a collective will. Discussion among equals operated as rumor, while public life was dominated by ritual and by centrally controlled forms of publicity.

In most peasant communities, in contrast, we have both a ritualized display of community and a public sphere based on discussion and deliberation. This public sphere has had various forms, with institutions such as town meetings, meetings of the *juntas de mejoras*, the Lion's Club, or the *asociaciones de padres de familia* serving as forums of discussion. Discrimination by sex in these forums varies and has received little systematic attention from either anthropologists or historians.[7] Although my impression is that they are usually dominated by men, there is also plenty of female participation, and many key instances where women are the central players.[8] But it must be noted that, in addition to the various community-wide forums, there are sex-specific forums of discussion and debate, including paradigmatic forums such as the *cantina* (bar) for men and the water well or the washing area *(lavadero)* for women, and these should alert us to the need to describe the gendered spaces of discussion and their interconnections in various local contexts.

In sum, the institutional spaces that stand out as having been arenas of discussion among equals are associated with village or urban life. The bar, the well, the village or school association, the *cofradía*, the Rotaries, or the town meeting allow for some public discussion that may have been somewhat less limited by the strictures of family authority on one side, and state authority on the other.

The articulation of various local forums into a national public sphere developed in distinct historical moments: (1) after independence, with the constitution of a national public sphere, (2) with the birth of modern industry during the *porfiriato*, (3) with the incorporation of a workers' sector into the reigning party after the revolution, (4) with the emergence of middle-class professional groups in the mid-twentieth century, (5) with the emergence of an independent union movement (1970s), (6) with the emergence of social movements that do not explicitly represent class interests but focus rather on selected issues such as housing, women's rights, defense against development projects, and so on.

Although I do not wish to go into each of these developments here, a few considerations on the transformation of the public sphere are needed. First, with independence, a nationally articulated public sphere emerged for the first time, with the commercial press and Congress as its two main forums. This transition meant that arbitration from the political center was no longer the only, or even necessarily the principal, way of arguing for the rights of a collective actor. Instead of merely expressing the collectivity's inclusion in the realm by way of the main fiestas, these collectivities sometimes found their *usos y costumbres* (traditional rights) being debated and changed in the new national public sphere, and this without any local imput. This was notably the case of indigenous communities, whose traditional institutions came under attack almost immediately after independence, and who lost most of their legal protection in just a few decades.

Moreover, most of the social actors of the period were illiterate and lacked property and other characteristics that were deemed central to being a citizen. Because of this, the ritualized representation of a national order continued to be of significance, although liberal governments fought hard to wrench this system of representation out of the hands of the church and into those of civil authorities. This process was politically painful and was never achieved in its entirety. The difficulty was in part owing to the fact that the civil framework set up by liberals had no room for formally recognizing the collective actors that were on the scene, whereas these had previously been acknowledged in the organization of *cofradías*, in the commemoration of patron saints, and in major religious fiestas such as Corpus Christi and Easter.

In other words, the creation of a national public sphere, "fictitious" and highly imperfect though it was, was a real threat to the traditional status of collective actors, because it set up an arena where new rules could be made that affected the very foundations of the collectivities in question. In this respect, the struggle against the clergy in the nineteenth and twentieth centuries takes on special significance, for the conflicts were not only connected to the power of the church as it has usually been considered (land, wealth, influence through schooling), but they issued, much more subtly, because the church had provided spaces of representation and political mediation for a series of collectivities. This ran headlong against the liberal project of creating a national citizenry that was shaped by individual opinion. The ultimate results of this clash in the nineteenth century are well known: a de jure separation of church and state, and a convulsive history of struggle over local rights between various classes and communities.

The second significant consideration on the transformation of the public sphere concerns the formation of a modern proletariat and its historical connections to the public sphere. In the initial phases of modernization, the Mexican proletariat found little room for expression or representation in government. A proletarian public sphere did emerge, however, around trade unions and with the help of the penny press, and it produced two of Mexico's most noteworthy intellectuals, the anarchist revolutionary Ricardo Flores Magón and the artist José Guadalupe Posada.

In other words, the early stages of modernization—especially in mining and in textiles—saw the constitution of proletarian collective actors and the articulation of the proletariat to the national public sphere, although both of these processes were hindered by state repression, as well as by low literacy rates and by the many social ties that Mexican workers have with nonproletarian kinsmen and friends.

After the 1910 revolution, such proletarian organizations and voices found much support from government, which took a leading role in organizing and coordinating union confederations—first the Confederación Regional de Obreros Mexicanos (CROM) and later the Confederación de Trabajadores de México (CTM), which still hobbles along today. This process, however, also led to the formal inclusion of unions in the official party apparatus, a situation that ultimately weakened that class's internal forums of discussion and compromised proletarian inclusion in civic, nongovernmental forums. A comparable process occurred with peasants who, thanks to the political strings that were attached to land reform, were effectively incorporated in the state's "masses." Thus we get relatively weak presence of these two classes in the nationally articulated public sphere. This meant that these collectivities maintained arbitrated and ritualized relationships with the state that were in some respects comparable to those that existed in the colonial era, except for the fact that the state— through a particularly rich development of nationalist mythology—was able to wrench most of these ritual functions away from the church.

Among the first collective actors to run headlong against this "neobaroque" system were the new middle classes. Ricardo Pozas Horcasitas has described this process in his study of the medical doctors' movement of early 1960s. These doctors cared little for revolutionary rhetoric. They had already been trained in a fully modern era, and expected the benefits of modernity without the forms of state tutelage that had been imposed on most peasant and working-class collectivities. They also expected to control their own discussions and to have free access to the press.[9]

The government showed a distinct unwillingness to open up to these new political actors, either by conceding liberties for self-organization or by allowing greater freedom of access to media and policymaking. Repression of the emerging middle classes continued throughout the 1960s and into the early 1970s, after which point the government began to embark on a series of political reforms that are collectively known as "the transition to democracy."

Middle-class pressures on the Mexican corporate state (movements of doctors, schoolteachers, students, parents' associations, etc.) grew in tandem with the development of the "new social movements," which were no longer strictly class-based and were not directed toward the control or redistribution of the benefits of production, but rather centered on the conditions of reproduction: housing, urban services, pollution control, schooling, parks, transportation costs, women's rights, and so on.

It is important to note, with regard to these movements, that many of them were not new in a strict sense: Castells has described the renters' strike in Veracruz in 1915 as a case in point, and urban riots in the colonial and early national period were concerned with issues such as grain prices, conflicts between church and state, and abuses by priests.[10] What is new about the movements beginning in the 1970s is their scale, which reflects the vertiginous growth of cities, and particularly of Mexico City, the diversification of demands on government as an institution responsible for providing an ever-expanding set of services and forms of social protection, and the fact that, being goal-oriented, these movements sometimes lacked mechanisms for defining participants as stable members of collectivities. This final point means that movements usually jell around leaders and issues and can then decline to such an extent that they define a *generation* rather than a collectivity that reproduces through time.

All of these conditions meant that the "new" social movements had enormous potential for widening the base of discussion that made up national public opinion, and that they were not easy to incorporate to the sectorial apparatus of the official party and the state. The combination of these variegated pressures, including those from professional and protoprofessional middle classes and nonincorporated unions and peasant communities, forced the state to develop new strategies of encompassment and inclusion, as well as to expand forms of access to national public opinion.

I have provided a historical overview of Mexico's main "collective actors" and have pointed to their internal forums of discussion and their connections to the state through ritual, closed-door discussion and decision making, and to the national public sphere. In addition, I have given some elements with which to imagine these various collectivities in their regional locations. It is in connection to these factors that a profitable discussion of the place and role of political rituals can take place.

## Political Ritual in National and Regional Space

A poignant introduction to the role of ritual in consolidating Mexican political communities can be found in the early contact period, which was a time when the capacity for dialogue between Spaniards and Indians was minimal, and powerful interests were vested in maintaining some miscommunication between them.[11]

At that time, a Franciscan friar, Jacobo de Testera, sought to create an atmosphere that was propitious for the rapid conversion of Indians, an atmosphere that would not require extensive communication between Indians and priests. To this end he used a form of pictographic writing in which icons were to be spoken out in indigenous tongues, while the sounds that were thereby emitted approximated those of the Latin orations of the Mass. Through a mock form of reading, Testera put Christian orations in the Indians' mouths: they read out "flag" and "prickly pear" (*pantli, noxtli*), he heard something quite like *"Pater noster,"*[12] and this misunderstanding allowed both parties to participate in a critical communitarian ritual: the Mass. Thus, at a time when there was no bourgeois public sphere in Mexico, before the existence of a national language or even of a coherent project for a national language, rituals were a fundamental arena for constructing political boundaries and relations of domination and subordination within the polity.

Gruzinski has written extensively on the crucial significance of nondiscursive forms of communication in the conquest and colonization of the Indians. He has shown the centrality of icons in this communicative process, and has even spoken of a "war of images" in lieu of public debate. At the level of images, and especially in ritual, pragmatic accommodations between participants may occur without any corresponding accommodation at the level of formally stated policy or discourse. This sort of politics—pragmatic accommodation while formally adhering to a discursive orthodoxy—has been insistently remarked upon by observers of Mexico, some of whom trace its beginnings to Hernán Cortés, whose dictum to King Charles—"I obey, but I do not comply"—has become famous.[13]

In fact, historian Irving Leonard felt that this was a defining characteristic of the dominant aesthetic sensibility of the so-called Baroque era
(roughly 1580–1750), which was based on rigid adherence to a few basic
principles of Catholic dogma and to the application of wit to embroider-
ing around them.[14] Likewise, Gruzinski argues that the transition into the
Baroque era of representation was accompanied by an attack on Indian
learning, by the decline of the book among the popular classes, and its
substitution by images that were conventional.[15]

This profoundly antidialogic trend did not die along with the Counter-
Reformation. Mexico's Enlightenment and Positivist eras were also characterized by the use of modernity as a rhetoric that departs from everyday
practice in civic life.[16] Generally speaking, anthropologists and historians
have recognized that Mexico has a legalistic, formulaic tradition that is
combined with keen political pragmatism, a pragmatism that has often
been compared to Machiavellianism.[17] The flexibility that Mexicans may
lack at the level of formal political discourse and discussion they have in
political practice, and these accommodations are enacted in ritual and
its imagery. Correspondingly, the study of ritual allows us to witness the
ideological articulations of a society that has always been both highly segmented and systematically misrepresented in formal discourse.

In sum, ritual is a critical arena for the construction of pragmatic political accommodations where few open, dialogic forms of communication
and decision making exist. In other words, there is an inverse correlation
between the social importance of political ritual and that of the public
sphere. Moreover, one could add a culturalist argument to this sociological one: once the Spaniards abandoned all serious attempts truly to convince and assimilate Indians into their society, certain aesthetic forms were
developed (the colonial versions of "baroque sensibility"), and these became values that permeated the society deeply, affecting family relations,
forms of etiquette, and other social forms in all social strata. Thus Mexican
ritual and ritualism would have both sociological and cultural roots.

This very general appreciation is merely a starting point, however, for
in order to organize the variegated literature on political ritual and, furthermore, to propose an agenda for future research, we need to arrive at a more
precise formulation of the specific sorts of political work that ritual does
and has done in different regional and historical contexts. I focus on three
main points here: First, I argue that political ritual reflects the dialectics of
opposition and appropriation between state agencies and collectivities.
This point leads us away from a simple opposition between popular and
state ritual. Second, I discuss some of the interconnections between ritual

and rumor. Specifically, I argue that both ritual and rumor can be seen as occupying spaces of expression that cannot find other ways into the public sphere. Ritual can serve as a way of constructing a high level of regional integration with only a minimum substratum of common culture and, especially, of discussion. This view leads away from looking at Mexican history as a simple secular process toward democracy and modernity. Third, I discuss the connections between ritual and corruption. This point helps to clarify the ways in which the state is locally appropriated and in which a hegemonic order is constituted.

## Ritual and the Expansion of State Institutions

A good starting point is to explore the relationship between Foucauldian institutions (with their techniques of bodily discipline) and rituals that aim to construct an image of consensus around a notion of "the people" (*el pueblo*). In a study of the history of patriotic festivals in the state of Puebla (1900–46), Mary Kay Vaughn shows that the interconnection between schools and festivals passed through two stages: during the *porfiriato*, festivals were organized by the local *jefe político* with the aid of the local elite of hacendados, ranchers, and notables. Civic fiestas emphasized the patriotic participation of Pueblans especially (May 5—the battle of Puebla—was the main celebration). At the same time, schools catered mainly to the notable families and, to a lesser extent, to inhabitants of the main *cabeceras* (municipal seats), but they decidedly excluded the rural and poor majority.[18]

After the revolution, the strength of schools was undermined concomitantly with the strengthening of the agrarian community and the weakening of the regional elites. Schoolteachers did not have the coercive power that prerevolutionary *jefes políticos* once had, so they could not organize local work parties in support of the school and federal funds were insufficient. This situation began to turn around in the 1930s through the revival of the patriotic fiesta by the teachers, who now used competitive sports to draw in a wide constituency. These sporting competitions became a venue for local social life as well as for traditional forms of competition and sociability between villages and barrios. As a result, local agrarian communities vied in getting schools built and provided the badly needed support for their sustenance.

Hence, perhaps the most fundamental modern institution of discipline and uniformity, the school, spread not so much as a result of state imposition as by its capacity to bridge and reconcile state plans with various forms of local politics. The school became, in fact, an alternative arena for giving materiality and visibility to local communities in a way that is analogous to the role that the church had played in the colonial period, and ritual (the patriotic festival, with its attractive sports features) played a central role in the expansion of schools just as the religious fiesta, with its secular and spiritual attractions, had been central to the earlier expansion of the church.

Vaughn provides a valuable clue for understanding the ways in which the revolutionary state succeeded in taking representational functions over from the church. In the Porfirian arrangement, schools and patriotic festivals were mainly organized by and for regional elites, and the church still provided the broadest arena for the political assertion of collective force in its fiestas. It is only after the revolution, with the decline in the coercive power of local politicians and the introduction of competitive sports, that the civic fiesta became a forum in any way comparable to the church fiesta, and, interestingly, it is only at this point that rural schoolteachers mustered the local support they needed to really expand the school system with the tight budgets that they have always had.[19]

In other words, state institutions expand in a fashion that is dependent on the local, regional, and national politics of culture. The institutions that create an idea of simultaneous national development are also constrained by the various local cultural and political forces.

The results of this situation have varied historically as the force of modern institutions has grown, but overall they may be synthesized as follows: in Mexico, public opinion and national sentiment still have public popular ritual as a critical forum, and the leveling media of the bourgeois public sphere (newspapers, television, Congress) have generally been used as a tool for providing a discursive interpretation and solution to the ritual manifestations of "popular will."

Evidently, this situation had been intermingled with the lack of a formal democracy in Mexico, but it would be a mistake to attribute this lack of democracy exclusively to a dictatorial imposition from the presidency: authoritarianism is the product of complex interconnections between various local, national, and international forces. Moreover, there developed a culture of accommodation to these circumstances, including well-established forms for expressing political demands, for interpreting them, and for resolving them.

This does not mean, however, that the role of political ritual has remained constant in Mexico since the Baroque era. Nor does it imply a simple substitution of church ritual by state ritual. The extension of schools has long-term effects on the local community that are distinct from those of the church, because schooling eases movement across the national space in search for work, and therefore ultimately contributes to weakening the agrarian community. I merely suggest that the system of political and cultural representation of the Baroque needs to be taken seriously as a precedent in order to understand the role of political ritual to this day, and that this is because religious and civic ritual is a key to understanding the expansion of state institutions in Mexico.

## Rumor, Ritual, and the Public Sphere

I have argued that throughout Mexican history there have been various social organizational forms and collective actors that have not developed the sort of open discussion of the classical bourgeois public sphere. This does not imply, of course, that communication does not exist within these groups, or that they are incapable of arriving at collective agreements or of representing these agreements in public. It means simply that public sentiment is formed in communicative contexts other than those of an open dialogue between equal citizens.

Hierarchical organizations such as landholding families, haciendas, or factories do not have free internal discussion, nor can their individual members always participate in the formation of national public opinion because they have usually had restricted access to the media. For the members of these subaltern groups, opinion is formed in the sort of context that Erving Goffman has called a "backstage": in the kitchen, in the washroom, while bending down to plant or pick, in the marketplace, or in the anonymity of a crowd.

These are the spaces where information flows. Because they are "backstage," they are typically seen as subversive of official truths as well as of the national public sphere, and they are correspondingly feminized. Thus, in Mexico, "frank," "open" talk at public meetings is often contrasted to "washerwoman's gossip" (*chismes de lavadero o de asotea*), and political dialogue is characterized as "manly" (direct, open, rational), whereas rumor is cowardly (it occurs behind one's back), it is "women's talk" (*chisme de viejas*).

This form of mapping gender onto the frontstage/backstage relationship between public spheres and the multistranded currents of rumor can be understood as a ploy for undermining the validity of rumor and it should not be taken as a de facto correspondence between a feminine/masculine dichotomy and public sphere/rumor. The same rumors that are feminized and called "washerwomen's gossip" one day can be hailed as the egregious "sentiments of the nation" the next day. Moreover, backstage communication is not a prerogative of women, just as many women engage in public speaking.

It is useful to think of rumor as following the negative mold of the various public spheres that have been discussed. Wherever civic discussion and open argument are precluded by the asymmetries of power, alternative communicative relationships emerge and rumor predominates. In Mexico, the nationally articulated public sphere has never achieved widespread credence—too many voices are excluded from it. Because of this, people usually prefer a personal source of information ("gossip") to a merely official one.[20]

This situation leads to Mexico's classical legitimacy crisis: how to interpret, conform, or channel what José María Morelos called "the sentiments of the nation." As we have seen, intellectuals have had a leading role in filling this communicational void, just as newspapers became a privileged media for the interpretation of national sentiment.

Nevertheless, intellectuals, like the oracles of old, need *signs*. Going out and asking citizens in a systematic fashion was always seen as problematic, and has only gained ground in recent years.[21] This is because the poll involves making the backstage front stage; in other words, it involves constructing a free-flowing, confessional relationship between citizens and the state, a relationship that involves a corresponding notion of governmental accountability. Because this accountability did not exist under authoritarian forms of corporativism, neither could a candid relationship be built except in cases where "citizens" felt that they had little to lose, and perhaps something to gain.

The signs that intellectuals and politicians read are therefore complex, for political manifestations are interpreted mainly in their expressive and symptomatic dimensions. Hence the work of interpreting national sentiment does not end with the gathering of opinions, for opinions that are unlinked to action, opinions that have no practical consequence, are easily discounted as "women's gossip" or "talk." The true national sentiment is only meaningful in connection to public action, to political ritual. I say "ritual" because the weakness of Mexico's national public sphere guarantees that political events will be interpreted symbolically, with expressive dimensions counting at least as much as instrumental ones.[22]

Moreover, significant differences emerge between political manifestations that are geared to the media and events that are oriented to direct action in smaller-scale collectivities. Interesting in this respect is the use of masks in two recent cases, that of "Superbarrio" in Mexico City and that of the neo-Zapatistas in Chiapas. The use of masks allows for a more abstract identification of a movement with "the people," and as such its demands can be put forward in a clearer way to the public and the specter of co-optation of a specific leader or of a small constituency diminishes. The use of masks is a Brechtian sort of strategy, effacing the individual and stressing the social persona by relying on images derived from the mass media.

This is entirely different from ritualized social movements that are not directed to the media that represent national public opinion, for example, in small towns. In those cases, "the people" are represented directly by known people, and it is the presence of particular *individuals* that convinces others to join in. Consequently, these movements are not mediated by a national public; they are direct expressions of local opinion and, although at times they seek support from national media and public opinion, they do not usually entertain high hopes for the efficacy of these mediations.

Also interesting is the use of inversions of public and domestic realms in mediated versus face-to-face movements. Whereas in local movements these sorts of inversions are direct appeals to revolt, in mediated movements they serve as pointed appeals to public opinion and are thus *gestures* of revolt. Thus, middle- and upper-class women take to the streets of Mexico City to protest the construction of a highway or to protest the high costs of a devaluation. This provides powerful "photo opportunities" for an urban movement. Similarly, ranchers from the Altos de Jalisco fill Guadalajara's central square with tractors to protest new agricultural policies. The inversions of public and domestic spheres are usually more sharply subversive in smaller communities, where local opinion can immediately be swayed. For example, when women took to the streets in Tepoztlán in 1978, the men backed them and took over the municipal presidency. In the mediated urban context (which is an ever-growing field, given the current expansion of the national public sphere into ever-deeper levels of the regional system), inversions are used as appeals to a public opinion that will then exert pressure on government by nonviolent means.

In sum, whereas many collectivities are routinely recognized and reconstituted in rituals that can substitute open internal discussion, there are also political manifestations of public sentiment that are created in backstage contexts, socialized through rumor, and converted into specific movements that can be analyzed as political ritual because their significance depends on their mode of insertion in a body of public opinion that is not smoothly created out of discussions in the public sphere. The theatrical element is therefore of special importance.

The centrality of ritual in the constitution of polity can therefore be understood in two dimensions: on the one hand, rituals can be expressions of collective vitality and interests within the sanctioned political order; on the other hand, public political manifestations are understood as expressions of a public sentiment that is constructed in the backstage, and that has therefore not (yet) been harnessed by the state. This second dimension means that political movements are heavily ritualized. They are in fact the main signs that political interpreters read.

### Corruption and Ritual

I have suggested three important roles that ritual has in the constitution of political communities in Mexico. First, on the most general level, ritual is crucial because social segmentation and power relations undermine dialogue in the national community. Second, ritual has been used to build alliances between local collectivities and state and church. The dialectics of this process involves competition or struggle between collectivities or classes, and alliances with state or church are used to further local interests in those struggles. Third, ritual is critical to the constitution of national public opinion in an authoritarian state because it is the principal sign that interpreters read, occupying a role that is analogous to that of the poll (and that is no less manipulable); ritual substitutes for a bourgeois public sphere. In this section, I inspect the relationship between ritual and corruption in the Mexican system.

The problem of corruption can be understood on three levels: first, on a functional level (what it does for government, what it does for individual participants and victims); second, at the level of accusations of corruption (what a discourse of corruption does in the world of politics); and third, at the level of the moral sensibility of a people (how discourses and practices of corruption affect personal attitudes and definitions of self).

Throughout Mexican history, corruption has consisted of appropriating portions of state or church machinery for private benefit (arguably), to the detriment of the state's interest as well as that of the public. However, these appropriations serve various functions and have varying implications during different periods. For example, throughout the colonial period, official governmental posts were seen as prizes that the crown handed down in recognition either of social proximity or of past favors, or else in exchange for money. Correspondingly, officials were expected to profit from their posts: they were not civil servants, but rather royal servants. Comparable situations have existed well into the modern period.

Because the church was the fundamental arena for collective expression, and because it had its own independent sources of taxation, corruption in the church was also important. Local constituencies could at times play these two sets of ambitions off against each other. Villagers participated fervently in their fiestas in part as a show of alliance with the church, which might then intervene in their favor against the abuse of landowners or officials, whereas suits against priests could be brought to civil authorities. Local ritual could also stand as an affirmation of local rights against both church and state, both of which could easily conspire against the subaltern classes. Ritual had a mediating role in the colonial period, where the boundaries, strength, and rights of a collectivity could be expressed at the same time that alliances were forged with the church or the state.

In this context of negotiation, corruption was reflected in what might be called an extended "cargo system." Anthropologists have been prone to take a narrow view of what religious cargos are about, stressing their significance in indigenous communities and their links to forms of prestige that are allotted only within the limits of traditional communities. In fact, variations of "cargo systems" exist and have existed throughout the national space, and the burden of paying for celebrations has usually reflected the expected distribution of the benefits of reigning. For example, Mexico City notables and officers had to come up with money for all sorts of commemorations of the royal family's affairs, as well as those of the viceroy. Smaller towns and villages had to incur parallel expenditures to commemorate their saint's day. But it was these very forms of public festival that also gave political recognition to these places and allowed for the funneling of resources to the community leadership.

This same logic survived into the national period. In Tepoztlán, for instance, carnival became the most expensive fiesta and was bankrolled to a large degree by the local notables. This contrasted with the humble barrio fiesta, which was paid for by collective contributions. Local notables funneled their money into *comparsas* (dance organizations) that represented their barrio of origin; thus notables created solidarity with poorer members of their barrios and subsequently depended on this local basis of support to successfully control municipal offices during the nineteenth century and most of the twentieth century.

In the Morelos highlands, de la Peña has described how hacienda owners increased their popularity and that of the municipal notables by contributing resources to the local fiesta.[23] Finally, in Zinacantán, the classic and much-debated instance of the traditional "cargo system," Cancian has shown that financing local fiestas was a crucial item of prestige and local power for many years, and that the system only came into crisis when the local economy diversified and the population grew, creating a split between the older peasant notables and younger capitalist entrepreneurs.[24] The elders have kept the young generation from sponsoring the fiestas, and the cargo system has therefore declined as a locus of political expression.

The correlation between financing festivities and reaping the benefits of the state (or of appropriating local branches of the state) has parallels in the ways in which the PRI's political campaigns are financed. Until the democratic reforms of the 1990s, calculating costs of official party campaigns was impossible, because, instead of working with a centralized coffer and budget, campaign costs were diffused among supporters, all of whom expected to benefit from the state in exchange for these expenditures. Governors and municipal presidents used up their budgets to show their personal support of a presidential candidate and, through that personal support, the support of the collectivities to which they were linked. Union leadership that had privileged support from the government used union funds and working hours to support the candidate. As in the fiesta, participants in campaign events were also meant to gain things for themselves: a day off work, free food, and a fiesta, or at least a renewed relationship with their immediate patron.

Thus, political ritual has been tied to corruption because the financing of ritual reflects the actual or expected ways in which local leaders and communities appropriate portions of the state apparatus—these rituals are enactments both of a personalized style of state redistribution and of the power of the whole constituency vis-à-vis the more abstract national state.

The connection between fiesta and corruption does not end here, however, for most fiestas combine a controlled and an unrestricted aspect. Solemn Masses are followed by turkey in mole sauce, drinking, and dancing; carnival ends with the High Mass of Ash Wednesday; political rallies typically are followed by free-flowing streams of alcohol. Even the most Apollonian rituals, such as the once popular oratory contests, were peppered with occasional comic or lyric moments, and secular festive events such as the bullfight or the cockfight tended to receive some governmental supervision, with formal moments where supervision was asserted.

This combination of political control and unrestrained popular expression made the fiestas occasions where a certain complex hegemony was enacted, for popular expression was at once unrestrained and encompassed by the authorities. This is the most subtle sense in which political ritual can be said to be tied to the history of corruption: fiestas assert the significance of a collectivity vis-à-vis the state and thus they have been used to jockey for position on the national map. On the other hand, once a collectivity is receiving some benefits from the state, once it has a leader or a class that appropriates the state and represents it locally, these leaders are expected to foot the bill of much political ritual, for the ritual will serve as a manifestation of the collectivity's continued vitality to higher officials. Thus fiestas are usually signs of the vitality of both "the people" and "the state." "Corruption" underwrites this whole relationship because the state is only extended into these collectivities on the condition that it be locally appropriated (usually by local elites) and that some of the benefits of this appropriation spill over to the rest of the local population.

Finally, rituals present popular moral standards regarding corruption. Ungenerous leaders are shunned, as are leaders who do not finance fiestas or do not recognize or acknowledge their own people.[25] In general, an ethics of respect, generosity, and communion is enacted, and these values provide the rudiments of a technology that is used for articulating the national polity. In this respect, the Catholic ritual is a standard that continually haunts the politician.

These pervasive connections between ritual and corruption, both in relation to local appropriations of state machinery and in the construction of an ethics of those appropriations, demonstrate the critical significance of the study of ritual for understanding hegemony in the Mexican national space.

## Conclusion

I have explored the connection between ritual and political communities by looking at public spheres developmentally. In the process, I have suggested relationships between rumor, ritual, and corruption. This analysis leads us away from three trends in the study of political ritual. The first is the one that divides rituals into state versus popular ritual. The second is the trend that tries to construct a secular progress between premodern ritual and modern democracy. Against the first trend, the perspective developed here stresses the dialectics of opposition and appropriation between state agencies and various collectivities. This dialectic affects both the constitution of subjectivities by the state and the ways in which state institutions are locally appropriated. Against the second trend, our perspective stresses the persistent obstacles to the creation of a bourgeois public sphere in Mexico. Mexican modernity continues to segment and exclude large numbers from the promised benefits of citizenship and modernization, and this has allowed for a continuous reconstitution of a ritual life that has its origins in the Baroque era.

For these reasons, the specter of an "ancien régime" seems never to die in Mexico: it survived the 1857 constitution, it survived the revolution, and it may even survive the current transition to democracy. The regional study of ritual offers a way of specifying these relationships, of understanding their historical evolution, and of clarifying the nature of social change in the polity.

Finally, a third trend that must be modified is the one that seeks to synthesize national culture by way of the study of national rituals. Our contribution to this perspective is to show the significance of developing an overall geography of ritual as a necessary prior step. Once this is done (and this chapter is only a beginning of such a geography), the social and political referents of rituals can be clarified and placed in their proper perspective. Because our fundamental thesis is that political ritual is substituting for arenas of discussion and argumentation—creating hegemonic idioms of agreement between various and diverse points of view (cultural and political)—the study of these rituals can serve as an entry to understanding hegemony geographically, but rituals cannot be used to homogenize the culture of their participants in any simple way.

# 8

## Center, Periphery, and the Connections between

## Nationalism and Local Discourses of Distinction

It is now commonplace to recognize that centers and peripheries have historically constituted each other: "the Orient" was as critical for the formation of a narrative about "the West" as European colonialism was to the formation of Asian nationalisms, the Americas and Spain mutually constituted each other, and, much more generally, ideas regarding cultural and economic modernity and modernization rely on constructions of "tradition" and therefore on producing peripheries.

A somewhat less understood dimension of center–periphery relationships is how peripheralization and centralization are practices that can help us to understand the ways in which localized idioms of distinction and political language are created. This point is often overlooked because of the strong temptation to portray centers and peripheries as stable and homogeneous and then to make these categories into vast abstractions: "the West" is central, "the Rest" is peripheral; "the First World" is central, "the Third World" is peripheral. If prompted for greater detail, then a speaker may say, within the Third World, metropolises are central, rural areas are peripheral, or formal sectors are central, informal sectors are peripheral. Such attempts to classify places as central versus as peripheral tend to bracket the fact that center and periphery are always coexisting as elements in idioms of power and of distinction throughout the social system, because center–periphery tropes are hierarchical in Louis Dumont's sense, that is, they involve complementarity and encompassment.[1] Thus, although one may agree that in the late nineteenth century Britain could, on the whole, be classified as central to the world system, while India could be counted as a periphery, we can also recognize that center–periphery discourses were equally relevant for the development of distinction in both places.

In this chapter I explore the historical transformation of center/periphery as a value-laden system of organizing social space in the anthropologically famous village of Tepoztlán, Mexico.[2] My purpose is to show historical changes in the ways in which "the center" has been locally constructed. I also aim to demonstrate a few of the competing strategies for centralization and marginalization as they have played out in local politics of distinction and in the enunciation of local demands to state agencies or for national public opinion.

By focusing on center/periphery as a key metaphor in the dialectics of distinction within Tepoztlán, I wish to leave a nagging paradox behind. When analysts rely on center–periphery metaphors in order to understand what Redfield called "folk societies," they tend either to exoticize the marginal society by analyzing it as if it were culturally coherent, or to deny the existence of a collectively generated "culture" and to substitute that notion with a more atomized, individualistic culture of multiple adaptations. In other words, they tend either to "orientalize" a reified local culture or to dispense with the notion of a locally generated collective culture in favor of something like "adaptation" or even "rational choice." In the case of Tepoztlán, Robert Redfield fell into the orientalizing trap by overdrawing the separation between "folk" and "urban" societies, while Oscar Lewis dissolved Tepoztecan "culture" into a set of pragmatic adaptations to an environment that was shaped by nationally dominant classes and politicos.

This theoretical bind emerges in numerous forms throughout the anthropological and historical literature. Often, differences map onto the opposition that Marshall Sahlins called "culture versus practical reason," where the culturalist will emphasize the internal coherence of local culture (and thereby construct a sharp break between the culture of peripheries and that of centers), while the economic reductionist will emphasize rational adaptations that generate statistically verifiable differences within and between localities that do not add up to a holistic local culture.

Nevertheless, the conceptual origins of this muddle are not restricted to the (by now largely transcended) opposition between a Saussurean-inspired notion of "culture" and practical reason. Part of the conceptual difficulty stems also from lack of attention to the analysis of spatial systems, and specifically to the distinction between various uses of center/periphery as an organizational scheme. The conflation of a center–periphery scheme for the organization of production with a center–periphery scheme for political domination and a center–periphery logic of cultural distinction leads inevitably to the sort of abstracted and idealized cores and peripheries that we seek to reject. It is the muddle in the spatial model—a confusion that can be shared by culturalists and pragmatists—that sets the stage for this ethnographic paradox.

## Consciousness of a Peripheral Status

Tepoztlán is located about seventy kilometers south of Mexico City, in what was until recently the agricultural periphery of the state of Morelos, whose capital is Cuernavaca. Until the early 1960s, this meant that villagers were primarily peasants, many of whom were called "Indians" by city folk. The town as we know it was created between 1550 and 1605 in response to Spanish authorities, who concentrated the more scattered indigenous inhabitants of the jurisdiction called Tepoztlán into a nucleated settlement. Thus, the very constitution of this agricultural village was to some degree orchestrated from without. Later, investors and power holders organized the region that is today called Morelos in such a way that irrigated sugar fields in the lowlands would benefit from cheap seasonal labor, firewood, and grazing lands provided by an impoverished highland peasantry that was concentrated in villages such as Tepoztlán. This decision was renewed from the time of the formation of Spanish landed estates in the late 1500s to the moment of industrialization, beginning in the 1950s.[3]

In short, Tepoztlán occupied a peripheral position from the time of its colonial reconstruction. Economically, it was to serve as a source of tribute, of revenue through commercial exploitation, and of cheap seasonal labor in lowland plantations. Politically, it was defined as an indigenous jurisdiction that was to be controlled from a distance by a Spanish *alcalde* mayor who was, in turn, named by the heirs to Hernán Cortés's estate, the Marquesado del Valle.

"The center" has thus been "in the periphery" for most of Tepoztlán's post-Conquest history, both in the sense that it has had a critical role in fashioning the place, and directly through specific institutions and individuals that have been charged with administering this peripheral status, including evangelizing priests, indigenous rulers, merchants, schoolteachers, policemen, and municipal officers. It is perhaps not surprising, then, that both centrality and marginality have been elaborated in Tepoztecan mythology.

One revealing set of stories that deal with these aspects of Tepoztecan society are about El Tepoztécatl, the mythical "man-god" of Tepoztlán who was meant to be both the local ruler in the pre-Conquest period and the first Indian to become evangelized in the region (on September 8, day of the Virgin of the Nativity, who is said to be his mother and who is also the patroness of Tepoztlán).[4]

The story of El Tepoztécatl has two main portions. One occurs before and at the time of Conquest when El Tepoztécatl vanquishes the lords of major surrounding towns, thereby gaining centrality for Tepoztlán. A second refers to the period shortly after Conquest, and it runs roughly as follows:

> Tepoztécatl's life was exemplary. He helped and protected all of his subjects and Tepoztlán thrived more during his reign than ever before. One day Tepoztécatl went to visit Mexico City and he found that people were having great difficulties in raising the main bell to the tower of Mexico's cathedral. Since Tepoztécatl was a friend of the god of wind, he enlisted his help and the wind god blew a strong whirlwind that blinded everyone while it raised Tepoztécatl into the air, bell and all. When the people looked around, Tepoztécatl was already in the church tower sounding the bell, much to everyone's amazement.
>
> In order to thank Tepoztécatl for his help, they gave him a box and told him to bury it in the main square of his village. Tepoztécatl received it with joy and walked back to Tepoztlán. When he arrived there, people asked him what was in the box. He answered that they had given him the box and that he could not open it, but rather had to bury it, which is what he did. However, people's curiosity was too great and they dug the box up that night and opened it the next morning. When they opened it, four white doves flew out in different directions. One posed itself on the church tower, another on the tower of Mexico's cathedral, a third on the hill where Tepoztécatl lives, and the fourth in the town of Tlayacapan. That is why no one discovered what Tepoztécatl had been given, but allegedly it was a great treasure.
>
> Upon receiving the news of what the curiosity of the keepers of the treasure had brought them to, Tepoztécatl said: "The doves that flew out of the village were fortune, but they now went to enrich other towns, and our

village shall always be poor. There shall be intelligent people, but they shall leave the place just as the doves that you freed left."[5]

As a whole, the story provides a genealogy of Tepoztlán's poverty and of its destiny always to lose its brightest lights to other towns. More subtly, the story also notes the role of Tepoztecans in the construction of the center. In point of fact, a number of Tepoztecans did work in corvée labor to build Mexico City's cathedral during the colonial period,[6] but Tepoztécatl's role with the cathedral's bell is also potent symbolically because the bell was the principal marker of time in the period, and, ultimately, of the dominion of the Spanish faith. Finally, the story makes Tepoztécatl a staunch ally of the church (Tepoztécatl as the first convert, Tepoztécatl as idol basher, Tepoztécatl as son of the Virgin of the Nativity), thereby representing Tepoztlán as a voluntary subordinate to the colonial regime, despite the fact that the village was burned to the ground by Cortés during his campaign against the Aztecs in 1521 because its lord would not become his ally.[7]

In sum, the legend of Tepoztécatl is a story about Tepoztlán's terms of submission. These terms, which are performed yearly on the day of the Virgin of the Nativity, include, first, public acknowledgment of hierarchical encompassment of the village by a larger political society centered in Mexico City and identified with the church; second, a recognition of what Tepoztlán has brought to the center; third, an emphasis on voluntary subordination to and adoption of this order; fourth, a proud affirmation of the continuity of local tradition, a continuity that is enunciated in the very act of recalling Tepoztécatl as man-god, as ally of the wind god, as lord of the mountain and guardian of the village. The story of El Tepoztécatl thereby reflects, to a significant degree, the prolonged vitality of a colonial discourse of hierarchy and marginality.

It would be mistaken, however, to imagine that this colonial discourse of encompassment is the only way in which center–periphery relations have been constructed by Tepoztecan ideologues. In fact, there are several center–periphery discourses operating simultaneously, and their signs and artifacts are constantly manipulated in local jockeying for status, wealth, and power. By way of illustration, I shall consider one example of a more modern formulation of Tepoztlán's peripheral status, beginning with a story written by Joaquín Gallo titled "The Intruder."

"The Intruder" is an allegory. A group of blond foreigners whose characteristics make them a composite of communist spies, evangelists, and anthropologists has come to Mexico with the mission of "study[ing] the customs, the psychology of the people of the villages, their ways of life, their thought, their degree of culture, and, above all, their religiosity. They believed that it was easier to convince simple and poor villagers and to attract them to their own point of view."[8] The leader of the group (who has been named "Ivan") goes to Tepoztlán. He asks villagers all sorts of questions that are intended to subvert the dominant order by implying that Tepoztecans are being exploited by capitalists, by government, and by priests.

After his initial inquiries, Ivan goes to Cuernavaca to cable a message that reads: "Tremendous success. It is easy to attract these sandal-wearers [*huarachudos*]: they can't read, they only eat tortillas, beans, and their explosive *mole*." Nonetheless, this impression of Tepoztecan ignorance and pliability proves deceitful, because, with their kindness, the purity of their faith, the beauty of their ways, and, predictably, their women, the Tepoztecos succeed in converting Ivan to their persuasion:

> He became convinced that people are happier in liberty, in peace and tran-
> quillity. He found that although there is poverty [in Tepoztlán], conditions
> are not wretched and that people's convictions are worth more, much
> more, than promises of equality that are never kept because those that
> manage the party rule the lives and goods of others.

Ivan takes a job in a nearby hacienda and courts Catalina, "a pretty dark girl with large eyes," but he is murdered by the men from his party.

This story is not especially popular or well known in Tepoztlán, but it rehearses a number of themes that are popular among romantic enthusiasts of the place, who stress both the ignorance and humility of the people and their greater purity and simplicity. The story also usefully summarizes a discourse that has been deployed by Tepoztecans themselves in their political dealings with outsiders, a strategy that involves mimicry of the idealized "Indian" of Mexican nationalist discourse.

One early instance of this mimetic strategy occurred in 1864 when "Tepoztecan Indians" went to pledge allegiance to Maximilian of Hapsburg and simultaneously petitioned him to solve a land dispute with neighboring haciendas. These "Tepoztecan Indians" were led by members of the local elite.[9]

The portrayal of Tepoztlán as "Indian" is central in the cultural construction of a class of notables during the *porfiriato*, whose members fled to Mexico City during the revolution and founded a Tepoztecan colony that was active in Tepoztecan politics and cultural affairs during the 1920s and 1930s, reviving local *indigenismo*. An idealized Indianness was deployed again in the early days of Tepoztecan tourism, beginning in the 1940s, when prominent artists and intellectuals settled in Tepoztlán and found in the place a kind of prototype of the true Mexico. More recently, in the 1960s, local movements against "hippies" deployed a similar discourse of rustic purity and traditionalism, a purity that has also been mobilized at times against Protestant missionizing, in discourse highlighting the value of life in Tepoztlán as against the migratory experience in the United States and, in the 1990s, for mustering local and external allies in massive mobilizations against two modernizing projects: a suburban train that was to link Mexico City with Tepoztlán and a development project that was to build a golf course and an urban development on communal lands.

This most recent social movement has been of such proportions that it led, among other many things, to the overthrow of the municipal council and to the promotion of a "popular council" in its stead. The ceremony in which the new council was sworn in makes powerful usage of the ideological mechanisms discussed here:

> Before a crowd of three thousand in a popular assembly [asamblea popular], Lázaro Rodríguez Castañeda took office today as the first mayor of the "free, constitutional and popular municipio of Tepoztlán." In a symbolic act, the Lord of the Wind, El Tepoztécatl, gave Rodríguez the rod of rulership [bastón de mando] as the new tlatoani of the community. The new popular municipal president, who shall lead Tepoztlán's destiny, swore that on no account shall he allow the Club de Golf El Tepozteco to be built, nor shall the municipio become "the patrimony of any oligarchy."[10]

Although "the intruder" of Joaquín Gallo's story is ambiguously portrayed as communist agent, U.S. evangelist, and foreign anthropologist/psychologist, and the story is true to some of the political usage to which the discourse of Tepoztecan "simplicity" has been put, one must add key agencies of the Mexican government itself as critical targets of this discourse of cultural purity. This distinctly modern peripheralizing discourse involves the double move of portraying ordinary Tepoztecans as Indians and as true representatives of the national ("popular") soul, thereby legitimating political mobilizations that can serve to negotiate the terms of the law and of state policy. The discourse is also for aspiring politicians, insofar as it does not deny the ignorance of the villager, and thereby provides political leaders with ample room for negotiation or manipulation. It is an ideology that can be deployed both to defend the village against actions of an "external agent" and to call for progress.

In short, Tepoztlán's position as an agricultural periphery, as a source of migrant workers for the United States, Mexico City, and Cuernavaca, as a poor *municipio* within the state system, and as tourist site—is recognized culturally in complex discourses of marginality. Nevertheless, it would be mistaken to take this as justification for labeling Tepoztlán simply as "a periphery," a simplification that obscures more than it reveals. Instead, the complexity of even the two peripheralizing discourses that we examined thus far signals that Tepoztlán has occupied several peripheral situations, often simultaneously, corresponding to varying ways of organizing economic and political space. As a result, one symptom of economic marginality—for instance, peasant production—can serve to claim centrality in political discourse in the shape of "Indianness." In the sections that follow, I shall review the relationship between center–periphery ideologies and the dynamics of distinction in Tepoztlán.

## Indio, de razón, *and* notable *in the Organization of Urban Space*

One key element of Spanish colonialism was the equation of urbanity with civilization. The extreme opposite of the urbane and civilized person was, of course, the uncivilizable barbarian who, following Aristotle, was thought of as a "natural slave," that is, as a creature entirely devoid of reason whose best hope was to be ruled by a rational person and harnessed to civil society (see Pagden 1982). The barbarian was an entirely physical being, of brutish force, ruled by his own emotions—a wild man alone in nature. Between the wild man and the cultivated aristocrat there were, of course, gradations of civility and coarseness. A logical corollary of this view was that signs of urbanity became a factor in local and regional politics of distinction: the construction of churches, of squares, and of public offices are an example, but there are others, including the official status awarded to a town (be it *ciudad, villa,* or *pueblo; cabecera* or *sujeto,* etc.), the proximity of houses to the central square and church, the durability of materials with which houses were built, the layout of streets, the layout of a graveyard, and, not least, the general bearing of the inhabitants.

In Tepoztlán these elements and others have been deployed in varying ways and for diverse purposes and, although we do not yet have continuous evidence for the history of these uses, there is sufficient documentation to sketch a general outline of the role of urbanity (and thus "centrality") in local politics of distinction.

The first major colonial census of Tepoztlán was carried out around 1540 and has been translated from Nahuatl into Spanish by Ismael Díaz

Cadena.[11] Although the interpretation of this document is demanding, a few interesting elements emerge with clarity. First, "Tepoztlán" was, at that time, the name of a jurisdiction roughly equivalent to today's *municipio* of Tepoztlán, but perhaps not the name of a nucleated village.[12] The jurisdiction was made up of nine *calpulli*. In other words, Tepoztecans of this period did not yet call their primary neighborhood units *barrios* (a term that is in use in the 1580 "Relación de Tepoztlán"), but still used the Nahuatl term that designated a social organizational unit that was conceived as a patrilineage with an attached territory. Of these nine *calpulli*, Atenco was that of the local *tlatoani*, and thus the highest-ranking *calpulli*. By the time of the 1540 census, a number of Tepoztecans had already been baptized, presumably by the Dominican Fray Domingo de la Asunción, who allegedly baptized El Tepoztécatl of the story narrated earlier, and who brought down and shattered the main idol dedicated to the tutelary god Ome Tochtli, building a provisional church at the foot of the steps leading to Ome Tochtli's hilltop temple.[13]

The census shows, too, that the households of nobles included *mayeque* serfs or slaves, and that not all of the local population were ethnic Tlahuica Nahuas (Carrasco 1964, 1976). Thus, this first census suggests a class structure in which the principal divisions were those between the nobility, *macehuales* (commoners), and *mayeque* serfs or slaves. The village was further divided into Christianized and pagan people, a social fact that was marked in the villagers' names, which appear as either Christian or indigenous in the census.

Around 1550, the Dominicans began construction of a convent and church with a spacious open-air chapel. Although we know little regarding the specific location of each of the nine *calpulli* prior to this time, it is clear that these units begin to be identified as barrios around this time, keeping both the name of the *calpulli* and adopting a patron saint. The noble *calpulli* of Atenco thus became Santo Domingo Atenco, taking the name of the mendicant order that dominated the village until the parish was secularized in the mid-eighteenth century.[14] Three other *calpulli* became the barrios of San Miguel, La Santísima Trinidad (*calpulli* Tlalnepantla), and Santa Cruz (*calpulli* Teycapa). The other five *calpulli* became the outlying hamlets of Santa Catalina, Santa María, Santo Domingo, San Juanico, and San Andrés. Thus, four *calpulli* were aggregated into the nucleated Villa de Tepoztlán as barrios, while the other five became *sujetos* of that villa. The difference between the villa and its *sujetos* was subsequently marked in terms of urbanity: the villa (which I shall henceforth call "Tepoztlán") had the main church and monastery. It was also the seat of the government of the *república*, established according to the New Laws of 1542.

The identity of Santo Domingo as a barrio of nobles may slowly have been undermined, beginning with the early Spanish prohibition against Indian nobles keeping slaves. On the whole, the internal structure of the barrios tended toward structural equivalence, each barrio being inhabited by a series of noble *principales* and *macehual* commoners, while the whole jurisdiction was under the political dominion of one or two major noble families that took up Spanish last names. The most famous and continuously important of these families was the Rojas family, whose members held the principal political offices with great frequency from the seventeenth to the twentieth centuries.[15]

Thus, centrality and marginality were slowly redefined during the sixteenth century. A city center, with the church, a square, and government buildings was established, and the most worthy subjects lived close to it. On the other hand, hierarchy between barrios tended to dissolve and was substituted by a relationship of structural equality and competition between them. This relationship of competition is expressed in each barrio's efforts to build its own chapel.

Thus, centrality was indexed by urbanity, and cultural distinction was arranged in some consonance with this idiom of centrality. Correspondingly, Tepoztecan elites (including a few Spaniards) tended to occupy the village center. They also were bilingual Spanish and Nahuatl speakers, dressed in the Spanish mode, rode horses, and so on, thereby occupying a nodal position in a political organization of space that had Spanish towns as cores and Indian jurisdictions as peripheries. Moreover, although for several centuries the outlying *sujetos* of the jurisdiction of Tepoztlán were in positions almost entirely analogous to those of the villa's own barrios, this began to change slowly, as some inhabitants of the central barrios of Tepoztlán became Hispanicized and identified more closely with Tepoztlán's urban institutions.

The whole process can be imagined as a shift from an initial hierarchical relationship between *calpulli*, to a tendency for structural equivalence between barrios (and hierarchy between the villa's Hispanicized center and the barrios), to a tendency for some inhabitants of barrios around the center of Tepoztlán to see themselves as more urbane and less "Indian" than inhabitants from outlying barrios and hamlets. This third phase gained momentum after independence, with the introduction of an ideal of democratic politics.

## Two Local Strategies for Reworking "Centrality"

Center–periphery dialectics in Tepoztlán have usually been experienced as a set of local distinctions, and not as a mere replica of a system of distinction that has its center in Cuernavaca or Mexico City. One of Robert Redfield's firmest convictions when he observed Tepoztlán in 1926 was that this was a "folk society," that is, a place that was its own cultural center, where information and cultural artifacts from outside the village were reprocessed and assimilated in a highly discriminating way. Although Oscar Lewis was more concerned with the impact of national conditions and events on local society than was Redfield, he did not question the fact that these conditions were reworked locally.[16] Both authors perceived that the connections between the interests of regionally dominant classes and local dynamics of distinction were actively mediated by Tepoztecans. In this respect, the indiscriminate application of the term *subaltern* for local Tepoztecans and for Tepoztecan culture would present some difficulties, because Tepoztecans have often combined wage labor with more independent forms of work, such as subsistence farming, artisanal production, and petty commerce. They have therefore preserved political and cultural spaces that have been limited—but not necessarily occupied—by regionally dominant classes.

Correspondingly, the constructs of centrality that we have reviewed were contested since their inception in the early colonial period and well into the second half of the twentieth century, when the very definition of centrality began to shift significantly. In this section, I wish briefly to identify two local strategies for manipulating centrality. The first is a form of asserting a disjunction between political centrality and social-moral centrality; the second is a way of appropriating the center for discretionary local usage. I review these two forms here in order to demonstrate that ideological mechanisms of contention and appropriation are well established. In later sections, I will review the transformation of center–periphery dialectics in modern Tepoztecan history.

The first strategy is to reject professional politics and political discourse entirely.[17] By relying on traditional ideas about the nature of sickness and health, about the necessary complementarity within the peasant family and the central importance of reciprocity for social and cultural reproduction, this strategy convincingly casts peasant agriculture as an inherently "clean" activity and politics as a necessarily "dirty" one. Peasant production is "clean" because its goal is to fulfill an entire cycle of production and consumption within the household, exploiting no one, and relying instead on a "natural" complementarity between the sexes, between young and old within the household, and on reciprocity between households.[18] These relations of complementarity and equality resonate in a powerful way with local ideas concerning health, nutrition, and the body.[19]

Politics, on the other hand, is inherently "dirty" because the politician's livelihood is based on producing and mediating conflict. As a result, political speech is to be systematically distrusted because it is always masking the politician's interest. The popular aphorism "A río revuelto, ganancia de pescadores" (roughly, Muddied waters benefit the fisherman) is used to describe the politician: his job is to generate confusion and then exploit societal conflict for his own benefit.

On the whole, these ideas reinforce a habitus that has local society as its center, insofar as they orient people's actions toward strengthening relations of complementarity and reciprocity within and between households and provide, in the process, a view of the meaning and goals of life that is not brokered or mediated either by the city or by the state. Moreover, the state, its representatives, and its activity ("politicians" and "politics") and capitalist merchants and producers are seen as living off of the contradictions of clean people, contradictions that are the unlucky result either of necessity (as when an individual is landless) or of foolish disregard for the precepts of local wisdom. This ideology does not deny the power of the state and the market, but rather sees its power as an evil that must perhaps be endured, sometimes resisted, but never emulated. The relation of local society to state agents is cast not as a relation of complementarity, but rather as a relation of exploitation. As a result, regional loci of power are not seen as the center of local society, but rather as external to it.

The second strategy for reworking the relationship between Tepoztlán and the centers of power that encompass it I call the "artificial flowers strategy," in honor of an episode in the local school during the 1860s, when a community member was dispatched on the long walk to Mexico City to purchase artificial flowers that would serve as floor prizes for student contestants. The strategy consists of enshrining urbanized or industrialized objects that represent items that are found profusely in a natural state in the local environment (such as flowers). This is then used to link local society to the national community or to elite culture in a highly discretionary fashion, both to make claims on powerful individuals or state agencies and to hector the local population toward more involvement in state institutions or in idioms of distinction that come from dominant centers.

For instance, the self-identification of Tepoztecans as "Indians" before emperor Maximilian of Hapsburg was a form of enshrining an urban category ("Indian") that refashioned elements of the local life-world. In identifying with the romanticized Indian of national mythology, Tepoztecans could stake a claim for special treatment within the national state. At the same time, however, utilizing this strategy also meant learning nationalist discourse and exhibiting this learning in public. It is not coincidental, then, that Tepoztecans who used this strategy since the 1860s promoted schooling actively, while insisting simultaneously on activities such as learning the Mexican national anthem in Nahuatl, or performing local folklore in schools or political rallies.

This strategy has also been used to market local products for outsiders and to protect selected resources from unleashed market forces. The adoption of urban discourses regarding the value of pure air, of the picturesque beauties of the village, or even of the "vibrations" of the mountains and the pyramid have served simultaneously to defend local resources against the intrusion of unwanted corporate investors and to commodify local resources.

The very same discourse that is used to sell an agriculturally worthless piece of land with a good view at an exorbitant price is used to bar the construction of a building that will block that view. The same discourse that is used to convince fellow villagers to "work for progress" is used to bar unwanted forms of investment or state intervention from the village.

Thus, although a center–periphery dialectic has been at the core of local cultural history since the early colonial period, and although Tepoztlán as a whole can plausibly be described as "a periphery" because its centers are outposts of more significant centers, and because local conditions of production have been dictated by dominant groups who have privileged other spaces, we must also recognize the existence of local ideologies and practices that rework dominant center–periphery ideas in significant ways, ranging from a rejection of centers of power as legitimate centers of value, to a discretionary refashioning of center–periphery relationships that serves to transform and to reposition local society vis-à-vis the state and the market.

## Class Strife and Redefinitions of Centrality

I have argued that, although it is legitimate to classify Tepoztlán as an economic and political periphery, power centers have always been present there both indirectly (shaping the contours of Tepoztlán as a productive space) and directly (in the form of agents and agencies and in local ideology and cultural production). I have also singled out two alternative strategies that are deployed to reframe or manipulate center–periphery relationships locally. In this section, I wish to clarify the social import of these strategies by inspecting the way in which centrality was contested in an especially conflicted moment, in the aftermath of the Mexican Revolution.

Class conflict is often a latent theme in Tepoztecan political history. It has usually been subsumed into political battles that cut across classes, making the language of class strife into the sort of discourse that James Scott has called a "hidden transcript," referring to the fact that most forms of class struggle involving peasants are not articulated openly or explicitly, favoring instead more oblique forms of enunciation through resistance. One significant historical exception to this rule did occur, however, in the years immediately following the Zapatista revolt of 1910–19.

Tepoztecans suffered terribly during the Mexican Revolution. The village was burned down on several occasions, many were abducted by the federal army, others fought alongside Zapata. Peaceful villagers were forced to live in the mountains for months at a time, where they suffered famine and plagues, while others fled to Mexico City, Cuernavaca, and Yautepec.[20]

In many ways, the revolutionary process destroyed the central institutions of the *porfiriato*. In 1911, local Zapatista commanders burned the municipal archives, where land records were kept. The houses of local caciques and of the church fathers, even the church building itself, were periodically turned into barracks, and the region's main haciendas went up in smoke. Nevertheless, the destruction of the region did not lead to a simple collective takeover. Instead, Zapatistas were divided among themselves and much of Tepoztlán's local leadership was killed in internal frays. Moreover, the unpredictability of the outcome of the war between Zapatistas and Federales was such that villagers had to learn to live with both factions. Although most of the town's *pacíficos* sympathized with Zapata, they usually portrayed both Federales and Zapatistas as a menace.

By the time the pacification of the village came in 1918, local Zapatistas did not contest the command of a relatively benign federal army officer. Instead, his main opposition came from elites who wanted to regain control of local government. They expected to be reinstated now that the defeat of Zapata was certain. Moreover, most Tepoztecans who fought with Zapata left the village to do so, and often came back to Tepoztlán almost as strangers, finding that many of their possessions had been taken by those who had stayed, and fearing overt political identification as rebels both because of the military defeat of their movement and because most local Zapatistas had dispersed in various armed bands and did not return to the village as organized units.[21]

However, the military defeat of Zapatismo did not lead to the reconstruction of the Porfirian system. The seizure of the national presidency by general Álvaro Obregón in 1920 instated the remaining Zapatistas in the Morelos state government. Zapatista general Genovevo de la O became military commander of the region, all of which allowed Tepoztecan Zapatistas to express their convictions and hopes for land reform and political change openly.

The village's notable families had emigrated to Mexico City at the start of the revolution and lived in the neighborhood of Tacubaya, where a Tepoztecan colony of exiles was established. These exiles, including not only the town's main caciques, but also its principal intellectuals and many people of more humble origin, formed an association, the "Colonia Tepozteca," which was simultaneously a historical society, a philanthropic society, and a political group. The Colonia took an active role in reactivating local education, and it published a newspaper on Tepoztlán using rhetorical formulas that were reminiscent of the prerevolutionary intelligentsia's *indígenismo*.

However, not even the intellectuals and politically active individuals of the Colonia Tepozteca were united under the banner of an old-style *cacicazgo*. On the contrary, at least two prominent ones were affiliated with the socialist and Obregonista labor confederacy that dominated Mexico City politics in the early 1920s, the Confederación Regional de Obreros Mexicanos (CROM). This combination of factors allowed for the conformation of a sort of local Zapatista politics that had never emerged in a coherent fashion during the highly uncertain years of armed insurrection.

Local Zapatistas allied themselves to the Mexico City CROM leadership, raised the red-and-black banner of Mexican anarcho-syndicalism, and created a CROM-affiliated "Unión de Campesinos Tepoztecos" (UCT) that gained the support of the Zapatista state governor and of President Obregón himself. Moreover, there was a family of Tepoztecan peasants, the Hernández brothers, who had been officers in Genovevo de la O's army and who quickly became the armed branch of this movement. I do not have space to detail the ways in which these political relationships unfolded in the highly turbulent 1920s, and shall turn instead to the ways in which social space and centrality were reconfigured during this decade.[22]

We have seen that representations of civilization relied on symbols of urbanity, symbols that were concentrated in the center of the town, which is where state, church, and market had their seat and where the most substantial citizens resided. This view of civilization had the potential of expanding outward from that center, a tendency that was manifested in the urbanization of barrios, the improvement of barrio chapels, the expansion of education, and the adoption of urban ways, including shoes and dress, and the adoption of certain pieces of furniture (mainly beds, in the early twentieth century, but also sofas, tables, and later radios, television, etc.). The adoption of modern status symbols occurred principally at the individual level, through education, language practices, and forms of consumption that pitted "Indians" against "proper folk," "sandal-wearers" (*huarachudos*) against "dandies" (*catrines*), and users of the fork, the bed, and the table against users of tortillas as eating implements, mats (*petates*) for sleeping, and stools around the hearth for eating. However, the movement of "progress" was also visualized in aggregate form, making some places more civilized and modern than others, according to whether they had roads, houses built with solid materials, and so on.

In the Tepoztlán of the *porfiriato* and of the 1920s and 1930s, progress was correspondingly expressed in barrio competition. The fact that local elites lived in the three "lower barrios" that are adjacent to the plaza allowed those barrios to be identified as stronger, wealthier, and more civilized, despite the fact—demonstrated by Lewis—that there were numerous poor residing in them.[23] It is not surprising, then, that postrevolutionary conflicts over the definition of centers and of their place in local society were manifested in the very conception of local urban space.

The political situation of the 1920s produced intense conflict between the old Porfirian elite and the members of the new Unión de Campesinos Tepoztecos, a conflict that revolved around control over the municipal presidency, over the local militia, and over the exploitation of the communal forests.

Members of the Unión de Campesinos Tepoztecos felt that local peasant demands could articulate with a national and regional movement, represented by the CROM and Zapatismo (respectively). Radicalized Tepoztecan peasants imagined a community without a local landholding elite but that could still be part of national politics. As a result, they tried to marginalize the old class of caciques that had traditionally represented the national center in the village. Activists called for the death or expulsion of local caciques as they rallied under the red-and-black banner. Significantly, these caciques were also referred to in this period as "*los centrales*," that is, as the people from the town's center.

In their turn, the *centrales* defined supporters of the UCT as "Bolsheviks" and, in a stunning strategic move, as "*los de arriba*," that is, as inhabitants of the four upper barrios that were removed from the plaza and could not compete successfully in expressions of urbanity such as the expensive carnival celebrations. In doing so, the *centrales* sought to maintain the older core–periphery ideology that saw "the party of progress" as a movement that expanded from the center outwards and successfully encompassed a portion of the local poor, at the very least those who inhabited the same barrios as the rich.

In other words, the *centrales* strongly resisted being identified either as rich or as the old caciques. Instead, they wished to be seen as progressives who were interested only in improving local conditions. They tried very hard not to appear hostile to the local poor. In a characteristic example of what I earlier called the "artificial flowers strategy," for instance, a writer who used the pseudonym of El Tepoztécatl, and who routinely addressed Tepoztecans from the pages of *El Tepozteco*—a paper put out by the cacique-dominated Colonia Tepozteca—wrote: "Even our most humble neighbors—once they have been invested with the representation of public functions—are owed unconditional obedience, not only because of the representation of authority that they wield, but because they wield this authority because of the morality of their public actions and because of their good personal habits" (*El Tepozteco*, December 1, 1921).

Taking on the voice of El Tepoztécatl to address his compatriots, this political writer apparently favors peasant political power, but is in fact subtly stressing the critical importance of "progressive" behavior in political posts:

> What can be expected of a town that is ruled by authorities plagued with vice that, forgetting the investiture of which they are unworthy, and having lost all dignity . . . instead of making public show of their morality and good conduct create public scandals in such a drunken state that, because of their indecent acts, they deserve not only immediate demotion but also exemplary punishment?

This apparently neutral call for civilized behavior subtly reasserted a pre-revolutionary politics of distinction, by calling for reinstating religion,[24] public morality, the significance of education and of literacy.[25]

The care with which the old elite dealt with this issue, never discounting local leadership out of hand because of their class origins, but judging them instead on their distinction, reflects the power of the movement pitted against them. It is not coincidental that almost all political articles in *El Tepozteco* are signed with pseudonyms (mainly "El Tepoztécatl" and "Alexis": the Aztec and the Hellenic) and that they take on an impersonal and allegedly impartial voice. By presenting their faction as the party of education, the *centrales* mapped the factionalism of the period onto a distinction between the "backward" upper barrios and the "progressive" lower ones, and rejected the map that pitted peasants from all barrios against inhabitants of the center.

This illustrates the vulnerability of centers in the periphery, as well as the existence of alternative criteria for marginalization and inclusion in a system of distinction, for, whereas sympathizers of the Unión de Campesinos Tepoztecos stressed class as their criterion of inclusion or exclusion ("the people" versus "the caciques," "the people" versus "los centrales"), their opponents invoked a distinction based on urbanity that was then mapped onto the lower versus the upper barrios: inhabitants of upper barrios were portrayed as ignorant, poor "Indians."[26] In this way, an apparently innocuous call for progress in fact was used to reconfigure urban space against the peasant core–periphery model that was based on class.

A significant innovation of 1920s politics is that there was a concerted attempt by some poor villagers to control local government, and thereby to disentangle the connections between the power of the state and the power of money. Redfield unwittingly reflected this novelty when he ingenuously classified politics as a *tonto* occupation (that is, as uncouth or Indian).[27] Although this may have been true in 1926, it was entirely false in the prerevolutionary era. In fact, the idea of making the village as a whole into a peasant outpost within a broadly based workers' union whose main source of governmental support was in the national presidency was a deep change from the prerevolutionary spatial model, when the Morelos state governor, who came from the region's hacienda-owning elite, named the subregional *jefes políticos* and dominated the municipal presidency in an alliance with local economic elites. Thus, the terms and the very nature of the presence of state and market power were the object of a local politics that was manifested in a struggle over local categories of centrality and marginality.

## Recent Reconfigurations of Centrality and Marginality

In an earlier work, I suggested that the analysis of regional culture can proceed by looking at the ways in which residual, dominant, and emergent forms of organizing economic and administrative space are interwoven in a specific place.[28] In the case of Morelos, there clearly was a long-lasting economic organization of regional space based on interdependencies between lowland sugar and rice plantations and poorly irrigated highland villages. This organization entered a critical stage during the final decades of the nineteenth century when a series of factors—ranging from the intensification of production in sugar haciendas to increased pressure on land resulting from population growth and the rise of a small-town agrarian bourgeoisie—steadily increased tensions between villages and haciendas. It was at this junction that the revolution broke out, destroying the region's haciendas and initiating a new stage in the organization of economic space.

Although some aspects of the old economic system were revitalized after the revolution (see Warman 1976), the economic organization of Morelos never regained the clear-cut features of earlier periods. Industrialization of selected areas began in the 1950s. Tourism, construction, and real estate have picked up steadily, crops have shifted, seasonal migration to the United States has ebbed and flowed. These and other factors have contributed to a much more diversified set of economic relations, which in turn translate into a multiplication of economic "centers."

On the whole, these twentieth-century transformations have altered the hierarchical order that once existed between localities, moving progressively away from a system that was characterized by a neat overlap between economic and political space to a system with important disjunctures between various economic interests and the hierarchy of political administration. In some cases, these changes in the spatial organization of economic production have been overlaid on the old agrarian core–periphery organization of the region. Such was the case, for instance, of industrialization, which proceeded in such a way as to take advantage both of the preexisting infrastructure of the region's main towns and of the cheap labor that could be gotten from peasant peripheries. Other activities, such as tourism and construction of weekend homes for people from Mexico City, operate according to a logic that is largely independent of the principles used to organize space in the agrarian era.

In this section, I shall review aspects of the reconfiguration of center–periphery dialectics in Tepoztlán since the 1950s. I shall argue that although the old dialectics of distinction successfully spread the ideals of progress throughout the village, transcending the old divisions between the center and the barrios and even between *los de arriba* and *los de abajo*, the result has not been a simple incorporation of Tepoztlán and of Tepoztecans into a standardized idiom of distinction (if, indeed, such a standardized form can be said to exist). Instead, the space that was historically shaped in the struggle over local power and distinction has left room for forms of subjectivity that are not shaped in a simple fashion by state discourses and institutions.

I have argued that since independence there has been a progressive civilizational movement in Tepoztlán. This movement was spurred through competition between individuals and by competition between villages and barrios. "Progress" also involved attaching local culture and history to national mythology, a move that served multiple, and not always commensurable, purposes, including enhancing the position of the local intelligentsia and political elite, marketing local resources for outsiders, and defending Tepoztlán against specifically targeted state and private development projects. I have also noted the existence of an antipolitical, and to some extent "antiprogressive," discourse that upholds the autarkic community composed of independent households as its ideal. This discourse can be allied to that of the progressive nationalist's, since the very existence of a traditional culture is a significant instrument for claiming positions vis-à-vis the state, but it can and has also stood against "progress," opposing numerous state and private schemes leading up to the massive protests against a golf course.

When rumors first circulated regarding plans to build a road linking Tepoztlán to Cuernavaca, they were received with much enthusiasm: "If this [project] comes to fruition, it will be of great importance, because Tepoztlán will be visited by foreign and domestic *excursionistas*."[29] The image that Tepoztecans had then was of tourists who would come to spend the day (*excursionistas*), visit the pyramid, and leave a few pesos behind in local food stalls or perhaps in an inn. Matters developed quite differently, however.

The road connecting Tepoztlán and Cuernavaca was finished in 1936, and Tepoztlán did receive some *excursionistas* in the 1940s and 1950s, as well as a small number of prominent artists and intellectuals, some of whom helped bring state resources to the village.[30] Beginning in the 1960s, however, the nature and scale of tourism and colonization changed dramatically.

In 1965, a direct freeway to Mexico City was built, leaving Tepoztlán less than an hour away from the city. As a result, weekend homes proliferated, and the price of land began to rise. Large portions of the Valley of Atongo, just east of the village, had been bought up by three investors in the 1940s and they resold plots slowly, favoring settlement by families who maintain a relatively rustic look but who are wealthy by village standards. Beginning in the 1980s, and especially after the devastating 1985 earthquake in Mexico City, a number of middle- to upper-class people moved permanently to Tepoztlán, forming schools for their children and engaging in varying degrees with local Tepoztecan society. By the early 1990s, land prices in Tepoztlán were among the highest in the country, and the village had a number of famous homeowners in its midst, including intellectuals, artists, financiers, and politicians. At the same time, the large number of daily visitors that come to the pyramid and the market have been a boon for local commerce, especially in the market and around the plaza, and for several hotels, restaurants, discos, and video stores. Tourism and colonization produced changes in the center–periphery dialectic.

First, the colonists and homeowners have acquired a collective identity that is separate from the village. Although a number of these individuals have good ties in the village, when tensions arise, people in the valley are spoken of as "foreigners" or as "Tepoztizos" (false Tepoztecos). At the same time, social and cultural differentiation by the traditional eight barrios has been erased thanks to this same process, because barrios are all roughly equally urbanized and land value is roughly equal throughout. The premium placed on scenic beauty no longer makes living close to the plaza particularly desirable, and the wealth of the local elite is overshadowed by that of the new inhabitants. As a result, the last several decades have brought the traditional divide between the city center and the barrios to a close. In its stead there are now divisions between the village and the valley, as well as between the traditional old barrios and some of the new settlements on the margins of the village, which are poorer, have fewer urban services, and include significant numbers of migrants from outside the village.

Second, the growth of the real-estate market has made agricultural value a secondary consideration in the organization of space. This has combined with long-term shifts in family economies to almost completely sever Tepoztlán's identity as a periphery of a lowland agricultural core. Growth in the local construction industry, in petty commerce for tourists, and in services for weekend homes began making Tepoztlán into a receptor of migrant workers, and wage labor in lowland agriculture has all but disappeared. This process did not occur without conflict or resentments— for instance, in connection to water usage by weekenders for lawns and pools while local agriculture lacked irrigation—but it has continued inexorably, making agriculture into a complementary economic activity.

Third, tourism and colonization also involve the adoption of a series of values that come along with commodification: the construction of Tepoztlán as a "natural," "traditional," and "picturesque" place has had its truth-value confirmed in the market. So has the idea of the place as a site for an alternative lifestyle to that of the modern city, a process that opened a market for earrings, incense, crystals, tarot reading, and tai chi lessons, as well as for crafts that are made elsewhere but sold to tourists locally.

From the perspective of center–periphery relations, this process gave a new twist to the earlier nativism, which had mainly served to tie the village to a national mythology and was used in appeals to the state. The commodification of Tepoztlán as a setting of scenic beauty and of an alternative cultural tradition opens the place up to a kind of multiculturalism whose paraphernalia includes Guatemalan jackets, incense, masks from Guerrero, herbal medicine, Kung Fu, Guru Mai, and so on. The construction of place now combines the nativist identification of Tepoztlán as a center of Mexicanness with constructs emerging from the hippie movement, and especially that mixture of spiritual traditions known as "New Age."

In sum, tourism and colonization have dramatically reshaped the dynamics of distinction in Tepoztlán. Although tourism does not employ the whole village by any means, it has affected land prices, patterns of urbanization, and the definition of what constitutes a local resource. From the perspective of economic cores, the town has gone from being a place where agricultural labor was cheaply produced to a place where city folk can find reprieve and alternatives to their lives. As such, Tepoztlán has moved from being a periphery of Morelos's irrigated lowlands to being a posh periphery of Mexico City; it has also gone from providing labor, grazing lands, and wood to lowland haciendas to providing scenic beauty, goods, and services for tourists and colonists. These processes have helped to expand urban services in Tepoztlán at a quick rate and, as a result, economic differences between the village center and the barrios, or between upper and lower barrios, have practically disappeared. New divisions, however, have emerged between colonists of the valley, who are sometimes portrayed as "foreign," as rich, or as eccentric or sexually promiscuous, and "real" Tepoztecos. These divisions between true locals and new arrivals at times also spill into antagonism against migrant workers, who come mostly from Guerrero, but can come from as far away as Oaxaca or even Guatemala. Finally, peasant agriculture has diminished in importance (not only because of tourism), although it does remain as a complementary activity for families.

Another shift that accounts for a modification in local core–periphery dialectics has been the rise of wage labor and of professionalism. Beginning in the 1930s, villagers invested in the education of their young. This process, which was aided by connections with politically influential visitors, gave Tepoztlán an educational edge over the vast majority of Morelos. In the 1970s, there was a relatively large number of Tepoztecan schoolteachers; today there are also many Tepoztecan professionals in a host of fields. The growth in local education was first financed by the sale of charcoal and wood from the communal forests but, beginning in the 1950s, it received support from income coming from local construction and from work in the burgeoning new industries around Cuernavaca.

This process did not, however, lead to the full assimilation of Tepoztecans into formal-sector white- and blue-collar jobs because the biggest growth in high school and college graduates—beginning in the late 1970s—coincided with the slump in employment for these sectors. As a result, reliance on self-employment and/or on trying to control local sources of employment has grown, making these educated sectors highly oriented to community life and to Tepoztlán as a place that can provide a crucial space for reproduction. This is reflected in the fact that some, though by no means all, of the leadership and militancy against projects such as the golf course and the fast train has come from these educated Tepoztecos.

This apparent paradox can be better understood if we acknowledge that professionalization and skilled industrial wage labor present Tepoztlán with yet another alternative core–periphery structure, wherein the so-called formal-sector jobs that are controlled by the state and industries are a core to an "unemployed," "underemployed," "self-employed," or "informally employed" periphery. In this context, Tepoztlán is a home in the periphery that deserves to be defended against intruders who not only will change the face of Tepoztlán, but will also not employ skilled Tepoztecos and ruin a valued community and lifestyle by flooding the town with educated and higher-income colonists who will impact further on scarce local resources, including water and land, and eventually squeeze local inhabitants out of their homes. The expansion of education in a period of economic uncertainties has strengthened many an educated Tepozteco's resolve to re-create a local tradition.

The sense of a new investment in the locality has also been strengthened by migrants who spend months working in the United States and Canada. A significant proportion of migrant dollars are invested in bettering homes, buying furniture, and in domestic infrastructure in the village, thereby reaffirming the value of Tepoztlán as locus of cultural and social reproduction, and once again casting Tepoztlán as a periphery to new centers, this time in the United States and Canada, while retaining the place's desired and cherished value as the site of reproduction, as the end of their investments.

These three elements—tourism, the rise of an underemployed educated class, and migratory labor to the United States—have transformed the center–periphery logic in significant ways. Internally, the spatial layout of the village is no longer part of an idiom of centrality, except in the distinction between valley and center and, in a more subtle tone, between neighborhoods of poor migrants from Guerrero and the rest of the barrios. Centrality is, however, asserted in the way in which Tepoztlán's status as a "pure" place gets reconstituted, and here we see a confluence between the symbols that attract tourists to Tepoztlán and the ways in which professionals and migrants invest themselves in the place. I next illustrate the nature of this confluence with changes that have transpired in the ways in which the local carnival is celebrated.

## Carnival

In earlier sections, we saw that neighborhood and village have been social organizational units that embodied distinctions such as those that separate Indianness from urbanity, wealth from poverty, and so on. These dynamics generated competition between barrios, a competition that tended to make them homologous with one another: each barrio had (and has) its chapel with its patron saint; each barrio was meant to have its own character, reflected in an animal nickname (specifically, toads, lizards, ants, opossums, badgers, and maguey worms); each barrio organized its own fiesta; and barrios organized collective work parties for various purposes. In addition to this tendency toward homology between barrios, we noted that center–periphery dialectics were once expressed in an opposition between the lower barrios around the plaza and the poorer upper barrios. This opposition found ritual expression in carnival because the biggest expenditure for that fiesta, the fabrication of *chinelos* (elaborate carnival costumes) and paying for prestigious bands, was bankrolled by barrios and not by the village as a whole. Only the three lower barrios had sufficient resources to organize successful dance *comparsas.*

Anthropologist Phillip Bock did a Lévi-Straussian analysis of barrio symbolism in Tepoztlán.[31] He argued that the signs of barrio identity, including animal nicknames, barrios saints' names, barrio fiestas, and carnival *comparsas*, were part of a "traditional Tepoztecan cosmovision" that was alive and well when he studied it in the early 1970s. According to such a view, the distinctions between barrio animal names and the separation of the village into an upper and a lower portion are all part of an elaborate symbolic code that represents the organization of Tepoztlán as an indigenous agrarian village. If we pay attention to the dates of the fiestas and organize barrio symbols along an axis of symmetry that corresponds with the above/below division, then these symbols suggest distinctions between night and day, between wet and rainy seasons, between rich and poor, and between Indian and mestizo. However, the symmetry that is so crucial to the kind of coherent worldviews that are posited by structural analyses such as Bock's prove to be historically precarious when we try to articulate them to the history of distinction. Instead of trying to find such a transcendental symmetry, we can look to the carnival, to the barrio fiesta, and to the symbolism associated with place in Tepoztlán as arenas in which the changing relations between places are manifested.

In recent years, for instance, the barrio of Los Reyes changed its carnival sign from a badger (a nocturnal animal associated with the mountains and with the dry season) to a little king (representing the Three Magi whom the barrio is named after). San Sebastián, who once shared the opossum with the barrio of Santa Cruz, has since changed to a scorpion, and San José adopted a leaf instead of sharing Santo Domingo's frog. Although these changes alter the apparent symmetry and neat intertextuality of the previous arrangement, they are not a reflection of the decline of carnival or of barrio fiestas. Quite the contrary, these fiestas are perhaps even better attended today than they were a couple of decades ago.

If we inspect recent changes in the carnival carefully, we note three significant items: first, carnival *comparsas* now incorporate all eight barrios of the village and no longer exclude the upper barrios; second, today's barrios never share their nicknames in carnival (it used to be that San José and Santo Domingo shared the frog, and Santa Cruz and San Sebastián shared the opossum); third, some barrios have taken up symbols that are simply indices of the barrio's name, relinquishing the obscure symbolism of animal names: San José is a neighborhood that was always known as "La Hoja" (the leaf), and it is no longer represented by a toad but by a leaf; Los Reyes is no longer represented by a badger but by the Magi; and San Pedro abandoned its maguey worms for a representation of its chapel.

These shifts reflect several facts that relate to our discussion of centers and peripheries. Barrios are no longer an index of differential urbanity. There is no longer an opposition between the central and the upper barrios, a fact that is reflected not only in that *comparsas* now bring together upper and lower barrios, but also in the fact that barrio symbolism is used strictly as a form of individuation, and not as a way of expressing alliances, as was the case when San José and Santo Domingo, two lower barrios, shared the toad, or when Santa Cruz and San Sebastián, two upper barrios, shared the opossum. Also, the new version of carnival reflects a loosening of the ties between the ritual cycle and the agricultural cycle, a fact that is manifested in the current discomfiture in handling and understanding the traditional animal nicknames. The significance or even the range of associations of some of these animals is lost on most local people, and so they tend to weed out difficult or unpleasant symbols, such as San Pedro's maguey worms, that could set them up for ridicule. Instead of being in the hands of barrio elders, much official barrio symbolism today has fallen into the hands of schoolteachers who see the carnival symbolism not as a reflection of traditional productive techniques and social organization, but rather as part of a timeless local tradition celebrating the village.

In short, barrio symbolism in carnival manifests several of the changes we have been discussing. Urbanity is no longer the principal sign of centrality in local idioms of distinction. Neither is there a clean-cut spatial division between the party of progress and the party of tradition. The enormous vitality of "tradition" masks the fact that agriculture has been steadily receding as a defining activity for Tepoztecans. The key position taken by educated Tepoztecans in reshaping barrio symbolism makes the fiesta a celebration of an idealized tradition whose links to older forms of production and social organization are increasingly tenuous.

This picture, however, does not reflect the vitality of local society even as it can be gleaned from fiestas such as carnival, for along with the decline of the core–periphery dialectic that was based on an agrarian political economy, we find new personal investments in the place and its significance vis-à-vis "the outside world." These pulsations are obvious not only in the huge crowds of tourists and locals who are present, who are dancing, who are drinking and eating, but also in some of the symbolism of the carnival itself, particularly in the costumes.

Lavish expenditure on elaborate carnival costumes (chinelos) is a common investment among Tepoztecos who work as migrant laborers in the United States and Canada. Their savings allow them not only to improve their houses and to buy consumer products, but also to participate lavishly in this expensive fiesta. Many other Tepoztecans, educated and noneducated, wage earners and petty merchants, also invest in these expensive costumes.

In 1993, chinelo carnival costumes were embroidered mainly with four kinds of motifs: (1) stereotypical (calendar-like) images of Aztec princes, princesses, and pyramids that reaffirm the village's lineage in the dominant nationalist discourse; (2) figures from cartoons such as Donald Duck, Tweety, and so on; (3) voluptuous women—either in the sexy Indian or in the Barbie-doll modes; and (4) beer cans, tequila bottles, or Coke. These images play with the diversification of economic centers that Tepoztecans deal with, reaffirming an idealized image of the Indian, appropriating ready-made images from the media that circulate as widely as Tepoztecans can hope to circulate, playing with consumption, and fantasizing with exotic sexual affairs. All are dreams that are shared while dancing in the carnival of Tepoztlán.

## Conclusion

*Center* and *periphery* are mutually dependent terms. More important, they are in a relationship that is constantly renegotiated. This fact is sometimes forgotten because of the political dividends that accrue from reifying centers and peripheries. It was expedient in the 1960s to define the whole of Latin America as a periphery to a northern Europe and North America. But the very ease with which we fall prey to such reification is a sign of the conceptual difficulty involved in spelling out the ways in which center–periphery relations are intertwined. This difficulty stems in part from the tendency to collapse economic, political, and cultural core–periphery structures as if these relationships all mapped onto each other neatly. They need not do so.

In the case of Mexico, for one, nationalism was built not on the culture of the bourgeoisie or of the urban proletariat, but rather around the romanticized figure of the Indian and peasant. As a result, the cultural core–periphery structure (which can be abstracted out of an analysis of the dynamics of distinction) is impacted and thus does not follow neatly from economic considerations. For instance, Tepoztecans have claimed, at times effectively, a special tie to *lo popular* in order to negotiate conditions with the state. Economic marginalization can place a particular group of people in a politically advantageous position as potential representatives of "national culture."

Theoretical positions that take only economic factors as their criteria for organizing core–periphery models tend to render the complex politics of center–periphery invisible. Instead of visualizing a politics of distinction that permeates most of the world system at every level, this strategy tends to envision regional blocks competing with each other. For instance, Immanuel Wallerstein (1974) used countries as units in his classification of the core–periphery structure of the capitalist world system. This makes sense to the degree to which, as Wallerstein argued, the transfer of capital between nation-states has been a crucial mechanism for capitalist expansion. Following this same logic, analysts who seek to go beyond an international core–periphery structure and into peripheralization within a particular country have been logically drawn to concepts such as "internal colonialism," which still allowed a relatively clear-cut division between centers and peripheries. Unfortunately, these views tend to imagine places as distinctly "central" or "peripheral," instead of as loci with different kinds of center–periphery dialectics.

I hope to have shown here that "the center" has always been present in Tepoztlán, but that the processes of claiming centrality and of peripheralization have changed historically. In fact, in at least one key moment during the 1920s, a traditionally defined center's capacity to encompass and, hence, to successfully peripheralize the whole village was seriously called into question—this despite the fact that, from a macroeconomic point of view, Mexico (and Tepoztlán) remained as "peripheral" as ever.

I also showed that peripheralization in the period following industrialization, especially since the 1960s, has become an increasingly complex phenomenon due to the coexistence of competing logics and loci of "centrality": the relationship with the nation-state is now strongly influenced by transnational currents of Tepoztecan migrants, by urban middle- and upper-class colonists, by educated and wage-earning Tepoztecans, and by the very process of commodifying local culture and resources. This diversification of economic centers and the definitive decline of the old agrarian core–periphery structure have produced significant ideological alterations, even though some of these are masked by the apparent continuity of traditions such as the carnival.

Not long ago, local politics of distinction differentiated the uncouth peasant *indio* from the urbanized and educated citizen. At the same time, some Tepoztecan intellectuals were involved in dignifying Indianness using the "artificial flowers" strategy, that is, by teaching Nahuatl, literacy, learning the national anthem in Nahuatl, and so on. This strategy allowed these intellectuals simultaneously to reinforce their position as what Redfield called *"correctos"* and to stake a political claim for the town vis-à-vis the state. From a peasant perspective, however, all of these strategies were best kept at arm's length, separate from the morality of reciprocity and of household production that was at the center of their lives. In this period, the term *indio* was indeed what Judith Friedlander (1975) called a "forced identity"; in other words, it was a discriminatory term used to discount a peasant's authority as a public speaker or as a progressive citizen.

Today it is increasingly difficult to categorize Tepoztecans as Indians, as peasants, or as subjects in need of civilization. There is no unified local elite. There is no single encompassing economic center. At the same time, the importance of Tepoztlán as a site of social reproduction is as strong as it ever was. Migrants want their (modernized) homes to come back to.

Families with construction workers, petty merchants, or skilled laborers in their midst still like to grow some corn for their own consumption, and all are worried about having sufficient water or about retaining or acquiring a small plot for their children to build on.

In this context, claiming peripheral status from one angle can serve to challenge a competing form of peripheralization. Nativism is used to counter large corporations and large-scale development projects that threaten Tepoztlán as a site for social reproduction, while economic necessity is used to legitimate commercialization of local culture and resources. The ideal of personal progress helps spur migrants on their difficult journey north, and the ideal of coming back to celebrate the fiesta helps to keep them going. It should not be entirely surprising, then, that so many Tepoztecans—peasants or wage-earning, educated or not—are willing publicly to take on an indigenous identity that was described by Judith Friedlander only three decades ago as "forced identity," for this is part of what it takes to reproduce at the margins.

# PART III

# Knowing

# the Nation

# 9

## Interpreting the Sentiments of the Nation:

## Intellectuals and Governmentality in Mexico

My aim in this chapter is to inspect the sources of legitimation that have allowed Mexican intellectuals to represent national sentiment or public opinion. It is common to contrast the role of intellectuals in Mexico with their role in the United States: Mexican intellectuals are thought to be more involved in public debate and in political society, while intellectuals in the United States are thought to be cloistered off from that world by a well-greased academy that makes them into erudites or technicians. This opposition often leads, in turn, to an argument regarding whether the social position of the Mexican intelligentsia in fact follows a more European, and specifically French, model. These contrasts can be misleading, however, since they may be taken to imply that the differences between Mexico and the United States are simply the result of the application of distinct models of knowledge production.

Both French and American examples have been chosen by technicians and policy makers to model Mexican governmental institutions. The hospitals, educational establishments, and prisons that were created or reformed during the *porfiriato* (1876–1910) were often imaged on French models. The establishment of El Colegio Nacional, which is a more recent creation, was inspired by the Collège de France. The influence of the United States as provider of institutional models has been equally great, especially since World War II, and the newer universities and research facilities have often followed American examples. French and United States institutional models have thus coexisted in Mexico since the late nineteenth century, and so they cannot be made fully to account for the strategies that Mexican intellectuals have used to represent national sentiment.

Instead, a more general analysis of the historical connections between state-formation and intellectuals is required. In this chapter, I contribute to this endeavor by inspecting the relationship between intellectuals' representation of popular sentiment and the history of what Michel Foucault called "governmentality," that is to say the history of the ways in which the state described and administered Mexico's population. My general contention is that the economic and political circumstances surrounding Mexican independence produced a long delay in the effective implementation of a governmental state.[1] During this protracted period, a style of intellectual representation that gained its authority from political revolt complemented the sort of scientific representations of the Mexican people that are associated with governmentality. The representation of national sentiment was produced not only by reference to a set of indicators culled from censuses and questionnaires, but also by giving meaning and direction to the cacophany of popular social movements and insurrection.

My general claim is that although statistics were generated and populations were cared for and managed by Spanish administration since the sixteenth century, the state and the church kept their information on the population and deliberations on general policies private. Systematic information on towns and provinces was centralized in offices such as that of the royal cosmographer, or placed in the hands of high royal officials such as *visitadores* or viceroys, but they were not scrutinized by a "public." In the ancien régime, public sentiment was a phenomenon associated with towns or cities, and there was no consolidation of opinion at the level of the realm, much less of the entire empire. Correspondingly, statistics, maps, or reports could be controlled by specific communities or corporations, but not in the name of a broader polity.[2]

The notion of a public that transcended the bounds of the town or city and extended into the broader realm was consolidated slowly only during the late eighteenth century. With this development, statistics became a matter of general interest, because they measured the common good. However, the tension between the notion that statistics were privy to the king and his representatives and the idea that they were the mirror in which the public could measure its own improvement extended to the end of the colonial period. As late as 1791, the Inquisition barred Viceroy Juan

Vicente Güemez Pacheco y Padilla from publishing the results of a Mexico City census that he had commissioned, and freedom of the press was only granted for a few brief months in 1812. As a result, the first major publications presenting the Spanish colonies from the viewpoint of a governmental state, the works of Alexander von Humboldt, had a powerful effect on American nationalists.[3] Humboldt's portrayal of the Spanish-American realms as functioning wholes, complete with an aggregate population (divided into races), maps of the realms, and discussions of their compounded resources helped nationalists imagine their countries as autonomous units, and themselves as their would-be administrators. The dialogue between scientifically aggregated knowledge of the population, public discussion, and state administration thus had only a short, and rather explosive, colonial history.

This fact is coupled with another, which is of equal significance. At independence, most Spanish-American countries were not well integrated economically. The new national elites were usually landowners, and the commercial and financial concerns that had tied the empire together were most often controlled by Peninsular Spaniards. Independence therefore inaugurated processes of territorial disarticulation and disaggregation, and national consolidation would be won only after a protracted sequence of *pronunciamientos*, caste wars, civil wars, and foreign interventions. As a result, peaceful administration was encumbered, census taking was irregular, and the consolidation of a working scientific establishment was slow. Mexican independence was won in 1821, but a securely functioning governmental state did not exist until the 1880s.

There is thus an extended period in Mexican history when a commonly accepted scientific image of the population, of its desires and its propensities, was not attainable. Intellectuals' reliance on the instruments of governmental administration was thus necessarily mixed with the interpretation of public sentiments on the basis of their attachment to revolts, revolutions, and social movements, and these movements were commonly endowed with authority to discredit "scientific" representations of public opinion.

In the Mexican case, this nineteenth-century phenomenon (which was common to Spanish America and indeed to portions of Europe) was extended far into the twentieth century thanks to the Mexican Revolution of 1910–20, and to the fact that the state that was spawned by the revolution was a one-party regime that was led by an inordinately powerful president. Thus, regardless of French or American influences, both of which have provided critical instruments for the representation of national sentiment,

Mexican intellectuals have spoken for the people with some autonomy vis-à-vis the classical instruments of governmentality. This is my argument at its most general level.

## Populations, States, and Nationalities

Benedict Anderson argued that New World nationalisms were the first of the modern era, that nationalism moved from the periphery of empires to their very core. Although this contention is debatable, it is undoubtedly true that American nationalisms sprang up relatively early on the world scene. What is less clear is the nature of the relationship between nationalism, sovereignty, and statecraft, because the dogma that nationalism spawned independence movements can just as easily be inverted, and one could just as readily claim that it was the prospect of severing ties with Spain that shaped Spanish-American nationalisms.

It is tempting to resolve this question by pointing to a dialectic between nationalism, the push to independence, and then the further propagation of nationalism as a result of the contest for independence itself. However, it is worth considering this matter more closely, because the specific contents of "nationalism" vary significantly according to its connections to the various aspects of statecraft, and these variations in turn afford a perspective on our theme, which is the specific spaces for intellectual production that are characteristic of Latin American, and specifically Mexican, modernity.

In the last decades of the eighteenth century, New Spain underwent a significant shift in the ways in which publicity and "the public" were discussed, with an emergent class of "reasonable people" (gente sensata) rejecting so-called baroque forms of ceremony and championing enlightened views of the common good. They were aided by enlightened monarchs who shared their suspicion of the "obscurantist church" and of sectors of the old nobility. This shift corresponds to a recomposition and expansion of New Spain's upper classes, with new individuals entering the Mexican nobility and the expansion of urban classes of merchants and artisans as the country's economy grew.[4]

Late-eighteenth-century conceptions of "the public" can be culled from the *Gazeta de México*, Mexico City's periodical, which reappeared in 1784 in a novel form after a lapse of two decades in which no regular newspaper was published. The earlier *Gazeta* of Mexico City and the *Gazeta de Lima* had dealt almost exclusively with public ceremony and commercial information, with coverage of commemorations of royal births and deaths, deaths of principal inhabitants of the cities, masses pleading for the welfare of the Spanish fleet, and *Te Deums* of thanks for being spared from plagues, but also with lists of the cargo and names of the ships that entered Veracruz and other ports. In the second era of the Mexico City *Gazeta*, this genre of reporting was complemented with discussion concerning "the public" and its improvement.[5]

Perhaps the best way of capturing this novel concern with the progress and welfare of "the public" is a genre of writing that I am tempted to call "the scientifically marvelous." We know, today, of the curious genealogy of discourses of the marvelous in the Americas, of their deployment as propaganda and as a silencing mechanism in the sixteenth century, and of their centrality in the perception of contemporary Latin America as the site of a disjointed modernity, in the literary movement of the *real maravilloso*.[6]

In the late eighteenth century, we have a specific subgenre of writing the marvelous—which is, of course, found also outside of the Iberian world—that exalts the wonders of nature and of science. The pages of the *Gazeta*, a paper whose dedication to useful things was decreed by the king himself, are replete with examples:

> In the measles epidemic, whose remnants still sting this jurisdiction, a child of age seven was sickened by it and by smallpox simultaneously, such that the right side of his body was pocked by measles, while the left side was filled with smallpox, with not one grain of smallpox mixed with one of measles.(November 17, 1784, 186; my translation)

In this case, the exact separation of the infant's body in halves is the object of wonder. As in so many instances of what is judged to be marvelous, it is the combination between the infinite and the exact that is awe-inspiring, the precision that denies randomness and thereby allows the viewer a glimpse of a higher order. This report is an item from a broad genre in which natural phenomena are shown to be motivated by a divine order, and inquiry into the natural world is thereby made compatible with religion.

Another kind of example of the "scientifically marvelous" dwells on the unsuspected potency of the ordinary:

> Don Ángel de Antrello y Bermúdez, inhabitant of this city (of Guadalajara) with a letter dated on the fifteenth of the past month (of October) notifies the Supreme Government with the goal that this news be published, that the plant called Ajenjo, which in Sonora is called Estafiate, ground and mixed with water, together with the root of Palo Blanco, or, if this root is

lacking, that of Chamisa, or Jarilla, known in Sonora (where it grows in abundance) as Batamote, is highly efficacious, if drunk, to cure rabies. (Ibid., 193; my translation)

In the same way that natural harmony revealed heavenly intervention, so too did the unsuspected potential of nature, its marvelous uses and the promise to heal and to help.

The genre of the scientifically marvelous as it is found in the *Gazeta* combines an interest in public welfare and confirmation of the role of God and of religion in the transition to modernity and toward the progressive improvement of living conditions. The intervention of God is manifest in the uncanny. Science, in this sense, has a double mission: discovering and proclaiming God's hand in nature and serving a public whose very adoption of all that is true and useful is a ratification of a deep and mysterious rationality. The people who subscribed to the view that public acclaim was the measure and proof of having discovered a divine rationality were known as *gente sensata*, or "reasonable people." They opposed the pomp and ceremony of the retrograde church with a modernized Catholicism in which the progressive discovery of God's ways was tied to the improvement of the living conditions of the public. In this respect, Miguel Hidalgo, leader of the first armed revolt for Mexican independence in 1810, is paradigmatic: a mystic of national independence, a priest, and a man impassioned by the useful sciences. Scientifically inclined nationalists and nationalistic scientists were commonplace at this time.

This particular form of validating truth is compatible with Michel Foucault's ideas concerning governmentality: states define a population, establish parameters to measure its progress, introduce new productive techniques, and then legitimize their own existence on the basis of the adoption of these improvements. In this sense, governmentality creates characteristic spaces and roles for intellectuals: for the engineer and the inventor, for the economist, the hygienist, and the statistician, and, indeed, these are some of the main sorts of intellectuals who appear in debates during the late-eighteenth- and early-nineteenth-century *Gazetas*.

As if to illustrate the social composition of the lower echelons of this intelligentsia, an editorial response to a technical debate that filled entire issues of the *Gazeta* invents a hypothetical readership in an imaginary village:

In the town of Cozotlán, abundant in sadness and scarce in amenities, there resided a curate who combined a satisfactory level of comprehension with great diligence, because of which he remained unsatisfied with mere devotion to his obligations, and sought always to be instructed in the useful natural sciences, which were not incompatible with his office . . . Our curate gathered in his house a very modest salon [*tertulia*], made up of the notary and the barber—the only two champions who had any polish in a country filled with thorns and roughness. (December 29, 1784, 2; my translation)

The country's intellectuals clearly had the public welfare in mind. This was to be attained through the application of sciences and arts that were compatible with religion. The pious technician was the personification of the useful citizen.

*Dialectics between the Technician and the Spirit Medium*

Certainly these ideas regarding the public as the site where truth about nature is put to its ultimate test were related to the development of nationalism in Mexico, though one might note that they were also broadly compatible with Spanish absolutism and, indeed, with any form of modern statecraft. Independence, however, brought with it a dizzying political instability—an instability, moreover, that led to the dramatic increase in the relative backwardness of the new Spanish-American countries, with respect to the United States and northern Europe.[7] The relative decline of Mexico came along with unmitigated competition for control and appropriation of state institutions, and this contest made the simple adoption of material improvements by "the public" an insufficient basis for interpreting national sentiments. The strategy of governmentality, though centrally important throughout the modern era, was insufficient once independence destabilized government.

It is in this context that a second method for interpreting public sentiments became important. This method maintains that popular will is visible during times of revolution and revolt, but is difficult to ascertain in times of apparent peace because systems of coercion over individual opinion are in place. In peaceful times, the people were ruled by the existing powers: political bosses, hacienda owners, mine owners, who each had a ferrous hold on their workers and dependents. The vote merely echoed the wishes of this political class.

The establishment of a state based on democratic representation was always a distant goal, never an accomplished fact. Although numerous attempts were made to establish a system of representation based on reliable ways of counting the population and on the capacity to guarantee equality before the law to all citizens, the successful establishment of credibility was another matter.[8] It is arguably the case, for instance, that the 1994 and 1997 elections were the first fair elections in Mexican history. Polls and polling were not being used widely in Mexico before 1988.[9]

These difficulties stemmed principally from the force of various corporate structures in the society, ranging from haciendas, to the church, to the army, to indigenous communities. Underlying their strength was the weakness of the private sphere of vast numbers of Mexicans. There have always been many people who were dependents in Mexico, either because they were servants, or sharecroppers, or peons living on their master's property. Dependents have never made ideal liberal citizens, for the defense of individual rights is meant to be based on secure property and a competitive labor market (servants were explicitly barred from citizenship in early legal codes). In the twentieth century, the "urban informal sector," which is enormous, produces other forms of dependency. The state was thus incapable of upholding the ideals of liberal citizenship for the poorer sectors of society, and therefore political representation depended, and was perceived as depending, on the muscle of regional and local elites.[10]

An example that clarifies the nature of the problem is the case of Texas before its secession in 1836. The Mexican constitution of 1824 abolished slavery. Nevertheless, as tensions between Anglo-American colonists in Texas and the Mexican government mounted in the late 1820s, the Mexican government repealed the prohibition of slavery in the case of Texas as a way of appeasing the colonists. In short, the Mexican state did not have the power to guarantee citizenship to its population, but relied instead on the power of various local elites who could mobilize or demobilize popular classes to such an extent that in certain instances they might even be able to enslave them without effective state restrictions.[11]

In a more general way, one might argue that the continued presence of a vast peasantry and, especially in the twentieth century, of a populous urban informal sector has meant that the state culture of governmentality, based on censuses and on other forms of state ethnography, as well as on the construction of measures of progress, has never been intellectually sufficient for founding credible political representation. These standard mechanisms for measuring popular will are effective only to the extent that the state has the means for regulating the lives of its people.

What is more, the growing concern with backwardness—a concern that began to develop about ten years after independence and that became acute after the war with the United States in 1847—meant that some of the forms of state culture that one associates with governance in more developed countries became an aspect of state theater in the more backward ones.

Early national statistics in Mexico mobilized the study of variation around a mean in order to demonstrate that the people of Mexico City were as educated as those of London, that levels of prostitution in Mexico were lower than those of Paris, and that levels of prosperity were comparable to those of the same capitals. These statistics were not reliable or useful for internal social engineering, the way that colonial statistics had been. Instead, they were intended to create a mystique of modernity that would help secure a place for Mexico in the concert of nations.

Any bid for being taken seriously in the international arena involved such forms of state theater. During the *porfiriato* (1876–1910), which was the first time in which such a credible bid could be sustained, there was much display of the visible signs of modernity. Díaz created an elite police corps, the *rurales*, whose uniforms and organization gave a semblance of order to a country whose association with banditry was legendary. The first national census was taken in 1895 and then regularly every ten years beginning in 1900; and the capital city became the site of government interventions that were oriented to making the city into a credible capital of a modern nation. I shall dwell briefly on certain aspects of this strategy.[12]

The national state was only lightly inscribed in Mexico's landscape before the 1880s. In many of the most important state capitals, institutes of science and arts existed as an educational and intellectual counterpart to the structure of state legislatures. These Institutos Científicos y Literarios tried to recruit students from each municipality every year, thereby creating a structure of education that would impact the whole of each state's political life. This method of intellectual representation, which was parallel to the ideal of democratic representation, has not yet received much attention from historians, and we do not have a good comparative view of its operation, but it is clear that it did not achieve a nationally integrated public sphere.

This fragmentation of the public sphere, which corresponds to the lack of a national dominant class (that can only be said to have emerged after the construction of the railroads, beginning in the 1880s), is reflected in the fragility of the state's inscription in the landscape. According to Carlos Monsiváis, there were only seven statues of heroes in the whole of Mexico's public squares before 1876.[13]

With Díaz, however, effective centralization of the state was achieved, along with the consolidation of a national bourgeoisie. These achievements coincided neither with a florescence of democratic institutions nor with the universal extension of civic virtue—except, of course, at the level of state theater. The *porfiriato* may have been the heyday of bonded labor, but in Mexico City, Díaz presented an image of federal democracy by lining the new Paseo de la Reforma boulevard with two busts of notables from each of the republic's states. The capital city thus became a site where local leaders were transormed into the metonymic signs of an imaginary democracy.

The strategy of political representation that was first consolidated under Díaz is still used today. During ethnographic work on the staging of public rallies during the presidential campaign of Carlos Salinas in 1988, I noticed that in each state tour, the presidential candidate delivered speeches that contained a simple formula: he would begin by acknowledging the greatness of the state in which he was, by naming prominent historical figures of the state, who were usually political heroes or prominent artists, intellectuals, and the like. Then he would value their contribution in terms of what they meant for the nation. For instance, Salinas said that he was proud to be in Puebla, the region of Aquiles Serdán and the birthplace of the Mexican Revolution; Chihuahua was the state that harbored Benito Juárez during his campaign against the French invaders; Veracruz was the land of poets and popular artists who, like Agustín Lara, had brought international recognition to Mexico. In each speech, the region was recognized, but its value was only realized at the level of the nation.[14] This is a legacy of Díaz's regime, when Mexico City was effectively set up as the site in which national value was realized.

However, although the centralization of the state under Díaz allowed for the development of a more reliable set of measurements with which to count, poll, and represent "the people," capital accumulation in the period relied on labor repression, and the stability of the central state itself depended on robust authoritarian practices. As a result, the governmental intellectual whose infancy we have tracked all the way back to the pages of the *Gazeta de México* in the 1780s had only limited credibility and was used as much as an element of state theater as the means for actual governmental administration. The tension between the representation of the people by way of the state's governmental sciences and its representation through direct and unmediated access to national sentiment thus became a structural feature of Mexican development.

The figure of Francisco I. Madero, the revolutionary leader who toppled Díaz in a vast popular movement, provides a curious instance of the intimate and unsolvable contradiction between a governmental intellectual and one who represents popular opinion through a more mystical tie.

Madero was famously upright, a guardian of impartiality and of the rationality of justice, as is evident in this fragment from one of his speeches pronounced soon after toppling Díaz:

> To the suffering and working people, this is to say that I expect everything from your wisdom and prudence. That you should consider me as your best friend: that you make moderate and patriotic use of the liberty that you have conquered and that you have faith in the justice of your new governors . . . because from the political point of view your situation has undergone radical change, going from the miserable role of pariah and slave to the august heights of that of the citizen. Do not expect that your economic and social situation shall improve sharply, because this cannot be attained through decrees or laws, but only by the constant and laborious effort of all social elements . . . Know that you shall find happiness in yourselves, in dominating your passions and repressing your vices, and in developing your willpower in order to act always according to the dictates of your conscience and of your patriotism, and not according to the ways of your passions. Finally, I urge you to seek strength in unity and to make the law the norm of all of your acts.[15]

However, there were not yet any reliable mechanisms for feeling the pulse of this new world of august citizens and impartial judges. Knowing the popular will was, in the end, a matter of faith, it required the ability to tap into the secret reservoirs of national sentiment. In this respect, the other, private face of Madero as a religious man and especially as a spiritualist is not as contradictory as it has been made out to be.[16] As a leader who proved capable of mobilizing a broadly based national movement in entirely undemocratic conditions, Francisco Madero the progressive democrat needed the guidance of his alter ego, Francisco Madero the spiritualist and medium. The duality of the governmental intellectual and of the intellectual as spirit medium of the popular will is here conjoined in a single, politically explosive figure.

In sum: Whereas an early form of interpreting national sentiments is based on the public's adoption of useful and progressive measures, Mexico's instability, its increasing backwardness, and the authoritarianism that was its most readily available remedy all conspired to produce a second method of interpreting the sentiments of the nation. This method recognizes that political representation in the public sphere is insufficiently developed, so that popular will is conceived of as a rumor that can be interpreted through exegesis of popular actions, with revolutions as ultimate loci of authenticity.

In times of unrest, as during the period between 1821 and 1876 or between 1910 and 1940, or again since the revolt in Chiapas in 1994, appeal
to social movements and to revolutions as the privileged sites of public
opinion is quite extended, while the capacity to build legitimacy on the
productive effects of a state culture of governmentality declines, turning
the scientists and technicians of those periods into objects of ridicule
whose pretense of method is broken by a reality that will not cede to positivist inspection. During moments of stability and progress, however, the
public acceptance of these technicians grows, but even then their material
dependence on a state that relies on the mediation of a political class for
the management of a large "dependent" population occasionally undermines their credibility.

*Interpassivity and Governmentality*

The concept of "interpassivity" is useful for understanding the dialectic
between the two forms of intellectual production and the two kinds of
spaces for intellectuals that I have outlined so far.[17] Interpassivity is a kind
of relationship in which the anticipated reaction of an interlocutor is acted
out by the emissary of the original message. Žižek gives canned laughter
on television as an example.

In the Mexican case, both of the techniques for interpreting the sentiments of the nation that I have outlined (and that I am tempted to call
"bureaucratic" and "charismatic") are built on the silence, or at the very
least on the incoherence, of popular expression. The will of the people is
read either by interpreting silence as complacent appeal of the governmental state, or according to the interpretations of intellectuals, whose
speech is meant to be the symptom of the expected reaction of a public
that is unable to articulate views in the public sphere.

In this sense, the role of intellectuals in Mexico is not limited to that of
technicians of governmentality—which differentiates the country to some
degree from the United States. The role of somatizing national sentiments,
the interpassivity of national intellectuals, is based not so much on the
professional drive for specification, isolation, and classification as on developing narratives about the progress of popular will that conform to the
circumstances of social movements and state policies. We thus have as
national intellectuals both the technician and the medium, the bureaucra-
tized professional and the "interpassive" charismatic intellectual.

The state subsidy of intellectual "mediums" or agents entrusted with
acting out expected popular sentiments is a historical fact that is worthy of

note, since many modern states subsidize only the bureaucratic, "governmental" intellectuals. In Mexico, governmental subsidies to the press are substantial, and there are a number of institutions, ranging from state-funded presses to universities, cultural institutes, museums, fellowships, and scholarships that are routinely used to fund this kind of intellectual.[18] The significance of these "interpassive" intellectuals for the Mexican nation is a function of the state's capacity to create a working relationship between the country's diverse corporate sectors.

In this sense, postrevolutionary government investment in interpassive intellectuals can be clarified if we contrast Mexico's situation to Ortega y Gasset's (1921) famous analysis of the breakdown and decomposition of Spain. Ortega described a situation, which he named "particularism" and described as a breakdown of the consciousness of interdependence between the nation's principal segments. This breakdown was caused by the lack of an attractive and viable national project. In that context, the various sectors of society—the army, the proletariat, the bourgeoisie, the intelligentsia—turned inward and did little to seek intersectorial alliances. This inward turn was led by parochial leaders, each of whom imagined a perfect identity between his own sectorial interests and those of the general public. The famous military *pronunciamientos* of the nineteenth century were, for Ortega, paradigmatic of the phenomenon of particularism:

> The *pronunciados* (military rebels) never believed that it was necessary to struggle to obtain victory. They were sure that almost everyone secretly held their same opinions, and so they had blind faith in the magical effect of "pronouncing" a phrase. They rose, then, not to struggle, but rather to take possession of public power.[19]

Mexico's situation in the postrevolutionary era had both similarities to and differences with the Spanish case. On the one hand, it was, and to some extent remains, a deeply segmented country. On the other hand, the revolutionary state was able to put forth a more or less viable and attractive national project. National unity, however, still rested on a culturally segmented and inwardly oriented set of sectors, most of which had weak intellectual representation. In this context, it is perhaps not so surprising that the state took such an interest in fostering an intelligentsia that could somatize these various sectorial interests and place them into a single, though highly restricted, discussion that in Mexico has been called "public opinion."

## Conclusion

The analysis of the spaces for intellectuals in one backward country allows us to look at the relationship between politics and antipolitics in Latin America under a different light. In Mexican politics of the past century, a dialectic between so-called *técnicos* and *políticos* has been widely noted. Similarly, in countries such as Chile, Argentina, and Brazil, military governments developed elaborate "antipolitical" discourses: their governments were cast as technical administrations, not as properly political.[20] This discourse of antipolitics is associated with a specific kind of anti-intellectualism: Chilean universities and culture spheres were dismantled in all but their most technical wings during the military government, and an appreciation of the bureaucratic, as against the charismatic, intellectual has remained there to this day.

Similarly, during the *porfiriato* in Mexico, the intellectual-cum-political elite took on the pretentious name of *científicos*. Porfirio's policy would be founded in a positive science, that is, on the hegemony of the governmental state. Even then, however, these pretensions were understood to be at least in part an aspect of state theater, and a distance between the *país real* and the *país legal*, between the state's image of the country and the country itself, was at times grudgingly acknowledged. As a result, charismatic intellectuals, though dangerous to the regime, were not entirely alien to it. The Mexican Revolution, however, provided a new fount and bedrock for popular will, one that brought back the claims of all past revolutions, and revolutionary governments took it upon themselves to create spaces and to provide resources for an intelligentsia whose role has been to function as an interpassive agent of popular opinion. These spaces include an "autonomous," but state-funded, National University, and government-backed spaces for relatively free artistic expression and publication. This contrast might provide a key for understanding why the Mexican state has fostered a certain sort of intellectual and artistic production, whereas other Spanish-American countries have invested much fewer resources in these activities. It also frames the question of the connection between engaged public intellectuals and academics or technicians in relation to a set of issues that transcend the question of which models—French, British, German, Spanish, or American—were imported. All were imported, and all were subordinated to the logic outlined here.

Michel Foucault's idea of governmentality is of special pertinence for understanding the strategies with which intellectuals have represented national sentiments because Mexico's entry to modernity was highly turbulent. As a result, the instruments of governmentality have usually been unevenly applied, owing to the state's insufficient resources and the nature of capitalist development in the region. Moreover, given Mexico's position in the international arena, given its need to attract foreign capital and to gain a measure of respect from the great powers, governmentality itself became something that needed to be convincingly exhibited. The sciences of state administration needed to be presented as developed and effective, a fact that in itself has generated the suspicion that they are neither. This complex history of governmentality in Mexico thereby provided a relatively secure space for nongovernmental intellectuals.

# 10

## An Intellectual's Stock in the

## Factory of Mexico's Ruins:

## Enrique Krauze's *Mexico: Biography of Power*

*This essay was first published in the* American Journal of Sociology *103, no. 4 (1998): 1052–65. It was subsequently translated and published in Mexico in the newsmagazine* Milenio *(May 11, 1998), where it generated a broadly publicized exchange with Enrique Krauze.[1] This debate became something of a curiosity for those who follow the affairs and daily practice of intellectuals. Although it gravitated toward the ad hominem remark more than to proper intellectual argumentation, the episode is itself a performance of the central themes of this book: the role of intellectuals in nation building, the role of scientific disciplines (in this case, of history) in this process, and the significance of zones of contact as points of tension were all dramatically enacted. Mr. Krauze countered the claims that I make in this essay by arguing, among other things, that his book could not be called a "ruin" because it had sold 1 million copies, and that my review, which he chose to frame as an attack by "an academic" on "a public intellectual," was motivated by a sense of personal frustration with the Mexican milieu. I was portrayed as having accepted a position in the American academy because I lacked viable alternatives in Mexico's university system and, finally, as "Míster" Lomnitz, that is, as a foreigner or, what is much worse, as a Mexican who had chosen the United States over Mexico.*

*This chapter is thus itself an example of the relationship between contact zones and the production of the nation. Its publication also generated some debate around the category of "official history." In his response to this essay, Mr. Krauze declared himself to be amused by my arguments in this regard: How could he, who had denounced the 1968 student*

*massacre and been a champion of democracy since the 1980s, be accused of writing offi-*
*cial history? In an interview with* Milenio *regarding this debate, historian Lorenzo*
*Meyer went further and argued that in Mexico there has never been an official history.*[2]
*And yet, I would argue, it moves.*

*I call the history that is written to provide the pedigree, to identify the imaginary sub-*
*ject, and to provide the governmental horizon of the state "official history." In Michel*
*Foucault's terms, this is a "history from the present," as opposed to a "history of the pres-*
*ent." Its function is to give the state its proper certification, and to shape and direct a na-*
*tional community. Enrique Krauze's criticism of Mexican presidents and presidentialism*
*has left the revolutionary regime's national mythology intact in its most important points;*
*invigorated in its central dogmas, it is now ready for its new tenants.*

*This chapter concerns the practice and use of history in Mexico's great epochal transi-*
*tion. It is about the relationship between intellectuals, the state, and the market, and espe-*
*cially about the privatization of Mexico's cultural apparatus. As such, this essay and the*
*debate that it provoked are one of the early episodes of what has become a battle over the*
*cultural policies of the Mexican state. I reproduce here my original text with no modifica-*
*tions, though I have added two new footnotes to call attention to mistakes in my original*
*text that were pointed out by Mr. Krauze in his responses. They are of little consequence.*

At the end of every presidential term (*sexenio*), Mexican presidents become
involved in a frenetic race of inaugurations; their posterity depends on it.
Hospitals, museums, universities, dams, highways, subways—all of the
signs of modernization and progress that every president promises—must
be inaugurated, along with a large bronze plaque giving credit to the
president, whether the building is finished or not. My brother, a scientist,
once witnessed the inauguration of a research facility by outgoing president López Portillo in 1981. The inauguration occurred in a building that
was made to look finished, complete with lawns, potted plants, and the
rest of it. As soon as the president left, a presidential team came in, rolled
up the grass, picked up the potted plants and took them to the site of the
next inauguration.

This practice, which betrays so much about the economy and legitimacy of Mexican presidentialism, is certainly one of the sources of what
Brazilian literary critic Beatriz Jaguaribe has called "modernist ruins." The
rush to legitimize a presidency or a governorship is enmeshed with the
economy of public expenditure, and both conspire to produce veritable
monuments to the grandiloquence and corruption of the governing elites
that are, at the same time, inhospitable and alienating for the intended user
("the public"). The fascinating thing about these modernist ruins is that
they betray the gestural quality of much of Mexico's state-led modernity.

The central tenet of architectural modernism (utility, practicality) serves as a screen for a second rationale, which is political: the story of Mexico's progressive state veils an enormous pork barrel.

This aspect of Mexico's modernity was most poetically captured by the Scottish eccentric and surrealist Mr. Edward James, who built majestic cement ruins for the jungles of the Huasteca to swallow up. When he was asked why he built this costly extravagance, Edwards claimed that it was to confuse the archaeologists of the future.

Like Mr. James's ruins, Mexico's "modernist ruins" have very personal signatures, which are often those of the president who sponsored them. So, whereas archaeologists of the pre-Columbian past use site names to label historical epochs (e.g., Monte Albán I, II, III, or Tlatilco IV, V, and VI), archaeologists of Mexico's modernist ruins would be wise to rely on the names of the presidents who sponsored them, for example, Alemán I and II, or López Portillo I, II, and III.

Although the discussion of modernist ruins usually brings to mind housing projects, hospitals, bridges, and basketball courts, Mexico's cultural world is also littered with these ruins. The central axis of cultural modernity—which is a productive relationship between science, art, and the constant improvement of the quality of life ("progress")—was historically so feeble in Mexico that, beginning in the 1920s, the state took a proactive role in strengthening it. This role has been as open to demagogy and corruption as any other modernizing project.

Until the 1960s, the state's function as patron of the sciences and the arts had met with relative success—the National Autonomous University was built, as was the National Polytechnical Institute. The arts flourished under state patronage, and Mexico began to make a credible bid for a place among modern nations. The revolutionary prestige of government and the accelerated modernization that began around 1940 fostered a relatively snug relationship between middle-class ideals of mobility and the state's self-image as the prime engine of modernization.

Mexican sociologist Ricardo Pozas has shown how this relationship first cracked in 1964, when medical students and young doctors rejected the state's authoritarian forms of decision making and embarked on a series of strikes that were violently suppressed.[3] The sequel and culmination of this conflict occurred in the student movement of 1968, which ended with the massacre of hundreds of students at Tlatelolco square, in Mexico City.

The killings at Tlatelolco provoked a new spurt of construction of modernist ruins. Under President Echeverría the whole of Mexico's university system expanded way beyond the country's capacities, which meant filling the university with a staff that was not always well qualified. Although the results of this huge expansion of the educational system in the 1970s were mixed, criticisms of its perverse effects were particularly harsh, because the formula of state-driven expansion was no longer sustainable after the state's fiscal crisis in 1982.

The National University and other public institutions came under severe scrutiny, and their ruinous aspect was widely publicized as the de la Madrid administration slashed its support of Mexican public institutions of higher learning. This was the dawn of a new era in Mexican cultural life, an era marked by privatization and by growing differences between an increasingly proletarianized mass of low-prestige teachers, a somewhat fancier stratum of publishing academics, and a new cultural elite that fuses writing with business.

Changes in Mexico's cultural world have been so deep that the analysis of their impact on the quality of cultural production has been suspended to a surprising degree. There is so much that is new in the institutional arrangement of Mexican cultural life since the 1980s: changes in training programs and in the profile that is expected for entering a university career, growth of private and public universities, and the emergence of cultural groups with wide media access.

There are signs, however, that the time is ripe for a critical look at today's cultural milieu, for the era's first monumental modernist ruins are now becoming clearly visible. This year it seems that Mexico City's main private art museum may close its doors.[4] It is also clear that most Mexican private universities are not funding research. However, in the world of culture, the most significant ruins are always the cultural works themselves. The appearance of Enrique Krauze's *Mexico: Biography of Power* (Harper-Collins, 1997) is a landmark in this respect; it is a "period piece" that allows us to scrutinize the effects of power on intellectual production in a sector of Mexico's intelligentsia.

I propose to do just this. A discussion of the organization of Krauze's book, of the connections between Krauze's intellectual project and his position in Mexico's cultural milieu, and an appraisal of the value of this book as a work of history opens a clear perspective on the use of history as a gesture in the struggle over who gets to represent Mexico.

*Organization*

*Mexico: Biography of Power* is Enrique Krauze's most ambitious book. It combines into a single work three books in Spanish (*Biografías del poder*, about the leadership of the Mexican Revolution, *Siglo de Caudillos*, about the Mexican presidency in the nineteenth century, and *La presidencia imperial*, which covers the Mexican presidency from 1940 to the present). In addition, *Mexico: Biography of Power* offers a brief synthesis of political power and political culture in the colonial period. This is the only work available, in English or in Spanish, that covers such vast territory.

The complexity of the subject matter is made manageable by giving history a direction and a premise. Both of these are offered with disarming simplicity. For Enrique Krauze, the history of Mexico is the history of the struggle for democracy. So much so that, echoing Fukuyama, he ends this book by asking Mexicans

> to bury once and forever Cuauhtémoc with Cortés, Hidalgo and Iturbide, Morelos and Santa Anna, Juárez with Maximilian, Porfirio with Madero, Zapata and Carranza, Villa and Obregón, Calles with Cárdenas, all of them reconciled within the same tomb. But Mexico would have to be less pious toward its modern actors. There can be no reconciliation with Tlatelolco.[5]

Krauze feels that the 1968 massacre at Tlatelolco should not be forgotten because that conflict was largely about governmental democracy. However, the fact that the 1968 movement did not involve or affect Mexico's peasants nor the majority of its poor does not seem to matter: Mexico's peasants are asked to "bury Zapata," who called for land for those who work it, but never to forget a middle-class movement that demanded democracy.

The organization of political history around the story of democracy is highly problematic in a country whose fundamental viability was in question during most of the nineteenth century. Moreover, although democracy has been a significant political issue during most of Mexico's modern history, it has often not been the principal political aim or site of contention.

For instance, the Mexican Revolution (1910–20) begins as a democratic revolt under Madero, but it quickly turns into a broadly based and rather inchoate social revolution with variegated demands, ranging from agrarian reform, to labor laws, to national control over resources, to radical state secularism. On the whole, it is fair to say that these demands, and the dynamics of the struggle for power itself, overshadowed democracy as the main issue. This fact is confirmed in the political success of the official state party (PRI), a party that was deeply undemocratic but that left considerable room for social demands. In short, although the organization of Mexico's political history around the epic of democracy is pleasing for

American readers, and to some political groups in Mexico, it is not defensible as the key to understanding that history.

The book's central premise shares the pleasing simplicity of its teleology:

> This book threads the lives of the most important leaders during the last two centuries into a single biography of power, but I am in no way subscribing to an outmoded (and unacceptable) great-man theory of history.[6]

Thus, while writers and academics the world over worry about the "death of the subject," Krauze is busy anthropomorphizing national history and providing it with a "biography."

> What I hope to convey is that in Mexico the lives of these men do more than represent the complexities and contradiction of the country they came to govern or in which they took center stage for a time at the head of armies fighting for change or for a return to the past (or for both). The accidents of their individual lives also had an enormous effect on the directions taken by the nation as a whole. Personal characteristics and events that in a moderately democratic country might be mere anecdotes— interesting, amusing, or trivial—can in Mexico acquire unsuspected dimensions and significance. An early psychological frustration, a physical defect, a family drama, a confused prejudice, a tilt one way or the other in a man's religious feelings or his passions, even a local tradition automatically accepted could literally alter the fate of Mexico, for better or for worse.[7]

According to Krauze, then, presidential biographies in Mexico collectively shape what he mystically calls the nation's "biography of power." However, he does not want this to be identified with a "great-man theory of history" but wishes instead to provide the premise with a kind of cultural specificity. This is because Mexico's historical roots combine "two traditions of absolute power—one emanating from the gods and the other from God [he means the Aztec and the Spanish tradition]—this political mestizaje conferred a unique connection with the sacred on Mexico's succession of rulers."[8] What we have, then, is a great-man theory of history with validity confined to Mexico.

As a result, Mr. Krauze continually asserts that Mexico is unique and fundamentally different from the rest of the world. This exceptionalism is convenient because it allows him to ignore the parallels between Mexican history and other histories, parallels that would diminish the force of the contention that presidential biographies have systematically "altered the fate of Mexico." On the other hand, since Krauze claims exception for Mexico on the basis of the peculiarities of the Aztec and Spanish mixture, this leads straight back to Mexico's official history, which this book distinctly reproduces: Martín Cortés (son of Hernán Cortés and La Malinche) was "the first Mexican" (p. 52); Hernán Cortés was "the spiritual antithesis" of Moctezuma (p. 44); Moctezuma and Cortés "created a new nationality the instant they met" (p. 47); there was no "true ethnic hatred" in Mexico from the colonial period forward (p. 49); slavery in Mexico was sweeter than in the United States (p. 50), and so on. In short, the fabricated saga of the mestizo as national protagonist is swallowed whole, hook, line, and sinker. The authoritative narration of Mexico's fate and fortune rehearses and reaffirms official history, but with a twist: instead of culminating with the progress wrought by the Mexican Revolution (which had been the End of History until recently), it culminates with the democracy that Krauze's 1968 generation is supposed to have engendered.

## Krauze: Biography of Power

Krauze's history can be read in two keys: the first key is the the saga of democracy into which he wants to shoehorn Mexican political history; the second is the saga of his own intellectual genealogy. This second epic, which is barely visible to an English-speaking audience, is nonetheless critical, because Mr. Krauze is in the business of representing the nation to the outside, trying hard to garner credentials with which to construct himself as the kind of privileged interlocutor that other Mexican intellectuals have been: Octavio Paz, Carlos Fuentes, Diego Rivera, Rufino Tamayo.

Enrique Krauze began his career with a book on what he called "intellectual caudillos" of the Mexican Revolution (the term *caudillo* originally referred to military leaders whose charisma allowed them to vie for control over countries and regions; it is a political form that was characteristic of Spanish America's nineteenth century). Krauze then hitched his wagon to the star of Daniel Cosío Villegas, a prominent liberal historian who directed El Colegio de México and who created a workshop that was known as the "factory of Mexican history," where much of the history of the *porfiriato* and the Mexican Revolution was written.[9] After Cosío's death, Mr. Krauze became the impresario and subdirector of *Vuelta*, Octavio Paz's cultural magazine, from which he derived most of his intellectual cachet.

In an effort to create a voice for himself, and perhaps to emerge from under the long shadow of his mentors, Krauze identifies as a member of the 1968 generation, a generation that was marked by the student movement and by its violent end at the hands of the Mexican state. Like a number of others, Krauze relies on this identity to acquire the semblance of purity. He sees himself as a liberal and even as a "heretic,"[10] an independent intellectual who criticizes Mexican authoritarianism from the sanctity of his private world.

In fact, however, Krauze's prestige and cultural power do not come from 1968, nor is he comparable on an intellectual plane to Cosío Villegas, let alone to Octavio Paz. Krauze's prominence is, instead, an effect of a more recent story. With the debt crisis in 1982, the Mexican government came down hard on all salary earners, real minimum wages plummeted to half in less than five years (a fact that, like almost every economic consideration, goes unnoted in Krauze's book). Among the wage-earning population, one of the sectors that was hit hardest was the educational sector, and the universities in particular.

When the debt crisis hit, the government was unwilling to maintain university salaries at in their traditional middle-class levels, and so it created a system of evaluation that sidestepped university regulations of promotion and that rewarded only productive academics. "Publish or perish" came to have a very literal meaning in the Mexican academy. However, the process of internal stratification in the university system did not come without a substantial cost both for the prestige of academic work and for the possibility of surviving as a beginning scholar. As a result, whole generations of potential scholars were either significantly slowed down or destroyed.

At the same time that the Mexican state strangled its universities, it did not abandon its patronage and contact with intellectuals. The de la Madrid (1982–88) and Salinas (1988–94) governments coupled their tight policies toward the university with generous contracts and subsidies to specific intellectual groups. The principal groups gravitated around two literary/political journals: *Vuelta* and *Nexos*. These two groups accumulated vast cultural power in the 1980s and 1990s: Héctor Aguilar Camín, former director of *Nexos*, member of the '68 generation and erstwhile leftist, was a close friend to Carlos Salinas de Gortari. He created a publishing house, Cal y Arena, whose books were widely distributed, publicized by *Nexos*-controlled public TV Channel 22.

On his side, Enrique Krauze, the principal entrepreneur of the *Vuelta* group, received support from President de la Madrid for his "biographies of power" project (comprising the *porfiriato* to Cárdenas sections of *Mexico: Biography of Power*), a project that was printed by the government-owned publishing house Fondo de Cultura Económica, a prestigious press that sidestepped its traditional role of publishing scholarly work.

During that same period, Krauze and *Vuelta* began doing business with

Televisa, Mexico's television giant that had effectively been a communications monopoly for decades, thanks to its special ties to government. Televisa had a largely negative role in Mexico's transition to democracy, a fact that has been widely recognized by independent political observers of Mexico, including the United Nations. This did not stop self-styled democratic hero Enrique Krauze from becoming one of the company's partners. Krauze is co-owner of Clio, a publishing house devoted to popularizing his version of Mexican history, and producer of historical soap operas that have devoted some effort to rehabilitating Porfirio Díaz (1876–1910), the liberal dictator and former archvillain of official history.

In short, Krauze's power was amassed in a moment in which the government turned its back on public education and research and subsidized a process of cultural privatization that had similar characteristics to other privatizations: enormous concentration of power in very few hands, and the formation of a new elite.

Whereas Daniel Cosío Villegas's "factory of history" was built in a public institution, and whereas his factory produced books that were signed by the individuals who did the research, Krauze's factory of history is private, and only he takes the credit. For big rollers in Mexico's cultural enterprises, research is a menial task. Thus, where most historians work alone or with one or two assistants, Mr. Krauze lists sixteen in his acknowledgments, two of whom are as accomplished as historians as Krauze himself.[11] His heavy reliance on this private "factory" is the reason why this book is such a good mirror of presidential power: the resources that Krauze musters have allowed him to write a monumentally ambitious work, but his methods make him unsure at every turn. *Mexico: Biography of Power* is a hollow monument.

## Krauze as Historian

This book's main empirical contribution is a set of interviews that the author or his assistants made with important political figures as well as a much-publicized, but rather disappointing, diary of President Díaz Ordaz. Most of the book, however, is based on published documents, as well as on secondary sources. The use of these secondary sources provides another key for the archaeologist of Mexico's modernist ruins.

During the past twenty years or so, U.S. and British historians have written a sizable proportion of the most relevant works on Mexican history, yet the work of historians such as John Coatsworth, Alan Knight, Eric Van Young, Gilbert Joseph, Anthony Pagden, John Tutino, Florencia

Mallon, and Stephen Haber is not cited, nor—in most cases—are their ideas assimilated in the text, despite their indisputable relevance to the subjects covered.[12] Like the politicians who have always stressed Mexican exceptionalism, Krauze too is interested in Mexico's insularity; by turning his own coterie of friends and mentors into the principal thinkers and actors in Mexican history, he can easily aspire to become Mexico's representative in the media.

The use of the work of Mexican scholars is equally problematic. For instance, in his treatment of the 1968 movement, a chapter that is meant to be the high point of the book, Krauze gives preeminence to two intellectuals—Cosío Villegas and Octavio Paz—both of whom were marginal to the movement and of an older generation, but were nonetheless central to Krauze's own development. Cosío Villegas gets no fewer than thirty-three mentions in the text of this book; Mexican historian Edmundo O'Gorman, who was arguably a more profound thinker, gets none.[13] Perhaps the oversight is due to the fact that O'Gorman publicly disapproved of Krauze's biographies of power. Citations of significant books written by members of a younger generation of Mexican scholars are another notable absence—they are potential competition.

In addition to the political motives behind these oversights, there is another likely cause for Krauze's sloppy use of secondary sources: the factory. This hypothesis comes to mind because there are a number of instances when a key historical work is indeed cited, but its conclusions are not assimilated in the analysis. Or else a work is cited in one context (perhaps being worked on by one of his research assistants) but then fails to appear as a source in another part of the book where it could have done a lot of good.

For example, French historian François Xavier Guerra has developed quite a complex view of the modernization of the Mexican state in the nineteenth century. Guerra's view is that between independence (1821) and the revolution (1910), Mexican political society changed from being made up of corporations that were built around personal ties in villages, guilds, and haciendas, to a modern society in which these personal ties could no longer hold the country together. As a result, the personal power of Porfirio Díaz (1876–1910) is, for Guerra, both the culmination and the swan song of what Krauze calls a "biography of power." Guerra is cited on a factual matter, but his general argument is ignored. Moreover, Guerra fails to appear in Krauze's discussion of political theory in independence, where he would have been very helpful. In sum, the cavalier use of secondary sources is possibly the only true sense in which Krauze can be called liberal.

## The Authority of Opinion

Enrique Krauze has had two principal mentors, Daniel Cosío Villegas and Octavio Paz. Krauze took Cosío Villegas's factory of history, privatized it, and made it into his own political machine. From Paz, Krauze has tried to emulate grandeur, scope, and boldness. The result is not always bad. *Mexico: Biography of Power* is certainly a readable book. However, Krauze's attempts at Paz-like boldness also have a very perverse effect, which is that they liberate this book from the usual strictures of historical evidence.

Krauze has made a name for himself in Mexico by calling for a "democracy without adjectives," but he seems entirely incapable of offering a history without opinions.[14] More often than not, these opinions are stated as if they were facts. In *Mexico: Biography of Power* we are asked to believe, for instance, that there were only two "true ethnic wars" in Mexican history (p. 780), and that Cosío Villegas's criticisms of President Echeverría (1970–76) were the bravest thing any Mexican had published in one hundred years (p. 746); we also learn that "Juárez the Indian" "was all religion" (p. 167) and that his invocations of God and Providence were carried out "without hypocrisy" (p. 166). In short, the dictatorship of what might usefully be labeled "the Krauzometer."

The translator, Hank Heifetz, has done a commendable job not only in avoiding the annoying changes in register that characterize Krauze's Spanish prose, but also in trying to tone down the Krauzometer as much as possible. So, for instance, in *La presidencia imperial* (the Spanish-language book that comprises Parts IV and V of *Mexico: Biography of Power*, and which appeared simultaneously with it in the spring of 1997), Octavio Paz's *Labyrinth of Solitude* is "the most important book of the Mexican twentieth century" (100 on the Krauzometer, p. 152), but it is only "one of the most important books of the Mexican twentieth century" in English (p. 364, and an 80 on the Krauzometer). Similarly, in Spanish, Krauze asserts boldly (100 on the Krauzometer) that President Díaz Ordaz (1964–70) did not lie in his memoirs (p. 355), but in English he asserts that "[i]t is unlikely that they are all lies" (pp. 728–29, and only a 55 on the Krauzometer). In Spanish, Miguel de la Madrid won his election because the people voted for him personally, and not for the PRI (p. 402, and 100 on the Krauzometer—president de la Madrid was a generous patron to Krauze); in English, the people voted not for de la Madrid personally, but rather for his platform of moral renovation (p. 763, and 80 on the Krauzometer). Moreover, in Spanish, de la Madrid won the election with 76 percent of the vote (p. 402), whereas in English he seems only to have received 68 percent (p. 763). In this book, opinions are facts, and they both change along with the intended readership.

## Biography and Power

Certainly, Krauze's factory has produced a readable book, with much information in it, including some new information and a wealth of anecdotes. Although none of this information makes a significant mark on the historical interpretation of modern Mexico, it does add richness and legibility to this facile and ideologically loaded text. In Mexico, Krauze's version of history is being massively consumed in soap operas, which is an appropriate—though perhaps not harmless—venue for it.

There is, in addition, another good selling point for this book, which is the idea that biography is a useful vantage point for political analysis. I have already argued that this interest in biography led Mr. Krauze to the great-man view of history that he allegedly rejects, but more attention to Krauze's biographies is warranted.

The first thing to note about these presidential biographies is that they rarely provide the kind of psychological insight that the author was hoping for. This unevenness is due not only to the space and detail devoted to various presidents (Miguel Alemán gets seventy-five pages, Manuel Ávila Camacho gets twenty-seven, Miguel de la Madrid gets eight pages), but also to the format of the chapters. For instance, whereas we get an attempt to portray the family history and youth of presidents and caudillos between Porfirio Díaz and Gustavo Díaz Ordaz (1876–1970), there is no parallel information for the more contemporary presidents (beginning with Echeverría). Krauze thereby declines any attempt to provide a more profound portrait of the three presidents with whom he has had a personal relationship (de la Madrid, Salinas, and Zedillo).

The irregularity of the quality of biographical insights is also a product of Krauze's rush to represent, which leads inevitably to an imprudent reliance on common sense. For instance, Krauze tells us that

> [r]evolutions have been organized around ideas or ideals: liberty, equality, nationalism, socialism. The Mexican Revolution is an exception because, primordially, it was organized around personages . . . The local histories from which they [these personages] began, their family conflicts, their lives before rising to power, their most intimate passions—all are factors that might have been merely personal, though perhaps representative, if these were merely private lives. But they could not be in Mexico, a country

where the concentration of power into a single person (*tlatoani*, monarch, viceroy, emperor, President, caudillo, *jefe*, *estadista*) had been the historic norm across the centuries.[15]

The trouble with this is that no distinctions are made regarding the significance of biographies, say, for a *tlatoani* and for a president, or for a caudillo and a monarch. Instead of attempting to specify these different forms of power, and then seeing their connection to biography, they are constantly collapsed into a single composite, which is then—sometimes anachronistically—turned into the quintessence of Mexicanness.

Throughout the book terms such as *monarch, tlatoani, theocratic,* and *caudillo* are used as metaphors for other forms of power. The Mexican presidency is "like a monarchy." The president is "like a *tlatoani*." Presidential power is "almost theocratic." José Vasconcelos and Daniel Cosío Villegas were intellectual "caudillos," and communications magnate Emilio Azcárraga was a "caudillo" of industry.

These comparisons and metaphors may be innocent enough in daily parlance, but if your thesis is that there is a special connection between the details of a leader's biography and the country's destiny (p. xv), then the difference between an actual monarchy and something that has similarities to a monarchy, an actual caudillo and someone who is compared to a caudillo, an actual *tlatoani* and a president, becomes critical.

For example, the power of a revolutionary caudillo like Emiliano Zapata was, especially in its origins, charismatic. People followed him because they shared his cause, were often in desperate straits, and because they believed in him. Zapata's biography is critically important because it is the source of the social connections of his inner circle (whose biographies in turn affect outer circles), and because his persona gave credibility and direction to the movement as a whole. As a result, the epic of Zapata's life takes a messianic turn, similar to what we find in a number of revolutionary caudillos in Mexico, beginning with Miguel Hidalgo, whose political usage of the passion play was perceptively analyzed by Victor Turner (also not cited by the author).

Krauze argues that the biography of Zapata and of Hidalgo is critical for understanding their movements' destinies, but one might argue, conversely, that the construction of their personas was shaped by the context in which they arose as leaders. It is certainly no biographical accident that led Zapata, Hidalgo, and even Madero to take up a messianic, Christian narrative and construct their persons around it. Specific forms of power such as presidencies, monarchies, grassroots leadership, and so on imply different kinds of relationships between the leader's biography and the exercise of power.

For instance, in European monarchies, the idea of "the king's two bodies" implied full identity between the king's well-being and the prosperity of the land. The king was like an embodiment of his kingdom. Indeed, in the case of Spanish America, Philip II decreed the production of censuses and maps of the entire realm (the famous *Relaciones geográficas*). The maps and descriptions he received were concentrated in his palace at El Escorial and in the office of the royal cosmographer, and the information in those censuses and maps was privy to the king. At the same time as he received the maps, he sent out portraits of his person to the four corners of the realm: the king concentrated the full image of the realm in his palace; the realm received, in its stead, the bodily image of the king.[16]

The relationship between biography and the application of power in this case is certainly distinct from that of Mexico's nineteenth-century presidents. The connection between presidential power and personal benefit inverted the central dogma of monarchy. Nineteenth-century caudillos like José María Morelos and even Santa Anna wanted to be thought of as *servants*, not as lords, of the nation. As a result, nineteenth-century presidents ("caudillos") routinely modeled their public personae after Cincinnatus—a renouncer (much as George Washington did in the United States, and Rosas did in Argentina). However, Krauze wrongly reduces Santa Anna's constant show of retreating from the presidential chair to a psychological quirk ("he detested the direct and daily exercise of power"), when in fact it was a variation of a classical theme in the theater of presidential power in nineteenth-century Spanish America.[17] Whereas the monarch identified his personal welfare and prosperity with that of the realm, early presidents and revolutionary caudillos used personal sacrifice as a legitimating device. As the presidency became a stable political institution, the office began to require less dramatic personal sacrifices and the image of the "civil servant" became more prominent—this was the image that Juárez adopted for himself, but it was not routinized in Mexico until well into the twentieth century.

Krauze ignores all of this. For him, charismatic power is a constant in Mexican history, the product of a mythified fusion of Aztec and Spanish "theocracies." As a result, he reduces the differences in the persona of various leaders to the details of their biographies. This error leads to the kind of Mexican exceptionalism that I objected to earlier (to the proposition that there is something about Mexico that makes all of its leaders into *tlatoanis*—or did, until the fateful events of 1968, which brought about a new generation, led by Krauze, among others, who have finally brought democracy to Mexico, the End of History). It also leads him to curious attempts to differentiate "authentic" from "inauthentic" leaders.

Antonio López de Santa Anna for Krauze is the epitome of the fake. His power was theatrical, operatic, and worse, it was divorced from the nation's roots—never mind that "the nation" did not yet effectively exist. Thus, commenting the rise of Benito Juárez (who, unlike Santa Anna, is portrayed here as being 100 percent authentic—"a pure-blooded Indian"), Krauze says that "[t]he country would now be governed by a group of young mestizos who were closer to Mexican soil, closer to indigenous roots" (p. 151). Which brings us back to the fundamental characteristic of this ruin: it is little more than a reenactment of the national myth for the 1990s.

In *The Critique of the Pyramid*, a post-1968 reflection on what had gone awry in Mexico, Octavio Paz wrote a trenchant criticism of Mexico's National Museum of Anthropology. His main complaint was that the architecture of the building and its layout made the museum's Aztec hall into the culmination and synthesis of all pre-Hispanic culture. This construction of the Aztec empire as both the centerpiece of the pre-Hispanic world and the antecedent of the independent Mexican nation negated cultural pluralism, idealized a strong central state, and falsified the pre-Columbian past.

Krauze's book is very much like that museum. The fusion and confusion of *tlatoanis*, caudillos, viceroys, and presidents, and the thesis that the course of Mexican history was dictated by Díaz Ordaz's ugliness, by Santa Anna's theatricality, and by Juárez's religiosity and purity, makes this book as much of a Mexico City–centered account of the history of power in Mexico as the Museum of Anthropology ever was. In this allegedly critical review of the Mexican presidency, the presidents are fetishized, and the social history of the country is collapsed into nationalist myth.

The peculiarity of Krauze's generation of mythmakers is that they are not builders of state institutions, but have instead used state patronage to build private niches for themselves. Two Mexican intellectuals of the 1968 generation have been emblematic in this transition, Héctor Aguilar Camín (former editor of *Nexos*) and Enrique Krauze (former subdirector of *Vuelta*).[18] These intellectuals have been in the business of creating their own "factories of culture." They now speak from these niches and ventriloquize "Civil Society," much as Maya priests once interpreted the commands of a Talking Cross.

So far this new mode of cultural production has counted on the support of the Mexican state, of some powerful—government-related—business-men, and, by now, on its own private resources. The system also benefits, however, from the fact that the readership in the United States—and to some extent in Europe—has preferred to have a small handful of author-ized voices on Mexico rather than to take the country seriously as a site of cultural and intellectual production. It has been economical and conve-nient for Americans and others to simply tune in to Carlos Fuentes, Octavio Paz, or Enrique Krauze and to take whatever they say as repre-sentative of what José María Morelos called "the sentiments of the nation." However, the power to represent Mexico in this way, to embody it in a single intellectual, is as dead as the autocratic power of the president.

When he was at the height of his power, President Miguel Alemán wanted the Nobel Peace Prize. President Luis Echeverría tried for the secretary-general of the UN, and Carlos Salinas wanted to be president of the World Trade Organization. These un-kingly desires reflect the nature of presidential power and the limits of presidential biographies: they are not the main axis in the history of Mexico. I like to think that this book is the intellectual counterpart of these desperate presidential moves: the concentration of cultural power in the hands of a few intellectuals has been linked to the authoritarian power of Mexican presidents, and the current democratization and debilitation of the presidential office prom-ises to end this form of "intellectual *caudillismo.*"

# 11

## Bordering on Anthropology:

## Dialectics of a National Tradition

The current sense of crisis in U.S. and European anthropology has been widely debated. Beginning with a series of criticisms of the connections between anthropology and imperialism in the 1970s, the critique of anthropology moved to deeper epistemological terrain by interrogating the narrative strategies used by ethnographers to build up their scientific authority and their role in shaping "colonial" discourses of self and other. The field of anthropology in the United States and Europe is still reverberating from these discussions.[1]

Less well known and less understood, perhaps, is the quieter sense of unease and transformation in anthropological traditions that one might call "national anthropologies." By "national anthropologies" I mean anthropological traditions that have been fostered by educational and cultural institutions for the development of studies of their own nation. These traditions began to be the object of reflexive interest in the United States and Europe during the 1970s, alongside vocal criticisms of colonialism. Their significance for reshaping anthropological theory was brought to the fore in the 1980s.[2]

Noteworthy among these interventions were two short pieces by Arjun Appadurai arguing against holism in dominant metropolitan anthropological traditions. Holism, for Appadurai, was "a glaring example of the making

≈ 228 ≈

of theoretical virtue of a range of infirmities of practice,"[3] infirmities that included the "tendency for places to become showcases for specific issues over time."[4] This tendency was weaker in peripheral anthropological traditions, because they developed not so much for the production of a general account of "Man" or of "Culture," but rather to confront social problems in the ethnographer's own society, a society that was always problematically integrated to "the West." Thus, in the 1980s, peripheral anthropologies became part of a process of diversification and specification of anthropology, a process that countered the grand holistic narratives of earlier generations that used India as an excuse to reflect on hierarchy, Africa to reflect on lineage structures, or the Mediterranean to think about honor and shame. This movement against grand holistic narratives and toward the diversification of the field is perhaps the principal symptom and effect of globalization on "metropolitan" anthropological traditions.

However, the effects of "globalization" on national anthropologies is not so well understood. Globalization has involved a number of powerful changes in these places, including transformations in the role of national governments in development and educational projects, the demise of "national economies" as being even ideally viable, and changing publics for anthropological works. These general tendencies seem to produce differing effects in distinct countries. These differences are influenced by factors such as national language (former English colonies having some comparative advantages here), the role of local anthropologies in managing national development, and their impact on nationalist narratives. In this chapter, I provide a historical interpretation of the gestation of the current malaise in one national tradition, which is Mexican anthropology.[5]

Peripheral nations with early dates of national independence, such as most countries of Latin America, have had national traditions of anthropology that evolved in tandem with European and American anthropology from its inception. The histories of these national anthropologies is still not very well known, in part because of the disjunction between the ways that anthropology is taught in the great metropolitan centers and in national anthropological traditions. Whereas in Britain, France, or the United States, anthropological histories are traced back in time within their native traditions, "national anthropologies" often emphasize ties to great foreign scholars, thereby placing themselves within a civilizational horizon whose vanguard is abroad. Commenting on this phenomenon, Darcy Ribeiro once said that his fellow Brazilian anthropologists were *cavalos de santo* (spirit mediums who spoke for their mentors in Europe or the United States). The works of anthropologists of the "national traditions" thus appear to be discontinuous with each other. To use a Mexican illlustration, the influence of Boas on Gamio and of Comte on the earlier Chavero tends to mask the genealogical relations between Gamio and Chavero.

It is therefore not surprising that, although the existence of this class of "national anthropologies" is well known, it has not been sufficiently theorized. How does a discipline that owes so much to imperial expansion and "globalization"—indeed, a discipline that has often conceived of itself as the study of racial or cultural "others"—thrive when its objects of study are the anthropologist's co-nationals? How are theories and methods developed in American or European anthropologies deployed in these national traditions? Is there a relationship between the current transformations of national anthropologies and "the crisis of anthropology" writ large?

The study of Mexican anthropology is instructive for the broader class of national anthropologies. Mexico developed one of the earliest, most successful, and internationally influential national anthropologies.[6] The institutional infrastructure of Mexican anthropology is one of the world's largest and its political centrality within the country has been remarkable. This is linked both to the critical role that Mexico's archaeological patrimony has played in Mexican nationalism and to anthropology's prominent role in shaping national development. However, the success of Mexican anthropology in that nation's project of national consolidation is today its principal weakness.

The sense of crisis in contemporary Mexican anthropology moves between two related concerns: the high degree of incorporation of anthropology and anthropologists into the workings and designs of the state, and the isolation and lack of intellectual cohesiveness of the academy. The concern with the co-optation of Mexican anthropology in particular is a recurrent theme. In addition, there appears to be the sort of disjunction between research, criticism, and useful and positive social action ("relevance") that has also been the subject of recent attention.

This chapter claims that Mexican anthropology has reached the point where it must transcend the limitations imposed by its historical vocation as a national anthropology. In order to lend credence to this normative claim, I explore the development of Mexican anthropology from the mid-nineteenth century to the present by focusing on four dynamic processes: the historical relationship between the observations of foreign scientific travelers and the production of a national image (materials used for this section range from the 1850s to the early 1900s); the relationship between evolutionary paradigms and the development of an anthropology applied to the management of a backward population and its incorporation into "national society" (materials from the 1880s to the 1920s); the consolidation of a developmental orthodoxy (materials from the 1940s to the 1960s); and the attempt to move from an anthropology dedicated to the study of "Indians" to an anthropology devoted to the study of social class (materials from the 1970s to the 1990s). I begin by contextualizing the current unease in Mexican anthropology, and move from there to the historical discussion.

*1968–95: "Criticism has been exchanged for an official post"*[7]

The 1968 student movement produced a generational rupture in Mexican anthropology. Its manifesto carried the disdainful title of *De eso que llaman antropología mexicana* (Of that which they call Mexican anthropology), a book that was penned by a group of young professors of the National School of Anthropology who were playfully known in those days as "The Magnificent Seven." The *magníficos* had had the daring to criticize that jewel on the crown of the Mexican Revolution that was *indigenista* anthropology.

By 1968 the identification of Mexican anthropology with official nationalism was at its peak. The new National Museum of Anthropology, which was widely praised as the world's finest, had been inaugurated in 1964, and the National School of Anthropology (ENAH) was housed on its upper floor. The institutional infrastructure of Mexican anthropology was firmly linked to the diverse practices of *indigenismo*, including bilingual education, rural and indigenous development programs throughout the country (concentrated in the Instituto Nacional Indigenista, INI), and a vast research and conservation apparatus, housed mainly in the Instituto Nacional de Antropología e Historia (INAH). Mexican anthropology had provided Mexico with the theoretical and empirical materials that were used to shape a modernist aesthetics, embodied in the design of buildings such as the National Museum of Anthropology or the new campus of the National University. It was charged with the task of forging Mexican citizenship both by "indigenizing" modernity and by modernizing the Indians, thus uniting all Mexicans in one mestizo community. In Mexico, this is what was called *indigenismo*.

According to the *magníficos*, Mexican anthropology had placed itself squarely in the service of the state, and so had abdicated both its critical vocation and its moral obligation to side with the popular classes. The 1968 generation complained that Mexican *indigenismo* had as its central goal the incorporation of the Indian into the dominant system, a system that was called "national" and "modern" by the *indigenistas*, but that was better conceived as "capitalist" and "dependent." Mexican anthropology was described as an orchid in the hothouse of Mexico's authoritarian state, coopted and entirely saturated by its needs and those of foreign capital.

Moreover, the legitimate actions of early *indigenistas*, their ties to the Mexican Revolution, had been exhausted. In the words one of the *magníficos*, Guillermo Bonfil:

> Today we can contrast the reality of Mexican society with the ideals of the revolution and establish the distance between the two . . . It would be difficult to doubt that these days we can no longer do justice to the future by maintaining the same programs that were revolutionary sixty years ago. Those programs have either run their course or else they have been shown to be ineffective, useless, or, worse yet, they have produced historically negative results.[8]

Thus, the authors of *De eso que llaman antropología mexicana* called for Mexican anthropologists to keep their distance from the state. They should steer clear of a policy (*indigenismo*) that had the incorporation of the Indian into "national society" as its principal aim. "National society," noted Arturo Warman, was always an undefined category that simply stood for what Rodolfo Stavenhagen and Pablo González Casanova had called "internal colonialism" as early as 1963. The aim of Mexican *indigenismo* had been the incorporation of the Indian into the capitalist system of exploitation, and in so doing it had abandoned the scientific and critical potential of the discipline.[9]

Not surprisingly, tensions grew strong in the National School of Anthropology, and they culminated in the expulsion of Guillermo Bonfil from the school by director Ignacio Bernal. The fact that a number of *indigenistas* remained loyal to the government during and after the 1968 movement was seen by the *sesentayocheros* as a final moment of abjection, and it marked the end of that school's dominance in Mexican academic settings. Twenty years later, however, Arturo Warman, who was the most famous of the *magníficos* and author of a number of books that were critical of Mexico's agrarian policies, accepted the post of director of the Instituto Nacional Indigenista, and later that of Secretary of Agrarian Reform under President Salinas. From this position, Warman conducted the government's agrarian policies, which were directed precisely to incorporating Mexican peasants into forms of production that are geared to the market. Thus the co-optation of the anthropological establishment seemed to repeat itself, complete with its own moment of drama: in March 1995 the

Mexico City papers reported that Arturo Warman was charged with pleading with former President Salinas on behalf of President Zedillo to put an end to a one-day hunger strike.[10]

## Principal Thesis

My contention is that the image of anthropology's history repeating itself in a never-ending cycle of state incorporation is misleading. In this chapter, I seek to elucidate the origins and historical evolution and current exhaustion of Mexican anthropology as a confined, national, tradition.

The concerns that characterized anthropology in Mexico even before its institutional consolidation in the late nineteenth century related to the historical origins of the nation and to the characteristics of its peoples. The study of the origins and of the attributes of the nation's "races" was especially important in Mexico, where independence preceded the formation of a bourgeois public sphere. Until very recently, at least, Mexico has been a country in which public opinion is to a large degree subsidized and dramatized by the state. Anthropological stories of national origins and of racial and cultural difference were therefore useful to governments and they were routinely projected both onto the nation's internal frontiers and abroad. Anthropology has helped to reconfigure the hierarchical relations that develop between sectors of the population, and it contributed to the formation and presentation of a convincing national teleology. However, in Mexico, as elsewhere, the strategies and role of the state in shaping the contours of society have been deeply transformed from the 1980s on. The crisis in anthropology today is not as much about the discipline's absorption by the state as it is about its uncertain role in the marketplace. An enlightened vanguard may no longer realistically aspire to fashion and shape public opinion for internal purposes, and discourses regarding cultural origins and social hierarchies are no longer central to the allure of the country for foreign governments and capitalists. In this context, there is a real need for invention.

## Anthropology and the Fashioning of a Modern National Image

Shaping an image of national stability, of collective serenity, security, and seriousness of purpose, has never been an easy task in Mexico. It was absolutely impossible to accomplish in the decades following independence (1821), when governments had to operate with unstable and insufficient revenue, a foreign debt that was impossible to pay, constant internal

Figure 11.1. *The Horse and the Zapilotes*, in Evans (1870), p. 506. The buzzard (here misspelled) became a regular motiv in travel writing on Mexico during the nineteenth century. Buzzards figure in the first Mexican impressions of both Fanny Calderón de la Barca and E. B. Tylor. Here, Colonel Albert Evans uses the image to end his book on a suitably pessimistic note: "As we went down by rail from Paso del Macho to Veracruz, we looked from the window of what had been Maximilian's imperial car, upon a scene by the roadside which struck me nearer to the heart, and filled my soul with sadness . . . a poor old steed—who may have borne Santa Anna and his fortunes in his day, or better served the world by drawing a dump cart for a grading party—had been turned out to die. The *zapilotes [sic]*—which are among the institutions of the country—watching from afar saw death's signal in his glazing eye, and wheeling down from their airy heights, came trooping from all directions to the coming feast" (Evans 1873: 505–6).

revolutions, a highly deficient system of transportation, and frequent foreign invasions. The image of Mexico abroad, an image that had been so important to Mexican politicians and intellectuals even before Baron von Humboldt published his positive accounts of New Spain, had turned very contrary indeed. Naturalists and ethnographers who followed Humboldt's steps took a decidedly negative view of Mexico's present and a pessimistic view of its future.[11]

A useful point of entry for understanding the labors of early Mexican anthropologists is a discussion of Edward B. Tylor's travel book on Mexico, which recapitulates the adventures and impressions that he and the collector Henry Christy had on their trip to Mexico in 1856. To my knowledge, this book has never been published in Spanish, and it is not widely known or read in Mexico. This is odd at first glance, given Mexico's legitimate claim to have been the muse that inspired the discipline that in Oxford was at times referred to as "Tylor's science."[12] The lack of attention to Tylor's Mexican connection seems even stranger given the need that countries like Mexico have had to remind the world that they have not been absent in the process of shaping the course of Western civilization.[13]

Mexico's failure to appropriate Tylor's *Anahuac* seems less perplexing when we actually read the book. Tylor described a Mexico whose presidency had changed hands once every eight months for the previous ten years, a country whose fertile coastal regions were badly depopulated, and whose well-inhabited highlands were bandit infested and difficult to travel. Mexico was also a country that was sharply divided by race, where the whites and half-castes were hated by the Indians whom they exploited.

Tylor's first vista of Mexico is the port of Sisal, in the Yucatán, and it gets the Mexican reader off to an uneasy start, suggesting the fragility of Mexico as a polity and its lack of cohesiveness as a nation:

> One possible article of export we examined as closely as opportunity would allow, namely, the Indian inhabitants. There they are, in every respect the right article for trade: brown-skinned, incapable of defending themselves, strong, healthy, and industrious; and the creeks and mangrove swamps of Cuba only three days' sail off. The plantations and mines that want one hundred thousand men to bring them into full work, and swallow aborigines, Chinese, and negroes indifferently—anything that has a dark skin, and can be made to work—would take these Yucatecos in any quantity, and pay well for them.[14]

Tylor's first impression was a disturbing reminder of the fragility of the links between Mexico's people and its territory. His observation revealed what is still today something of a dirty secret, which is that Mayas were indeed being sold as slaves in Cuba at the time. But if Tylor's first impressions were unsettling, Mexican nationalists would find little solace in his conclusions:

> That [Mexico's] total absorption [into the United States] must come, sooner or later, we can hardly doubt. The chief difficulty seems to be that the American constitution will not exactly suit the case. The Republic laid down the right of each citizen to his share in the government of the country as a

Figure 11.2. *Porter and Baker in Mexico*, in Edward B. Tylor, *Anahuac* (1861), p. 54.

universal law . . . making, it is true, some slight exceptions with regard to red
and black men. The Mexicans, or at least the white and half-caste Mexicans,
will be a difficulty. Their claims to citizenship are unquestionable if Mexico
were made a State of the Union; and, as everybody knows, they are totally
incapable of governing themselves . . . [M]oreover, it is certain that
American citizens would never allow even the whitest of the Mexicans to be
placed on a footing of equality with themselves. Supposing these difficulties
got over by a Protectorate, an armed occupation, or some similar con-
trivance, Mexico will undergo a great change. There will be roads and even
rail-roads, some security for life and property, liberty of opinion, a flourish-
ing commerce, a rapidly increasing population, and a variety of good things.
Every intelligent Mexican must wish for an event so greatly to the advantage of his country . . .[15] As for ourselves individually, we may be excused for
cherishing a lurking kindness for the quaint, picturesque manners and customs of Mexico, as yet un-Americanized; and for rejoicing that it was our
fortune to travel there before the coming change, when its most curious
peculiarities and its very language must yield before foreign influence.[16]

Tylor's Mexicans were in most respects an unenlightened people.
Mexican schooling was dominated by an obscurantist and corrupt church
(Tylor mentions the case of a priest who was a highwayman, and discusses
the laxity of priestly mores).[17] The legal system gave no protection to ordinary citizens, who were at a structural disadvantage with respect to soldiers and priests. The population avoided paying taxes because the government was ineffective. The country as a whole was in the hands of
gamblers and adventurers, and Mexican jails offered no prospect of reforming prisoners.

Ethnologists and historians of the period must have been struck by the
Mexican government's incapacity to control the connections between the
nation's past and its future, a fact that is demonstrated by Tylor and
Christy's activities as collectors of historical trophies, but even more potently by Tylor's remarkable description of Mexico's national museum:

> The lower story had been turned into a barrack by the Government, there
> being a want of quarters for the soldiers. As the ground-floor under the
> cloisters is used for the heavier pieces of sculpture, the scene was somewhat
> curious. The soldiers had laid several of the smaller idols down on their
> faces, and were sitting on the comfortable seat on the small of their backs,
> busy playing at cards. An enterprising soldier had built up a hutch with
> idols and sculptured stones against the statue of the great war-goddess
> Teoyaomiqui herself, and kept rabbits there. The state which the whole

Figure 11.3. *Hon. William H. Seward Traveling in Mexico,* in Evans (1870), p. 18.
A characteristically uncritical representation of American power in the period.

place was in when thus left to the tender mercies of a Mexican regiment
may be imagined by any one who knows what a dirty and destructive animal a Mexican soldier is.[18]

Mexican anthropology has had multiple births: the writings of the
sixteenth-century friars, and especially of Bernardino de Sahagún, are frequently cited, but so are those of Creole patriots and antiquarians writing
in the seventeenth and eighteenth centuries, or the foundation of the
International School of American Archaeology and Ethnology in 1911 by
Franz Boas, and the creation of the first department of anthropology by
his student, Manuel Gamio, in 1917.[19] *Anahuac* represents an unacknowledged, but not a less important, point of origin, for Tylor's first book was
the sort of travel narrative that anthropologists, including Tylor himself,
tried to trump with the scientific discipline of anthropology, retaining the
sense of discovery and of daring of the genre while reaching for systemati-
zation and emotional distance.[20] For Mexican intellectuals, however,
*Anahuac* named the unspeakable but omnipresent nightmare of racial dismemberment, national disintegration, and the shameful profanation of the
nation's grandeur by the state itself. *Anahuac,* in other words, is a work that
both British and Mexican anthropologists would write against. As in a
Freudian dream, the primal scene has been carefully hidden, but the devel-

opment of anthropology in Mexico (and, indeed, in Britain) was to a significant degree shaped by the negative imprint of this book and others like it.

After the publication of *Anahuac*, things in Mexico took a different turn than the one that Tylor had envisioned. Instead of being invaded by the United States, Mexico was occupied by France, which made the best of the American Civil War to regain a foothold on the continent; and, although Tylor was not entirely wrong in thinking that a number of Mexicans would welcome the intervention of a great power, civil strife and resistance against the French proved stronger than he had anticipated, and the turn of world events frowned upon Mexico's second empire. After its "second independence," however, Mexico had yet to show that it was a politically viable country, a country that was capable of attracting foreign investors, a country that could embrace progress.

One important move in this direction is a book written by Vicente Riva Palacio and Manuel Payno, both of whom would later lead the manufacture of a new history of Mexico.[21] *El libro rojo* (The red book) (1870) was among the first of a series of lavishly printed and illustrated volumes of the final third of the nineteenth century. It is a brief history of civil violence in Mexico, told by way of an illustrated look at executions and assassinations, much as if it were a book of saints. *El libro rojo* is remarkable for its ecumenical reproach of civil violence. Illustrated pages are dedicated equally to Cuauhtémoc and to Xicotencatl (Indian kings who fought on

Figure 11.4. *Dolce far niente*, unsigned etching from Felix L. Oswald, *Summerland Sketches, or Rambles in the Backwoods of Mexico and Central America* (Philadelphia, 1880), p. 185. The image of a lazy and obscurantist church was a staple of anglophone writing on Mexico from the time of Thomas Gage's work in the seventeenth century to the writings of Edward B. Tylor and beyond. Here the priest's siesta illustrates Oswald's observations on Mexico in the 1870s.

Figure 11.5. *Statue of the Mexican Goddess of War (or of Death) Teoyaomiqui* (1861), in Edward B. Tylor, *Anahuac,* p. 221. Soldiers used this stone to build a rabbit hutch.

opposite sides during the Conquest), to conquistador Pedro de Alvarado and to the Aztec emperor Moctezuma, to Jews who were burned by the Inquisition and to priests who were massacred by Indians, to marooned African slaves and to a Spanish archbishop. Even more remarkably, the pantheon of martyrs includes heroes on alternate sides of Mexico's civil struggles of the nineteenth century: Father Hidalgo and Iturbide; the liberals Comonfort and Melchor Ocampo, and the conservatives Mejía and Miramón. Even Maximilian of Hapsburg, who had been executed by the still-reigning president, Benito Juárez, was given equal treatment.

El libro rojo sought to shape a unified Mexico by acknowledging a shared history of suffering. Ideologically, this was the course that was later taken under General Díaz (1884–1910).[22] El libro rojo was primarily directed to unifying elites, as is shown by the book's guiding interest in state executions, rather than in the anonymous dead produced by civil strife or exploitation. The unification of elites involved taming the nation's war-torn past and projecting this freshly rebuilt past into the present in order to shape a modernizing frontier. It is therefore not surprising that the pacification and stabilization of the country that followed slowly after the French intervention required the services of an enlightened elite, which came to be known as the científicos, in order to shape Mexico's image.

This is the subject of detailed work by Mauricio Tenorio-Trillo, in his book Mexico at the World's Fairs and elsewhere. I will illustrate the kind of work that was accomplished by this intelligentsia by referring to a book that was published in English and French by Justo Sierra and a team of illustrious científicos in 1900, Mexico: Its Social Evolution. This work is of special interest not only because Sierra was such a prominent and influential figure in Mexican culture and education, but also because it was printed especially in foreign languages, and its lavishly produced illustrations seem to answer point by point the negative comments and images of Mexico offered by Tylor and other travelers.

The first, most fundamental strategy followed by Sierra's team was to make Mexico's evolution comprehensible and parallel to that of France, Britain, or the United States (that is, to readers of French and English). Thus, the names of the authors and historical personages were anglicized, from "Jane Agnes de la Cruz" to "William Prieto," and parallels between Mexico's evolution and that of the civilized world were explicitly or implicitly established. Carlos ("Charles") de Sigüenza y Góngora is placed alongside Isaac Newton, Río de la Loza is followed shortly by Auguste Comte, and photographs of museums, hospitals, and courthouses built in Victorian or the latest Parisian styles were displayed on page after page. This mimetic strategy was common among Mexico's elite literary and scientific circles of the Belle Epoque, but it is taken up in a punctual manner by Sierra, who endeavors to show that each of the hallmarks of progress exists in Mexico.

Tylor complained of the state of abandon of Mexican education and its subordination to a retrograde church; Justo Sierra provided discussions of the development of Mexican positive science. Tylor smiled ironically at the lack of attention that was given to Mexico's history and patrimony; Sierra shows the National Museum of Anthropology and the ways in which Mexico's once conflict-torn races have been neatly studied and organized in it. Finally, Tylor noted the arbitrariness of Mexico's government and the lack of justice and institutions of social reform. Sierra shows the rapid and impressive development of courts of law, of councils, hospitals, schools, museums, and prisons. In short, while Tylor spoke of a country that had been ravaged by revolution, Sierra's book spoke of evolution.

In this dialectic between Tylor's and Sierra's books one can catch a glimpse of the central role that anthropology has had in Mexico's history. In a rather simplified way, one could say that the international aspect of anthropology has the capacity to destabilize nationalist images of Mexico. Mexico's national anthropology has worked hard to curb these tendencies by imaging the parallels between Mexico's development and that of the nations that produce anthropologists who travel.

*Shaping Narratives of Internal Hierarchy, Organizing Governmental Intervention in the Modernizing Process*

In addition to shaping and defending the national image, Mexico's anthropology had from the beginning a role to play in the criticism and organization of internal hierarchies.

Even before the rise of any solid institutional framework for the development of Mexican anthropology, discussions and writings on race and on the historical origins of Mexico's peoples were constantly deployed in order to orient strategies of government. The *Boletín de la Sociedad Mexicana de Geografía y Estadística*, Mexico's oldest scientific periodical (founded in 1839), has many examples of this. Statistical and population reports that were drafted in the 1850s and 1860s often carried sections on race, for instance. Thus, Juan Estrada, in his report on the Prefectura del Centro of the state of Guerrero, says that "[O]f the 25,166 souls in the prefecture, 20,000 are Indians. However, what is painful is that the remaining 5,000 are not educated, nor do they refrain from uniting with the Indians in their designs to exterminate the Hispano-Mexican race."[23]

Figure 11.6. *The National Preparatory School,* from Justo Sierra, ed., *Mexico: Its Social Evolution,* tome 1, vol. 2, p. 480. Finely printed photographs of modern hospitals, laboratories, libraries, prisons, schools, courtrooms, town halls, and railroad stations fill the pages of Sierra's book.

In the same period (1845), the Constitutional Assembly of the Department of Querétaro gives a more nuanced account of the racial question in its state: "The wise regulatory policy of our government has proscribed forever the odious distinctions between whites, blacks, bronzed, and mixed races. We no longer have anything but free Mexicans, with no differences among them except those imposed by aptitude and merit in order to select the various destinies of the republic."[24] However, the authors go on:

> We would abstain from making this sort of classification [i.e., racial classification] were it not true that just as politics prefers to treat citizens as essential parts of the nation, so does economics prefer to consider their specific condition, not in order to worsen it but, on the contrary, to seek its improvement. Without a practical knowledge of the peoples [*los pueblos*], we cannot improve their civilization, their morality, their wealth, nor the wants that affect them.[25]

The congress then proceeds to discuss the qualities and deficiencies not only of Querétaro's three main races (Indians, mixed-bloods, and

Figure 11.7. *National Museum, Salon of the Monoliths*, from Justo Sierra, *Mexico: Its Social Evolution*, tome 1, vol. 2, p. 488.

Creoles), but also important distinctions within the Creole race according to levels of education. Thus, while the highest class of Creoles is circumspect, controlled, and similar to the ancient Spartans, the classes beneath them can be fractious.

Statistics supplied by the state of Yucatán for the year 1853 include detailed discussions of the relationship between race and criminality, showing that Indians are less likely to commit violent crimes than *castas* or Creoles, because the Indian race is belittled (*apocada*), either naturally or as a result of degeneration. Correspondingly, Indians indulge in petty theft, and they do so systematically: "The Indian steals. More than anything he is a thief, and this he is without exception, and in as many ways as he can. However, because of their petty nature, these thefts escape the action of justice, and so are not recorded in the annals of crime."[26] Statistics from the department of Soconusco in Chiapas in the same period divided local races into *ladinos*, Indians, blacks, and Lacandones.[27]

It is clear from these reports that there was not a fixed national system of racial composition, but that the races, and even to some extent the specifics of their character, varied substantially by region. Even Edward B. Tylor's classification of Mexican races reflects this, for although he foregrounds the relationship between Indians, half-castes, and Spanish-

Mexicans, he also mentions the black population in the Veracruz region, and divides Mexican Indians into three types: brown Indians, red Indians, and blue Indians. These "blue Indians," known in Mexico at the time as *pintos*, were the troops of general Juan Álvarez that had overrun Mexico City shortly before Tylor's visit, and they were "blue" because many of them had a skin disease that erases pigment in large patches.

One of the principal tasks of anthropology as it began to develop in the 1880s was to put order into these regional hierarchies of race and to tie them into a vision of national evolution of the sort that was so successfully displayed in Sierra's *Mexico: Its Social Evolution*. A key strategy for this can be found in Alfredo Chavero's work on pre-Columbian history in *Mexico a través de los siglos* (1888), a work that develops an evolutionary scheme for pre-Columbian history that implicitly organizes hierarchical relations between the races in the present.

Chavero describes Mexico's pre-Columbian past as if it had been waiting underground for his patriotic generation to bring it back to life. Throughout the ravages of colonial destruction and the revolutions of the nineteenth century, the colossal Mexican past slept under a blanket of soil:

> But our ancient history had been saved, and all that could have perished in oblivion shall today rise to our hands. Even if these hands be guided more by daring than by knowledge, they are also moved by love of country, a love that embraces the desire to preserve old memories and ancient deeds just as the great hall of a walled castle keeps the portraits of each of its lords, the sword of the conquistador and the lute of the noble lady.[28]

After claiming the possession of the noble treasures of the past for his country, Chavero proposed an evolutionary story for pre-Columbian Mexico. This story had blacks as the initial inhabitants. However, these blacks were weaker and less well suited to most of Mexico's environment than the race that expelled them from all but the torrid tropical zones: the Otomis. For Chavero, it is the Otomis who can be truly called Mexico's first inhabitants. However, the Otomis were not much better than the blacks: they were a population of troglodytes who spoke a monosyllabic tongue, a people that was contemporaneous with humanity's infancy:[29]

> Life in those days could be nothing but the struggle for sustenance. Families were formed only by animal instinct. Intelligence was limited inside the compressed crania of those savages . . . And just as nothing linked them to heaven or to an eternal god, so too did they lack any ties to the earth; there was no fatherland [*patria*] for them.[30]

Despite these unpromising beginings, the inferiority of the Otomis did not deeply scar the nation's pride. Instead, it actually proved useful to understanding contemporary racial hierarchies, for the Otomis initiated an evolutionary movement that culminated with the magnificent Nahoas, a race whose appearance was, according to Chavero, contemporaneous with that of the great civilizations of Egypt, India, and China. Moreover, the Otomis offer a valuable perspective from which to comprehend the condition of the Indians during Chavero's present, for the Otomis were the Indians' Indians: they were the conquered peoples of those who were later, in their turn, conquered. Because of this, they allow the Mexican to relativize the Spanish Conquest and to diminish its weight in national history:

> But did these first peoples acquire any culture? We are not surprised to find them degraded and almost brutish in the historical period. They were torn apart by invasions without receiving new life-blood [savia] from the conquerors, and inferior peoples descend and perish when they come into contact with more advanced people. We would be wrong to judge the state of the ancient kingdom of Mexico before the Conquest on the basis of our present-day Indians.[31]

In one stroke Chavero has established both the grandeur of the Mexican past and the key to comprehend its fall, and so has put aside the painful image that foreigners still projected of Mexico in Chavero's day. Mexico's prehistory and its contemporary moment mapped onto each other, they completed one another. The images of the Negro, Otomi, and early Nahoa races in figures 11.8a–c illustrate this point: whereas Chavero used archaeological pieces to portray the early Negro and Nahoa races, he relied on a drawing of a contemporary "Indian type" to portray the ancient Otomi. The contemporary "degenerate" Indian type maps onto and indeed substitutes for the missing image of the early and unevolved Otomi, just as the ancient grandeur of the Nahoa completes the image of Mexico's future as it is being shaped by the *científico* elite.

Moreover, there is a striking similarity between Chavero's description of the degraded Otomis and contemporaneous descriptions by foreigners of the Mexican Indian. For example, U.S. historian Hubert Bancroft wrote a diary of his travels to Mexico at the time when *México a través de los siglos* was in preparation, and he makes the following comment regarding the pervasive fears of U.S. annexation among Mexicans:

> But what the United States wants of Mexico, what benefit would accrue from adding more territory, what the nation has to gain from it I cannot

Figure 11.8a. *Cabeza gigantesca de Hueyápan,* in *México a través de los siglos,* vol. 1, p. 63.

fathom . . . If there were nothing else in the way, the character of the Mexican people would be objection enough. The people are not the nation here as with us; the politicians are absolute. There is no middle class, but only the high and the low, and the low are very low indeed, poor, ignorant, servile and debased, and with neither the heart or the hope ever to attempt to better their condition. I have traveled in Europe and elsewhere, but never have I before witnessed such squalid misery and so much of it. Sit at the door of your hotel, and you will see pass by as in some hellish panorama the withered, the deformed, the lame and the blind, deep in the humility of

Figure 11.8b. *Tipo otomí,* in *México a través de los siglos,* vol. 1, p. 66.

Figure 11.8c. *Cabecita de Teotihuacán,* in *México a través de los siglos,* vol. 1, p. 69.

debasement, half hidden in their dingy, dirty rainment as if the light of heaven and the eyes of man were equally painful to them, hunchbacks and dwarfs, little filthy mothers with little filthy babes, grizzly gray headed men and women bent double and hobbling on canes and crutches.[32]

In the face of these devastating impressions, Chavero and his generation strived to make Mexico presentable to the patriot, to make it defensible vis-à-vis the foreigner, and especially to attract foreign allies. The success of this great concerted effort of the Porfirian intellectual elite has been discussed by Tenorio-Trillo, who calls the team of Mexican intellectuals and politicians who pulled it off "wizards." This is perhaps not much of an exaggeration. Fernando Escalante has reminded us that during most of the nineteenth century, Veracruz, a town that was so plague-ridden that it was known as "the city of death," was nevertheless the favorite city of the Creoles, because going there was the best way to get out of country.

The special role of Chavero and other early anthropologists was to suggest a certain isomorphism between the past and the present. By creating a single racial narrative for the whole country, these anthropologists could shape the internal frontiers of modernization while upholding a teleology that made progress and evolution an integral aspect of Mexican civilization. Moreover, this strategy involved using history to moralize about the present, which was an immensely popular activity in Mexico that had significant grassroots appeal.[33]

The generation of Porfirian anthropologists would use this evolutionary theory as a frame for shaping Mexico's image, but revolutionary anthropologists would use it to intervene directly in native communities. The key figure in this development is Manuel Gamio, who was so successful that he is generally considered the "father" of Mexican anthropology. Because Gamio's story is well known, I shall only briefly recapitulate. Manuel Gamio met Franz Boas when the latter founded the International School of American Archaeology and Ethnology in Mexico City in 1910. Boas, as Guillermo de la Peña has shown, felt that Gamio was the most promising of the young Mexican scholars and invited him to do his doctoral work at Columbia.[34] Gamio also received support from Carranza's government even before its final triumph over Villa, and in 1917 he created the Department of Anthropology of Mexico's agriculture and development ministry. From this position, Gamio organized a monumental study of the population of the Valley of Teotihuacán.

In San Juan Teotihuacán, Gamio found a perfect parable for the Mexican nation. The valley of Teotihuacán was rich, but its people were poor; the ancient city was the site of astonishing civilizational grandeur, but the current inhabitants had degenerated as a result of the Spanish Conquest, exploitation, and the poor fit between Spanish culture and the racial characteristics of the Indians. Just as important, perhaps, the setting offered up the raw materials for the presentation of a national aesthetics, a strategy that had already been implemented by the authors of *México a través de los siglos* and the architects of Mexico's exhibit at the Paris World's Fair of 1889. This work is continued and deepened by Gamio, who attempts not only to extend the use of an Indian iconography in Mexican publishing and architecture, but also to adopt an indigenizing aesthetic for enlightened classes, and to bring a serious engagement with indigenous culture to bear on modern technologies in architecture and cinema.[35]

The elevation of traditional culture for the consumption of elite classes was a matter of some controversy and it was often disdained in the restored Republic and during the *porfiriato* (it can still be controversial today). For example, when a critic of 1871 described Guillermo Prieto's poetry as "versos chulísimos oliendo a guajolote" (beautiful verses that smell of the indigenous term for turkey), this was taken as an insult.[36] Gamio's involvement in the revalorization of indigenous culture was part of a long-term civilizational process for the Mexican elite. Unlike his Porfirian predecessors, however, Gamio felt that the role of the anthropologist was not only to present the past as a vision of a possible future, but also to intervene as the enlightened arm of government, as the arm of science that was best equipped to deal with the management of population, with forging social harmony and promoting civilization. Thus, for Gamio, the actions of the anthropologists were the actions of the nation itself. In a prologue to a booklet that published the international reactions to *La población del valle de Teotihuacán,* Gamio explains that he puts this compendium of flattering comments into print not as an act of self-promotion, but rather because *La población del valle de Teotihuacán* "is a collective work that has national dimensions." Moreover:

> The opinions and critical judgments not only praise the scientific methods that preside over the research brought together in this work and the social innovations and practical results that were obtained. There is also, in several of the most distinguished foreign judgments, the suggestion that a number of other nations follow Mexico's example in favor of the well-being and progress of their own people, a judgment that will undoubtedly satisfy the national conscience.[37]

On the other hand, the fact that Teotihuacán and the Department of Anthropology of the Secretaría de Agricultura y Fomento were both national symbols did not make them equal, for whereas Teotihuacán stood for the nation because of the wealth of its territory, the grandeur of its past, and its racial and cultural composition (which reflected a four-hundred-year process of degeneration), the Department of Anthropology was the head of the nation from which the promotion of civilization was to come. This is most potently brought home in the instructions that Gamio gave to his researchers before they began fieldwork in Teotihuacán:

> We then suggested to our personnel that they shed the prejudices that can arise in the minds of civilized and modern men when they come into contact with the spirit, the habits and customs of the Teotihuacanos, whose civilization has a lag of four hundred years. We advised that they should follow strict scientific discipline in the course of their actions, but that they should make every effort to temporarily abandon their modes of thought, expression, and sentiments in order to descend in mind and body until they molded to the backward life of the inhabitants.[38]

The pioneering works of Alexandra Stern have shown the connections that existed between the work of Gamio and other "mestizophilic" nationalists and the eugenics movement.[39] One of the aspects of this relationship that is pertinent here is that the view of the current population as degenerate, as having been made to depart from the best developmental possibilities of its race, went along with quite a challenging and revolutionary set of policies. Indeed, as a high government official leading an official project, Gamio had an interventionist role in local society that was entirely different from that of foreign anthropologists. By his recommendation, the government raised the salary of the area's four hundred government employees (mostly employed in the archaeological dig and in the various development projects that Gamio promoted) in order to nudge up the salaries that local hacendados paid their peons. Gamio had lands distributed to peasants. A new road, a railroad station, medical facilities, and educational facilities were built.

The combined power of an integrative scientific method, embodied in anthropology, and its practical use by a revolutionary government was so dizzying that Gamio compared the mission of the Department of Anthropology with the Spanish Conquest:

> We believe that if the attitude of governments continues to be of disdain and pressure against the indigenous element, as it has been in the past, their failure will be absolute and irrevocable. However, if the countries of Central and South America begin, as Mexico has already begun, *a new conquest of the indigenous race*, their failure shall turn into a triumphal success.[40]

Thus, the discontinuities between Gamio and Porfirian ethnohistorians or ethnolinguists such as Chavero or Pimentel are as interesting as their convergences: both believed in the degeneration of Mexican races after the Conquest; both believed in the grandeur of Mexican antiquities; and both placed their knowledge in the service of national development. However, the Porfirians did so mainly as part of an effort to present Mexico in the international arena, as a contribution to efforts to bring foreign migrants, foreign investments, and tourism to Mexico, whereas Gamio took these theses and applied them not only to shaping the national image, but also to the art of governing.[41] By doing field research, by creating his own, "integral," censuses, and by intervening in a direct and forceful manner in local reality, he could at once participate in the Porfirian imaging process and help fashion internal frontiers.[42] The similarities and differences between the two anthropological styles parallel the similarities and differences between the Porfirian and the revolutionary governments:

Figure 11.9a. *Tipo de hombre indígena del valle de Teotihuacán,* from Manuel Gamio, *La población del valle de Teotihuacán,* vol. 2, plate 41. These samples from a series of mug shots illustrate Manuel Gamio's concern with race and racial types. Gamio celebrated indigenous culture and *mestizaje,* but he shared the scientific establishment's concerns with racial degeneration.

Figure 11.9b. *Tipo de hombre mestizo del valle de Teotihuacán,* from Manuel Gamio, *La población del valle de Teotihuacán,* vol. 2, plate 48.

Figure 11.9c. *Tipo de mujer indígena del valle de Teotihuacán,* from Manuel Gamio, *La población del valle de Teotihuacán,* vol. 2, plate 50.

both were modernizing regimes that wished to portray the republic as being led by enlightened and scientific vanguards, but whereas the Porfirian regime placed its bets mostly on providing every possible convenience to foreign capital, the revolutionary governments tried to balance their efforts to attract foreign investors and their commitment to internal social and agrarian reform. This latter formula was seen in the twentieth century as the more attractive and desirable in Mexico.

## Consolidation of a National Anthropology

When the 1968 generation accused Mexican *indigenistas* of shaping a strictly national anthropology, Gonzalo Aguirre Beltrán was probably right to accuse them in turn of not having read the *indigenistas* closely.[43] Aguirre went ahead and named a number of cases of studies that had been done by Mexican anthropologists abroad; he could also have listed the active interest that *indigenistas* from Gamio and Sainz on showed in exporting Mexican anthropology to other locations. Nevertheless, one can still argue that the 1968 generation was correct on this point, for the anthropology that Mexican *indigenistas* exported was a national anthropology, geared to shaping connections between the ancient past, contemporary ethnic or race relations, and national modernizing projects. As the Mexican governments moved from the early proactive stages of the revolutionary period to institutional consolidation in an era of much industrial growth, the position of anthropology became at once more institutionalized and less capable of challenging the status quo.

The period that runs roughly from 1940 into the late 1960s is a time when a nationalist orthodoxy prevailed. This is also the time when most of the great state institutions that house Mexico's large professional establishment were built: the Instituto Nacional de Antropología e Historia (1939), the Escuela Nacional de Antropología e Historia (1939), the Instituto Indigenista Interamericano (1940), the Instituto Nacional Indigenista (1949), the National University's Sección de Antropología (1963), and the new Museo Nacional de Antropología (1964). The growing strength of the Mexican state and the institutional consolidation of anthropology, alongside foreign (principally U.S.) anthropologists' interest in alterity and the delicate position of American researchers in Mexico during the Cold War, are all factors that conspired to take the sting off of foreign anthropologists as harsh critics.[44] It is impossible to imagine the kind of candid commentary that we read in Tylor's book regarding, for instance, "what a destructive animal a Mexican soldier is" being published by a prominent United States, British, or French anthropologist in this period (which has rather revealingly been labeled the "golden age" of Mexican anthropology).[45]

Instead, foreign anthropologists sought mutually beneficial collaborations, or else they were as unobtrusive as possible. They worried about being able to pursue their research interests and about being able to send students to the field. Even so, the orthodoxy of Mexican official anthropology still faced an external challenge, a challenge that is endemic to the very proposition of a nationalized scientific discipline. In this period of industry and progress, the challenge of foreigners was threefold: they could uncover the dark side of modernization, in the tradition of John Kenneth Turner's *Barbarous Mexico*; they could adhere to the Indian and reject the modern; or they might further the political interests of their nations at the expense of the Mexican government. I will briefly exemplify how these dangers were perceived in this period by examining two incidents.

In December 1946, President Miguel Alemán had just taken office. University of Chicago anthropologist Robert Redfield and two high officials of the Mexican government (Mario Ramón Beteta and Alejandro Carrillo) were invited to discuss the president's inaugural speech on Mexican national radio. The event generally went off without a hitch, except for a newspaper article attacking Redfield's position that appeared *La Prensa Gráfica*.

After reciting Redfield's impressive scientific credentials, Fernando Jordán focused on a question that Redfield had raised, which was whether the industrialization of Mexico would not carry with it a radical change in the mores of the Mexican people. Would industrialization not involve the standardization of indigenous cultures? Would it not diminish the beauty of a people that had well-defined ethnic characteristics, a people who gave great personality to Mexico? The radio host who was interviewing Redfield responded quickly that "the traditional moral structure of the Mexican people is so strong that not even three centuries of Spanish domination were able to change it in the least." However, Fernando Jordán reacted less defensively:

> If Mr. Smith, Mr. Adams, or any other tourist who had spent one month in our country had raised the same question, he would have reaffirmed the conception that we have of many of them. We would have thought him superficial and naive.
>
> However, the question was raised by Dr. Redfield, a professional ethnologist, a renowned sociologist, and author of a number of books about

Mexico and its aboriginal cultures . . . It is thus impossible to believe that Redfield's question was foolish or idle. But in that case, what does it mean?

In our view, it means several things at the same time: . . . that Mexico, for the scholar, only has a proper form when it is viewed through the kaleidoscope of native costume, dance, and through the survivals of pre-Hispanic cultures and the "folkloric" misery of indigenous people. But if this is part of Mexico, it is not Mexico itself, and it is not what our nation wishes to preserve.

Jordán is shocked that a famous sociologist could replicate the superficial opinions of a tourist, but he offers an explanation of Redfield's true motives:

> From another point of view, and given the trajectory of American anthropologists, Redfield's question can be interpreted in a different way. We feel that it expresses the researcher's fear of losing . . . the living laboratory that he has enjoyed since the days of Frederick Starr [another University of Chicago anthropologist]. He fears that he will no longer be able to vivisect the Otomi, Tzotzil, Nahua, or Tarahumara cultures. He trembles at the thought of seeing the Tehuana's dress, or the "curious" rags of the Huichol, being replaced by the overall that is necessary on the shop floor or the wide pants needed in agriculture. He is expressing his ideal of stopping our nation's evolution in order to preserve the colorful misery of our Indians, a misery that will provide material for a series of books—most of which are soporific—in which the concept of culture will be represented by a set of isolated and static "ethnic" attributes that have no relation to the Indian's dynamism.

The foreign anthropologist is interested in exoticizing Indians, in maintaining Mexico as a kind of laboratory or ecological preserve, and not in solving the country's pressing social and economic problems. As such, his opinions and research ideals should be rejected in favor of a more interventionist approach, an approach that is committed to modernization and social improvement. Foreign interest in traditional cultures is welcome insofar as it explores the roots and the potential of the Mexican people, or insofar as it adds its efforts to the practical guidelines set by governmental projects, but when foreigners begin to value the traditional over the modern, what we have is a pernicious form of colonialism.

We should note that Fernando Jordán's own implicit program for the Indians (and this was a journalist who studied anthropology in the National School and was favoring President Alemán's modernization program) denies anthropology as Redfield understood it. The "internal colonialism" of

Figure 11.10. *Untitled photograph of a Maya woman,* by Frances Rhoads Morley, from Robert Redfield, *The Folk Culture of Yucatan,* 104. This portrait of indigenous beauty is the kind of romanticization that Fernando Jordán objected to. It was also a source of friction between Robert Redfield and Oscar Lewis in their diverging portrayals of Tepoztlán and of poverty.

Mexican anthropology could not uphold diversity over progress, whereas the postcolonial U.S. or European anthropologist could not intervene directly in Mexico, and thus had a vested interest in diversity. National anthropology and metropolitan anthropological traditions relied on each other, but they also denied each other. Thus Gamio could not be a true cultural relativist like his mentor Franz Boas and still retain his brand of applied anthropology, nor would Boas fully approve of the bewildering variety of applied projects that Gamio liked to juggle. As a result, the degree of mutual ignorance that is tolerated between these traditions generally, and between Mexican and U.S. anthropologies in particular, rests on epistemological conditions that run deeper than mere patriotic rejection or language barriers.

For example, after the publication of the Spanish-language edition of *Five Families* in 1961, Oscar Lewis remarked:

> Some of the [Mexican] reviews [of *Five Families*] seem excellent to me and others very negative. But even in the good ones I feel there is some resentment of the fact it was a North American, a gringo, who has acquainted the world, and even Mexicans, with a little of the misery in which so many families live.
>
> I regret it very much if I have offended some Mexicans with my work. It was never my intention to hurt Mexico or Mexicans because I have so much affection for them . . .
>
> Many times I have suggested that it would be good if some Mexican anthropologists would be willing to leave their Indians for a while and come to my country to study the neighborhoods of New York, Chicago or of the South. I have even offered assistance in getting grants for them.[46]

Nevertheless, the project of Mexicans studying the United States has not yet come to fruition. The very idea of a national anthropology runs against it: what would a book by a Mexican on the United States be used for? Unless, of course, it were a book about Mexicans in the United States, or about American interests in Mexico. There is no public in Mexico, no institutional backing for this product, which would then be destined to be either an erudite curiosity, or worse, a Mexican anthropologist doing the Americans' job for them.[47] There was no possible symmetry of the sort imagined by Lewis in his well-meaning but also slightly disingenuous comment.

Thus, the threat of a scientific indictment of Mexican modernization by foreign scientists remained, and Mexican reactions to the publication of Oscar Lewis's *Children of Sánchez* (1964) were even more severe than they were to *Five Families*. In a letter to Vera Rubin, Lewis summarized the attack that the Sociedad Mexicana de Geografía y Estadística mounted against his book:

1  The book was obscene beyond all limits of human decency;
2  The Sánchez family did not exist. I had made it up;

3   The book was defamatory of Mexican institutions and of the Mexican way of life;

4   The book was subversive and anti-revolutionary and violated Article 145 of the Mexican Constitution and was, therefore, punishable with a twenty-year jail sentence because it incited to social dissolution;

5   The Fondo de Cultura Económica, the author, and the book were all cited for action by the Geography and Statistics Society to the Mexican Attorney General's Office; and

6   Oscar Lewis was an FBI spy attempting to destroy Mexican institutions.[48]

Much of the Mexican intelligentsia rallied to the cause of Oscar Lewis at this point, including some anthropologists such as Ricardo Pozas, who had been highly critical of *Five Families*, because they saw in the Society's attack the hand of the government trying to keep all eyes off of the destructive effects of Mexican modernization, that is, off of urban poverty. Nevertheless, Arnaldo Orfila, the great Argentine editor and then director of the state-owned Fondo de Cultura Económica, Mexico's most prestigious publisher, was forced to resign from his post, and Lewis published the third edition of *The Children of Sánchez* with a private publisher.

The implications of these two cases are clear. The whole set of views that in Mexico came to be called "officialist," and which more or less served to demarcate the limits of mainstream Mexican anthropology, had a tense relationship both with anthropologists who might romanticize Indians to the degree of rejecting modernization, and with those who studied the wrong end of the acculturation process, that is, the unhappily modernized end. If the anthropologists doing the work were American, then these tendencies were all the more menacing. Moreover, the rejection of these foreign works was also a way of reining in work done by Mexicans, work that could be seen as unpatriotic or as bookish and irrelevant. This was, in fact, pretty much what the official attitude to the 1968 movement boiled down to: student unrest was creating a poor image of Mexico abroad precisely at the time when the nation was on display, at the time of the Olympic Games.

*Conclusion: The Exhaustion of a National Anthropology?*

I began this chapter by noting the sense of estrangement, of being condemned to eternal repetition, that has surfaced on occasion in recent

Figure 11.11. *The Sánchez Family*, in Oscar Lewis, *Five Families*, p. 213. The Sánchez family opens a vista to the underside of modernization: crowded living, unhygienic conditions, promiscuity, and the disaggregation of communities.

years—the sense that anthropology in Mexico is destined to take its place inside a government office, regulating the population, writing the governor's speeches, or presenting a dignified face for the tourist; the sense that Mexican academic anthropology will always be confined to its preexisting public, to a national public that cares only about the solution to the "Great National Problems"; the uneasy feeling that nags the student of Mexican anthropology when she realizes that Francisco Pimentel was a high official in Maximilian's court, that Alfredo Chavero was the president of the Sociedad de Amigos de Porfirio Díaz, that Gamio was the founder of the Departamento de Asuntos Indígenas, undersecretary of education, and director of the Instituto Indigenista Interamericano, that Caso was founding director of INAH and ENAH, that Aguirre Beltrán was director of INAH, that Arturo Warman is Minister of Agrarian Reform . . .

This atavistic sensation is, nonetheless, to some degree a false one. There is a useful corollary of Marx's *Eighteenth Brumaire* that I think can be usefully applied here, which could be something like "moins ça change, moins c'est la même chose" (the less things change, the less they remain the same). The pattern of absorption of Mexican anthropology by the state is in some respects quite different today from the times when anthropology had a central role to play in national consolidation. The multiplication of state-funded anthropological institutions in the 1970s and 1980s seemed to respond more to the growth of the educational apparatus and to state relations with certain middle-class sectors than to the need for an-thropologists as technocrats. The existence of certain highly visible anthropologists in government masks the relative decline of the political significance of national anthropology for the Mexican state.

Moreover, in the stages that I have outlined, there is a distinct sense of exhaustion of the possibilities of the national anthropology paradigm: it began with the task of fashioning a credible national image that could do the work of harnessing the transnational machinery of progress. From there, national anthropology complemented this task with an active role in the management of the indigenous population (which in the early twentieth century could mean a concern with the vast majority of the na-tion's rural population). This development of the anthropological function gained much prestige from the revolutionary government's capacity to distribute land and to mediate in labor and land disputes.

The year 1968 marked a watershed for Mexican national anthropology because the student movement reflected a shift in the relative importance of Mexico's urban population. Correspondingly, the *magníficos* and others no longer called for absorbing Indians into the nation, but argued for a more theoretically inclined anthropology. In fact, each of the major mo-ments of Mexican anthropology, from the *científicos* to the revolutionaries, to the anthropology that blossomed after 1968, has involved a "theoretical inclination." Each has looked to the international field for inspiration or for authority, and intellectual leaders at least have had direct connections with the most prominent leaders of the international field. The apparent paradox, however, is that once theoretical inspiration is channeled into the national anthropology model, dialogue with the international commu-nity gets reduced to conversations with area specialists at best. However, as I have shown in detail, there are causes of substance that restrict the relationship between national anthropology and its metropolitan counter-parts, for the relationship between these two sorts of anthropologies has more often been one of mutual convenience than of true dialogue, because anthropologies that are devoted to national development must consistently choose modernization over cultural variation, and they must balance stud-ies of local culture with a national narrative that shapes the institutional framework of the field.

In 1968 there was momentary awareness of the conceptual and politi-cal confinement that was embedded in "national anthropology." However, *De eso que llaman antropología mexicana* was still, unwittingly perhaps, a version of a national anthropology: "Our anthropology has been *indigenista* in its themes. Even today it is conceived as a specialization in particular problems. *Indigenismo* is atomizing and it tends to interpret its materials in an isolated fashion [*en sí mismos*]. *Indigenismo has rejected the comparative method and the global analysis of the societies in which Indians participate.*"[49] By emphasizing the comparative method, these critics retained the sense of the national whole that was indispensable both to metropolitan traditions and to Mexican nationalist anthropology. They retained, in other words, the holistic premises that were later criticized by Appadurai and others. Not surprisingly, then, the final phase of Mexican national anthropology (1970s–80s) was an expansive moment that had a number of things in common with the heady days of Gamio, for the anthropology of those years had to reinvent a nation that no longer had an indigenous baseline but was still centered on taking command of projects of national development. The call to develop a holistic and comparative study of "the societies in which Indians participate" was therefore just as prone to the vices of bureaucratization, theoretical sterility, parochialism, and co-optation by the state as *indigenismo* had been. Today there is no longer a viable way of isolating the nation as the anthropologist's principal political and intellectual object, and Mexican anthropology has to diversify its communitarian horizons and reinvent itself.

# 12

## Provincial Intellectuals and the Sociology

## of the So-Called Deep Mexico

In an eloquent book that quickly became Mexico's best-selling anthropological work, *México profundo* (1987), Guillermo Bonfil portrayed Mexican reality as an overlay of two opposed civilizations: a subordinated civilization that stems from the millenarian agrarian culture of Mesoamerica and that has a variegated set of locations and permutations in contemporary Mexican society, and another, Western and capitalist, civilization. Bonfil explored the characteristics of the Mesoamerican tradition in the contemporary setting, usefully disturbing categories such as *Indian* and *mestizo*, and then proceeded to show how that civilization has been shut out or marginalized from Mexico's dominant civilizational scheme. His book calls for the reassertion of the Mexican tradition in the critical contemporary moment, and thus his analysis feeds directly into today's political debates.

My argument with Bonfil's book is not merely academic. The image of a deep versus an invented Mexico is a key trope in a specific kind of nationalist language that stems from a justified rejection of the social and cultural impact that multinational capital has had on Mexican society. Despite the ample justification for a nationalist reaction to current trends in Mexico, however, the "deep" versus "artificial" imagery stands on very shaky sociological ground and therefore is an ineffective political alternative, despite its obvious ideological appeal.

There is a sense in which Bonfil's civilizational approach is merely a re-fashioned inversion of the modernist trope of tradition versus modernity, sharing premises with formulations such as "the Chinese road to socialism" or "the Japanese way to progress." It can be read as a call for pragmatic accommodations between local forms of social organization and grand strategies for progress and industrialization, while it simultaneously claims the moral preeminence of the local tradition over the grand narratives of capitalism and socialism. From an analytic perspective, however, Bonfil does not offer a detailed formulation of the dialectics that have existed between so-called tradition and modernity since the inception of a modern mentality in the late eighteenth century or since the inception of capitalism in the sixteenth century.

One worrisome consequence of this shortcoming is that the political application of the "deep versus invented" imagery must ultimately rely on a system of refined discriminations wherein certain privileged subjects, usually nationally recognized intellectuals or politicians, are placed in a position of interpreting the true national sentiment. Because it cannot extract Mexico from the world capitalist system, the "deep Mexico" image tends to re-create or revitalize the sort of authoritarian nationalism that was characteristic of the period of growth under import substitution, a nationalism that had many positive aspects, to be sure, but that is bankrupt as a viable political formula today.

However, the very ease with which I have formulated this criticism may obscure the intuitive appeal of the imagery of a deep versus an invented Mexico, an appeal that undoubtedly stems from the ascertainable fact that large sections of Mexico's population are and have historically been shut out of the national public sphere. They have been "muted," and are correspondingly absent from the dominant forums of political discussion and public debate and have little access to the media of publicity. These forms of exclusion have been denounced both as a rather subtle form of racism and as internal colonialism.

In sum, "deep" and "artificial" are images that re-create an obsolete and unpromising form of nationalism, while at the same time they are at least successful in indicating and denouncing profound rifts in Mexican society. The question is, how can we provide a well-grounded sociology of these processes of political and communicative exclusion? Conceptually, the challenge that we face involves understanding the ways in which the national space is articulated, both politically and culturally: the various and diverse forms of political representation and discussion that exist in different sorts of places and the major transformations that regional and national systems have undergone.

I propose to meet this challenge by focusing in this chapter on the geography of two interconnected social categories: intellectuals and public spheres. Specifically, I wish to exemplify how a fine-grained analysis of the dynamics of cultural distinction in a small region helps us to understand the ways in which local publics are articulated to a national public. Intellectuals and forms of public discussion depend on and reflect the geography of cultural distinction, and by studying their nature and contexts we can understand why some social groups have no voice in national public opinion. It is only by specifying these mechanisms that we can at once criticize the current political and social system and avoid a simple primordialist nationalism that offers little promise of efficacy and many political dangers.

I shall interrogate the history of distinction and community representation in localities from the *municipio* of Tepoztlán, Morelos, that, because of their varying size, location, economy, and position in the state's administrative hierarchy, represent different niches of Morelos's regional political economy.

By looking at the historical development of those communities' internal mechanisms of representation, I hope to help develop the rudiments of a geography of intellectuals in Mexico's national space.[1] I have chosen a rural and semiperipheral area to initiate this geography, because in such regions one can discern the contexts for the emergence of persons who can articulate local sentiment to state discourses and vice versa. In small towns it is also easy to specify some of the difficulties that aspiring intellectuals face in that process.

## *Definitions*

I wish to begin by clarifying my usage of two terms: *public sphere* and *intellectuals*. For the first term, I quote from an article by Geoff Eley who, following Habermas, says:

> By "the public sphere" we mean first of all a realm of our social life in which something approaching public opinion can be formed. Access is guaranteed to all citizens. A portion of the public sphere comes into being in every conversation in which private individuals assemble to form a public body. They then behave neither like business or professional people transacting private affairs, not like members of a constitutional order subject to

the legal constraints of a state bureaucracy. Citizens behave as a public body when they confer in an unrestricted fashion—that is, with the guarantee of freedom of assembly and association and the freedom to express and publish their opinions—about matters of general interest. In a large public body this kind of communication requires specific means for transmitting information and influencing those who receive it. Today newspapers and magazines, radio and TV are the media of the public sphere.[2]

As for the second term, I have found Max Weber's definition of intellectuals to be the most useful for my purposes here, for Weber once defined intellectuals as "a group of men who by virtue of their peculiarity have special access to certain achievements considered to be 'culture values,' and who therefore usurp the leadership of a 'culture community.'"[3] Thus we are concerned with two dimensions: the representation of communities, and the cultural values that can be sufficiently difficult to acquire and sufficiently important to authorize one individual's representation while disauthorizing another's.[4]

Because intellectuals as we define them here are concerned with the representation of communities by virtue of specific culture values, an understanding of local-level intellectuals necessarily requires a look at local systems of class and cultural distinction. I will discuss localities that correspond roughly to two major types of places in the region of Morelos: the village of Tepoztlán, which was until recently a peripheral agricultural town and is a seat of municipal power (*cabecera*); and the hamlets of Santo Domingo, Amatlán, and San Andrés de la Cal (all of the *municipio* of Tepoztlán), which are small nucleated villages that surround the municipal *cabecera* and that were, until recently, occupied almost exclusively by peasants and farm laborers. I begin with a discussion of the hamlets, and will proceed from there to the municipal seat.

### Intellectuals and the Representation of Community in Morelos: The Hamlets

For most of their colonial and modern history, inhabitants of the hamlets in the *municipio* of Tepoztlán have been part of a single class, of a single culture. During the whole colonial period, there were no economic elites in the hamlets.[5] Inhabitants were peasants; they were also involved in animal husbandry and in selling wood to nearby haciendas and ranches. Villagers paid tribute to the Marquesado del Valle, and for some years also sent workers to the mines at Taxco and Cuautla under the *repartimiento* system of corvée labor. Local land bases were meager, villagers were forced to rent land from Spanish hacendados or ranchers, and I have found not one Spaniard, or anyone using the title of "Don" or "Doña," registered in the birth, death, and marriage records found in the local parish (starting in the early seventeenth century and continuing with some interruptions into the mid-nineteenth century).

There was some basis for gaining greater prosperity in those communities through politics. The post of *alcalde* carried with it exemption from tribute payments, and there are documents that suggest that these *alcaldes* may occasionally have pocketed some money in their mediations with the *cabecera* and, particularly, in their organization of cooperative efforts for the *cabecera's* church and church festivities: some *alcaldes* paid villagers less than they in turn charged for candles and wax presented to the church, for example.[6] However, the most substantial cases of corruption in Tepoztlán's history all occur in the Villa of Tepoztlán and not in its dependent hamlets (*sujetos*).

In the hamlets, political bosses gained their positions because of their centrality in a kinship network: they were elected from and by the local elders.[7] They were thus centrally located and deeply identified with local society, and internal rifts probably reflected divisions between families who aspired to those central positions, much as they do today.

This situation changed only in certain respects with independence. Local inhabitants were no longer legally classified as "Indians" then. Moreover, starting in 1856 with the creation of the civil registry, people adopted Spanish last names en masse, and privately controlled plots of communal land were registered for the first time in 1857, and then again in 1909.[8] On the other hand, the political equivalent of the old Indian *alcalde* was now named by the municipal presidents to the post of *ayudante municipal* and received no remuneration.

Although we know little about the expansion of haciendas in early-nineteenth-century Morelos since John Womack's view was first contested, in the case of Tepoztlán there is evidence that haciendas encroached on the *municipio* shortly after independence.[9] In fact, the ejido land that was given back to Tepoztlán after the revolution in 1927 was a restitution for this postindependence land invasion. It is possible that hacendados of that period either wanted to force more laborers to work for wages or, quite simply, that they felt that the chaotic political situation at the national and regional level allowed them to get away with invading Indian communities. Thus, inhabitants of those villages that bordered on hacienda lands were possibly more land-hungry in the nineteenth century than they had been earlier.

On the other hand, internal community differentiation does not seem to have grown during this period. The registration of lands would seem to point to a tendency for a weakening of communal links in favor of the formation a "private sphere" and its corresponding inhabitant: the "citizen." This was, in any case, the liberal agenda behind policy changes. However, it is difficult to ascertain whether or not those changes had a significant impact either on community or on local society in the nineteenth century, for these villages were all highly endogamous, and there seem to have been communal policies not to sell local lands to outsiders.[10] Moreover, the registration of plowable lands as private property in fact simply formalized the arrangement that existed in the colonial period, while land that was not arable retained its communal status.

These policies were reinforced after 1927, with agrarian reform, when inhabitants of some of the hamlets received lands in restitution for what the haciendas had taken a century earlier. Communal tenure was also officially reinstated, and a new local official, the Representante de Bienes Comunales, was charged with overseeing an assembly that made all decisions concerning local communal lands. Resistance against selling large tracts of private lands to outsiders remains a factor even today, as land developers have discovered on more than one occasion.[11] In sum, the hamlets were socially quite homogeneous during the whole colonial period, and into the mid-twentieth century.

In the decades following the introduction of the first industries in the region, beginning in the mid-1950s, two new economic groups have emerged: out-migrants who retain local ties (returning either on weekends—if they live in Mexico City or Cuernavaca—or seasonally, if they are working in the United States or Canada), and political mediators who acquired new significance in the processes of connecting the villages to modern life (in the construction of the village's road, in bringing schools and electricity, etc.).

Major political divisions, which in the hamlets have always been linked to competition between major families, now pitted "conservative" factions—who sought to maintain communal land, forest, and water resources intact—against *progresistas* (or "modernizers"), who justified compromising some of these resources, or even consuming them entirely, in exchange for the advantages and comforts of progress and civilization.

These factions are common both to the municipal *cabecera* at Tepoztlán and to all of the hamlets. However, the specific connection between conservative and *progresista* factions on the one hand, and the history of cultural distinction on the other, was somewhat different in the hamlets than in the municipal seat, and this was reflected in the issue of intellectuals and the intellectual representation of communities.

There are no known local intellectuals from these villages for the preindustrial period. Schoolteachers who worked on and off in these places were hired irregularly by local families and stayed even more irregularly. Starting in the 1950s, the villages began producing a few schoolteachers of their own. However, the ministry of education's placement policy works against hiring natives in local schools—at least in the early stages of a teacher's career. None of the hamlets ever had a resident priest, and the posts of *ayudante* and—after 1927—of communal lands representative were not particularly associated either with literacy or with intellectual leadership (although reading was always an asset), but rather with social centrality within the hamlet or with personal ties to Tepoztlán's municipal president.

We can understand a little more about the social spaces that were available to aspiring intellectuals in these hamlets by looking at recently generated ethnographic information. In the early 1980s, Santo Domingo was divided into two factions, one that had sided with a modernizing Presidente de Bienes Comunales, who had opened the communal forests to commercial exploitation in order to pay for the road that allowed motor vehicles and electricity to come up to the town for the first time, and the faction that opposed him.[12] Interestingly, these two factions were identified in spatial terms with two sides of the village, and each side was known by an animal name: the *tecolotes* (owls) were on the eastern side, and the *xintetes* (lizards) on the western side. The reasons why this factionalism between conservatives and *progresistas* could be made to coincide with a spatial division of the whole village can be found in the relations of kinship and patronage around the political leader—whose core of support was mainly near his own residence.

Now, up to this point, the category of "intellectual" would be very problematically applied in Santo Domingo: local cultural values were not susceptible to being controlled or monopolized. The people who had gained the respect of the entire community had done so on a strictly consensual basis, and they could not lord their knowledge over anyone without losing their capacity to represent that person.

In my own ethnographic work in the *municipio* in the late 1970s and the early 1990s, I learned that there is a discourse on "respect" that is often generated when one interviews a person; for, in interviewing someone, there is implicit acknowledgment of the other's authority. Many people who want to reaffirm their right to represent the community to the outsider, and especially to an educated outsider, begin or end their parley by saying something like: "In this town everyone respects me. That's because I respect everyone. Everyone knows me and greets me, and I greet everyone. There is no one who doesn't respect me," and so on. However, it sometimes happens that when someone else discovers who you have been talking to, he or she proceeds to discredit the individual in question and to warn you about taking him seriously. It is little wonder that Oscar Lewis's informants told him that Redfield's main informant had "a head full of air." I, in turn, have been told that Lewis's informants were pulling his leg, and I know that it has been said that I spoke too much with a man who is not even a "real Tepozteco." When authority is based on *respeto*, it is always consensual, and if an intellectual bases his or her authority exclusively on *respeto*, he or she will only very occasionally be successful in "usurping the representation of a culture community." An intellectual whose basis is strictly consensual can never be professionalized.

In the hamlets, positions of leadership and access to knowledge were limited to a certain circle of people, composed usually of married men, and often of married men with many grown brothers and sisters or children. Within those circles, however, the only roles that involved controlling cultural values that were not easily accessible to the whole age group were those of healer (*curandero*) and witch (*brujo*). Since the 1950s, schooling has become another way of acquiring some scarce cultural values, but schooling also tends to lead one out of the community and into skilled urban jobs or bureaucracies that have very few local institutional spaces.

Having good or evil powers over health and the body was traditionally seen as being available to people by one of two means: either one is born with a calling (it is said in Santo Domingo that a child who is born with a *morral*, or pouch, under her arm is destined to become a person of knowledge; twins too are believed to be born with these powers), or one could acquire power by revelation, either through possession by *los aires*, by touching lightning, or by ingesting psychotropic substances near a cave—where *los aires* dwell—and finding healing powers there. The knowledge that healers and witches have is thought to be revealed in dreams or in conversations with plants or spirits. In other words, there is no socially standardized route that leads to this position of knowledge.

Moreover, connections between the knowledge of *curanderos* and political power can be quite problematic: *curanderos* often try to disengage themselves from local infighting for fear that they may eventually be isolated as witches. This is probably why it is so common in the Mexican countryside to find people claiming that they have *curanderos* in their village, but witches are almost exclusively found in the town next door. On the other hand, in some factionalized villages, like Santo Domingo during the 1970s and early 1980s, *curanderos* identified closely with local factions, and witchcraft accusations flowed between them.

In other words, either *curandero* power is closely associated with political power and can be used as an instrument of it, or else the *curandero* seeks to be disassociated from political identification and use his or her knowledge for the benefit of any caller. If the *curandero* uses his art to gain worldly power, he will be called a witch by his political enemies and in this way his authority to represent the community gets subsumed under the power of a political faction. It is only in the second case, when the *curandero* renounces the active pursuit of political power for himself, that the *curandero* can become a successful local intellectual.

Because of the fact that curing is seen as a gift that is magically revealed, the whole organization of *curanderismo* as a system of knowledge is spatially simple and not amenable to building a bureaucratic or quasi-bureaucratic hierarchy: localities have one or more *curanderos*, whose power and effectiveness for both good and evil purposes are contrasted with those from nearby villages and hamlets. These *curanderos* are all members of the peasant community and they are usually not devoted exclusively to their curing powers: the money or species that they get from healing complements what they earn from farming, wages, or small-scale commerce.

There is a second level of healers who have regional, or sometimes even national and international, reputations. These healers sometimes live in larger towns, and they can charge very steep prices. A healer of this kind who operated in Yautepec in the 1980s, and who was much sought after by Tepoztecans, earned roughly the equivalent of three months of minimum wages each working day.[13]

These professionalized healers or witches have clients from the hamlets (people who were not cured by their local healer, or who mistrust the local healer because of his or her connections to possible enemies) or from other healers, as well as from their local cities and elsewhere. The greater degree of commercialization of their practices also tends to separate them from local politics: they have a clientele they cater to in exchange for money, and their sustained connections to local community factions are often tenuous.

In sum, the small peasant hamlets of Morelos traditionally had only two social roles that could successfully amass knowledge that was not available to everyone. One was that of the local politician, whose mediating position in the power network made him privy to information and news that was not necessarily accessible to all; the other was the healer or witch, whose powers are not believed to be reproducible at will, and who is confronted with a tough choice: either to subsume his or her powers under those of internal factional and political divisions, or to withdraw from political and factional affairs as much as possible.

Consequently, in these hamlets there has usually been a large extent of democracy in the form of town meetings and discussions—a firm basis for the representation of the collectivity—coexisting with a very narrow platform for the formation of professional intellectuals. Moreover, the values that need to be cultivated to gain respect within the community involve a kind of humility that limits the capacity of a respected man to serve an articulatory function for any extended period of time. Any attempt at monopolizing such a representation by an average person is susceptible to mockery and ridicule. Solemnity and respect at the community level are only achieved by representing group feeling in a low-key, unpretentious manner, because representation gained through *respeto* can be taken away at will.

Thus, the cultural homogeneity of the hamlets produced a kind of paradoxical effect: on one side, the hamlets had an inordinately open forum of local discussion and debate—as other ethnographers who have worked in these sorts of places have recognized;[14] on the other side, there is no local basis for any privileged intellectual representation of the community and, what is much worse, the cultural values that have been accessible to all in the village have not been the ones that allow access to the mediated national public sphere.

Because of this, the hamlets were always vulnerable to representations by individuals who had agendas that were not constructed in local public discussion. This fact, which can be glossed simply by saying that the hamlets had no local intellectuals who could effectively mediate between the local community and state or private institutions, had two sorts of effects. First, it made the inhabitants of the hamlets easily available to stereotyping by outsiders. Second, in the most recent period, following the industrialization and urbanization of much of Morelos, it has meant that newly educated individuals who reside locally can also indulge in this sort of appropriation.

For example, the hamlet of Amatlán now has an intellectual, a schoolteacher who married into the village and who has been the most active Nahuatl revivalist in town. Don Felipe has promoted the idea that the pre-Columbian priest-god Quetzalcoatl was born in Amatlán. There is a happy coincidence between Don Felipe's nativism, the regional promotion of tourism, and a local ethnic revival that has been produced by intensified economic dependence on cities and on wages, so his project has met with success.

Recently, Amatlán was officially declared by the state of Morelos to have been the birthplace of Quetzalcoatl, renamed "Amatlán de Quetzalcoatl," and now dons a polychromed cement statue of the god next to the town's basketball court. Don Felipe also sold a plot of land to an investor who built the village's first hotel and restaurant: "La Posada de Quetzalcoatl," which offers tours to visit a famous local *curandera*, traditional *temaxcal* baths, and a naturalist diet.

Not content with these accomplishments, Don Felipe teaches schoolchildren the Mexican national anthem in Nahuatl, and invented a "Fiesta de Quetzalcoatl" celebrating Quetzalcoatl's birthday, held on the last Sunday of May. When a friend of mine asked a young man about his participation in the fiesta, he undermined Don Felipe's legitimacy as a representative of local society by saying, "Oh, that's just 'la fiesta de Don Felipe'" (Don Felipe's fiesta).

In this example, we perceive the emergence of a system of internal cultural difference in Amatlán—a difference between those who are keyed in to local history as a way of refashioning the relationship of the locality to the national state (and thereby to tourism and other forms of investment) and those who are not. However, it is still the case that the local assembly and public sphere are politically connected to the outside through the *ayudante*, through schoolteachers, and through the communal lands representative, but they have no reliable quotidian mechanism for having their voices heard in the national or regional public sphere.

### Intellectuals and the Representation of Community in the Cabecera

This situation was never the same in agrarian political and market centers such as the village of Tepoztlán, which always had greater internal cultural distinctions than its politically dependent hamlets and, consequently, more of a platform for generating its own intellectuals. Because Tepoztlán was the seat of a pre-Columbian polity, it was made into an administrative center in the colonial period. Tepoztlán had an Indian governor, who presided over the whole jurisdiction (including the hamlets), as well as a convent that housed at least one priest and, until the mid-eighteenth century, several monks. In addition to this, the population density of the village and the availability of some land in the jurisdiction attracted Spanish settlers, of whom there appear to have been three or four families at any one time.[15]

Thus, in the colonial period, Tepoztlán had two axes around which cultural distinctions were organized: an ethnic axis (mainly opposing Spaniards and Indians), and an axis of wealth and power.[16] Indian governors in this area, as elsewhere in central Mexico, tended to come from a single family, in this case the Rojas family, which came to acquire a substantial amount of wealth in land, cattle, plows, horses, and houses. This family and a couple of others took on many markers of cultural and ethnic distinction: the richer members of the Rojas family spoke and wrote Spanish as well as Nahuatl, rode horses, lived in the center of town, married Spaniards, and adopted a Spanish last name as well as the titles of *Don* and *Doña*.

The question of last names is interesting for our purposes here, because the idea of lineage was crucial to Spanish notions of nobility and honor: being able to trace one's line back to a knight who warred with the Moors, who was a conquistador or early settler of New Spain, or who had on some occasion served Christendom was often critical for claiming noble status, and Spanish commoners who came to the New World sometimes transformed their place of origin into a last name that became the initial point of such a line.

In contrast to this, Indians in Tepoztlán did not bear last names at all, but rather were baptized with compound first names, such as José Diego or María Gertrudis, and these names were not inherited. Thus, when a census taker or a local inhabitant wanted to specify which José Diego was being referred to, the name of the plot on which his house was built was uttered: José Diego Limontitla, for example, or José Diego Tlalnepantla. However these house-sites could not function strictly as a paternal last name for the purposes of honor and lineage because—although the preferred form of residence after marriage is and was patrilocal—there always has been some neolocal as well as uxorilocal residence after marriage. In other words, the house name could not function as a reliable marker of lineage; indeed, the image of a line or lineage among most Indians was difficult to maintain.

Instead of this, there were large barrio families that were mainly but not exclusively connected through the paternal line, and communal—quasi-familial—identity at the level of the barrio or village was thereby enforced. Thus, if an Indian commoner left his or her own village he or she would have nothing but a given name—no family history, only communal history. The ensuing lack of familial honor was sure to disauthorize that person's speech and had the effect of blending the individual into an urban mass. One could not speak publicly if one was a "nobody." The voice of these villagers was therefore anchored sturdily to their position within the community; outside the village they were merely *indios*.[17]

This issue has been significant into the modern era, for when a peasant is asked to speak authoritatively by someone of a higher status, the response will sometimes be something like "I don't know anything, I have no education, I am foolish." In this light, Robert Redfield's division of the Tepoztecans of 1926 into two categories, *tontos* (fools) and *correctos* (proper people), is more informative than Oscar Lewis thought, for *tonto* in this context is someone who is not authorized to speak publicly, someone who is incapable of holding a cultivated conversation with an outsider, while *correcto* means well-mannered, and referred to people who had a status from which to converse with representatives of the state, foreigners, and so on.[18] In the colonial period, the possession of a last name often indexed this distinction.[19]

In contrast to the namelessness of the commoners, to their lack of position outside of the local community, some Indian governors sought to create a line, a mechanism of distinction that would allow them to reproduce their privileges transgenerationally. They thereby took on a last name and became *ladinos*, that is, they became deft at the ways of the Spaniards. Thus, the language of distinction through blood, honor, and civilization was also adopted within the indigenous sphere by the Indian governors, whose representation of the indigenous community, ironically, was founded on the Spanish notion of lineage.

The cultural values that these Indian governors controlled and used in order to represent the community lay precisely in their bicultural adeptness: their constructed Spanishness vis-à-vis the Indians and local Spanish society, and their constructed rootedness in the Indian community by way of the Spanish notion of lineage. Arij Ouweneel (n.d.), who has studied Indian governors in the Valley of Mexico, has found documents certifying lineage and family trees for these Indian governors.

Despite the paucity of our knowledge of the question of intellectual representation in the eighteenth century, it seems likely that there were no channels available for an institutionalized production of local intellectuals that might represent the community by virtue of their cultural values. All mediation was in the hands of the Indian governor, who was elected by virtue of his lineage and wealth and was not the representative of a "culture community." The only local intellectuals that could access privileged cultural values and use them to represent the community were either those listed in our discussion of the hamlets (i.e., the "respected man" and the *curandero*, with all of their intrinsic limitations) or the priest and the teacher.

However, in the colonial period, access to these latter offices was denied to Indians. Thus, the intellectual representation of the community toward the outside was monopolized by Creoles and Spaniards. The rest were mostly *tontos.*

Given all of this, it is easy to understand how and why open contestation of the representation of the community could lead to violence. In 1777, Manuel Gamboa, Tepoztlán's resident priest, decided to give limestone that had been collected by villagers in communal *faenas* to the priest of nearby Tlayacapan for his church. The women of the village, who felt abused by the priest on many counts, turned over the lime cart, provoking the priest into a rage that he vented by beating one of the women with his cane. This prompted Tepoztecan men into action, and was the spark of a rebellion that led to the destruction of much property and to several deaths. The lack of a communal voice that could authoritatively counter that of the priest made way for a violent confrontation. On the other hand, the presence of a priest (and of schoolteachers in some periods) meant that there was an authoritative voice that could represent the village, and this voice would be heard regardless of the assessment of Indian governors and of the villagers themselves, as is obvious in the trials that followed the rebellion. In these trials, Gamboa used his authoritative portrayal of the villagers as part of his defense: the Indians were idle drunkards, couples lived in sin for two years before getting married, they sold their children to pay their debts, and so on. Meanwhile, villagers were not asked or authorized to produce a counterrepresentation of themselves and their defense was limited to a series of accusations against the priest.[20]

In sum, Tepoztlán had a firm system of internal cultural and class distinction that contrasted with that of the hamlets. Tepoztlán also had intellectuals from early on, most importantly, its priests. However, in the colonial period, these intellectuals were outsiders, and so we get the same sort of cleavage we had in the hamlets between the authority of village public opinion and the authority of (external) intellectuals representing the village.

Independence brought some changes to this situation. Most important, the fusion that had been under way between the wealthy members of the Indian nobility and the local Spaniards seems to have been accomplished rapidly. Tepoztlán was socially and culturally divided into two groups: the common people (or "the vulgar class") and *los notables.* This latter term is interesting not only because it was the national term for prominent citizens, but also because it effectively fused the political preeminence of the old Indian political elite (who used to be known as *principales*) with the racial-cultural pretensions of the Spanish ethnic elite (that used to characterize itself as a class of *gente de razón*). The term *notable* implies both the political preeminence of a *principal* and cultural distinction of a *de razón*. In the 1860s, Tepoztlán's *notables* were a group of about thirty men and their households, all of whom belonged to six or seven families that descended both from the old Spanish and Indian elites.

These *notables* monopolized the function of political representation (municipal officers and distinguished members of the militia of this period), as well as at least some of the intellectual functions: local schoolteachers came from this group, as did the one or two Tepoztecan professionals who were trained during the *porfiriato*. Furthermore, although priests continued to come from outside the community, which was standard church policy, the church's policing and representative functions were much diminished by the latter half of the nineteenth century, and we find the priest acting in consultation with the *notables*; he becomes one of them.

In other words, in the nineteenth century we get for the first time a space for what could be legitimately called small-town intellectuals in Tepoztlán: the internal dynamics of distinction produced cultural values that could be controlled and used to "usurp the representation of the community." These values were by and large the inherited marks of civilization from the colonial era (literacy, urbanity), but they were now included in an ideology of progress that opened the way for a dialectic between community development and nation building.

The main intellectuals of nineteenth-century Tepoztlán belonged to the same Rojas family that had sired Indian governors since the seventeenth century. Shortly after independence, a Rojas was involved in helping the village organize litigation against neighboring haciendas that had misappropriated village lands. Literacy, the Spanish language, and membership in the local political class allowed him to represent the village to the outside in a move to protect its communal lands.

The second, and best-known, intellectual of the family was José Guadalupe Rojas, who was the village's main schoolteacher for about forty years, and who was centrally involved in giving shape to all of the "progressive" social events and organizations of the new positivist age, including educational church missions, cultural societies (usually named after national or state political figures of the time), and the publication of several short-lived periodicals.

José Guadalupe's brother, Vicente Rojas, was also a schoolteacher in the village's second school. His nephew Mariano became a teacher of

Nahuatl in Mexico City's National Museum in the 1920s and authored a short Nahuatl wordbook that is still in circulation. Another member of the family, Simón Rojas, was said to have been present at the signing of Zapata's Plan de Ayala.

It is significant to note that the role of many of these *notables* centered on the defense of the community against hacienda encroachment, as well as the defense of the community's political will and vote at the state level. In this regard, there is a collapsing of the interests of local intellectuals and local politicians that comes with independence.

This is owing to the fact that the local *notables* were by no means wealthy from a regional point of view, being vastly overshadowed by hacienda owners and rich merchants. Moreover, retaining control of the local political apparatus remained crucial for much of the local elite for, like the Indian governors before them, perks from control of the new municipal offices, including the possibility of appropriating communal resources, were a significant source of wealth and resources—as, indeed, they still are today.

The case of the teacher José Guadalupe Rojas helps to illustrate the dynamics of intellectual representation in this era for, although his diaries span a short period (1865–72), an important transformation occurs in his outlook during that period. In the early portion of the diaries, Rojas is continually redeeming the people. He sees the "vulgar class" as being composed basically of peace-loving people who wished to work in peace, and whose limitations (what we today would call their "culture") could be remedied through titanic efforts in education. This education was meant to pull the lower class out of its lethargy and ignorance: the habits of the vulgar class (including their language, which at this time was still Nahuatl) were markers of ignorance.

In 1869, a visiting priest who was on a cultural mission publicly asked Rojas to make simultaneous translation into Nahuatl for him. Rojas says that he was ashamed to have been put in this position, but that he complied. However, only one year later, Rojas decided to teach reading and writing in Nahuatl in his school, and generally began to emphasize the grandeur of the native culture and its noble position at the root of Mexican nationality.

This is an important moment in the history of local intellectuals for, until 1870, Rojas was still fundamentally inspired by the teachers and priests of the colonial period: representing the community to the outside, while trying to destroy its native culture. Starting with the movement for Nahuatl literacy, Rojas—and most local intellectuals who have followed him—became involved in a dialectic that rooted the local community in nationalist mythology while it invoked urban values (shared in the national public sphere) such as literacy and urbanity, both to redeem the community of its ignorance and to construct the intellectual's own social importance. This strategy is exemplified in a little event that Rojas recorded on January 29, 1865. The school's board had collected money to pay for prizes that were to be distributed to the students and the teacher at the end-of-the-year celebration. These collections were a financial burden for the members of the board, most of whom were poor (even when *notable*): the schoolteacher had gone several months without pay. The board met to discuss what prizes to buy, and, after careful deliberation (these deliberations being, as they were, taken as signs of instruction, morality, etc.), sent Juan José Gómez on a sixteen-hour hike to Mexico City to buy twenty-nine bouquets of artificial flowers.

This event epitomizes the cultural relationship between the country and the city, at least as it was seen from the intellectual's point of view. The prizes are flowers, which are very much a local product (Tepoztlán is full of flowers, all year round), made permanent through specialized work. Artificial flowers were, in this context, an urban commentary on flowers (and, metonymically, on Tepoztlán): they are worth re-creating, they are worth enshrining, they are worth cultivating. They are valuable. And this, more generally, is what local intellectuals set about trying to do to local traditions and culture. By taking a local product or value and elaborating it in the city, and by taking a local product that was so valued in the city that it was the subject of elaboration, Rojas was simultaneously building a link between the local and the national culture and constructing his own role as representative and mediator.

Like the villagers who authorize their speech by insisting on how much they are respected, Rojas too was preoccupied with being taken seriously. To say that an event had been solemn was, to him, the highest praise, and yet the fact that he persistently noted whenever solemnity had been attained suggests that his capacity to represent was fragile, and that laughter could shatter all his efforts and expose him to public ridicule—a fact that reflects the limitations of the authority of small-town intellectuals of this period.

In Morelos, the revolutionary outbreak of 1910 in some ways produced a temporary dissolution of local communities, but it also intensified regional intercommunication between what we might call the popular public spheres. This was achieved through media such as the *corrido* ballads that circulated throughout the region, through the publication of leaflets whose contents were shared in the same meetings where *corridos* were sung, and in the installation of a kind of peasant common law in Zapata's headquarters and camps that was then transmitted to the villages as common law.[21]

In the case of Tepoztlán, participation in this regional peasant public sphere was consolidated in the immediate aftermath of the revolution. Agrarian reform laws enshrined communal land tenure and led to the formation of regional peasant confederations. Moreover, the political legitimacy that Zapatismo attained in the 1920s, and the flight to Mexico City of a significant portion of the old cacique class, also strengthened peasant representation of their communities.

However, it was still certainly the case that the main tensions surrounding the intellectual representation of the community were between a faction of modernizers and the more humble "conservatives" who sought to retain communal independence from politics and from the outside world. In this region, the main novelties of the period were (1) that the postrevolutionary *progresistas* were now much more persuaded of Rojas's nativism than they had been in the past, because the idea of totally ignoring and depreciating the native culture was politically much less sound after the revolution than it had been earlier, and (2) that the local peasant assemblies had more power than they had ever had in the past.

I first encountered the local conservative perspective during field research in 1977. At that time, the dominant view of politics among the local peasantry was that there were three types of political actors: politicians (who were exploitative and lived off of other people's work and did not fully belong to the local community), *campesinos* (who lived in households, belonged to barrios and villages, and respected each other), and *pendejos*, or idiots, who took what politicians *said* at face value, and therefore lent themselves to their abuses.

In this view, the campesino was the only "clean" social persona available to a Tepozteco, for the campesino eats what he produces, minds his own business, and defends his communal rights. On the other hand, the only honest politicians are necessarily risking their lives. Martyrdom is the only ultimate proof of cleanliness in politics. Because of this, unless and until martyrs such as Zapata returned, the best form of political participation was believed to be collective revolt and resistance around the defense of specific rights.[22] Tepoztecans have revolted on many occasions against encroachment on communal lands, against state management of communal water, and against several urban development projects.[23]

Contrary to what occurred in most hamlets, the institutional basis for local Tepoztecan intellectuals grew significantly as early as the 1940s. Many peasants were able to educate their children, and a fair number of

Tepoztecan schoolteachers and—beginning in the 1960s—professionals returned to the village and forged some links of communication with the local peasantry, both because they belonged to that social group and by using the "artificial flowers" technique. Moreover, the decade of the 1930s was one in which peasant revolutionaries began to lose their grip on the Morelos state government, and increasing bureaucratization and professionalization set in. In this context, intellectual mediators were required to communicate between state bureaucratic agencies and local constituencies.

Beginning in the 1950s, the literati became aspirants to municipal power, and they effectively edged out peasants from the main municipal offices. This process was accomplished, no doubt, because university-trained Tepoztecans had a much better chance of knowing people in the governor's inner circle than peasants did, but it was also the result of pressure exerted by people within government in favor of naming only officials who were professionals, *preparados*. Peasants were believed to be incapable of managing the paperwork and the legalities of public administration.

As long as the position of the educated Tepoztecans prospered, which was until about 1980, the split between *correcto*-like local intellectuals and the peasant public sphere was largely maintained, although coexistence was usually peaceful, and alliances were often made to defend common interests. This was largely because the power base of the local peasantry—its control over communal lands and its privileged position in revolutionary nationalism—was maintained to a significant degree.

The situation of the local intelligentsia has changed since that time for several reasons. On the one hand, the peasantry has been in a true state of siege. Planting has become too expensive. Work options as wage laborers in Tepoztlán (in the construction industry, in gardening, and in housekeeping), or in Cuernavaca, Mexico City, the United States, and Canada, have become increasingly important, even to educated Tepoztecans. Land prices have skyrocketed along with tourism and with the suburbanization of Tepoztlán, making selling very attractive and buying back almost impossible, and the legal framework for local communal tenure is now threatened.

On the other hand, teachers' salaries have plummeted and competition between local professionals has intensified, so that pressure on the local and state government from these sectors is increasingly unmet. As a result, in the 1980s, Tepoztlán got its first full-time journalist, who began writing a biweekly column on Tepoztlán in a Cuernavaca paper, and who had a local weekly significantly called *El Reto del Tepozteco* (the challenge of El Tepozteco). This name contrasts with the names of various previous, very short-lived periodicals such as *El Grano de Arena* or *El Tepozteco*, because whereas earlier leaflets stressed only that Tepoztlán was a microcosm of the nation (like a grain of sand), and that it could stand for the native roots of the nation, *El Reto del Tepozteco* makes these native roots (symbolized by El Tepozteco) into a political challenge (*reto*).

Tepoztlán has today become divided between two political parties. Conservative peasants, such as the current representative of communal lands, complain that the people have become divided, forsaking community and peasant livelihood and dignity for a factionalism that reflects national politics and national interests.

## Analysis

By looking at two different types of settlements in the *municipio* of Tepoztlán I have argued that the existence of small-town intellectuals, their nature, and their connections to both local politics and the national public sphere can be appreciated by inquiring into the history of distinction in these localities, and by connecting the mechanisms of cultural distinction to the policies of the state.

The contrast between Tepoztlán and its surrounding hamlets unfolds in the following manner: Because of its position as the administrative center of an indigenous jurisdiction, colonial Tepoztlán had a relatively powerful Indian nobility that was absent in the villages. Tepoztlán also had a resident priest, several Spanish families, and an occasional schoolteacher, all of whom promoted a complex system of internal cultural difference, which nonetheless could produce no local intellectuals. This was because (1) community cultural values were easily accessible to all adult men, (2) some cultivated values could not serve as a basis for community representation because they were banned by the church, and (3) the niches that could be occupied by intellectuals—that of priest and that of teacher—were off-limits to Indians.

The hamlets of the *municipio* had no such system of internal cultural and class difference, and, owing to that very fact, they had no way of generating intellectuals who could effectively articulate local opinion to influence Spanish policy. In both cases, then, one found political mediation, which relied on state power, serving also as the main form of cultural mediation.

After independence, the situation changed. Tepoztlán's cultural and politico-economic elite became unified, and this allowed for the emergence of the first truly local intellectuals. In the hamlets, the lack of an internal economic or cultural elite, as well as of local schoolteachers or priests, meant a prolongation of the rift between local public opinion, which was in certain respects formed quite democratically, and the national or regional spheres of discussion, deliberation, and policy formation. Liberal policies tried to change this situation by doing away with communal lands, and the institution of surnames and the registration of private property signal some degree of success in these policies. However, in the *municipio* of Tepoztlán, the erosion of the communities was not successfully completed by the end of the *porfiriato*, and the split described earlier was strongly reaffirmed with Zapata's revolution and its populist aftermath.

In the village of Tepoztlán, on the other hand, the nineteenth century spurred a new development of forms of cultural mediation. Whereas in the colonial period the priest was the utmost intellectual authority, and whereas in that era collective religious ritual was the main forum of mediation, nineteenth-century schoolteachers used nationalism and progress as the tools for building ties between the locality and state and private institutions. This explains why José Guadalupe Rojas, whose acts were initially comparable to those of a Spanish schoolteacher or priest, decided to take a nativistic turn and to identify the local popular culture with the nation's historical roots. His move has a family resemblance to the one that insists on seeing Mexico as divided into a "deep" and a "modern" country: in both cases, cultural and political marginality is equated to historical antecedence. Rojas, however, used his outlook as a modernizing device: position in the nation would strengthen Tepoztecan social life; Tepoztlán could claim such a position because of its pre-Hispanic roots, but the whole purpose of the claim was to modernize. This dialectic guaranteed a position for local intellectuals, because they could stand between national opinion and the local community, as indeed they still do.

There has been still one important change since the mid-1980s, though. The abundance of trained Tepoztecans combined with shrinking state resources and very significant transformations in the overall class composition of the locality led to factionalism within the professional classes. At that point, access to media became crucial, and this explains the revitalization of the local press.

*Conclusion: Intellectuals and Political Mediation in the National Space*

The historical analysis of the spatial fragmentation of Mexico's public sphere can be achieved by studying the ways in which culture communities have created or failed to create spaces for local intellectuals who can speak in and to the national public sphere and who are not themselves simply power brokers. This history is a complex one, but I suggest that there is a form to it, and that this form can be discovered if we look closely at the formation of regional cultures and back off from the homogenizing image of one deep Mexican civilization.

The postindependence project of creating a national public sphere, that is, a "media-scape" where civic opinion could be expressed, involved creating a unified cultural community where none existed. This is why Iturbide, who was Mexico's first national sovereign, complained that there was no Mexican public opinion, but rather a handful of diverse private opinions that claimed the status of being a national opinion. It is also why Iturbide felt that Mexican national sentiments were only truly expressed during popular uprisings. In other words, the channels for communicating between different local communities were extremely limited and accessible only to a few. People could only express their opinions effectively by force. The image of a "deep" Mexico, of a Mexico that finds no expression in either national political forums or in the mass media, can thus be traced back to independence.

In this chapter, I have developed the rudiments of a historical sociology of the silence that has characterized the relationship of certain sectors of the Mexican population and state institutions. The methodological premises of my analysis can be summarized in three points.

1   A geography of muteness needs to be developed to give well-pondered content to the "deep versus official" imagery. If such a geography goes undeveloped, the imagery necessarily devolves into the nationalist miasma that Iturbide and all of his successors were inextricably caught in.

2   Such a geography can be developed by analyzing the emergence of intellectuals in various types of communities or localities. It involves specifying the systems of internal cultural distinction that exist in each localized community, and then identifying the culture values that can serve as the basis for the formation of an intelligentsia that can aspire to represent the community.

3   The analysis also involves ascertaining whether the culture values in question articulate smoothly with those that prevail among intellectuals in the centers of national power, as well as with the state's culturally constituted idioms of representation.

When applied to the case of the municipal seat of Tepoztlán and to the hamlets of that *municipio*, these propositions yielded rich results. I would like to conclude by summarizing a few of them.

1　For long periods, the hamlets could only produce intellectuals by a kind of internal consensus that was formulated around a language of respect, whereas the municipal seat had a more sophisticated form of internal differentiation that fostered an intelligentsia from the very early colonial period on.

2　During the colonial period, the institutionalized positions for intellectuals in the village of Tepoztlán were all in the hands of Spaniards, and off-limits to the local population. Because of this, it is fair to say that a truly local intelligentsia with an institutional base did not emerge there until the national period.

3　Identification of local society with national culture became fundamental for the reproduction of local intellectuals during the nineteenth century, and it has remained critical to this day. The formula at which Tepoztecan schoolteachers arrived at was simple: local traditions are at the very root of Mexican nationality, but only the developed branches can instruct and extract the unpolished province from its sleepy backwardness. Local intellectuals were the needed mediators of this relationship: they rendered the image of the "deep Mexico" back to the urbanites, national intellectuals, and state officials who so esteemed it, and in return became effective brokers. The "deep" versus "artificial" imagery is therefore a favored trope of intellectual mediators, and it is a tool that has been used both to defend local culture and to argue for "progress" and modernization.

4　Despite the persistence of this formula of mediation, it has always had limited local appeal. Tepoztecans have at times disidentified both with the modernizing impulses of some intellectuals and with their insistent nationalist nativism. Don Ángel Zúñiga, a local intellectual who is devoting some efforts to teaching Nahuatl, has found more interest among middle-class urbanites who have migrated to Tepoztlán than he has among native Tepoztecos. Similarly, Don Felipe's celebration of Quetzalcoatl has received a range of responses, including a fair amount of apathy from many villagers. The fluctuations in the acceptance and fervor with which the projects of these intellectuals are embraced are a necessary object for future study.

5　The formula of the intellectual as the respected man is undoubtedly the one that has most internal appeal in peasant communities. However, it is this very democratic appeal, combined with the class and cultural chasm that divides peasant communities from urban centers, that guarantees an unstable, contested, and ultimately unroutinizable intellectual leadership.

Significant portions of the population of both Tepoztlán and its hamlets still have no voice as citizens. Instead, they are represented by political mediators and intellectuals whose negotiations with the government occur in a different language: no one should believe what politicians say, according to peasant conservatives. Instead of conversing with them, local constituencies have little choice but to engage in very pragmatically calculated transactions, where they receive certain resources or concessions in exchange for their voice.

The preceding discussion suggests, I think, that the term "silent Mexico" is more useful and precise than "deep Mexico." The silent Mexico has no historical priority over the rambunctious participants in the public sphere. Nor is it a root of nationality. It simply comprises the various populations that live beyond the fractured fault line of Mexico's national public sphere. This situation does not imply that these populations are marginalized from participation in state institutions; it means that they have no public voice. The "silent Mexico" is organized around certain systemic principles that can be perceived in the organization of cultural distinction in the national space.

# Notes

INTRODUCTION

1 José Limón, *American Encounters: Greater Mexico, the United States, and the Erotics of Culture,* 52–57.

2 A standard philosophical reference for this general point is Gilles Deleuze and Félix Guattari, *A Thousand Plateaus: Capitalism and Schizophrenia.* A detailed anthropological study that develops this criticism closely around a specific case is Lisa Malkki, *Purity and Exile: Violence, Memory, and National Cosmology among Hutu Refugees in Tanzania.*

3 Octavio Paz, *El laberinto de la soledad,* 13.

4 A nation-state is made up of a sovereign people, its state, and its territory. However, "a people" is not a stable entity, and neither are its connections to a state and territory. Ideally, the nation-state is a territory in which the inhabitants are communicated in such a way that they can concert opinions that give direction to government (this is called "the public sphere"). Government, in turn, is organized in such a way that it can rationally administer the entire population. Both of these imply spatial hierarchies that should, in theory, be isomorphic. Thus, the public should be smoothly integrated from local levels up to the national level, with no regard for class differences, while the national state should have an organized system of administration down to local levels requiring no additional mediation for the implementation of its authority. Finally, this unit as a whole needs to shape its representation in an international arena in such a way that foreigners and foreign interests operating in the national territory can be managed, and that national interests that reach beyond territorial frontiers are protected. *The national space is the intersection between the geography of the national public, the spatial organization of government, and the nation-state's situation in the international arena.*

5 See Dipesh Chakrabarty, "Provincializing Europe: Postcoloniality and the Critique of History," 337–57; and Harry Harootunian, *History's Disquiet: Modernity, Cultural Practice, and the Question of Everyday Life.*

6 Javier Garciadiego summarizes the driving aims of the National University's founder, Justo Sierra, as follows: "For don Justo the aim of the new institution was the integral education of the students and not only the advance of science, a fact that distanced him from the positivists. Moreover, the university should devote much attention to the social reality of the country" (*Rudos contra técnicos: la Universidad Nacional durante la revolución mexicana*, 41; my translation). The definition of the "Great National Problems" has varied substantially since the inauguration of the National University in 1910, but the university's rhetorical commitment to studying and to solving them is a constant. See David Lorey, *The University System and the Economic Development of Mexico since 1929*.

7 Lawrence Levine, *The Opening of the American Mind: Canons, Culture and History*, chapter 3.

8 Arjun Appadurai, "Theory in Anthropology: Center and Periphery," 356–61.

9 For a useful catalog of U.S. stereotypes of Latin America, see John Johnson, *Latin America in Caricature*.

10 For the significance of science as a sign in a parallel context (India), see Gyan Prakash, *Another Reason: Science and the Imagination of Modern India*, chapter 1.

11 Katherine Verdery, *National Ideology under Socialism: Identity and Cultural Politics in Ceausescu's Romania*, 167–68.

12 Paul Krugman, "Mexico's New Deal," *New York Times*, Op-Ed, July 5, 2000. Krugman somewhat disingenuously argues that the true purpose of free trade was to bring democracy to Mexico: "now we know that, whatever the sins of Mr. Salinas, the reformers he brought to power were sincere—and the reform was real."

13 On the similarities between the three candidates, see Jorge Castañeda's arguments in "Ésta no es una elección de principios; es un referéndum para el cambio . . .", *Proceso*, 10–13.

## 1. NATIONALISM AS A PRACTICAL SYSTEM

1 Anderson goes even further, and denies that racial identity and racism are connected in any essential way to nationalism: "[t]he fact of the matter is that nationalism thinks in terms of historical destinies, while racism dreams of eternal contaminations . . . The dreams of racism actually have their origin in ideologies of class, rather than in those of nation" (1994, 149–50). I shall argue that this assertion is untenable in the Iberian world.

2 "Out of the American welter came these imagined realities: nation-states, republican institutions, common citizenships, popular sovereignty, national flags and anthems, etc., and the liquidation of their conceptual opposites: dynastic empires, monarchical institutions, absolutisms, subjecthoods, inherited nobilities, serfdoms, ghettoes, and so forth . . . In effect, by the second decade of the nineteenth century, if not earlier, a 'model' of 'the' independent national state was available for pirating" (ibid., 81).

3 At times Anderson appears to believe that there is such a thing as a "concrete" versus an "imaginary" community: "The relatively small size of traditional aristocracies, their fixed political bases, and the personalization of political relations implied by sexual intercourse and inheritance, meant that their cohesions as classes were as much concrete as imagined. An illiterate nobility could still act as a nobility. But the bourgeoisie? Here was a class which, figuratively speaking, came into being as a class only in so many replications" (ibid., 77). Although Anderson is shrewd in

searching for differences in the social organization of communication in various classes as a key to understanding nationalism, he incorrectly assumes that some forms of community are "concrete" while others are "imaginary." All communitarian relationships are based on an idea of the social whole that is imaginary; and "the nobility" of his example was much more reliant on systemic "replications" than Anderson imagines. So, for example, all legitimate descendants of the conquistadors and early settlers of the Indies were officially considered nobles (*hijos dalgo*) (*Las Leyes de Indias*, book 4, title 6, law 6). Likewise, it was policy to recognize and maintain the status of the Indian "nobility" (ibid., book 7, title 7, law 1). In short, the nobility of the Spanish colonial era played as systemic a role as the bourgeoisie, which meant that it burgeoned wherever it was needed to maintain a local hierarchy and state organization. The grandees of Spain were surely as ignorant of the identities of the descendants of first settlers or of Indian nobles in Chile as the members of the bourgeoisie of Barcelona were of the identity of their class counterparts in the Río de la Plata.

4 Real Academia Española, *Diccionario de la lengua castellana en que se explica el verdadero sentido de las voces . . . Madrid*, 1726–39 (1737).

5 For an illuminating discussion of the relationship between ancien régime and modern ideas regarding sovereignty in the Spanish and Spanish-American world, see François-Xavier Guerra, "De la política antigua a la política moderna, la revolución de la soberanía," in François-Xavier Guerra and Annick Lamperière, eds., *Los espacios públicos en Iberoamérica: ambigüedades y problemas, siglos XVIII–XIX*, 109–39. Guerra has shown that throughout the nineteenth century, Spanish America combined elements of an ancien régime and of a modern polity. A similar point has been made by Fernando Escalante, *Ciudadanos imaginarios*. Contemporary Latin America is also not without examples of tensions between competing claims between state sovereignty and the traditional rights of corporations and communities.

6 See Annick Lamperière, "República y publicidad a fines del antiguo régimen," 55–60.

7 A good case in point is the use of the eagle eating the serpent as the symbol for Mexico City. Enrique Florescano (1996) has studied the evolution of this symbol in the colonial period, and he shows that the Aztec symbol was used preferentially over the coat of arms that has been assigned to the city since the early seventeenth century. The use of this indigenous symbol as the local symbol also buttressed creole identity. This symbol was eventually written into the flag of Mexico in lieu of Hidalgo's Virgin of Guadalupe, or of Morelos's "Viva la Virgen María."

8 Key works on this matter include Brading 1991, Lafaye 1977, and Lavallé 1993.

9 Indeed, the Spanish constitution that was promoted in Cádiz in 1812 defined Spanish citizenship in such as way as to include in equal terms those born in any part of the Spanish dominion (article 18; in Tena Ramírez 1957, 62). Aljovín (1997, 2–4) discusses the decline of Andean Curacas at the end of the eighteenth century in the context of the Bourbon state's goal of eliminating the power of all institutions that brokered the relationship between the state and its subjects.

10 For example, in both the Constitution of Cádiz (1812) and Mexico's Centralist Constitution (1836), servants have nationality (Spanish and Mexican, respectively), but in neither case were servants citizens.

11 For the salience of individual communities as primary referents of identity in the

wars of independence, see Eric Van Young 1986. For the ways in which community or corporate identities interlocked with nationalist discourses, see Florencia Mallon, *Peasant and Nation: The Making of Post-Colonial Mexico and Peru*, chapters 5 and 7; also Escalante, *Ciudadanos imaginarios*, 97–119 and 193–97. An early formulation of the problem was set forth by Edmundo O'Gorman, who argued that Benito Juárez's triumph over the French in 1867 must truly be considered a "second independence," not simply in the sense that Mexico was freed from a foreign invader, but, much more fundamentally, because it represented the triumph of liberal republicanism over a classical republicanism: "We could say, then, that if Miguel Hidalgo is the founder of [our] nationality, Benito Juárez is the founder of republican nationality, which is not, as we know, at all the same thing" (1969, 86).

12 See, for instance, Florencia Mallon's discussion of "popular liberalism" in nineteenth-century Mexico and Peru (1995, 130), and Guardino's discussion of popular federalism between independence and 1850 (1996, 179–94).

13 See Fleisher (1992). Clearly, early modern nationalism differed considerably in England, France, and the Netherlands. Stephen Pincus (1998) interprets the Glorious Revolution as the first nationalist revolution, rather than as a religious war. England's early separation of nationalism and religion reflects the fact that it never hoped to achieve a universal monarchy, as Spain and the Ottomans did; thus, to a certain degree one could say that a religious nationalism is at the origins of the Spanish imperial state, whereas a revolutionary, secular form of nationalism developed in England.

14 "It ought to be well pondered how, without any doubt, God chose the valiant Cortés as his instrument for opening the door and preparing the way for the preachers of the gospel in the New World, where the Catholic church might be restored and recompensed by the conversions of many souls for the great loss and damages which the accursed Luther was to cause at the same time within established Christianity . . . Thus it is not without mystery that in the same year in which Luther was born in Eisleben, in Saxony, Hernando Cortés saw the light of day in Medellín, a village in Spain—the former to upset the world and bring beneath the banner of Satan many of the faithful who had been for generations Catholics, the latter to bring into the fold of the church an infinite number of people who had for ages been under the dominion of Satan in idolatry, vice, and sin" (Mendieta 1876, 3:174–75; my translation).

15 Laws distinguishing subjects of the Spanish crown from foreigners were equally precise (e.g., book 3, title 13, law 8).

16 It should be noted, however, that these processes were by no means a simple constant, and that the politics of differentiation between "Peninsulars" and "Creoles" responded to varying kinds of interests (including, for instance, interests in prolonging *encomendero* privilege after the second generation; interest in keeping Creoles out of certain religious orders or away from certain political posts). These interests waxed and waned at various times and places, in such a way that there were places and times when a "Creole" was simply a Spaniard, other moments when "Creole" was used principally as a discriminatory term, and yet others when American-born Spaniards tried to affirm the equality, and even the superiority, of their land with respect to Spain, Rome, or other European locations (see Lavallé 1993).

17 The nature of American lands and of their influence on the character of the

Americans was a polemical subject in scientific circles from the time of initial contact to the early twentieth century. See Antonello Gerbi, *Nature in the New World: From Christopher Columbus to Gonzalo Fernández de Oviedo*, and *The Dispute of the New World: The History of a Polemic, 1750–1900*.

18  The literature exalting American lands at times also refashions the connections between the Americas and "Eden." This has been studied in detail for Mexico by Lafaye (1977, chapter 1) and by David Brading (1991, chapters 14 and 16). In the Andean world, Lavallé (1993, 122) notes that "Many Creoles believed that their *patria* could be compared to the Elysian Fields, with the Bible's paradise. There was in this, for some, a mere literary style . . . For others, there could be no doubt: America should not be *compared* to paradise, it *was* the earthly paradise of the Scriptures" (emphasis in the original).

19  Raphael Semmes, a soldier in the U.S. army, described the reception that was given to U.S. troops by Mexico City's elites in the following terms: "The Calle de Plateros, through which we marched to the grand plaza, is the street in which all the principal shops are found; and although these were closed, the gay curtains that fluttered from the balconies above . . . (almost every house had prepared and hung out a neutral flag—English, French, Spanish, etc.—as a means of protection), and the fashionably dressed women, who showed themselves without the least reserve at doorways and windows gave one the idea rather of a grand national festival, than of the entry of a conquering army into an enemy capital" (cited in Luis Fernando Granados, "Sueñan las piedras: alzamiento ocurrido en la ciudad de México, 14, 15 y 16 de septiembre, 1847.") The "neutral flags" were meant to signal to U.S. soldiers that the families in question were also foreign nationals, usually by virtue of descent.

20  Charles V famously claimed that whereas German was appropriate for speaking to horses, and Italian was ideal for courting women, Spanish was for speaking to God. The term *ladino* also provides a clue to the sacralization of Spanish, because it was used to refer to Jews, Moors, African slaves, or, later, Indians, who spoke (neo)Latin, that is, Spanish (Lavallé 1993, 19). A discussion of the history of the title "Rey Católico" and of its significance for Spain in its competition with France can be found in Pablo Fernández Abadalejo, "'Rey Católico': gestación y metamorfosis de un título." Jaime Contreras argues that Spain's persecution of heresy under the Reyes Católicos can be understood as a political appropriation of the church: "Concerns with 'heresy,' which were initially of little consequence, became a fundamental buttress to royal law" ("Los primeros años de la inquisición: guerra civil, monarquía, mesianismo y herejía," 703). On the identification between Christianity and Spanish civilization in the so-called spiritual conquest of Mexico, see Peggy K. Liss, *Mexico under Spain, 1521–1556: Society and the Origins of Nationality*, chapter 5, especially pp. 77–82.

21  Antonello Gerbi (1985:267–68) remarks that Fernandez de Oviedo contrasted the grandeur of Spain with that of ancient Rome, noting that Spanish Goths were Christians and were martyred while resisting Roman paganism. Thus, in the sixteenth century, Spain's national identification with the Christianity was made to rank higher even than Rome's.

22  Anthony Pagden has shown that talk of a universal monarchy was never universally accepted in Spain itself, and that it was extinguished as an impracticable ideal by the end of the seventeenth century. However, he also argues that Spain's ideological

role as guardian of universal Christendom "formed an important part of the ideological armature of what has some claims to being the first European nation state" (*Spanish Imperialism and the Political Imagination*, 5).

23 The *Laws of the Indies* provide an interesting example of how Spain reconciled the simultaneous development between empires through time with a Catholic universalism. Much of the legistature that was promoted by Philip IV (at a time of imperial decay) shows punctilious concern with public oration and repentence for public sins, as mechanisms to reanimate the empire and, perhaps, also as potential explanations of its political shortcomings. For example, book 1, title 1, law 23 (passed originally in 1626) orders viceroys and church authorities to celebrate of November 21 every year with a Mass to the Holy Sacrament, in which priests call on everyone to reform their "vices and public sins" in order to thank God for his clemency in allowing Spanish ships to reach the Indies unharmed.

24 More thorough and convincing than Anderson's emphasis on the popularization of "empty time" through the newspaper and the novel is Moishe Postone's discussion of the rise of "abstract time," a history that is related in part to the development of technology, in part to the Newtonian scientific revolution, and ultimately to the history of commodification, and especially to the rise of "abstract labor." At the most general level, Postone suggests that the emergence of time as an "independent variable" "was related to the commodity form of social relations" (1996, 211). If we apply these ideas to Spanish America, we conclude that the consolidation of "abstract time" has been a long process, that has only been unevenly achieved. The process began with devices such as administrative reforms, was strengthened in various waves of modernizing reforms, with the rise of a bourgeois public sphere in the late eighteenth century, and eventually with the consolidation of industrialism. Spanish-American independence occurred somewhere in the middle of this process.

25 Antonio Domínguez Ortiz illuminates this situation: "The social thought of enlightened Spaniards was not radical. It did not claim the total suppression of barriers between the estates, because these were crumbling of their own accord. Instead, it seemed more urgent to struggle against economic differences that condemned a great portion of the population to misery. This does not mean that pride in nobility had disappeared . . . but they no longer used nobility titles as excuses to refuse common charges; privileges could only be justified if they were employed for the good of the nation" (*Carlos III y la España de la Ilustración*, 120–21). Domínguez discusses the significance of state projects and knowledge production in this period in chapter 5. See also Stanley Stein and Barbara Stein, "Concepts and Realities of Spanish Economic Growth, 1759–1789."

26 The fact that a nationalism and a national program were not a common denominator even among Mexican insurgents has been demonstrated by Eric Van Young, who has shown the centrality both of local indigenous revolts whose claims with regard to state building were in fact the opposite of those of the creole directorate (1986, 386, 412), and of an unideological criminal or brigand element whose participation was entirely opportunistic (1989, 36–37). The role of opportunistic rogues and the criminal element in independence is also pungently demonstrated by Archer (1989). On the other hand, Spanish-American independence was predictable even before indigenous social movements got started and before nationalists really heated up. As early as 1786, Thomas Jefferson's main preoccupation regarding

Spanish America was that it should not fall out of Spanish hands too quickly. The fact that Spain would eventually lose those territories was, for Jefferson, a foregone conclusion. The United States needed time to gain strength in order to annex as many Spanish-American territories as possible (cited in Fuentes Mares 1983, 34–35).

27 For a description that illustrates some similarities between these ideas and those expressed in indigenous messianic revolts of this period, see Eric Van Young 1986, 402.

28 Silvia Arrom, "Popular Politics in Mexico City: The Parián Riot, 1828," is an illuminating discussion of popular politics and anti-Spanish sentiment in this period.

29 Masons appear to be present in Spanish America since the 1780s, though in the Mexican case it appears that the deputies who were sent to the Cortes of Cádiz in 1812 were critical in the formation of Mexico's lodges of the Scottish rite.

30 Joel Poinsett to Henry Clay, June 4, 1825. Dispatches from U.S. Ministers to Mexico National Archives, Washington, D.C.).

31 The lodges had achieved such a status, that at the news of the death of the Duke of York, President Guadalupe Victoria, who was a *yorquino*, published an edict ordering the president, the vice president, the members of the Supreme Court, state governors, district officers, and army officials from the rank of colonel up to wear a black band of mourning (Primera secretaría de Estado Departamento esterior Sección 2, May 19, 1827).

## 2. COMMUNITARIAN IDEOLOGIES AND NATIONALISM
This chapter has been translated from Spanish by Paul Liffman.

1 Max Weber, *Economy and Society*, vol. 1, 40, 41–43.

2 Annette Weiner, *Inalienable Possessions;* Marcel Mauss, *The Gift: Forms and Functions of Exchange in Archaic Societies.*

3 Alfredo López Austin (*The Human Body and Ideology: Concepts of the Ancient Nahuas*, vol. 1, 74, 79, and generally 68–83) summarizes the tensions between the communitarian ideology of the *calpulli* and the imperial ideology of the Aztecs.

4 Fray Bernardino de Sahagún, *Coloquios y doctrina cristiana*, 151.

5 López Austin, *The Human Body and Ideology*, vol. 1, 207. López Austin also mentions that "the hair of prisoners taken in battle could also be kept as relics for the purpose of giving the captive's powers to the captors" (221).

6 In this connection, it is interesting to note the determination with which Spanish missionaries combated polygamy: without polygamy, the possibility of constructing supracommunitarian alliances in the indigenous world was reduced. Perhaps it was not accidental, then, that the first play presented in New Spain was an *ejemplo* against the sin of bigamy and any infringement of the seventh commandment. For a discussion of the contents of this play, as well as of its production and impressive technical effects, see Othón Arróniz, *Teatro de la evangelización en Nueva España*, 23–30. Ross Hassig (*Aztec Warfare: Imperial Expansion and Political Control*) offers a number of examples of the use of marriage as a strategy of alliance among the Aztecs. Following this logic, Moctezuma himself tried to marry one of his daughters to Cortés, but the latter declined the offer on account of the fact that "he was already married" (244).

7 In this regard, the Aztec empire contrasts with both the classic Mayan kingdoms, where war was an exclusive activity of the aristocracy, and with the Teotihuacán model, where almost the whole system appears to have been meritocratic. For a comprehensive treatment of war in the pre-Hispanic period, see Ross Hassig, *Mesoamerican Warfare*.

8 However, early modern Spanish ideas of race were different from current notions. Although *raza* was related to heredity, the term often had a negative slant, because *raza* was sometimes understood as a visible defect in physical appearance that was a mark of spiritual inferiority. Thus, the term was more readily used to refer to Jews, Moors, blacks, or Indians than to Old Christians, who had *casta*. On the other hand, bad blood could be tempered to some degree by a favorable environment.

9 See, for example, Edgar Love on marriages between blacks and other castes in Mexico City: "Marriage Patterns of Persons of African Descent in a Colonial Mexico City Parish," 79–91.

10 For examples of the latter, see David A. Brading's discussion of the ways in which the Spanish merchants bequeathed their businesses to their daughters' Iberian husbands, while their creole sons became an idle aristocracy (*Miners and Merchants in Bourbon Mexico, 1763–1810*).

11 Gonzalo Aguirre Beltrán, *La población negra de México, 1519–1810*, 157, 160–61; the term *bozal* is the same as the word for bridle or muzzle in Spanish and has the connotation of inexperience when applied to a horse or mule. It also may be that the term referred to the fact that African speech sounded like gibberish (*voz* or *boz* referred to voice, speech, shouting, mouth, muzzle, etc.).

12 Ibid., 157.

13 Ibid., 280–92. See also Colin Palmer, *Slaves of the White God: Blacks in Mexico, 1570–1650*.

14 Jacques Lafaye, *Quetzalcoatl y Guadalupe: la formación de la conciencia nacional en México*, and David A. Brading, *First America: The Spanish Monarchy, Creole Patriots and the Liberal State, 1492–1867*, chapter 16.

15 José María Luis Mora, *Obras sueltas*, vol. 1, 152–53.

16 For a discussion of race issues in Mexico, Alan Knight, "Racism, Revolution and Indigenismo: Mexico, 1910–1940," in *The Idea of Race in Latin America, 1870–1940*, ed. Richard Graham, 71–114.

17 Andrés Molina Enríquez, *Los grandes problemas nacionales*, 344.

18 They were more Indian than Spanish for several reasons: first, because the number of Spaniards in colonial Mexico was always smaller than the number of Indians; second, because the Spanish component of the mestizo race was transmitted almost exclusively by males, whereas the indigenous element was reproduced by both females and males; and third, because indigenous races survived in large parts of the country that white races had been incapable of inhabiting. In this latter argument, Molina Enríquez formulates quite explicitly the idea that Gonzalo Aguirre Beltrán developed under the title of "regions of refuge" (ibid.).

19 "The mestizos will finally absorb the Indians and they will completely fuse the Creoles and the foreigners residing here with their own race. As a consequence, the mestizo race shall develop with liberty. Once this is so, not only will it resist the inevitable clash with the North American race, but in this clash, it will win" (ibid., 352).

20 Ibid., 343; my emphasis.

## 3. MODES OF MEXICAN CITIZENSHIP

1 Roberto DaMatta, *Carnivals, Rogues and Heroes*, 137–97, and, for a later and more elaborated version, *A casa e a rua: Espaço, cidadania, mulher e morte no Brasil*.

2 The same saying exists in Mexico and has been attributed to none other than Benito Juárez, Mexico's most famous liberal. Fernando Escalante (*Ciudadanos imaginarios*, 293) discusses what came to be known in Juárez's day as "La Ley del Caso," that is, the discretionary application of the law as the law.

3 Thus the relationship between the government and the press is most often described as one of "collusion," rather than of simple repression (though repression has always existed). A good summary of the relationship between the press and the government is provided in Raymundo Riva Palacio, "A Culture of Collusion: The Ties That Bind the Press and the PRI," 21–32.

4 "Bando de Hidalgo, December 10, 1810," in *Leyes fundamentales de México, 1808–1957*, ed. Felipe Tena Ramírez, 22.

5 These strictures are repeated by Morelos in his *Sentimientos de la nación* (1813): "Article 9: All [public] jobs shall only be obtained by Americans."

6 Rayón's constitution can be found in Tena Ramírez, *Leyes fundamentales*, 24–27.

7 Ibid., 127.

8 François-Xavier Guerra, "The Spanish-American Tradition of Representation and Its European Roots," 7.

9 Florencia Mallon, *Peasant and Nation: The Making of Post-Colonial Mexico and Peru*, 129–33.

10 Lorenzo de Zavala, "Viaje a los Estados Unidos del Norte de América, 1834," 156.

11 In Pantaleón Tovar, *Historia parlamentaria del cuarto congreso constitucional*, vol. 1, 400–401.

12 Ibid., 306–8.

13 The discussion occurs on December 28, 1867 (ibid., 122). In a related discussion a few days later, Deputy Zarco justifies the war in Yucatán by explaining that "From the days of Maximilian, it is well known that there were designs to create a viceroyalty in Yucatán, an asylum for reactionaries. These traitors toil to separate that territory from the republic and to instate it as a principality so that they can sell the Indians off as slaves" (ibid., 137). Ironically, in order to combat these reactionaries and the Maya rebels, Juárez and his liberals provisionally legalized corvée labor and/or slavery in the peninsula.

14 All citations of discussions of the First Constitutional Congress are from the facsimile edition titled *Actas constitucionales mexicanas (1821–1824)*. Dates of discussions will be cited rather than pagination, which is not entirely sequential.

15 Lic. Jesús Arellano, "Oración cívica que en el aniversario del grito de independencia se pronunció en el palacio de govierno de Durango el 16 de septiembre de 1841."

16 Ibid., 11. Curiously, the scorpion would later go on to become emblematic of the state of Durango.

17 Ibid., 6.

18 Ibid., 16.

19 Francisco Santoyo, "Opúsculo patriótico, que pronunció el ciudadano teniente coronel graduado Francisco Santoyo, como miembro de la junta patriótica de esta ciudad [de Orizaba] el día 11 de septiembre de 1842."

20 Escalante, *Ciudadanos imaginarios*, 290.

21 Andrés Reséndez shows how, in the case of Texas and New Mexico, altruistic appeals

to national identity and shared religion were the principal resources used by Mexico to try to keep those territories in the republic ("Caught between Profits and Rituals: National Contestation in Texas and New Mexico, 1821–1848."

22 On February 7, 1868, just a few months after the execution of Maximilian von Hapsburg, the project for a law trying to ritually enshrine the 1857 constitution was presented to Congress. The justification for this proposal is significant: "it is un-questionable that this *talisman* (the constitution of 1857) that is so loved by the Mexican people, was the cause of the prodigious valor that distinguished us in the bloody war that has just passed" (in Tovar, *Historia parlamentaria*, vol. 1, 398).

23 Descriptions of Porfirian state theater are plentiful: for the boulevards, see Barbara Tenenbaum, "Streetwise History: The Paseo de la Reforma and the Porfirian State, 1876–1910," 127–50; for the *rurales*, see Paul J. Vanderwood, *Disorder and Progress: Bandits, Police, and Mexican Development*; for a general appreciation of Porfirian state theater, see Mauricio Tenorio-Trillo, *Mexico at the World's Fairs: Crafting a Modern Nation*.

24 Samuel Ramos, "El perfil del hombre y la cultura en México," 131–35.

25 See, for example, Larissa Lomnitz, *Networks and Marginality: Life in a Mexican Shantytown*; Carlos Vélez-Ibáñez, *Rituals of Marginality: Politics, Process, and Culture Change in Central Urban Mexico, 1969–1974*; Antonio Azuela, ed., *La urbanización popular y el orden jurídico en América Latina*.

26 For a full description of these campaign rituals, see Larissa Lomnitz, Claudio Lomnitz, and Ilya Adler, "Functions of the Form: Power Play and Ritual in the 1988 Mexican Presidential Campaign," 357–402.

27 Today this version is common wisdom, but for a succinct synthesis of this per-spective, see Lorenzo Meyer, *Liberalismo autoritario: las contradicciones del sistema político mexicano*.

## 4. PASSION AND BANALITY IN MEXICAN HISTORY

1 François-Xavier Guerra, *México del antiguo régimen a la revolución*.

2 José María Luis Mora, *Obras sueltas*, vol. 2, 52.

3 Ibid., 50.

4 Fernando Escalante, *Ciudadanos imaginarios*, 97–109.

5 "Decreto de excomunión de los insurgentes dado por el obispo Abad y Queipo, 1810," in *Historia documental de México*, ed. Ernesto de la Torre Villar, Moisés González Navarro, and Stanley Ross, vol. 2, 36–40.

6 Ibid., 37.

7 "Manifiesto que el señor D. Miguel Hidalgo y Costilla, Generalísimo de las armas americanas, y electo por la mayor parte de los pueblos del reino para defender sus derechos y los de sus conciudadanos, hace al pueblo (1810)," in Torre Villar et al., *Historia documental de México*, vol. 2: 40–43.

8 Ibid., 42.

9 Ibid., 43; my emphasis.

10 José María Morelos, "Bando de Morelos suprimiendo las castas y aboliendo la es-clavitud, 17 de noviembre de 1810," 162–63.

11 Luis Cabrera, "Los dos patriotismos," 55–56.

12 See Ángel Delgado, *España y México en el siglo 19*, vol. 2, 192, for the views of the Spanish ambassador Ángel Calderón de la Barca on these matters. Ambassador

Poinsett, the first U.S. diplomat in Mexico, arrived in the country saluting its independence and hailing the republic that was "founded on the sovereignty of the people and on the inalienable rights of man" (cited in ibid., vol. 1, 303), which it arguably was not.

13 Francisco Bulnes, *El verdadero Juárez: la verdad sobre la intervención y el imperio*, 819.

14 This occurred to Father Mariano Balleza, a kinsman of Hidalgo; see Alejandro Villaseñor y Villaseñor, *Biografías de los héroes y caudillos de la independencia*, vol. 1, 58.

15 Antonio López de Santa Anna, *The Eagle: An Autobiography of Santa Anna*, 68–69.

16 Villaseñor y Villaseñor, *Biografías de los héroes*, vol. 2, 267–68.

17 Friedrich Katz, *The Life and Times of Pancho Villa*, 789.

18 Thus, according to Molina Enríquez (1978, 425), "the notion of patriotism will be determined and reduced to the following simple terms: all will be like brothers in a family, free to carry out their own actions, but united by the fraternity of a common ideal, and obligated by virtue of that fraternity, on the one hand, to distribute their common inheritance equally, and, on the other, to tolerate each other's differences."

19 Bulnes, *El verdadero Juárez*, 856–57.

20 Juárez's Indianness was not trumpeted by Juárez himself, who only wrote of this matter in a letter dedicated to his children; however, Juárez was identified by others as Indian. I am grateful to Paul Ross for pointing this out to me.

21 Agustín Sánchez González, *Los mejores chistes sobre presidentes*, 64.

22 Edmundo O'Gorman, Escalante notes that the pervasive belief in Juárez as a law-abiding president can be traced back to the *porfiriato*, and forward to historians such as Daniel Cosío Villegas and Enrique Krauze. He then demonstrates that the representation of Juárez and of the restored republic as an era governed by the law and the ideals of liberal citizenship is a false representation (*Ciudadanos imaginarios*, 233; 254; 259–86).

23 O'Gorman, *México: el trauma de su historia*, 33.

24 See Mayer-Celis 1995. For a superficial overview of the history of Mexican censuses, see Claudio Lomnitz, *Modernidad indiana: nación y mediación en México*, chapter 5.

5. FISSURES IN CONTEMPORARY MEXICAN NATIONALISM

1 Carlos Fuentes, *Where the Air Is Clear*, 21.

2 For an analysis of the work of Carlos María Bustamante, see David A. Brading, *Los orígenes del nacionalismo mexicano*; for a synthesis of the nature of postrevolutionary state intervention in shaping a modern citizenry, see Alan Knight, "Popular Culture and the Revolutionary State in Mexico," 395–444; and for the specific case of Michoacán, see Christopher Boyer, "The Cultural Politics of *Agrarismo*: Agrarian Revolt, Village Revolutionaries, and State-Formation in Michoacán, Mexico."

3 Studies of the historical relationships between intellectuals, political ritual, and the public sphere in Mexico are the focus of chapters 7, 9, and 10.

4 Claudio Lomnitz, *Exits from the Labyrinth: Culture and Ideology in Mexican National Space*, chapter 1.

5 During the 1980s, Mexico's intelligentsia experienced two contradictory tendencies: growth in the number of institutional contexts for intellectual production, on the one hand ("decentralization"), and, on the other, a concentration of cultural power in two allegedly stellar and mutually antagonistic "intellectual groups," represented by the journals *Vuelta* and *Nexos*. During the Salinas years (1988–94), both

groups had close relations with the government, but *Nexos's* people received more concessions from the state, while *Vuelta's* received more from Televisa.

6 Interestingly, this image resonates with the transformations that Roger Rouse describes for U.S. society in the current wave of globalization, whereby the U.S. class structure shifted away from a pyramidal shape and toward a distribution that he likens to the shape of a rocket. The similarities are not mere coincidence, reflecting instead a fundamental shift in the class structure of both countries, as well as changes in the ways states reconstruct an image of citizenship. One significant contrast between the two cases, however, is that in the United States the dominant *image* of the class and power structure has not been that of the pyramid. The class structure in the United States is usually portrayed (somewhat appropriately) as diamond-shaped, with a broad middle and narrow points at the top and the bottom. Thus, whereas in the United States the current transformation of the class structure is decried in mainstream newspapers as reflecting both "corporate greed" and the "formation of an underclass" (that is, the transformation of a diamond into a pyramid), in Mexico the dominant images are simply of pillage, of taking the jewels from the temple on top of the pyramid and depositing them in Switzerland. See Roger Rouse, "Thinking through Transnationalism: Notes on the Cultural Politics of Class Relations in the Contemporary United States," 353–403.

7 I have developed this point in connection to the varying implications of multiculturalism in Mexico versus the United States and Europe in "Decadence in Times of Globalization," 257–67.

## 6. NATIONALISM'S DIRTY LINEN

1 This interest in the international networks of national identity production has produced an exciting corpus of works on the history of mapping, of censuses, of standardization of scientific measurements, of world expositions, of nationalist strategies in a number of literary forms and genres, on architecture, on urbanism, and on the history of transnational scientific and artistic networks. Perhaps the finest methodological exemplar of this line of research is Daniel Rogers, *Atlantic Crossings: Social Politics in a Progressive Age*, but this tradition has also produced a number of more general and theoretically inclined works, such as Arjun Appadurai, *Modernity at Large: Cultural Dimensions of Globalization*, Homi K. Bhabha, "DissemiNation: Time, Narrative, and the Margins of the Modern Nation," 291–322, Néstor García Canclini, *Hybrid Cultures: Strategies for Entering and Leaving Modernity*, Gyan Prakash, *Another Reason: Science and the Imagination of Modern India*, Doris Sommers, *Foundational Fictions: The National Romances of Latin America*, and Edward Said, *Culture and Imperialism*, to name a few prominent examples.

2 In the recent anglophone literature, Edward Said's *Culture and Imperialism* is a wide-ranging exploration of the ways in which the colonial world was both critically important to the development of "Western civilization" and systematically diminished or denied by it. The poor nations' reaction to these practices is outlined by Katherine Verdery (1991), who explores what she calls "protochronism" among Romanian nationalist intellectuals, which is a tendency to assert that key inventions of civilization were invented their country first. Both of these aspects of nationalism have long been recognized by writers and politicians in the colonial and postcolonial world. As early as the seventeenth century, indigenous intellectuals such as Guaman

Poma and Fernando de Alva Ixtlilxochitl argued for a kind of "protochronism" with regard to Christianity, claiming that their ancestors recognized the true God before the arrival of the Spaniards. This tactic underlies much of Latin America's *indigenista* thinking since at least the nineteenth century, and was given playfully ironic treatment in early 1900s by the Brazilian writer Lima Barreto through the tragicomic nationalist hero Policarpio Cuaresma.

3 Benedict Anderson, *Imagined Communities*, 5.

4 For example, Roger Bartra's most recent book *(La sangre y la tinta: Ensayos sobre la condición postmexicana)* is a collection of essays on "the post-Mexican condition."

5 Dipesh Chakrabarty (1992) has argued for the need to "provincialize" Europe in the realm of theory and history. If his call to arms succeeds, then perhaps the sort of "grounded theory" that I espouse here will in some respects be more universal and social thought may go through a phase that is parallel to the one that religion was said to have had in antiquity: "The various modes of worship, which prevailed in the Roman world, were all considered by the people, as equally true; by the philosopher, as equally false; and by the magistrate, as equally useful" (Edward Gibbon, *The History of the Decline and Fall of the Roman Empire*, 35).

6 European travelers to Mexico usually collected pre-Columbian objects. Contemporary products that attracted their attention were generally seen as curious exemplars of crafts that were distinctly European in origin, made quaint because of their indigenous twist. Thus, in the 1850s, a Mexican spur was sent to Britain by Henry Christy and Edward B. Tylor where, because of its extravagance and size, it was exhibited in the medieval section of the museum. See Edward B. Tylor, *Anahuac, or Mexico and the Mexicans, Ancient and Modern*, 295–96.

7 In an earlier work (1992a), I developed some elements of this cultural geography, above all those having to do with the construction of cultural regions within a national space. To that end, I proposed a series of concepts including "intimate cultures" (cultural zones forged by social classes in specific interactive contexts) and "culture of social relations" (culture generated in the framework of interactions between different social classes and identity groups within the national space). The topography of zones of contact, which I did not develop in *Exits from the Labyrinth*, is an important part of the task of producing a geography of national identity. This is because national space is in itself an aspect of an international system, so frames of contact with the foreign have to be understood as a feature of production of national culture and identity and not as an element external to nationality.

8 For the case of the censorship commissions, see Anne Rubenstein, *Bad Language, Naked Ladies, and Other Threats to the Nation: A Political History of Comic Books in Mexico*, chapter 4. For anti-Semitism in the movements against itinerant salesmen during the Great Depression, see Gary Gordon, *Peddlers, Pesos and Power: The Political Economy of Street Vending in Mexico City*, 47, and Moisés González Navarro, *Los extranjeros en México y los mexicanos en el extranjero, 1821–1970*, vol. 2, 133–34. For the case of the Chinese, see Juan Puig, *Entre el río Perla y el Nazas: la China decimonónica y sus braceros emigrantes, la colonia china de Teorreón y la matanza de 1911*, 173–228; for the sacking of the Parián Market, see Romeo Flores Caballero, *Counterrevolution: The Role of the Spaniards in the Independence of Mexico, 1804–38*, 119–21.

9 For the case of drugs in the 1930s, see Luis Astorga, "Traficantes de drogas, políticos y policías en el siglo veinte mexicano." The Díaz Ordaz regime's hostility to the

disorder of Mexican pop culture is succinctly addressed in Carlos Monsiváis, *Mexican Post-Cards*, 23–27. For a more detailed and wide-ranging discussion, see Eric Zolov, *Refried Elvis: The Rise of the Mexican Counterculture*. The discussion of *Beavis and Butthead* appeared in the national press in 1993.

10 This is also the argument that runs through Eric Hobsbawm and Terence Ranger, eds., *The Invention of Tradition*. Any Herderian view of nationality involves a dialectic between tradition and modernity.

11 Liberals honored Hidalgo and celebrated independence on September 15; conservatives honored Iturbide and celebrated independence on September 27. A detailed catalog of ideas representing both sides of this rift can be found in *La dominación española en México*.

12 This relationship between tradition and modernity is not exclusively Mexican. In nineteenth-century England, Matthew Arnold argued that the British national spirit was composed of three elements: the Saxon, which lent it its seriousness and tenacity; the Roman, which lent it its energy; and the Celtic, which lent it its spirit and sentiment: "[The English genius] is characterized, I have repeatedly said, by *energy with honesty*. Take away some of the energy which comes to us, I believe, in part from Celtic and Roman sources; instead of energy, say rather *steadiness*; and you have the Germanic genius: *steadiness with honesty* . . . the danger for a national spirit thus composed is the humdrum, the plain and ugly, the ignoble: in a word, *das Gemeine, die gemeinheit*, that curse of Germany, against which Goethe was all his life fighting" (Matthew Arnold, "On the Study of Celtic Literature," 341). In this same essay, Arnold argues for the full assimilation of the Celtic peoples into British society and for the annihilation of Celtic as a living language. The assimilation of these defeated peoples into the national genius is thus an identical move to the one made by Mexican *indigenistas*.

13 Zolov, *Refried Elvis*, 145.

14 Examples of how government *indigenistas* sought to reconfigure this relationship can be found in Alexander Dawson, *"Indigenismo* and the Paradox of the Nation in Post-Revolutionary Mexico."

15 "And it was quite singular that those Americans who so guarded the privilege of their white caste, when it came to Mexico always sympathized with the Indians, and never with the Spaniards" (José Vasconcelos, *Ulises criollo*, 34).

16 Arjun Appadurai, "The Culture of the State," lecture notes, University of Chicago, 1997.

17 Arturo Escobar's *Encountering Development: The Making and Unmaking of the Third World*, is a critique of development as it has been organized since World War II. The role of development discourse (not only at the general ideological level, but, more importantly, as a set of categories and measurements) is central to this story.

18 Erving Goffman, *The Presentation of Self in Everyday Life*, 106–34.

19 "We don't think it is necessary to underline the disastrous impression that the arriving tourist will form upon seeing the spectacle of immorality that the brothels, in open air and established in an important city artery, an obligatory path, offer" (cited in Katherine Bliss, "Prostitution, Revolution and Social Reform in Mexico City, 1918–1940," 196).

20 Alexandra Stern, "Eugenics beyond Borders: Science and Medicalization in Mexico and the U.S. West, 1900–1950," and "Buildings, Boundaries, and Blood: Medicalization and Nation-Building on the U.S.–Mexico Border, 1910–1930," 41–81.

21  Pratt coins the term *contact zone* "to refer to the space of colonial encounters, the space in which peoples geographically and historically separated come into contact with each other and establish ongoing relations, usually involving conditions of coercion, radical inequality, and intractable conflict . . . 'contact zone' in my discussion is often synonymous with 'colonial frontier.'" (Mary Louise Pratt, *Imperial Eyes: Travel Writing and Transculturation*, 6). My own usage leaves the question of domination and of the nature of inequalities in transnational contact zones open, because the relationships of contact are of multiple sorts.

22  The case of architectural modernism's decrepitude in Brazil has been analyzed by Beatriz Jaguaribe, "Modernist Ruins." The challenges that Brasília's poor suburbs pose for the nationalist utopia that the city was meant to embody are treated in James Holston, "Alternative Modernities: Statecraft and Religious Imagination in the Valley of the Dawn."

## 7. RITUAL, RUMOR, AND CORRUPTION IN THE FORMATION OF MEXICAN POLITIES

1  The role of ritual in the construction of a national polity is a venerable line of inquiry, with Eric Wolf, "The Virgin of Guadalupe: A Mexican National Symbol," and Victor Turner, *Dramas, Fields and Metaphors* the most prominent founding ancestors. The role of ritual in the consolidation of local communities has received much more attention, notably in arguments over Wolf's typology of peasant communities, as well as in debates over the "cargo system" (for example, Frank Cancian, *Economics and Prestige in a Maya Community, The Decline of Community in Zinacantán;* and Waldemar Smith, *The Fiesta System and Economic Change* and in studies on the connections between ritual and local politics (for example, Guillermo de la Peña, *Herederos de promesas*, and Claudio Lomnitz, *Evolución de una sociedad rural.* Interest in political ritual has also emerged in ethnographies of various dimensions of Mexican urban life (for example, Carlos Vélez-Ibañez, *Rituals of Marginality: Politics, Process, and Cultural Change in Central Urban Mexico, 1969–1974;* Larissa Lomnitz and Marisol Pérez Lizaur, *A Mexican Elite Family*) and in the anthropology of social movements (for example, Jorge Alonso, *Los movimientos sociales en el Valle de México,* and Carlos Monsiváis, *Entrada libre.* Finally, there is also work on politics as spectacle and on the role of myth and ritual in bureaucracy (Alberto Ruy Sánchez, *Mitología de un cine en crisis;* Larissa Lomnitz, Claudio Lomnitz, and Ilya Adler, "Functions of the Form: Power Play and Ritual in the 1988 Mexican Presidential Campaign"). In the past decade or so, interest in these fields has also gained prominence among historians, who have attended similar themes in various periods and regions. See, for example, Juan Pedro Viqueira Albán, *¿Relajados o reprimidos? Diversiones públicas y vida social en la Ciudad de México durante el Siglo de las Luces;* William Beezley, Cheryl Martin, and William French, eds., *Rituals of Rule, Rituals of Resistance: Public Celebrations and Popular Culture in Mexico;* Serge Gruzinski, *La Guerre des images: De Christophe Colomb à 'Blade Runner';* and Gilbert Joseph and Daniel Nugent, eds., *Everyday Forms of State Formation.* These titles are only a sample of the literature.

2  François-Xavier Guerra, *México del antiguo régimen a la revolución,* 2 vols.

3  Viqueira Albán's, *¿Relajados o reprimidos?* is a description and discussion of the transformations of collective participation in public ritual during the eighteenth century.

4  For example, the legislation promoted by Charles III devoted a chapter to the

regulation of slave and freed black *cofradías* (Javier Malagón Barceló, *Código negro carolino*, chapter 10, 188–89).

5 Lomnitz and Pérez Lizaur (*A Mexican Elite Family*, 157–91) describe how family ritual is a forum for intrafamilial communication and decision making in the twentieth century.

6 This is why Larissa Lomnitz, who has studied Mexican families of various social strata, insists on the significance of "vertical" ties in that social organizational form ("Las relaciones horizontales y verticales en la estructura social urbana de México").

7 The best historical treatment of this question is Steve Stern, *The Secret History of Gender: Women, Men, and Power in Late Colonial Mexico.* Florencia Mallon (*Peasant and Nation: The Making of Post-Colonial Mexico and Peru*, 70, 76) explores the politics of gender in relation to citizenship and political mobilization in nineteenth-century agrarian communities.

8 Paul Friedrich makes the point that women are able to publicly articulate opinions that would get their men killed (*Princes of Naranja*). This argument would seem to be borne out by the historical work on rebellion in Mexico. In the most comprehensive study of colonial rebellions to date, William Taylor notes that "[t]he place of women [in village rebellions] is especially striking" (*Drinking, Homicide and Rebellion in Colonial Mexican Villages*, 116). Although Taylor speculates that this may be owing to the absence of men from the villages during agricultural seasons, Paul Friedrich's explanation would seem to account for their behavior more fully, because "[I]n at least one fourth of the cases examined, women led the attacks and were visibly more aggressive, insulting and rebellious in their behavior toward outside authorities [than men]" (ibid.).

9 Ricardo Pozas Horcasitas, *La democracia en blanco: el movimiento médico en México, 1964–1965*.

10 Manuel Castells, *The City and the Grassroots.*

11 Stephen Greenblatt argues that the discourse of the marvelous was used to avoid transcultural communication in the contact period (*Marvelous Possessions*, 135–36). Gruzinski (*La Guerre des images*, 169–71) argues that attempts to foster true dialogue between priests and Indians were more or less abandoned in Mexico around 1570. I have argued that ambivalence toward communication between urban elites and popular classes lies at the heart of the history of Mexican anthropology (Claudio Lomnitz, *Modernidad indiana*, chapter 4).

12 Julie Greer Johnson, *The Book in the Americas*, 15.

13 See, for example, John Elliott, "Spain and America in the Sixteenth and Seventeenth Centuries," 303. The tradition of pragmatic accommodations that coexist with a discursive orthodoxy has been prominent since that early period, and its force could be witnessed in the censorship that was meted out to Fray Bernardino de Sahagún's ethnographic studies of sixteenth-century native society on the grounds that to name that society was to preserve it. Instead of favoring dialogue, comprehension, and conversion through rational convictions, Testera's attitude toward conversion, which emphasized ritual compliance over intellectual conviction, triumphed.

14 So, in describing the contents of a poetry contest during the era known as "the long siesta of the seventeenth century," Irving Leonard states that "[t]he aim [of the contest] was adulation and glorification of the subject matter and it was best achieved by ingenious conceits, by bold juggling of phrases and excessive artifice, together

with a pedantic exhibition of classical and scholastic learning. Obscurity was a virtue and a vacuous jumbling of allusions a merit. With the topic in no way disputable, exaggerated panegyrics and bombast were the marks of esthetic excellence" (*Baroque Times in Old Mexico*, 137).

15 Gruzinski, *La Guerre des images*, 169–71, 175.

16 See Guerra, *México del antiguo régimen a la revolución*, vol. 1, 182–201 for the *porfiriato*. See also the significance of lip service to democracy in the PRI's 1988 presidential campaign, in Lomnitz, Lomnitz, and Adler, "Functions of the Form." Fernando Escalante deals squarely with this issue in *Ciudadanos imaginarios*.

17 Most prominently in Friedrich, *Princes of Naranja*, and in Fernando Escalante, *El principito*.

18 Mary Kay Vaughn, "The Construction of the Patriotic Festival in Tecamachalco, Puebla, 1900–1946," 213–46.

19 Vaughn mentions that these processes of negotiation between teachers and local communities also led teachers to avoid imposing the most anticlerical educational themes of the "socialist education" of the 1930s. At the national level "socialist education" was in no small part a crusade to finish off the key role of the church as cultural integrator; some aspects of this initiative found local support and civic festivals thrived along with a transformation in popular culture (the introduction of sports). However, this same success also gave local constituencies the strength to avoid the most draconian antireligious measures taken by the government.

20 Ilya Adler's discussion of the uses of the press in Mexico's bureaucracy is significant in this respect. He describes how bureaucrats constantly present information that they have read from the newspapers either as their own personal interpretation or as coming from a personal source. The backstage has greater claim to truth than official, public renderings in Mexico. See Ilya Adler, "Media Uses and Effects in a Large Bureaucracy: A Case Study in Mexico."

21 *Nuestro País* is the first journal devoted to public opinion in Mexico, and polls only began finding their way into newspapers since the 1988 presidential campaign. For accounts of the rise of polling in Mexico, see Federico Reyes Heroles, *Sondear a México*, and Roderic Ai Camp, ed., *Polling for Democracy: Public Opinion and Political Liberalization in Mexico*.

22 A full study of this phenomenon would have to focus on the press and its management of public manifestations, a work that is yet to be done. However, examples and illustrations are easily available to any reader of the Mexican press. Crucial instances of these processes have occurred in the aftermath of the 1985 earthquake (what was "the meaning" of the popular and the governmental reactions to the disaster?), during the Consejo Estudiantil Universitario (CEU) student movement, during the 1988 elections, after the imprisonment of oil workers' union leader "La Quina," after the assassinations of Cardinal Posada, Luis Donaldo Colosio, and José Francisco Ruiz Massieu, during the Zapatista rebellion, and after the devaluation of the peso in 1995. All these events (and an infinite number of smaller ones) are the foci of political contention through the interpretation of their "true" nature and meaning. An ethnographic description of the dynamics of political interpretation during Mexican campaigns can be found in Claudio Lomnitz, "Usage politique de l'ambigüité: Le cas mexicain."

23 Guillermo de la Peña, *A Legacy of Promises: Agriculture, Politics and Ritual in the Morelos Highlands*, 58.

24  Cancian, *The Decline of Community in Zinacantán*, 151–70.

25  The Mixe of Oaxaca discriminate between good and evil merchants, whose money is, respectively, good and evil, depending on whether they organize a series of pre-scribed rituals and on whether or not they are sensitive to the needs of community members. See James B. Greenberg, "Capital, Ritual, and Boundaries of the Closed Corporate Community."

## 8. CENTER, PERIPHERY, AND THE CONNECTIONS BETWEEN NATIONALISM AND LOCAL DISCOURSES OF DISTINCTION

1  Louis Dumont, *Essays on Individualism: Modern Ideology in Anthropological Perspective*, 279.

2  The main anthropological works on Tepoztlán are Robert Redfield, *Tepoztlán: A Mexican Village*, Oscar Lewis, *Life in a Mexican Village* and *Pedro Martínez*, and Claudio Lomnitz, *Evolución de una sociedad rural*, but there a number of shorter pieces on the place, including Pedro Carrasco, "The Family Structure of XVIth Century Tepoztlán," and Phillip K. Bock, "Tepoztlán Reconsidered." María Rosas, *Tepoztlán, crónica de de-sacatos y resistencia*, is a journalistic account of recent political conflict in the village.

3  For discussions of the history of the relationship between lowlands and highlands in Morelos, see Arturo Warman, "*We Come to Object*": *The Peasants of Morelos and the National State*, 33–41, and Guillermo de la Peña, *A Legacy of Promises: Agriculture, Politics and Ritual in the Morelos Highlands*, 20–37.

4  It is difficult to discern what the historical bases of the Tepoztécatl myth may have been. Local and regional intellectuals, such as Pedro (Pbo.) Rojas, *El Tepoztécatl legendario*, and Juan Dubernard, *Apuntes para la historia de Tepoztlán*, unequivocally identify El Tepoztécatl as the reigning *tlatoani* (indigenous ruler) of the time of Spanish Conquest and as the first Tepoztecan to take baptismal rites. Others, including Redfield and Lewis, have assumed that El Tepoztécatl was a mythical, and not a historical, figure. The interpretation is, in any case, difficult.

Several early sources refer to Tepuztécatl. Fray Juan de Torquemada names him as one of the lords that Moctezuma dispatched to the Gulf Coast with gifts for Cortés (*Monarquía indiana*, vol. 2, 59). Fray Diego Durán (*Historia de las Indias de Nueva España e islas de la Tierra Firme*, vol. 2, 292) mentions Tepuztécatl as one of the gods that priests impersonated, along with Quetzalcoatl, Huitzilopochtli, Tlaloc, and others. These god-priests were charged with the sacrifice of numerous victims. In the instance named by Durán, sacrifices were initiated by King Axayacatl (reigned 1468–81), who, after having had his fill of slaughtering, passed the knife over to General Tlacaelel, who in turn was succeeded in this honor by the various god-priests. Fray Berardino de Sahagún mentions Tepuztécatl as one of the men in-volved in the discovery of pulque after the Mexica departed from Temoanchan in their pilgrimage to México-Tenochtitlán (*Florentine Codex*, book 10, 193).

It is possible, therefore, that Tepuztécatl was simultaneously the name of a god and the title taken by the *tlatoani*-priest of Tepoztlán who was charged with the care of the temple to the pulque god Ome Tochtli. It is also possible that a single *tlatoani* appropriated this name, under the model of the high priest Ce Acatl Quetzalcoatl. Finally, Tepuztécatl may have referred generically to nobles from Tepoztlán. In any case, Tepuztécatl appears in several historic-mythical periods, beginning with the migration from Aztlán, to a god of the Aztec pantheon under King Axayacatl, to a lord who met Cortés, to numerous modern-day apparitions in the figure of an old, wood-carrying peasant who appeared in the mountains and warned his countrymen against a road, a fast train, a cable car, and a golf course.

5   Joaquín Gallo, *Tepoztlán: personajes, descripciones y sucedidos*, 15; translation and adaptation are mine.

6   Silvio Zavala, ed., *El servicio personal de los indios en la Nueva España*, vol. 1, 294–97.

7   Ross Hassig, *Aztec Warfare: Imperial Expansion and Political Control*, 249.

8   Gallo, *Tepoztlán*, 163.

9   "The *indígenas* of Tepoztlán present themselves before Maximilian and Carlota to offer personally their complete support, and simultaneously thank them for allowing 'some poor *indígenas*' to be worthy of seeing their faces" (in *Periódico Oficial del Imperio Mexicano*, 28 de junio de 1864; reprinted in Teresa Rojas Rabiela, *El indio en la prensa nacional del siglo diecinueve*, vol. 1, 22).

10  *La Jornada*, October 1, 1995.

11  Ismael Díaz Cadena, trans., *Libro de tributos del Marquesado del Valle (1540)*. These census materials have been analyzed by Pedro Carrasco in "The Family Structure of XVIth Century Tepoztlán" and "Estratificación social indígena en Morelos durante el siglo XVI."

12  Peter Gerhard discusses the shape of the pre-Columbian kingdoms in present-day Morelos in "A Method for Reconstructing Precolumbian Political Boundaries in Central Mexico." Lewis (*Life in a Mexican Village*, 21) shows the sites of pre-Columbian habitation in Tepoztlán in contrast with modern-day settlement patterns. Before the Conquest, and in all probability at the time of this census, Tepoztecans lived in a number of scattered settlements at the feet of the Sierra de Tepoztlán and were not concentrated in a village. This is consonant with James Lockhart's discussion of the *altepetl* (*The Nahuas after the Conquest*, 15–20).

13  See Fray Agustín Dávila Padilla, *Historia de la fundación y discurso de la provincia de Santiago de México*.

14  Serge Gruzinski provides an account of the ways in which secularization was understood and resisted in the Altos de Morelos in *Man-Gods in the Mexican Highlands: Indian Power and Colonial Society, 1520–1800*, 105–72.

15  See Robert Haskett, *Indigenous Rulers: An Ethnohistory of Town Government in Colonial Cuernavaca*, 153–60 for the colonial history of this family.

16  In fact, in *Five Families*, Oscar Lewis contrasts the mediation of local community culture on Tepoztecan family life with the unmediated effects of capitalism on the Mexico City poor. Lewis felt that the "culture of poverty" was an urban phenomenon not because material conditions in the city were worse than in Tepoztlán—they were not—but rather because the urban experience of poverty was not mediated by a traditional collectivity.

17  For a more detailed discussion of this strategy and its deployment in modern Tepoztecan history, see Lomnitz, *Evolución de una sociedad rural*, 292–307.

18  Although I have not had the opportunity of verifying this in Tepoztlán, I believe that these ideas regarding peasant production are easily transferred to some of the other activities that Tepoztecans now engage in, particularly artisanal work (masonry, self-employed mechanics, bakers, etc.) and petty commerce. Greenberg (1994) provides an example of this kind of transference in his discussion of distinctions between "clean" and "dirty" money that are drawn among Oaxacan Mixe merchants. His material suggests the capacity of this peasant ideology to expand

beyond agriculture and into other forms of work. Essentially, a merchant's money is "clean" if he or she redistributes profits into the local community and if prices and loans to community members are low.

19 For an explication of traditional ideas on health in this region, see John Ingham, "On Mexican Folk Medicine." Michael Taussig's well-known study of capitalism in Colombia (*The Devil and Commodity Fetishism in South America*) develops an analysis with many parallels to this Tepoztecan ideology.

20 Lewis, *Life in a Mexican Village*, 231–35.

21 Lewis, *Pedro Martínez*, 119–20.

22 For more information on this process, see Lomnitz, *Evolución de una sociedad rural*, 157–74, and Lewis, *Life in a Mexican Village*, 235–40.

23 Lewis, *Life in a Mexican Village*, 26, 119–23.

24 See, for instance, most of the articles signed by "Alexis" in *El Tepozteco* during the 1920s, in AHT. Alexis was the pseudonym of father Pedro Rojas.

25 In a revealing admonition, the same writer calls on municipal authorities to consult with the literate municipal secretary: "If our ignorance blocks the good intentions that inspire us, if our unfamiliarity with rules and such interferes with our aims, let us approach our enlightened municipal secretariat, which, in all goodness, will remove the veil of ignorance that overpowers and annihilates us" (*El Tepozteco*, February 1, 1921, 3).

26 Redfield, *Tepoztlán*, 220; Lewis, *Life in a Mexican Village*, 26.

27 Redfield, *Tepoztlán*, 68.

28 Claudio Lomnitz, *Exits from the Labyrinth: Culture and Ideology in Mexican National Space*, 130–32.

29 *El Tepozteco*, April 1, 1922, 4.

30 Poet Carlos Pellicer donated his private collection of pre-Columbian artifacts for a new archaeological museum in Tepoztlán—the village's earlier collection had been destroyed during the revolution. Oscar Lewis's research project brought medical assistance to the village in the 1940s, and help from prominent visitors was enlisted for getting electricity and a junior high school (see Lomnitz, *Evolución de una sociedad rural*, chapter 2).

31 Bock, "Tepoztlán Reconsidered."

### 9. INTERPRETING THE SENTIMENTS OF THE NATION

1 A governmental state will "set up economy at the level of the entire state, which means exercising towards its inhabitants, and the wealth and behavior of all, a form of surveillance and control as attentive as that of the head of the family over his household and his good" (Michel Foucault, "Governmentality," in *The Foucault Effect, Studies on Governmentality*, 92. The "population," which is measured through a variety of statistics and with the help of a number of sciences, is thus the central concern of administration.

2 On the ways in which "public" and "republic" were understood in the Spanish colonial world, and on their transformation with independence, see François-Xavier Guerra and Annick Lamperière, "Introducción," in *Los espacios públicos en Iberoamérica: ambigüedades y problemas, siglos XVIII–XIX*, 5–26. For a sketch of the history of Mexican censuses, see Claudio Lomnitz, *Modernidad indiana: nación y mediación en México*, chapter 5.

3  Theories of administration such as German cameralism, applied by the Baron von Humboldt to New Spain in 1803, are classical instruments of governmentality, because they are oriented to treating the whole of the polity as if it were a business. See Albion W. Small, *The Cameralists, the Pioneers of German Social Polity.*

4  For a rich discussion of the relationship between *gente sensata* and baroque ritual, see Pamela Voekel, "Scent and Sensibility: Pungency and Piety in the Making of the Veracruz *Gente Sensata.*" Hugo Nutini provides the only general overview of the history of Mexico's aristocracy. He argues that the Mexican aristocracy underwent three periods of expansion, each of which was related to significant economic transformations, one of these the mining boom of the eighteenth century (*Wages of Conquest: The Mexican Aristocracy in the Context of Western Aristocracies*).

5  For a statistical analysis of the contents of the *Gazeta de Lima*, see Tamar Herzog, "La gaceta de Lima (1756–1761): la restructuración de la realidad y sus funciones."

6  For the use of the discourse of the marvelous as a propagandistic device, see Greenblatt 1992. For connections between colonial discourses of the marvelous and the literary movement devoted to the *real maravilloso*, see Giucci 1992.

7  For contrasting accounts of the origins of underdevelopment in the nineteenth century, see John Coatsworth, "Obstacles to Economic Growth in 19th Century Mexico," and Jaime O. Rodríguez, *Down from Colonialism.*

8  In her thesis on statistics in the early postindependent period, Laura Leticia Mayer Celis (1995) shows that national independence generated a flurry of statistics, as well as an interest in comparative national statistics, but that the scientific basis of these statistics lacked credibility even in their own time.

9  For an account of the emergence of polling written by an ardent proponent of this method, see Federico Reyes Heroles, *Sondeara México.*

10  This point is carefully argued in Fernando Escalante, *Ciudadanos imaginarios*, and in François Xavier Guerra, *México del antiguo régimen a la revolución.*

11  Maya Indians were also sold into slavery in Cuba during the second half of the nineteenth century.

12  For the image of the *rurales*, see Paul J. Vanderwood, *Disorder and Progress: Bandits, Police, and Mexican Development.* On Porfirian urban intervention, see Barbara Tenenbaum, "Streetwise History: The Paseo de la Reforma and the Porfirian State, 1876–1910." The most comprehensive discussion of the strategies and politics of national presentation in the international arena during this period is Mauricio Tenorio-Trillo, *Mexico at the World's Fairs: Crafting a Modern Nation.*

13  Carlos Monsiváis, *Los rituales del caos*, 141.

14  See Larissa Lomnitz, Claudio Lomnitz, and Ilya Adler, "Functions of the Form: Power Play and Ritual in the 1988 Mexican Presidential Campaign."

15  Francisco I. Madero, "Manifiesto de Madero al Pueblo, a los capitalistas, a los gobernantes, al ejército libertador, al ejército nacional y a la prensa, México DF, 24 de junio de 1911," 237.

16  For a fascinating fictional account of Madero as a spiritualist leader, see Ignacio Solares, *Madero, el otro.* Solares's description of Madero's spiritualist sessions is based on Madero's diary. Other revolutionary leaders and presidents, such as Álvaro Obregón and Plutarco Elías Calles, were also spiritualists. Also pertinent to this question is the philosopher Antonio Caso's appeal to the powers of intuition via Bergson against the Porfirian *científicos'* faith in positivism.

17 For a useful discussion of this concept, see Slavoj Žižek, "Cyberspace, or, How to Traverse the Fantasy in the Age of the Retreat of the Big Other."

18 On the nature of government involvement and subsidy of the press, see Raymundo Riva Palacio, "A Culture of Collusion: The Ties That Bind the Press and the PRI. " The best-paid collaborators of the Mexican press are political columnists and well-known intellectuals who have regular columns.

19 José Ortega y Gasset, *España invertebrada: bosquejo de algunos pensamientos históricos*, 86.

20 On the politics of antipolitics as a strategy and historical phenomenon, see Ferguson 1994; for the relationship between technocracy and democracy in Mexico, see Miguel Ángel Centeno, *Democracy within Reason: Technocratic Revolution in Mexico*.

### 10. AN INTELLECTUAL'S STOCK IN THE FACTORY OF MEXICO'S RUINS

1 Enrique Krauze, "El mártir de Chicago"; Claudio Lomnitz, "Respuesta del Krauzificado de Chicago"; Enrique Krauze, "Adiós Míster Lomnitz." An interesting anti-Semitic coda to the debate occurred in a letter to the editor of the Mexican daily *Excelsior*: Augusto Hugo Peña, "Acerca de la fábrica de mentiras de Enrique Krauze," and my reply, "Respuesta al señor Augusto Hugo Peña."

2 Lorenzo Meyer, "En México nunca se hizo una historia oficial," interview with Arturo Mendoza Monciño.

3 Ricardo Pozas Horcasitas, *La democracia en blanco: el movimiento médico en México, 1964–1965*.

4 The Centro Cultural Arte Contemporáneo was in fact closed down in 1998.

5 Enrique Krauze, *Mexico: Biography of Power*, 797.

6 Ibid., xv.

7 Ibid.

8 Ibid., xiv.

9 In fact, the central thesis of *Mexico: Biography of Power* (i.e., the preponderance of the president's biography over Mexican history) is derived from an essay by Cosío Villegas that was written against Luis Echeverría—a president who had an especially strong delusion of omnipotence—titled *El estilo personal de gobernar* (1975). The theme of that essay, which was that in Mexico the president's personal whims had become a kind of *raison d'état*, is magnified by Krauze into *the* key to the whole of Mexican history.

10 See Enrique Krauze, *Textos heréticos* (1992).

11 These are Margarita de Orellana and Aurelio de los Reyes.

12 In the debate that followed the publication of this article, Krauze pointed out that he does in fact cite John Coatsworth once. He could not, however, dispute the fact that neither Coatsworth nor any of the others' ideas had any impact on his work. They did not. The Coatsworth citation in question is for factual information, and makes no direct or indirect reference to this author's ideas, many of which are incompatible with Krauze's.

13 Enrique Krauze misinterpreted this line to mean that he had not cited O'Gorman in his notes. I purposely counted only discussions in the body of the text, which is where Mr. Krauze deals with ideas. If we turn to the notes of *Mexico: Biography of Power*, O'Gorman is cited three times. On each occasion, the citation is for narrowly factual evidence, and not a discussion of any of Mr. O'Gorman's ideas; Mr. Cosío,

by contrast, gets discussed thirty-three times in the body of the text, and then is frequently cited in the notes for factual information.

14  See Enrique Krauze, *Por una democracia sin adjetivos* (1986). Not surprisingly, the phrase "democracy without adjectives" does not belong to Krauze, but is instead Rafael Segovia's, "La decadencia de la democracia," *Razones* 24 (March–April 1980).

15  Krauze, *Mexico: Biography of Power*, 243–44.

16  See Barbara Mundy, *The Mapping of New Spain: Indigenous Cartography and the Maps of the Relaciones Geográficas*, chapter 1.

17  See, for instance, my own book *Exits from the Labyrinth: Culture and Ideology in Mexican National Space*, part 2, chapter 2. For Argentina, see Jorge Myers, *Orden y virtud: el discurso republicano en el régimen rosista*. Other Latin American illustrations can be found in John Lynch, *Caudillos in Spanish America, 1800–1850*.

18  After Octavio Paz's death (and the initial publication of this essay, which appeared in print three months prior), Enrique Krauze purchased the shares of *Vuelta* and launched a new magazine, *Letras libres*, of which he is editor.

### 11. BORDERING ON ANTHROPOLOGY

1  Sherry Ortner reviews recent books on the crisis in anthropology in "Some Futures of Anthropology."

2  Notably, *Ethnos* devoted a special issue to peripheral anthropological traditions in 1983.

3  Arjun Appadurai, "Is Homo Hierarchicus?" 759.

4  Arjun Appadurai, "Theory in Anthropology: Center and Periphery," 358. This critique echoes Johannes Fabian's discussion of the practice of constructing anthropological sites as if they were "culture gardens" that were unconnected to the ethnographer's own society (*Time and the Other: How Anthropology Makes Its Object*). Similarly, Jonathan Friedman characterizes Geertzian cultural relativism in the following terms: "Each arbitrary anthropoplogical construction becomes a unique artifact to be cherished by its discoverer, a work of art in a gallery of distinct human species" ("Our Time, Their Time, World Time: The Transformation of Temporal Modes," 170).

5  The sense that Mexican anthropology is undergoing a difficult transition is reflected in different ways in a number of works, for example, Luis Vázquez León, "La historiografía antropológica contemporánea en México," and Claudio Lomnitz, *Modernidad indiana: nación y mediación en México*, chapter 4. Roger Bartra offers Mexicans a choice between four "intellectual deaths," one of which can be summarized as "death by academy" ( *La sangre y la tinta: ensayos sobre la condición postmexicana*, 43–48).

6  In 1973, Ralph Beals reviewed the field of Mexican anthropology and concluded that although it had had a relatively minor impact on anthropological theory, Mexican anthropology had played a critical role in the formation of a national conscience, and that the country had the third-largest number of anthropology professionals, after Japan and the United States (cited in Vázquez León, "La historiografía antropológica contemporánea en México," 139). In fact, however, a number of national anthropologies, especially in Latin America, but also elsewhere, have turned to Mexico for inspiration during the past century. It should be noted, nevertheless, that Mexico has never been a "pure model" but, as in the case of Mexico itself, Mexican-inspired national anthropologies shaped networks of national institutions

that were then connected especially to U.S., or occasionally European, missions: Cornell, Harvard, Chicago, Berkeley, Stanford, UNESCO, and French cultural missions have been some of the institutional partners of these national institutions. For the case of Peru, see Manuel Marzal, *Historia de la antropología indigenista: México y Perú*. The influence of Mexican anthropology on the anthropology of the United States receives subtle treatment in Mauricio Tenorio-Trillo, "Stereophonic Scientific Modernisms: Social Science between Mexico and the United States, 1880s–1930s," *Journal of American History*, and in José Limón, *American Encounters: Greater Mexico, the United States, and the Erotics of Culture*, chapter 2.

7  The reference is to Arturo Warman, "Todos santos, todos difuntos": "Criticism had been replaced by an [official] appointment *[un nombramiento]*. . . . Anthropology had been rewarded with lifelong benefits in the Instituto de Seguridad Social y Servicios a los Trabajadores del Estado" (34).

8  Guillermo Bonfil, "Del indigenismo de la revolución a la antropología crítica," in *De eso que llaman antropología mexicana*, 42.

9  Scientific research and critical discourse were subsequently (and erroneously, I think) counterposed to the practice of *indigenismo*: "The state doesn't care about the development of anthropology as a science that is capable of analyzing reality and modifying it deeply. At most it is interested in it as a technique to train restorers of ruins and taxidermists of languages and customs. However, it finds that the schools of anthropology . . . are centers where students gather and study reality in order to transform it, that they fight for democratic liberties, and that they maintain a militant attitude on the side of the oppressed" (Andrés Medina and Carlos García Mora, cited in Guadalupe Méndez Lavielle, "La quiebra política [1965–1976]," 362).

10  *Proceso*, March 13, 1995.

11  Foreign negative images of New Spain were the catalyst for some of the most distinguished eighteenth-century historical and anthropological writings by Mexican Creoles. For a discussion, see Antonello Gerbi, *The Dispute of the New World: The History of a Polemic, 1750–1900*.

12  The British Museum also calls the collector Henry Christy, who led Tylor to Mexico, the godfather of anthropology (*Henry Christy: A Pioneer of Anthropology*, 1).

13  Unveiling these connections is the painstaking subject of much of the scholarship of recent decades, from Latin American "dependency theory" to Edward Said's *Culture and Imperialism*, but it has also been a constant concern since the late nineteenth century.

14  Edward B. Tylor, *Anahuac, or Mexico and the Mexicans, Ancient and Modern*, 16–17.

15  It is worth noting that Tylor's viewpoint here coincides with that of Marx and Engels, both of whom saw the incorporation of Mexico into the United States as a desirable thing. Thus, during the Mexican-American War, Marx wrote: "We must hope that [the Americans] appropriate most of Mexico's territory and that they use the country better than the Mexicans have" (1847, in Domingo P. de Toledo y J., *México en la obra de Marx y Engels*, 28). Engels, in his turn, wrote on January 23, 1848: "We have witnessed the defeat of Mexico by the United States with due satisfaction . . . when a country is forcibly dragged to historical progress, we cannot but consider this as a step forward" (ibid.).

16  Tylor, *Anahuac*, 329–30.

17 The laxity of priestly mores is a theme that was well known to English readers since the publication of Thomas Gage's travels in seventeenth-century Mexico.

18 Tylor, *Anahuac*, 222. On the subject of the government's care for its antiquities, Tylor tells how he and Henry Christy literally created markets for antiquities: "At the top of the pyramid [of Cholula] we held a market, and got some curious things, all of small size however" (ibid., 275). Henry Christy's ethnographic collection became the most important of its time, and more than half of its registered pieces were Mexican (see British Museum, *Henry Christy*, 11).

19 For a standard recapitulation of this vision, see Warman, "Todos santos, todos difuntos," and Lomnitz, *Modernidad indiana*, chapter 4.

20 Mary Louise Pratt has tracked the connections between travel writing and anthropology in *Imperial Eyes: Travel Writing and Transculturation.*

21 Tenorio-Trillo's *Mexico at the World's Fairs: Crafting a Modern Nation* is the pathbreaking book on this subject.

22 Stacie G. Widdifield, *The Embodiment of the National in Late Nineteenth-Century Mexican Painting*, 61–64; Tenorio-Trillo, *Mexico at the World's Fairs*, 30.

23 Juan Estrada, "Estado Libre y Soberano de Guerrero; Datos estadísticos de la prefectura del Centro," *Boletín de la Sociedad Mexicana de Geografía y Estadística* (hereafter, BSMGE), vol. 3, 74.

24 Asamblea del Departamento de Querétaro, "Notas estadísticas del Departamento de Querétaro, formadas por la asamblea constitucional del mismo, y remitidas al supremo gobierno . . . ," BSMGE, vol. 3, 232. In a footnote, the Congress of Querétaro contrasts its enlightened view of race with the "horrible anomaly" of slavery in the United States.

25 Ibid.

26 Sociedad Mexicana de Geografía y Estadística, "Estadística de Yucatán, publicase por acuerdo dc la R. Sociedad de Geografía y Estadística, de 27 de enero de 1853," BMSGE 294.

27 Emilio Pineda, "Descripción geográfica del departamento de Chiapas y Soconusco," BMSGE 341.

28 Alfredo Chavero, *México a través de los siglos*, vol. 1, iv.

29 "Language is of great value for explaining ethnographic relations. Otomi is a language of an essentially primitive character. The Mexicans call it *otomitl*, but its true name is *hiá-hué*. All of the circumstances of this language reflect the poverty of expression of a people that is contemporaneous to humanity's infancy" (ibid., 65). In his views of indigenous linguistics, Chavero follows the work of Francisco Pimentel, ("Discurso sobre la importancia de la lengüística . . . , 370), who argues that monosyllabic languages, such as Chinese and Otomi, have no grammar and are the most primitive. Pimentel was also looking for even earlier evolutionary forms within Mexico, such as languages that combined mimicry and speech ("Lengua Pantomímica de Oaxaca . . . ," 473). In their disdain for Otomi and Chinese, Pimentel and Chavero were following racist trends in European romantic linguistics. See Martin Bernal, *Black Athena: The Afrocentric Roots of Classical Civilization*, vol. 1, 237–38. For a discussion of scientific stereotypes of Mexican Indians, see Robert Buffington, *Criminal and Citizen in Modern Mexico*, 149–55.

30 Chavero, *México a través de los siglos*, 69.

31 Ibid., 67.

32  Hubert Bancroft, "Observations on Mexico" (manuscript), 18–19.

33  Thus, Bancroft writes that "I am really astonished at the great number of pamphlets and books for the young relating to the history of this country, almanacs of history, catechisms of history, treatises on history, etc. These together with the numerous historical holidays and celebrations show as deep and demonstrative a love of country as may be found, I venture to assert, anywhere else on the globe. There is certainly nothing like it in the literature of the United States. Today, the 27th, one hundred years after the event, in this comparatively isolated capital [San Luis Potosí] there are two factions on the plaza almost coming to blows over an Iturbide celebration, the priests insisting that they will do honor to his memory, and the government party swearing that they shall not" (ibid., 40–41). In this instance, the date of the commemoration of Mexico's independence becomes the focal point for confrontations between liberals and conservatives. It is possible that Mexican obsessions with history had their roots in the civil wars, although there is certainly much influence from Spanish ideas of lineage and inheritance.

34  Guillermo de la Peña, "Nationals and Foreigners in the History of Mexican Anthropology," 279. Important sources on Gamio include Ángeles González Gamio, *Manuel Gamio, una lucha sin fin*; Mauricio Tenorio-Trillo, "Stereophonic Scientific Modernisms: Social Science between Mexico and the United States, 1880s–1930s"; Alexandra Stern, "Eugenics beyond Borders: Science and Medicalization in Mexico and the U.S. West, 1900–1950"; Aurelio de los Reyes, *Manuel Gamio y el cine*; Buffington, *Criminal and Citizen in Modern Mexico*; and José Limón, *American Encounters: Greater Mexico, the United States, and the Erotics of Culture*, chapter 2.

35  For example, for a wedding banquet in honor of the Gamio marriage, the Departamento de Antropología offered their honored guests dishes with titles such as "arroz a la tolteca," "mole de guajolote teotihuacano," "liebres de las pirámides," and "frijoles a la indiana." Invitation to the banquet is reproduced in González Gamio, *Manuel Gamio una lucha sin fin*.

36  See the debate in Ignacio Manuel Altamirano, *Diarios*, 108–45.

37  Manuel Gamio, *Opiniones y juicios sobre la obra La población del valle de Teotihuacán*, 2.

38  Ibid., 51.

39  Gamio was elected vice president of the Second International Eugenics Congress in Washington, D.C., in 1920 (Buffington, *Criminal and Citizen in Modern Mexico*, 154). For a full discussion of Mexican eugenics, see Alexandra Stern, "Buildings, Boundaries, and Blood: Medicalization and Nation-Buildings on the U.S.–Mexico Border, 1910–1930" and *Eugenics beyond Borders*, chapters 4 and 5.

40  Gamio, *Opiniones y juicios sobre la obra La población del valle de Teotihuacán*, 49; my emphasis.

41  The closest antecedent to Gamio's synthesis may have been the short-lived agrarian experiment carried out by Maximilian. See Jean Meyer, "La junta protectora de las clases menesterosas: indigenismo y agrarismo en el segundo imperio."

42  The difference between these two approaches was felt to be so sharp at the time that, in the 1917 constitutional convention, Porfirian *científicos* were seen as dubious Mexicans, as can be witnessed from the following speech by congressman José Natividad Macías on the proposed law of nationality: "Would any of you admit Mr. José Yves Limantour [Díaz's finance minister, born in Mexico of French descent] as a Mexican citizen by birth? Answer frankly and with your hand on your heart. (Voices: No! No!) Would you take as a Mexican by birth Oscar Braniff, Alterto

Braniff, or Tomás Braniff? *(Voices: No! No! We wouldn't take any científicos!)"* (in 50 *Discursos doctrinales en el congreso constituyente de la Revolución Mexicana, 1916–1917,* ed. Raul Noriega, 255; my emphasis).

43  Gonzalo Aguirre Beltrán, *Obra polémica,* 104.

44  The impact of the Cold War on Mexican anthropology has not yet been studied. The recent revelation that a former director of the National School of Anthropology, Gilberto López y Rivas, spied for the Soviet Union in the United States suggests that this is a significant topic. The effects of Plan Camelot on the intellectual climate in the region are better known (see Irving Louis Horowitz, *The Rise and Fall of Project Camelot).* Paul Sullivan's *Unfinished Conversations: Mayas and Foreigners between Two Wars* is a sensitive book on the relationship between anthropology and diplomacy in the first half of the twentieth century. On López y Rivas, see David Wise, *Cassidy's Run: The Secret Spy War over Nerve Gas,* chapter 12; Oswaldo Zavala, "Los pasos de López y Rivas como 'espía soviético' en Estados Unidos," *Proceso,* April 16, 2000; and Homero Campa, " 'Asumo mi responsabilidad y no me arrepiento', dice el ahora diputado," *Proceso,* April 16, 2000.

45  See, for example, Javier Téllez Ortega, "La época de oro (1940–1968)."

46  Oscar Lewis to Arnaldo Orfila, October 26, 1961, in Susan Rigdon, *The Culture Facade: Art, Science, and Politics in the Work of Oscar Lewis,* 288–89.

47  Mexican studies of Mexicans in the United States have a tradition, dating back to Gamio (1931). For a discussion of the ways in which these studies were subordinated to Mexican national interests, often at the expense of the Mexican-American perspective, see Limón, *American Encounters,* chapter 2.

48  Oscar Lewis to Vera Rubin, November 12, 1965, in Rigdon, *The Culture Facade,* 289.

49  Warman, "Todos santos, todos difuntos," 37.

## 12. PROVINCIAL INTELLECTUALS AND THE SOCIOLOGY OF THE SO-CALLED DEEP MEXICO

1  In this respect, this chapter is a prolongation of the work that I initiated in *Exits from the Labyrinth,* 221–41.

2  Geoff Eley, "Nations, Publics and Political Cultures: Placing Habermas in the 19th Century," 289.

3  Max Weber, *From Max Weber,* 176.

4  Gramsci's definition of intellectuals is more habitually used by anthropologists today (see *Selection from the Prison Notebooks,* 5). It is, in many ways, a useful definition, especially because it forces analysts to search for connections between processes of class formation and political discourse. I relied on Gramsci's definition in my earlier work on provincial intellectuals. However, Gramsci's famous definition says little about the nature of the work of intellectuals and, probably because of this, his followers can all too easily end up labeling anyone who makes an utterance that foments class awareness an "intellectual," thereby diminishing the utility of the category. For a more recent example of this, see Stephen Feierman, *Peasant Intellectuals: Anthropology and History in Tanzania.* I use Gramsci implicitly here as a useful supplement to Weber.

5  This description is based on a study of the documentation that is available on Tepoztlán in the Archivo General de la Nación (AGN), ramos de Tributos, Tierras, General de Parte, Hospital de Jesús, Indios and Criminal, as well as on local parish

records, and on ethnographic research done by myself in 1977–78 and 1992–93, and by others. Horacio Crespo and Enrique Vega published the 1909 Public Property Register of the whole of Morelos in *Tierra y propiedad en el fin del porfiriato*, vols. 2 and 3. From that census we can ascertain that in the hamlet of Santo Domingo, which will concern us here especially, the largest landowner owned a mere eight hectares, and 93 percent of the village's registered private agricultural plots were smaller than one hectare. The village's largest holding was 5.9 hectares. There is no reason to suppose that the land-tenure situation of Santo Domingo was any different in the colonial period.

6  AGN, Criminal, vol. 302, exp. 4, f. 206v–208.

7  In 1775, the *alcalde* of San Andrés de la Cal was selected by twenty-one electors. See AGN, Hospital de Jesús, vol. 9, fs. 27–28.

8  The vast majority of the *municipio*'s lands remained communal even to the end of the *porfiriato*. During that time, communal lands were classified into three types: forests, *texcal* (lava fields), and *agostadero* (grazing lands). All arable land was registered as private property. Texcal lands were used in a system of rotating, slash-and-burn agriculture that has been described in the detail by Oscar Lewis (*Life in a Mexican Village*, 148–54). Crespo and Vega (*Tierra y propiedad en el fin del porfiriato*, vol. 2, 212) reproduce the legal registration of these lands in 1909. Tepoztlán's retention of communal lands makes the village unusual in the Morelos region.

9  Womack's view was that most of the appropriation of pueblo lands by haciendas occurred after 1857 and, especially, during the early years of the sugar boom in the 1880s (*Zapata and the Mexican Revolution*). This position was first contested by Horacio Crespo and Herbert Frey ("La diferenciación social del campesinado como problema en la teoría de la historia"), who argued that Morelos's haciendas had expanded to their full extent as early as the seventeenth century. Crespo and Vega (*Tierra y propiedad en el fin del porfiriato*) reproduce the raw data from the 1909 property registrar that fostered these conclusions. Unfortunately, volume 1 of this work, which was to provide a full interpretation of this history, has not come to light. Florencia Mallon (*Peasant and Nation: The Making of Post-Colonial Mexico and Peru*, 137–41) shows that the *títulos primordiales* of several Morelos communities, including both Tepoztlán and Anenecuilco, were stolen during or immediately after the Wars of Independence, and that haciendas profited from this by invading village lands during the whole first half of the nineteenth century. A full synthesis of the relative importance of these three waves of land concentration has yet to be written. In addition, we need to know more about the history of changes in other forms of access to land, such as renting and sharecropping, although Womack's thesis regarding the pernicious role that capitalist intensification of sugar production had for traditional renting arrangements is still helpful in this regard.

10  Regarding endogamy, a few samples from the parochial archives are illustrative: of the 133 marriages that were celebrated in the church of Tepoztlán between 1684 and 1686, only one was between a Tepoztecan and someone from outside the *municipio*. Between 1792 and 1807, there were 694 marriages in the parish. Of these only 3.5 percent were between a Tepoztecan and an outsider, usually someone from a neighboring hacienda or village. Endogamy in the hamlets and the *cabecera* was also high, although the smaller hamlets often tended to marry villagers from another hamlet within the *municipio*. Oscar Lewis carried out a census in 1943 in which he

confirms the continued valence of these trends, and Sara Verazaluce, a Tepoztecan physical anthropologist working on this subject, has orally confirmed that there is still a very high level of village and municipal endogamy today (personal communication, March 1993).

11 In 1992, a Cuernavaca real-estate company wanted to purchase a sizable amount of land from peasants from San Andrés and Santa Catarina. It went about this in a secretive way, hiring insiders to purchase lands individually from farmers whom they knew. The same tactic had been taken earlier, in 1962, by the Montecastillo golf club development company (Claudio Lomnitz, *Evolución de una sociedad rural*, 201–4). When villagers woke up to these tactics, they rebelled and stopped the company's efforts. In 1995, attempts to resuscitate the golf-course project led to intense confrontations between the village and the state government, to factional strife within the village, and even to assassination.

12 Ethnographic information on Santo Domingo derives to a large degree from Pedro Antonio Velázquez Juárez, "Etnozoología y cosmogonía en los Altos de Morelos."

13 Ibid., 209.

14 See Roberto Varela, *Expansión de sistemas y relaciones de poder*, 111–54. The debates on Mexican democracy would do well to take such examples of local democracy into account. Authoritarianism must be understood as a regional system, and not simply as a mentality.

15 Records of Spaniards in the village extend back to the mid-sixteenth century. Martín Cortés built himself a house there (Silvio Zavala, ed., *El servicio personal de los indios in Nueva España*, vol. 2, 377–78), and there are other documented cases of Spaniards in the village even in this early period.

16 There were some periods in which there were mulattos in Tepoztlán. However, the parish records almost exclusively break the population down into Indian and Spanish, with a few mestizos and *castizos*. The 1909 property records show that whereas 93 percent of landholdings in Santo Domingo were plots of less than one hectare (and 78 percent were smaller than half a hectare), the corresponding figures for the *cabecera* are 62 percent and 37 percent. Whereas the three largest landowners in Santo Domingo owned between six and eight hectares, Tepoztlán had a number of proprietors who owned between twenty and forty hectares.

17 This was the case even into the *porfiriato*. One elderly Tepoztecan acquaintance who had worked on a hacienda before the revolution described the bad working conditions and culminated his story by saying, "And they called us Tepoztecan Indians!"

18 Lewis rightly criticized Redfield's reification of this distinction, and his identification of these categories with social class, but he was wrong in eschewing Redfield's observation altogether.

19 Translators for Spanish officials in the colonial period were also regularly from these *principales*.

20 AGN, Criminal, vol. 203, exp. 4, f. 159–66.

21 For the use of *corridos* in regional communication, see Robert Redfield, *Tepoztlán: A Mexican Village*, 180–93, and Catherine Heau, "Trova popular e identidad cultural en Morelos." For peasant common law in Zapata's camps, see Salvador Rueda, "La dinámica interna del zapatismo: consideración para el estudio de la cotidianeidad campesina en el área zapatista."

22 Lomnitz, *Evolución de una sociedad rural*, 299–307. James B. Greenberg, "Capital,

Ritual, and Boundaries of the Closed Corporate Community," is an interesting discussion of the way contemporary Mixes have developed mechanisms for distinguishing between "good" and "evil" merchants on the basis of the nature of their ties to local communitarian networks. This parallels good and evil politicians in Tepoztlán.

23 See Lomnitz, *Evolución de una sociedad rural,* chapter 3, for an account of these confrontations.

# References

*Archives*

AGN    Archivo General de la Nación
AHC    Archivo Histórico Condumex
AHT    Archivo Histórico de Tepoztlán
Claf    Colección Lafragua, Biblioteca Nacional, Mexico City
       Registro de la Propiedad del Estado de Morelos, 1909 (published by Crespo and Vega)
NARA  National Archives, Washington

*Primary Sources*

UNPUBLISHED SOURCES

Bancroft, Hubert. 1883. "Observations on Mexico" (manuscript). Bancroft Library, University of California Berkeley.
Primera secretaría de Estado Departmento esterior Sección 2. 1827. "Funeral real." May 19.
Rojas, José Guadalupe. n.d. (1870s). Personal diary. Valentín López González personal collection.

PUBLISHED SOURCES

*Actas constitucionales mexicanas (1821–1824)*. Mexico City: UNAM. 1980. 10 vols.
Altamirano, Ignacio Manuel. (1871). *Diarios*. In *Obras completas*, vol. 20. Mexico City: Conaculta.
Alva Ixtlilxóchitl, Fernando de. 1975. *Obras históricas*. 2 vols. Mexico City: UNAM.
Arellano, Lic. Jesús. 1841. "Oración cívica que en el aniversario del grito de independencia se pronunció en el palacio de govierno de Durango el 16 de septiembre de 1841." Claf.
Arenas, Francisco Javier. 1968. *Estado de Morelos*. Mexico City: Editorial Porrúa.

Asamblea del Departamento de Querétaro. 1852 (1845). "Notas estadísticas del Departamento de Querétaro, formadas por la asamblea constitucional del mismo, y remitidas al supremo gobierno. . . ." *Boletín de la Sociedad Mexicana de Geografía y Estadística*, vol. 3, 169–236.

Bulnes, Francisco. 1904. *El verdadero Juárez: la verdad sobre la intervención y el imperio.* Mexico City: Librería de la Viuda de Ch. Bouret.

Cabrera, Luis. 1910. "Los dos patriotismos." In *Obras completas*, vol. 2. Mexico City: Ediciones Oasis. 47–56.

Castañeda, Jorge G. 2000. "Ésta no es una elección de principios; es un referéndum para el cambio, dice el asesor foxista Jorge Castañeda." Interview by Antonio Jáquez, *Proceso*, June 4. 10–13.

Charles III of Spain. 1784. *Código negro carolino.* Ed. Javier Malagón Barceló. Santo Domingo: Ediciones El Taller.

Chavero, Alfredo. 1888. *Mexico a través de los siglos.* Vol. 1, *Historia antigua de la conquista.* Barcelona: Espasa.

Cortés, Ubaldo. n.d. *Leyenda de El Tepoztécatl.* Tepoztlán: No imprint.

Dávila Padilla, Fray Agustín. 1955 (1596). *Historia de la fundación y discurso de la provincia de Santiago de México.* Madrid: Academia Literaria.

Delgado, Ángel. 1953. *España y México en el siglo 19.* 3 vols. Madrid: Instituto Gonzalo Fernández de Oviedo.

Díaz Cadena, Ismael, trans. 1978 (ca. 1540). *Libro de tributos del Marquesado del Valle (1540).* Mexico City: Biblioteca Nacional de Antropología e Historia.

Durán, Fray Diego. (1967). *Historia de las Indias de Nueva España e islas de la Tierra Firme.* 2 vols. Mexico City: Editorial Porrúa.

Echagaray, Salvador. 1913. "El método estadístico y algunas de sus aplicaciones." *Boletín de la Sociedad Mexicana de Geografía y Estadística*, 5ª época, vol. 6, 62–78.

Estrada, Juan. 1852. "Estado Libre y Soberano de Guerrero; Datos estadísticos de la prefectura del Centro." *Boletín de la Sociedad Mexicana de Geografía y Estadística*, vol. 3, 71–75.

Evans, Colonel Albert S. 1870. *Our Sister Republic: A Gala Trip through Tropical Mexico 1869–1870.* Toledo, Ohio: Hartford Columbia.

Gage, Thomas. 1699. *A New Survey of the West-Indies.* London: M. Clark.

*La Gazeta de México*, 1ª y 2ª época. Various issues.

Guaman Poma de Ayala, Felipe. 1980 (1584–1614). *Nueve corónica i buen gobierno.* Mexico City: Siglo XXI.

Humboldt, Alexander von. 1984. *Ensayo político sobre el reino de la Nueva España.* Mexico City: Editorial Porrúa.

Jordán, Fernando. 1946. "En torno a la pregunta de un antropólogo." *La Prensa Gráfica*, December 16.

Krugman, Paul. 2000. "Mexico's New Deal." *New York Times*, Op-Ed, July 5.

*La dominación española en México.* 1878. Polémica sostenida por los periódicos *Diario Oficial* y *La Colonia Española* con motivo de la ley de colonización dada por el gobierno mexicano en 31 de mayo de 1875. 4th ed., vol. 4. Mexico City: Imprenta de *La Colonia Española*.

*Las Leyes de Indias.* 1890 (1680). Madrid: Biblioteca judicial.

Lima Barreto. 1997. *Triste fin de Policarpo Quaresma.* Paris: UNESCO.

López de Santa Anna, Antonio. 1988. *The Eagle: An Autobiography of Santa Anna.* Ed. Ann Fears Crawford. Austin, Tex.: State House Press.

Madero, Francisco I. 1911. "Manifiesto de Madero al Pueblo, a los capitalistas, a los gobernantes, al ejército libertador, al ejército nacional y a la prensa, México DF, 24 de junio de 1911." In *Fuentes para la historia de la Revolución mexicana*, vol. 4, *Manifiestos políticos, 1982–1912*, ed. Manuel González Ramírez. Mexico City: Fondo de Cultura Económica, 1950. 236–39.

Malagón Barceló, Javier. 1974 (1784). *Código negro carolino*. Santo Domingo: No imprint.

"Memoria de las Secretarías de relaciones y Guerra, Justicia, Negocios Eclesiásticos e Instrucción Pública del Gobierno del Estado de México, leida a la Honorable Legislatura en las sesiones de los días 1° y 2° de mayo de 1849 por el Secretario de esos ramos, C. Lic. Pascual González Fuentes." 1849, Colección Lafragua, Biblioteca Nacional.

Mendieta, Fray Jerónimo de. 1876 (1596). *Historia eclesiástica indiana*. 3 vols. Mexico City: Editorial Joaquín García Icazbalceta.

Mora, José María Luis. 1963 (1837). *Obras sueltas*. Mexico City: Editorial Porrúa.

Morelos, José María. 1965 (1810). "Bando de Morelos suprimiendo las castas y aboliendo la esclanitud, 17 de noviembre de 1810." In *Morelos: su vida revolucionaria a través de sus escritos*, ed. Ernesto Lemoine. Mexico City: UNAM. 162–63.

——. 1965 (1812). "A los americanos entusiasmados de los gachupines." In *Morelos: su vida revolucionaria a través de sus escritos*, ed. Ernesto Lemoine. Mexico City: UNAM. 197–200.

Noriega, Raúl, ed. 1967. *50 Discursos doctrinales en el congreso constituyente de la Revolución Mexicana, 1916–1917*. Mexico City: Instituto de Estudios Históricos de la Revolución Mexicana.

Oswald, Felix. 1880. *Summerland Sketches, or Rambles in the Backwoods of Mexico and Central America*. Philadelphia: J. B. Lippincott and Company.

Pimentel, Francisco. 1860a. "Discurso sobre la importancia de la lengüística, leido por el sr. D. Francisco Pimental al tomar asiento por primera vez en la Sociedad de Geografía y Estadística el 22 de agosto de 1861." *Boletín de la Sociedad Mexicana de Geografía y Estadística*, 1860, vol. 7, 367–71.

——. 1860b. Lengua Pantomímica de Oaxaca, en sesion del 19 de diciembre de 1861, leyó el sr. socio D. Francisco Pimentel la siguiente proposicion." *Boletín de la Sociedad Mexicana de Geografía y Estadística*, 1860, vol. 8, 473.

Pineda, Emilio. 1852. "Descripción geográfica del departamento de Chiapas y Soconusco." *Boletín de la Sociedad Mexicana de Geografía y Estadística*, 341.

*Proceso*. 1995. "Culmina el enfrentamiento con Zedillo: Carlos Salinas se va a un 'exilio convenido'." March 13, 6–7.

——. 2000a. "'Asumo mi responsabilidad y no me arrepiento', dice el ahora diputado," by Homero Campa. April 16.

——. 2000b. "Los pasos de López y Rivas como 'espía soviético' en Estados Unidos," by Oswaldo Zavala. April 16.

Real Academia Española. 1726–39 (1737). *Diccionario de la lengua castellana en que se explica el verdadero sentido de las voces . . . Madrid.*

"Relación de Tepoztlán." 1985 (1580). In *Relaciones geográficas de México*, vol. 1, ed. René Acuña. Mexico City: UNAM. 183–95.

Riva Palacio, Vicente, and Manuel Payno. 1870. *El libro rojo*. Mexico City: Díaz de León y White.

Rodó, Enrique. 1962. *Ariel*. Buenos Aires: Capelusz.

Rojas, Pedro (Pbo.). 1968. *El Tepoztécatl legendario.* Pamphlet, no imprint.

Rojas Rabiela, Teresa, ed. 1992. *El indio en la prensa nacional del siglo diecinueve.* Mexico City: Casa Chata.

Rouaix, Pastor. 1928. Algunas rectificaciones al Censo del Estado de Durango, practiado en el año de 1921. *Boletín de la Sociedad Mexicana de Geografía y Estadística,* 5ª época, vol. 37: 259–82.

Sahagún, Fray Bernardino de. 1961. *Florentine Codex.* Book 10. Trans. Charles Dibble and Arthur J. O. Anderson. Santa Fe: School of American Research.

Sánchez, González, Agustín. 1995. *Los mejores chistes sobre presidentes.* Mexico City: Planeta.

Santoyo, Francisco. 1842. "Opúsculo patriótico, que pronunció el ciudadano teniente coronel graduado Francisco Santoyo, como miembro de la junta patriótica de esta ciudad [de Orizaba] el dia 11 de septiembre de 1842." Claf.

Secretaría de Programación y Presupuesto. 1988. *El censo de población de Nueva España 1790, primer censo de México.* Mexico City: SPP.

Sierra, Justus, ed. 1900. *Mexico: Its Social Evolution.* 3 vols. Mexico City: J. Ballescá and Company.

Sociedad Mexicana de Geografía y Estadística. 1852. "Estadística de Yucatán, publicase por acuerdo de la R. Sociedad de Geografía y Estadística, de 27 de enero de 1853." *Boletín de la Sociedad Mexicana de Geografía y Estadística,* 238–339.

Tena Ramírez, Felipe, ed. 1957. *Leyes fundamentales de México, 1808–1957.* Mexico City: Editorial Porrúa.

Toledo y J., Domingo P. de. 1939. *México en la obra de Marx y Engels.* Mexico City: Fondo de Cultura Económica.

Torquemada, Fray Juan de. 1975 (1615). *Monarquía indiana.* 7 vols. Mexico City: UNAM.

Torre Villar, Ernesto de la, Moisés González Navarro, and Stanley Ross, eds. 1974. *Historia documental de México.* 2 vols. Mexico City: UNAM.

Tovar, Pantaleón. 1872. *Historia parlamentaria del cuarto congreso constitucional,* vol. 1. Mexico City: Imprenta de I. Cumplido.

Turner, John Kenneth. 1911. *Barbarous Mexico.* Chicago: C. H. Kerr and Company.

Tylor, Edward B. 1861. *Anahuac, or Mexico and the Mexicans, Ancient and Modern.* London: Longman, Green, Longman, and Roberts.

Vasconcelos, José. 1982. *Ulises criollo.* In *Memorias,* vol. 1. Mexico City: Fondo de Cultura Económico.

Villavicencio, Pablo. 1975. *The Political Pamphlets of Pablo Villavicencio, "El Payo de Rosario."* 2 vols. Ed. James McKegney. Amsterdam: Rodopi.

Zavala, Lorenzo de. 1976 (1834). "Viaje a los Estados Unidos del Norte de América, 1834." In *Obras,* ed. Manuel González Ramírez. Mexico City: Editorial Porrúa.

Zavala, Silvio, ed. 1987. *El servicio personal de los indios en la Nueva España.* 3 vols. Mexico City: El Colegio de México.

## Secondary Sources

Adler, Ilya. 1986. "Media Uses and Effects in a Large Bureaucracy: A Case Study in Mexico." Ph.D. dissertation, Department of Communication, University of Wisconsin, Madison.

Adorno, Rolena. 1986. *Guaman Poma: Writing and Resistance in Colonial Peru.* Austin: University of Texas Press.

Aguirre Beltrán, Gonzalo. 1972 (1946). *La población negra de México, 1519–1810.* Mexico City: Fondo de Cultura Económica.

———. 1992 (1976). *Obra polémica.* Mexico City: Fondo de Cultura Económica.

Alberro, Solange. 1988. *Inquisition et société au Mexique, 1571–1700.* Mexico City: CEMCA.

Aljovín, Cristobal. 1997. "Poderes locales en la primera mitad del XIX." *Histórica* 21(1): 1–25.

Alonso, Jorge. 1986. *Los movimientos sociales en el Valle de México.* Mexico City: SEP.

Anderson, Benedict. 1994 (1983). *Imagined Communities.* London: Verso.

Appadurai, Arjun. 1986a. "Is Homo Hierarchicus?" *American Ethnologist* 13(4): 745–61.

———. 1986b. "Theory in Anthropology: Center and Periphery. *Comparative Studies in Society and History* 28(2): 356–61.

———. 1996. *Modernity at Large: Cultural Dimensions of Globalization.* Minneapolis: University of Minnesota Press.

———. 1998. "Dead Certainty: Ethnic Violence in the Era of Globalization." *Public Culture* 10(2): 225–47.

Archer, Christon. 1989. "The Young Antonio López de Santa Anna: Veracruz Counterinsurgent and Incipient Caudillo." In *The Human Condition in Latin America: The Nineteenth Century,* ed. Judith Ewell and William Beezley. Wilmington, Del.: SR Books. 3–16.

Arnold, Linda. 1988. *Bureaucracy and Bureaucrats in Mexico City, 1742–1835.* Tucson: University of Arizona Press.

Arnold, Matthew. 1962. "On the Study of Celtic Literature." In *The Complete Prose Works of Matthew Arnold,* vol. 3. Ann Arbor: University of Michigan Press.

Arrom, Silvia. 1996. "Popular Politics in Mexico City: The Parián Riot, 1828." In *Riots in the Cities: Popular Politics and the Urban Poor in Latin America, 1765–1910,* ed. Silvia Arrom and Servando Otoll. Wilmington, Del.: SR Books. 71–96.

Arróniz, Othón. 1979. *Teatro de la evangelización en Nueva España.* Mexico City: UNAM.

Astorga, Luis. 2000. "Traficantes de drogas, políticos y policías en el siglo veinte mexicano." In *Vicios públicos, virtudes privadas: la corrupción en México,* ed. Claudio Lomnitz. Mexico City: CIESAS-Miguel Ángel Porrúa.

Azuela, Antonio, ed. 1993. *La urbanización popular y el orden jurídico en América Latina.* Mexico City: UNAM.

Bartra, Roger. 1993 (1987). *The Cage of Melancholy.* New Brunswick, N.J.: Rutgers University Press.

———. 1999. *La sangre y la tinta: ensayos sobre la condición postmexicana.* Mexico City: Editorial Oceano.

Batres, Leopoldo. 1888. *Clasificación del tipo étnico de las tribus zapotecas del estado de Oaxaca y Acolhua del Valle de México.* Mexico City: Imprenta del Gobierno Federal.

Beezley, William, Cheryl Martin, and William French, eds. 1994. *Rituals of Rule, Rituals of Resistance: Public Celebrations and Popular Culture in Mexico.* Wilmington, Del.: SR Books.

Bernal, Martin. 1987. *Black Athena: The Afrocentric Roots of Classical Civilization.* Vol. 1. New Brunswick, N.J.: Rutgers University Press.

Bhabha, Homi K. 1990. "DissemiNation: Time, Narrative, and the Margins of the Modern Nation." In *Nation and Narration,* ed. Homi K. Bhabha. New York: Routledge. 291–322.

Bliss, Katherine. 1996. "Prostitution, Revolution and Social Reform in Mexico City, 1918–1940." Ph.D. dissertation, Department of History, University of Chicago.

Bock, Phillip K. 1980. "Tepoztlán Reconsidered." *Journal of Latin American Folklore* 6(1): 129–50.

Bonfil, Guillermo. 1970. "Del indigenismo de la revolución a la antropología crítica." In *De eso que llaman antropología mexicana,* ed. Arturo Warman, Guillermo Bonfil, Margarita Nolasco, Mercedes Olivera, and Enrique Valencia. Mexico City: Editorial Nuestro Tiempo.

———. 1987. *México profundo.* Mexico City: SEP.

Boyer, Christopher. 1997. "The Cultural Politics of Agrarismo: Agrarian Revolt, Village Revolutionaries, and State-Formation in Michoacán, Mexico." Ph.D. dissertation, Department of History, University of Chicago.

Brading, David A. 1971. *Miners and Merchants in Bourbon Mexico, 1763–1810.* Cambridge: Cambridge University Press.

———. 1972. *Los orígenes del nacionalismo mexicano.* Mexico City: ERA.

———. 1984. "Bourbon Spain and Its American Empire." In *Cambridge History of Latin America,* vol. 1, ed. Leslie Bethell. New York: Cambridge University Press. 389–440.

———. 1991. *The First America: The Spanish Monarchy, Creole Patriots and the Liberal State, 1492–1867.* New York: Cambridge University Press.

Breckenridge, Carol. 1989. "The Aesthetics and Politics of Colonial Collecting: India at World Fairs." *Comparative Studies in Society and History* 32(2): 195–215.

Bricker, Victoria. 1985. *The Indian Christ, the Indian King.* Austin: University of Texas Press.

British Museum. 1965. *Henry Christy: A Pioneer of Anthropology.* London: British Museum.

Buffington, Robert. 2000. *Criminal and Citizen in Modern Mexico,* Lincoln: University of Nebraska Press.

Camp, Roderic Ai, ed. 1996. *Polling for Democracy: Public Opinion and Political Liberalization in Mexico.* Wilmington, Del.: SR Books.

Cancian, Frank. 1965. *Economics and Prestige in a Maya Community.* Stanford, Calif.: Stanford Unversity Press.

———. 1992. *The Decline of Community in Zinacantán.* Stanford, Calif.: Stanford University Press.

Carrasco, Pedro. 1961. "The Civil-Religious Hierarchy in Mesoamerican Communities." *American Anthropologist* 63: 483–97.

———. 1964. "The Family Structure of XVIth Century Tepoztlán." In *Process and Pattern in Culture: Essays in Honor of Julian H. Steward,* ed. Robert A. Manners. Chicago: Aldine. 185–210.

———. 1976. "Estratificación social indígena en Morelos durante el siglo XVI." In *Estratificación social en la Mesoamérica pre-hispánica,* ed. Pedro Carrasco and Johanna Broda. Mexico City: Sepinah. 102–17.

———. 1991 (1967). "La transformación de la cultura indígena durante la colonia." In *Los pueblos de indios y las comunidades,* ed. Bernardo García Martínez. Mexico City: El Colegio de Mexico. 1–29.

Castells, Manuel. 1983. *The City and the Grassroots.* Berkeley: University of California Press.

Centeno, Miguel Ángel. 1997. *Democracy within Reason: Technocratic Revolution in Mexico.* University Park, Pa.: Penn State University Press.

Chakrabarty, Dipesh. 1992. "Provincializing Europe: Postcoloniality and the Critique of History." *Cultural Studies* 6(2): 337–57.

Chevalier, François. 1970. *Land and Society in Colonial Mexico.* Berkeley: University of California Press.

Clifford, James. 1988 (1981). "On Ethnographic Surrealism." In *The Predicament of Culture.* Cambridge: Harvard University Press, 117–51.

Coatsworth, John. 1978. "Obstacles to Economic Growth in 19th Century Mexico." *American Historical Review* 79(1): 80–100.

Cohn, Bernard. 1996. *Colonialism and Its Forms of Knowledge: The British in India.* Princeton, N.J.: Princeton University Press.

Collier, William Miller, and Guillermo Feliú Cruz. 1926. *La primera misión de los EEUU en Chile.* Santiago: Imprenta Cervantes.

Comaroff, Jean. 1999. *Body of Power, Spirit of Resistance.* Chicago: University of Chicago Press.

Contreras, Jaime. 1995. "Los primeros años de la inquisición: guerra civil, monarquía, mesianismo y herejía." In *El Tratado de Tordesillas y su época,* vol. 2, ed. Luis Ribot García. Madrid: Junta de Castilla y Aragón. 681–703.

Cosío Villegas, Daniel. 1975. *El estilo personal de gobernar.* Mexico City: Joaquín Mortiz.

Crespo, Horacio, and Enrique Vega. 1982. *Tierra y propiedad en el fin del porfiriato.* Vols. 2 and 3. Mexico City: Centro de Estudios Históricos del Agrarismo en México.

Crespo, Horacio, and Herbert Frey. 1982. "La diferenciación social del campesinado como problema en la teoría de la historia." *Revista Mexicana de Sociología* 43(1) 285–313.

Crespo, Horacio, ed. 1984. *Morelos: cinco siglos de historia regional.* Mexico City: Centro de Estudios Históricos del Agrarismo en México.

DaMatta, Roberto. 1985. *A casa e a rua: Espaço, cidadania, mulher e morte no Brasil.* São Paulo: Brasiliense.

———. 1991 (1979). *Carnivals, Rogues and Heroes.* South Bend, Ind.: University of Notre Dame Press.

Dawson, Alexander. 1997. "*Indigenismo* and the Paradox of the Nation in Post-Revolutionary Mexico." Ph.D. dissertation, Department of History, State University of New York, Stony Brook.

Deleuze, Gilles, and Félix Guattari. 1987 (1980). *A Thousand Plateaus: Capitalism and Schizophrenia.* Minneapolis: University of Minnesota Press.

Díaz de León, Antonio. 1986. *Utopía y resistencia.* Mexico City: ERA.

Domínguez Ortiz, Antonio. 1989. *Carlos III y la España de la Ilustración.* Madrid: Alianza Editorial.

Duara, Prasenjit. 1995. *Rescuing History from the Nation: Questioning Narratives of Modern China.* Chicago: University of Chicago Press.

Dubernard, Juan. 1983. *Apuntes para la historia de Tepoztlán.* Cuernavaca: No imprint.

Dumont, Louis. 1986. *Essays on Individualism: Modern Ideology in Anthropological Perspective.* Chicago: University of Chicago Press.

Eley, Geoff. 1992. "Nations, Publics and Political Cultures: Placing Habermas in the 19th Century." In *Habermas and the Public Sphere,* ed. Craig Calhoun. Cambridge: MIT Press. 289–339.

Elliott, John. 1984. "Spain and America in the Sixteenth and Seventeenth Centuries." In *Cambridge History of Latin America,* vol. 1, ed. Leslie Bethel. Cambridge: Cambridge University Press. 287–340.

Escalante, Fernando. 1992. *Ciudadanos imaginarios.* Mexico City: El Colegio de México.

———. 1995. *El principito.* Mexico City: Cal y Arena.

Escobar, Arturo. 1995. *Encountering Development: The Making and Unmaking of the Third World.* Princeton, N.J.: Princeton University Press.

Ewell, Judith, and William Beezley, eds. 1989. *The Human Condition in Latin America: The Nineteenth Century,* Wilmington, Del: SR Books.

Fabian, Johannes. 1983. *Time and the Other: How Anthropology Makes Its Object.* New York: Columbia University Press.

Feher, Ferenc. 1992 (1989). "Revolutionary Justice." In *Regicide and Revolution,* ed. Michael Waltzer. New York: Columbia University Press.

Feierman, Steven. 1990. *Peasant Intellectuals: Anthropology and History in Tanzania.* Madison: University of Wisconsin Press.

Ferguson, James. 1994. *The Anti-Politics Machine: "Development," Depoliticization, and Bureaucratic Power in Lesotho.* Minneapolis: University of Minnesota Press.

Fernández Abadalejo, Pablo. 1995. "'Rey Católico': gestación y metamorfosis de un título." In *El Tratado de Tordesillas y su época,* vol. 1, ed. Luis Ribot García. Madrid: Junta de Castilla y de Aragón. 209–16.

Fleischer, Cornell. 1992. "The Lawgiver as Messiah: The Making of the Imperial Image in the Reign of Suleyman." In *Soliman le magnifique et son temps,* ed. Gilles Veinstein. Paris: Documentation française. 159–77.

Flores Caballero, Romeo. 1974 (1969). *Counterrevolution: The Role of the Spaniards in the Independence of Mexico, 1804–38.* Lincoln: University of Nebraska Press.

Florescano, Enrique. 1996. "Indian, Spanish, and Liberal Iconographic Traditions in Mexico and the Creation of National Symbols." MS presented at the Getty Center for the History of Art and the Humanities, Los Angeles.

Foucault, Michel. 1991. "Governmentality." In *The Foucault Effect: Studies in Governmentality,* ed. Graham Burchell, Colin Gordon, and Peter Miller. Chicago: University of Chicago Press.

Friedlander, Judith. 1975. *Being Indian in Hueyapan: A Case of Forced Identity.* New York: St. Martin's Press.

Friedman, Jonathan. 1985. "Our Time, Their Time, World Time: The Transformation of Temporal Modes." *Ethnos* 50: 168–83.

Friedrich, Paul. 1986. *Princes of Naranja.* Austin: University of Texas Press.

Fuentes, Carlos. 1982 (1960). *Where the Air Is Clear.* New York: Farrar, Straus and Giroux.

Fuentes Mares, José. 1983. *Poinsett: historia de una gran intriga.* Mexico City: Editorial Oceano.

Gallo, Joaquín. 1991. *Tepoztlán: personajes, descripciones y sucedidos.* Mexico City: Talleres Gráficos de la Cultura.

Gamio, Manuel. 1916. *Forjando patria; pro nacionalismo.* Mexico City: Editorial Porrúa.

———. 1922. *La población del valle de Teotihuacán.* 2 vols. Mexico City: Secretaría de Agricultura y Fomento.

———. 1924. *Opiniones y juicios sobre la obra La población del valle de Teotihuacán.* Mexico City: Secretaría de Agricultura y Fomento.

———. 1931. *The Mexican Immigrant, His Life-Story.* Chicago: University of Chicago Press.

García Canclini, Néstor. 1995. *Hybrid Cultures: Strategies for Entering and Leaving Modernity.* Minneapolis: University of Minnesota Press.

García Mora, Carlos, ed. 1987–88. *La antropología en México: panorama histórico.* 15 vols. Mexico City: Instituto Nacional de Antropología e Historia.

Garciadiego, Javier. 1996. *Rudos contra técnicos: la Universidad Nacional durante la revolución mexicana.* Mexico City: El Colegio de México.

Gerbi, Antonello. 1973. *The Dispute of the New World: The History of a Polemic, 1750–1900.* Pittsburgh: University of Pittsburgh Press.

————. 1985 (1975). *Nature in the New World: From Christopher Columbus to Gonzalo Fernández de Oviedo.* Pittsburgh: University of Pittsburgh Press.

Gerhard, Peter. 1970. "A Method for Reconstructing Precolumbian Political Boundaries in Central Mexico." *Journal de la Société des Americainistes* 49: 27–41.

————. 1981. "Un censo de la diócesis de Puebla en 1681." *Historia Mexicana* 30(4): 530–60.

————. 1993 (1972). *A Guide to the Historical Geography of New Spain.* Rev. ed. Norman: University of Oklahoma Press.

Gibbon, Edward. 2000 (1776). *The History of the Decline and Fall of the Roman Empire.* (abridged version) London: Penguin Classics.

Giucci, Guillermo. 1992. *La conquista de lo maravilloso: el nuevo mundo.* Montevideo: Ediciones de Juan Darién.

Goffman, Erving. 1959. *The Presentation of Self in Everyday Life.* New York: Doubleday.

González Gamio, Ángeles. 1987. *Manuel Gamio, una lucha sin fin.* Mexico City: UNAM.

González Navarro, Moisés. 1994. *Los extranjeros en México y los mexicanos en el extranjero, 1821–1970.* 3 vols. Mexico City: El Colegio de México.

Gordon, Gary. 1997. "Peddlers, Pesos and Power: The Political Economy of Street Vending in Mexico City." Ph.D. dissertation, Department of History, University of Chicago.

Gramsci, Antonio. 1971. *Selection from the Prison Notebooks.* New York: International Publishers.

Granados, Luis Fernando. 1998. "Sueñan las piedras: alzamiento ocurrido en la ciudad de México, 14, 15 y 16 de septiembre, 1847." Licenciatura thesis, Facultad de Filosofía y Letras, UNAM.

Greenberg, James B. 1994. "Capital, Ritual, and Boundaries of the Closed Corporate Community." In *Articulating Hidden Histories: Exploring the Influence of Eric R. Wolf,* ed. Jane Schneider and Rayna Rapp. Berkeley: University of California Press. 67–82.

Greenblatt, Stephen. 1992. *Marvelous Possessions.* Chicago: University of Chicago Press.

Gruzinski, Serge. 1989. *Man-Gods in the Mexican Highlands: Indian Power and Colonial Society, 1520–1800.* Stanford, Calif.: Stanford University Press.

————. 1990. *La Guerre des images: De Christophe Colomb à 'Blade Runner.'* Paris: Fayard.

Guardino, Peter. 1996. *Peasants, Politics, and the Formation of Mexico's National State: Guerrero, 1800–1857.* Stanford, Calif.: Stanford University Press.

Guerra, François-Xavier. 1988. *México del antiguo régimen a la revolución.* 2 vols. Mexico City: Fondo de Cultura Económica.

————. 1992. *Modernidad e independencias: ensayos sobre las revoluciones hispánicas.* Madrid: Mapfre.

————. 1994 "The Spanish-American Tradition of Representation and Its European Roots." *Journal of Latin American Studies* 26(1): 1–35.

————. 2000. "The Implosion of the Spanish American Empire: Emerging Statehood and Collective Identities." In *The Collective and the Public in Latin America: Cultural Identities and Political Order,* ed. Luis Roniger and Tamar Herzog. Brighton: Sussex Academic Press. 71–94.

Guerra, François-Xavier, and Annick Lamperière, eds. 1998. *Los espacios públicos en Iberoamérica: ambigüedades y problemas, siglos XVIII–XIX.* Mexico City: Fondo de Cultura Económica.

Habermas, Jürgen. 1991. *The Structural Transformation of the Public Sphere.* Cambridge: MIT Press.

Handler, Richard. 1994. "Is Identity a Useful Concept?" In *Commemorations: The Politics of National Identity,* ed. John R. Gillis. Princeton, N.J.: Princeton University Press. 27–40.

Harootunian, Harry. 2000. *History's Disquiet: Modernity, Cultural Practice, and the Question of Everyday Life.* New York: Columbia University Press.

Haskett, Robert. 1991. *Indigenous Rulers: An Ethnohistory of Town Government in Colonial Cuernavaca.* Albuquerque: University of New Mexico Press.

Hassig, Ross. 1988. *Aztec Warfare: Imperial Expansion and Political Control.* Norman: University of Oklahoma Press.

———. 1992. *Mesoamerican Warfare.* Berkeley: University of California Press.

Heau, Catherine. 1984. "Trova popular e identidad cultural en Morelos." In *Morelos: cinco siglos de historia regional,* ed. Horacio Crespo. Mexico City: Centro de Estudios Históricos del Agrarismo en México. 261–74.

Herzog, Tamar. 1992. "La gaceta de Lima (1756–1761): la restructuración de la realidad y sus funciones." *Histórica* (Lima), 16: 33–61.

Hobsbawm, Eric, and Terence Ranger, eds. 1983. *The Invention of Tradition.* Cambridge: Cambridge University Press.

Holston, James. 1989. *The Modernist City: An Anthropological Critique of Brasília.* Chicago: University of Chicago Press.

———. 2000. "Alternative Modernities: Statecraft and Religious Imagination in the Valley of the Dawn." *American Ethnologist* 26(3): 605–32.

Horowitz, Irving Louis. 1974. *The Rise and Fall of Project Camelot.* Cambridge: MIT Press.

Ingham, John. 1970. "On Mexican Folk Medicine." *American Anthropologist* 72: 76–87.

Jaguaribe, Beatriz. 1998. "Modernist Ruins." *Public Culture* 10(4): 294–317.

Johnson, John. 1980. *Latin America in Caricature.* Austin: University of Texas Press.

Johnson, Julie Greer. 1987. *The Book in the Americas.* Providence, R.I.: John Carter Brown Library.

Joseph, Gilbert, and Daniel Nugent, eds. 1994. *Everyday Forms of State Formation.* Chapel Hill, N.C.: Duke University Press.

Katz, Friedrich. 1998. *The Life and Times of Pancho Villa.* Stanford, Calif.: Stanford University Press.

Kirshenblatt-Gimblett, Barbara. 1998. *Destination Culture: Tourism, Museums, and Heritage.* Berkeley: University of California Press.

Knight, Alan. 1990. "Racism, Revolution and Indigenismo: Mexico, 1910–1940." In *The Idea of Race in Latin America, 1870–1940,* ed. Richard Graham. Austin: University of Texas Press. 71–114.

———. 1994. "Popular Culture and the Revolutionary State in Mexico." *Hispanic American Historical Review* 74(3): 395–444.

Krauze, Enrique. 1986. *Por una democracia sin adjetivos.* Mexico City: Joaquín Mortiz.

———. 1992. *Textos heréticos.* Mexico City: Grijalbo.

———. 1998a. "Adiós Míster Lomnitz." *Milenio* 40 (June 1).

———. 1998b. "El mártir de Chicago." *Milenio* 38 (May 18).

———. 1998c. *Mexico: Biography of Power.* New York: HarperCollins.

Lafaye, Jacques. 1977. *Quetzalcoatl y Guadalupe: la formación de la conciencia nacional en México.* Mexico City: Fondo de Cultura Económica.

Lamperière, Annick. 1998. "República y publicidad a fines del antiguo régimen." In *Los espacios públicos en Iberoamérica: ambigüedades y problemas, siglos XVIII–XIX*, ed. François-Xavier Guerra and Annick Lamperière. Mexico City: Fondo de Cultura Económica. 55–60.

Lavallé, Bernard. 1993. *Las promesas ambiguas: ensayos sobre criollismo colonial en los andes.* Lima: Pontificia Universidad Católica del Perú.

Leonard, Irving. 1959. *Baroque Times in Old Mexico.* Ann Arbor: University of Michigan Press.

Levine, Lawrence. 1996. *The Opening of the American Mind: Canons, Culture and History.* Boston: Beacon Press.

Lewis, Oscar. 1951. *Life in a Mexican Village.* Urbana: University of Illinois Press.

———. 1959. *Five Families.* New York: Vintage Books.

———. 1964a. *The Children of Sánchez.* New York: Basic Books.

———. 1964b. *Pedro Martínez.* New York: Random House.

Limón, José. 1998. *American Encounters: Greater Mexico, the United States, and the Erotics of Culture,* Boston: Beacon Press.

Lira, Andrés. 1983. *Comunidades indígenas frente a la Ciudad de México.* Mexico City: El Colegio de México.

Liss, Peggy K. 1975. *Mexico under Spain, 1521–1556: Society and the Origins of Nationality.* Chicago: University of Chicago Press.

Lockhart, James. 1992. *The Nahuas after the Conquest.* Stanford, Calif.: Stanford University Press.

Lomnitz, Claudio. 1982. *Evolución de una sociedad rural.* Mexico City: Sepochentas.

———. 1992a. *Exits from the Labyrinth: Culture and Ideology in Mexican National Space.* Los Angeles: University of California Press.

———. 1992b. "Usage politique de l'ambigüité: Le cas mexicain." *L'Homme* 32(1): 91–102.

———. 1994. "Decadence in Times of Globalization." *Cultural Anthropology* 9(2): 257–67.

———. 1998a. "Respuesta al señor Augusto Hugo Peña." *Excelsior-(El Buho),* August 8.

———. 1998b. "Respuesta del Krauzificado de Chicago." *Milenio* 39 (May 25).

———. 1999. *Modernidad indiana: nación y mediación en México.* Mexico City: Planeta.

Lomnitz, Larissa. 1975. *Networks and Marginality: Life in a Mexican Shantytown.* New York: Academic Press.

———. 1987. "Las relaciones horizontales y verticales en la estructura social urbana de México." In *La heterodoxia recuperada: en torno a Ángel Palerm,* ed. Susana Glantz. Mexico City: Fondo de Cultura Económica. 515–58.

Lomnitz, Larissa, Claudio Lomnitz, and Ilya Adler. 1994 (1990). "Functions of the Form: Power Play and Ritual in the 1988 Mexican Presidential Campaign." In *Constructing Culture and Power in Latin America,* ed. Daniel Levine. Ann Arbor: University of Michigan Press. 357–402.

Lomnitz, Larissa, and Marisol Pérez Lizaur. 1987. *A Mexican Elite Family.* Princeton, N.J.: Princeton University Press.

López Austin, Alfredo. 1988 (1980). *The Human Body and Ideology: Concepts of the Ancient Nahuas.* Salt Lake City: University of Utah Press.

Lorey, David. 1993. *The University System and the Economic Development of Mexico since 1929.* Stanford, Calif.: Stanford University Press.

Love, Edgar. 1971. "Marriage Patterns of Persons of African Descent in a Colonial Mexico City Parish." *Hispanic American Historical Review* 51: 79–91.

Lynch, John. 1992. *Caudillos in Spanish America, 1800–1850*. Oxford: Clarendon Press.

Machlachlan, Colin, and Jaime Rodríguez. 1980. *The Forging of the Cosmic Race: A Reinterpretation of Colonial Mexico*. Berkeley: University of California Press.

Macune, Charles. 1978. *El estado de México y la federación mexicana, 1823–1835*. Mexico City: Fondo de Cultura Económica.

Malkki, Lisa. 1995. *Purity and Exile: Violence, Memory, and National Cosmology among Hutu Refugees in Tanzania*. Chicago: University of Chicago Press.

Mallon, Florencia. 1995. *Peasant and Nation: The Making of Post-Colonial Mexico and Peru*. Los Angeles: University of California Press.

Márquez, Enrique. 1977. "La casa de los señores Santos." M.A. thesis: Centro de Estudios Internacionales, El Colegio de México.

Marzal, Manuel. 1981. *Historia de la antropología indigenista: México y Perú*. Lima: Pontificia Universidad Católica del Perú.

Mauss, Marcel. 1954. *The Gift: Forms and Functions of Exchange in Archaic Societies*. London: Coehn and West.

Mayer Celis, Laura Leticia. 1995. "Estadística y comunidad científica en México, 1826–1848." Doctoral thesis, Centro de Estudios Históricos, El Colegio de México.

Méndez Lavielle, Guadalupe. 1987. "La quiebra política (1965–1976)." In *La antropología en México: panorama histórico*, vol. 2, ed. Carlos García Mora. Mexico City: Instituto Nacional de Antropología e Historia. 339–438.

Meyer, Jean. 1971. "Los obreros en la Revolución Mexicana: Los 'Batallones Rojos'." *Historia Mexicana* 81: 1–137.

———. 1993. "La junta protectora de las clases menesterosas: indigenismo y agrarismo en el segundo imperio." In *Indio, nación y comunidad en el siglo diecinueve*, ed. Antonio Escobar. Mexico City: CIESAS. 329–64.

Meyer, Lorenzo. 1995. *Liberalismo autoritario: las contradicciones del sistema político mexicano*. Mexico City: Editorial Oceano.

———. 1998. "En México nunca se hizo una historia oficial." Interview with Arturo Mendoza Monciño. *Milenio* 37 (May 11).

Molina Enríquez, Andrés. 1978 (1909). *Los grandes problemas nacionales*. Mexico City: ERA.

Monsiváis, Carlos. 1987. *Entrada libre*. Mexico City: ERA.

———. 1995. *Los rituales del caos*. Mexico City: ERA.

———. 1997. *Mexican Post-Cards*. New York: Verso.

Mora, José María Luis. 1963. *Obras sueltas*. 2 vols. Mexico City: Editorial Porrúa.

Moreno, Rafael. 1989. "La ciencia y la formación de la mentalidad nacional en Alzate." *Quipú* 6(1): 93–108.

Morse, Richard. 1982. *El espejo de Próspero*. Mexico City: Siglo XXI.

Mundy, Barbara. 1995. *The Mapping of New Spain: Indigenous Cartography and the Maps of the Relaciones Geográficas*. Chicago: University of Chicago Press.

Myers, Jorge. 1995. *Orden y virtud: el discurso republicano en el régimen rosista*. Buenos Aires: Universidad Nacional de Quilmes.

Nutini, Hugo. 1995. *Wages of Conquest: The Mexican Aristocracy in the Context of Western Aristocracies*. Ann Arbor: University of Michigan Press.

Obeyesekere, Gananath. 1992. *The Apotheosis of Captain Cook: European Mythmaking in the Pacific*. Princeton, N.J.: Princeton University Press.

O'Gorman, Edmundo. 1969. *La supervivencia política novohispana: reflexiones sobre el monarquismo mexicano.* Mexico City: Condumex.

———. 1977. *México: el trauma de su historia.* Mexico City: UNAM.

Ortega y Gasset, José. 1921. *España invertebrada: bosquejo de algunos pensamientos históricos.* Madrid: Calpe.

Ortner, Sherry. 1999. "Some Futures of Anthropology." *American Ethnologist* 26(4): 984–91.

Ouweneel, Arij. 1990. *The Indian Community of Colonial Mexico.* Amsterdam: CEDLA.

———. N.d. "From Tlahtocayotl to Gobernadoryotl: A Critical Scrutiny of Some Characteristics of Indigenous Rule in Eighteenth-Century Mexico." Unpublished manuscript.

Pagden, Anthony. 1982. *The Fall of Natural Man: The American Indian and the Origins of Comparative Ethnology.* New York: Cambridge University Press.

———. 1990. *Spanish Imperialism and the Political Imagination.* New Haven: Yale University Press.

Palmer, Colin. 1976. *Slaves of the White God: Blacks in Mexico, 1570–1650.* Cambridge: Harvard University Press.

Paz, Octavio. 1981 (1950). *El laberinto de la soledad, Posdata, y Vuelta al laberinto de la soledad.* Mexico City: Tezontle, Fondo de Cultura Económica.

———. 1982. *Sor Juana Inés de la Cruz o las trampas de la fe.* Mexico City: Fondo de Cultura Económica.

Peña, Augusto Hugo. 1998. "Acerca de la fábrica de mentiras de Enrique Krauze." *Excelsior (El Buho),* July 26.

Peña, Guillermo de la. 1981 (1980). *A Legacy of Promises: Agriculture, Politics and Ritual in the Morelos Highlands.* Austin: University of Texas Press.

———. 1982. *Herederos de promesas.* Mexico City: Casa Chata.

———. 1995. "Nationals and Foreigners in the History of Mexican Anthropology." In *The Conditions of Reciprocal Understanding,* ed. James W. Fernandez and Milton B. Singer. Chicago: University of Chicago Center for International Studies. 276–303.

Phelan, John Leddy. 1970. *The Millennial Kingdom of the Franciscans in the New World.* Berkeley: University of California Press.

Pietschmann, Horst. 1996 (1972). *Las reformas borbónicas y el sistema de intendencias en Nueva España: un estudio político administrativo.* Mexico City: Fondo de Cultura Económica.

Pincus, Stephen. 1998. "The English Nationalist Revolution of 1688–1689." Unpublished manuscript.

Postone, Moishe. 1996. *Time, Labor, and Social Domination: A Reinterpretation of Marx's Critical Theory.* New York: Cambridge University Press.

Pozas Horcasitas, Ricardo. 1993. *La democracia en blanco: el movimiento médico en México, 1964–1965.* Mexico City: Siglo XXI.

Prakash, Gyan. 1999. *Another Reason: Science and the Imagination of Modern India.* Princeton, N.J.: Princeton University Press.

Pratt, Mary Louise. 1992. *Imperial Eyes: Travel Writing and Transculturation.* New York: Routledge.

Puig, Juan. 1992. *Entre el río Perla y el Nazas: la China decimonónica y sus braceros emigrantes, la colonia china de Teorreón y la matanza de 1911.* Mexico City: CONACULTA.

Ramos, Samuel. 1965 (1938). "El perfil del hombre y la cultura en México." In *Samuel Ramos: trayectoria filosófica y antología de textos,* ed. Agustín Basave. Monterrey: Centro de Estudios Humanísticos de la Universidad de Nuevo León.

Redfield, Robert. 1930. *Tepoztlán: A Mexican Village*. Chicago: University of Chicago Press.

———. 1941. *The Folk Culture of Yucatan*. Chicago: University of Chicago Press.

Reséndez, Andrés. 1997. "Caught between Profits and Rituals: National Contestation in Texas and New Mexico, 1821–1848." Ph.D. dissertation, Department of History, University of Chicago.

Reyes, Aurelio de los. 1991. *Manuel Gamio y el cine*. Mexico City: UNAM.

Reyes Heroles, Federico. 1995. *Sondear a México*. Mexico City: Editorial Oceano.

Ribot García, Luis, ed. 1995. *El Tratado de Tordesillas y su época*, 3 vols. Madrid: Junta de Castilla y de Aragón.

Rigdon, Susan. 1988. *The Culture Facade: Art, Science, and Politics in the Work of Oscar Lewis*. Urbana: University of Illinois Press.

Riva Palacio, Raymundo. 1997. "A Culture of Collusion: The Ties That Bind the Press and the PRI." In *A Culture of Collusion: An Inside Look at the Mexican Press*. ed. William A. Orme Jr. Miami: North-South Center Press. 21–32.

Rodríguez, Jaime O. 1983. *Down from Colonialism*. Los Angeles: Chicano Studies Research Center Publications, University of California.

Rogers, Daniel. 1998. *Atlantic Crossings: Social Politics in a Progressive Age*. Cambridge: Harvard University Press.

Rosas, María. 1997. *Tepoztlán, crónica de desacatos y resistencia*. Mexico City: Era.

Rouse, Roger. 1995. "Thinking through Transnationalism: Notes on the Cultural Politics of Class Relations in the Contemporary United States." *Public Culture* 7(2): 353–403.

———. 1996 (1995). "Mexican Migration and the Social Space of Postmodernism." In *Between Two Worlds: Mexican Immigrants in the United States*, ed. David G. Gutierrez. Wilmington, Del.: SR Books. 247–63.

Rubenstein, Anne. 1998. *Bad Language, Naked Ladies, and Other Threats to the Nation: A Political History of Comic Books in Mexico*. Durham, N.C.: Duke University Press.

Rueda, Salvador. 1984. "La dinámica interna del zapatismo: consideración para el estudio de la cotidianeidad campesina en el área zapatista." In *Morelos: cinco siglos de historia regional*, ed. Horacio Crespo. Mexico City: Centro de Estudios Históricos del Agrarismo en México. 225–50.

Ruy Sánchez, Alberto. 1981. *Mitología de un cine en crisis*. Mexico City: Premia.

Sahagún, Fray Bernardino de. 1991. *Coloquios y doctrina cristiana*. Traducidos del náhuatl por Miguel León-Portilla. Mexico City: UNAM.

Sahlins, Marshall. 1976. *Culture and Practical Reason*. Chicago: University of Chicago Press.

———. 1985. *Islands of History*. Chicago: University of Chicago Press.

Said, Edward. 1993. *Culture and Imperialism*. New York: Knopf.

Scott, James. 1985. *Weapons of the Weak: Everyday Forms of Peasant Resistance*. New Haven: Yale University Press.

Secanella, Petra María. 1983. *El periodismo político en México*. Barcelona: Editorial Mitre.

Segovia, Rafael. 1980. "La decadencia de la democracia." *Razones* 24 (March–April).

Seed, Patricia. 1988. *To Love, Honor and Obey in Colonial Mexico*. Stanford, Calif.: Stanford University Press.

———. 1995. *Ceremonies of Possession in Europe's Conquest of the New World, 1492–1640*. Cambridge: Cambridge University Press.

Small, Albion W. 1909. *The Cameralists, the Pioneers of German Social Polity*. Chicago: University of Chicago Press.

Smith, Waldemar. 1977. *The Fiesta System and Economic Change.* New York: Columbia University Press.

Solares, Ignacio. 1989. *Madero, el otro.* Mexico City: Joaquín Mortiz.

Sommers, Doris. 1991. *Foundational Fictions: The National Romances of Latin America.* Berkeley: University of California Press.

Spencer, Herbert. 1892 (1857). "Progress: Its Law and Cause." In *Essays, Scientific, Political and Speculative,* vol. 1. New York: Appleton and Company. 8–62.

———. 1967 (1893). "The Inadequacy of 'Natural Selection.'" In *The Works of Herbert Spencer,* vol. 17. Osnabrück: Otto Zeller. 1–69.

Stein, Stanley, and Barbara Stein. 1971. "Concepts and Realities of Spanish Economic Growth, 1759–1789." *Historia ibérica, economía y sociedad en los siglos XVIII y XIX* (1): 103–20.

Stern, Alexandra. 1998. "Measuring Modernity: Eugenics in Mexico's Classrooms, 1920–1940." Paper Presented at the Mellon Latin American History Conference, Harvard University, April 3–4.

———. 1999a. "Buildings, Boundaries, and Blood: Medicalization and Nation-Building on the U.S.–Mexico Border, 1910–1930." *Hispanic American Historical Review* 79(1): 41–81.

———. 1999b. "Eugenics beyond Borders: Science and Medicalization in Mexico and the U.S. West, 1900–1950." Ph.D. dissertation, Department of History, University of Chicago.

Stern, Steve. 1995. *The Secret History of Gender: Women, Men, and Power in Late Colonial Mexico.* Chapel Hill: University of North Carolina Press.

Stevens, Donald F. 1991. *Origins of Instability in Early Republican Mexico.* Durham, N.C.: Duke University Press.

Suárez Cortés, Blanca Estela. 1987. "Las interpretaciones positivistas del pasado y el presente (1880–1910)." In *La Antropología en México,* vol. 2, ed. Carlos García Mora. Mexico City: Instituto Nacional de Antropología e Historia. 13–88.

Sullivan, Paul. 1989. *Unfinished Conversations: Mayas and Foreigners between Two Wars.* New York: Knopf.

Taussig, Michael. 1980. *The Devil and Commodity Fetishism in South America.* Chapel Hill: University of North Carolina Press.

———. 1987. *Shamanism, Colonialism and the Wild Man.* Chicago: University of Chicago Press.

Taylor, William. 1979. *Drinking, Homicide and Rebellion in Colonial Mexican Villages.* Stanford, Calif.: Stanford University Press.

Téllez Ortega, Javier. 1987. "La época de oro (1940–1968)." In *La antropología en México: panorama histórico,* vol. 2, ed. Carlos García Mora. Mexico City: Instituto Nacional de Antropología e Historia. 289–341.

Tenenbaum, Barbara. 1994. "Streetwise History: The Paseo de la Reforma and the Porfirian State, 1876–1910." In *Rituals of Rule, Rituals of Resistance: Public Celebrations and Popular Culture in Mexico,* ed. William Beezley, Cheryl Martin, and William French. Wilmington, Del.: SR Books. 127–50.

Tenorio-Trillo, Mauricio. 1996. *Mexico at the World's Fairs: Crafting a Modern Nation.* Berkeley: University of California Press.

———. 1999. "Stereophonic Scientific Modernisms: Social Science between Mexico and the United States, 1880s–1930s." *Journal of American History* 86(3): 1156–87.

Todorov, Tzvetan. 1981. *La conquête d'Amérique: La question de l'autre*. Paris: Seuil.

Turner, Victor. 1974. *Dramas, Fields and Metaphors*. Ithaca, N.Y.: Cornell University Press.

Van Young, Eric. 1986. "Millennium on the Northern Marches: The Mad Messiah of Durango and Popular Rebellion in Mexico, 1800–1815." *Comparative Studies in Society and History* 28(3): 385–413.

———. 1989. "Agustín Marroquín: The Sociopath as Rebel." In *The Human Condition in Latin America: The Nineteenth Century*, ed. Judith Ewell and William Beezley. Wilmington, Del.: SR Books. 17–38.

Vanderwood, Paul J. 1992 (1981). *Disorder and Progress: Bandits, Police, and Mexican Development*. Wilmington, Del.: SR Books.

Varela, Roberto. 1984. *Expansión de sistemas y relaciones de poder*. Mexico City: UNAM.

Vasconcelos, José. 1983 (1936). *Ulises criollo*. In *Memorias*, vol. 1. Mexico City: Fondo de Cultura Económica.

Vaughn, Mary Kay. 1994. "The Construction of the Patriotic Festival in Tecamachalco, Puebla, 1900–1946." In *Rituals of Rule, Rituals of Resistance: Public Celebrations and Popular Culture in Mexico*, ed. William Beezley, Cheryl English Martin, and William French. Wilmington, Del.: SR Books. 213–46.

Vázquez León, Luis. 1987. "La historiografía antropológica contemporánea en México." In *La Antropología en México panorama histórico*, vol. 1, ed. Carlos García Mora. Mexico City: Instituto Nacional de Antropología e Historia. 176–94.

Vázquez Valle, Irene. 1975. "Los habitantes de la Ciudad de México vistos a través del censo de 1753." Master's thesis, Centro de Estudios Históricos, El Colegio de México.

Velázquez Juárez, Pedro Antonio. 1986. "Etnozoología y cosmogonía en los Altos de Morelos." Licenciatura thesis, Departamento de Antropología. Universidad Autónoma Metropolitana-Iztapalapa.

Vélez-Ibáñez, Carlos. 1981. *Rituals of Marginality: Politics, Process, and Culture Change in Central Urban Mexico, 1969–1974*. Berkeley: University of California Press.

Verdery, Katherine. 1991. *National Ideology under Socialism: Identity and Cultural Politics in Ceausescu's Romania*. Berkeley: University of California Press.

Villaseñor y Villaseñor, Alejandro. 1962. *Biografías de los héroes y caudillos de la independencia*, 2 vols. Mexico City: Jus.

Villoro, Luis. 1967. *El proceso ideológico de la revolución de independencia*. Mexico City: UNAM.

Viqueira Albán, Juan Pedro. 1987. *¿Relajados o reprimidos? Diversiones públicas y vida social en la Ciudad de México durante el Siglo de las Luces*. Mexico City: Fondo de Cultura Económica.

Voekel, Pamela. 1987. "Scent and Sensibility: Pungency and Piety in the Making of the Veracruz *Gente Sensata*." Unpublished manuscript.

Wallerstein, Immanuel. 1974. *The Modern World System*. New York: Academic Press.

Walzer, Michael. 1992. *Regicide and Revolution*. New York: Columbia University Press.

Warman, Arturo. 1970. "Todos santos, todos difuntos." In *De eso que llaman antropología mexicana*, ed. Arturo Warman, Guillermo Bonfil, Margarita Nolasco, Mercedes Olivera, and Enrique Valencia. Mexico City: Editorial Nuestro Tiempo.

———. 1980 (1976). *"We Come to Object": The Peasants of Morelos and the National State*. Baltimore: Johns Hopkins University Press.

Wauchope, Robert, ed. 1976. *Handbook of Middle American Indians*. Vols. 12–15. Austin: University of Texas Press.

Weber, Max. 1977. *From Max Weber.* Ed. H. H. Gerth and C. Wright Mills. London: Routledge.

————. 1978. *Economy and Society.* 2 vols. Berkeley: University of California Press.

Weeks, Charles. 1987. *The Juárez Myth in Mexico.* Tuscaloosa: University of Alabama Press.

Weiner, Annette. 1992. *Inalienable Possessions.* Berkeley: University of California Press.

Widdifield, Stacie G. 1996. *The Embodiment of the National in Late Nineteenth Century Mexican Painting.* Tucson: University of Arizona Press.

Wise, David. 2000. *Cassidy's Run: The Secret Spy War over Nerve Gas.* New York, Random House.

Wolf, Eric. 1958. "The Virgin of Guadalupe: A Mexican National Symbol." *Journal of American Folklore* 71(1): 34–39.

Womack, John. 1969. *Zapata and the Mexican Revolution.* New York: Knopf.

Žižek, Slavoj. 1998. "Cyberspace, or, How to Traverse the Fantasy in the Age of the Retreat of the Big Other." *Public Culture* 10(3): 483–513.

Zolov, Eric. 1999. *Refried Elvis: The Rise of the Mexican Counterculture.* Berkeley: University of California Press.

# Index

twin cities, 138; and U.S. economic interests, 139
Bourbon reforms, 21, 23, 82; administrative ideas, 21; and Alexander von Humboldt, 8; decentralization, 25; as enlightened despotism, 8; and independence, 25; as modernizing, 82; as reformist movement, 25; as a response to backwardness, 25; threat to American Revolution, 25; threat to British Navy, 25
*Bozales*, 44
Brading, David, 16
Bribes, 61, 62
*Brujos*, 270
Bullfighting, 66, 71, 147, 162; as cause of incivility, 66; as spectacle that dulls reason, 66–67
Bulnes, Francisco, 95, 96; portrayal of Benito Juárez, 95
Bulstos, Hermenegildo, 101
Bureaucratic procedure: as mechanism of exclusion, 61
Bustamante, Carlos María, xi, 114

*Caballero Águila*: sculpture of, 102
*Caballero Español*: sculpture of, 102
*Cabecita de Teotihuacán*, 249
*Cabeza gigantesca de Hueyapan*, 247
Cabrera, Luis, 53; critique of the centenary of independence, 86; "Los dos patriotismos," 138; as pro-mestizo nationalist, 53
Calderón de la Barca, Fanny, 233
Calles, Plutarco Elías, 94, 104; building of the state, 74; development of Cuernavaca, 104; residence in Cuernavaca, 137
*Calpulli*, 38, 40, 51, 173, 174; *calpulteotl*, 37; communitarian ideology of, 37; as cornerstone of community, 37; and kinship relations, 37; and lineage, 37; primordial unit of, 39
Cancian, Frank, 161–62
*Cantina*, 149
Cárdenas, Lázaro, 104, 105, 133, 137, 219; construction of Pan American Highway, 104; formula for modernization, 114; nationalization of oil industry, 74, 104

Carnival, 188, 189, 190, 192
Carranza, Venustiano, 98
Carrasco, Pedro, 73
Carrillo, Alejandro, 255
Caso, Alfonso: founding director of INAH, 260; founding director of ENAH, 260
Castells, Manuel, 152
Caste wars, 49, 199; Chan Santa Cruz, 50; Chiapas Highlands, 50; Huasteca of San Luis, Potosí, 50; Mixteca region, 50; as national movements, 49; Yaquis of Sonora, 50; of Yucatán, 50
Castille, 8
*Castizo*, 50
Catholicism, 23, 47, 63, 85, 86, 133
*Catrines*, 180
Caupolicán, xiii
Census, 3; of 1895, 205; and Viceroy Juan Güemes Pacheco, 198–99; in Tepoztlán, 172, 173
Center-periphery, 177; change to the dialectic, 185; coexistence of, 165; conflation of scheme, 167; decline in the dialectic, 190; discourses of, 165–66; paradox of, 166; and political language, 165; problems with, 191–93; shifts in, 186; and Tepoztlán, 165; transformation of, 187–88
Central power, 88, 105
Centralization, 165
CEPES (*Centro de Estudios Políticos y Sociales*), 76
Certificates of blood purity, 16, 42
Charles III, 9, 24, 25; subject category of, 9
Charles V, 15
Chavero, Alfredo, 230, 252; creation of racial narrative, 245–50; *México a través de los siglos*, 245; Otomis, 245, 246; portrayal of Negro, Otomi, and Nahoa races, 246; similarity with foreign descriptions, 246
Chiapas: neo-Zapatistas, 158
Chicago School of Economics, 140
*Chinelos*, 188, 190
Christian: patriarchs, 68; Tepoztlán census, 173

image, 138; Olympics, 133, 135, 138; ugliness of, 226

Discourse of the home, 58, 59, 61; according to DaMatta, 58; applied to the good *pueblo*, 67; familial idioms, 59

Discourse of the street, 58; according to DaMatta, 58; as discourse of liberal citizenship, 58

Dismodernity, 110, 122

*Dolce far niente* (1880), 239

Dumont, Louis, 166

Durazo, Arturo, 112

Earthquake of 1985, xi

Echeverría, Luis, 104, 222, 227; and Cosío Villegas, 222; electrification of the countryside, 104; highways, 133

Education, 60, 205

*Ejidos*: failure to create propertied citizenry, 75

Election of July 2, 2000, xxi

Elections: as sources of revenue, 78

Eley, Geoff: definition of public sphere, 265–66

Elites, 143, 200; construction of public opinion, 147; corruption of, 213; Creole, 30; discourse of messianism, 70; forms of discussion, 148; lack of public forum, 148; Masonic lodge membership, 30; portrayed as foreign, 144; and public opinion, 147; Tepoztecan, 174; virtuous and vicious, 70

*El pueblo*, 155

*El que se enoja, pierde*, 60, 78; meaning of, 60

ENAH (National School of Anthropology and History), 231, 254; expulsion of G. Bonfil, 232

*Encomendar*, 16

England, 15, 21

Enlightenment, 4, 154

Escalante, Fernando, 84, 249; arguments on citizenship, 71–72; fictitious character of the citizen, 84; opposition to Daniel Cosío Villegas, 72

*Español*, 17, 18, 33, 44, 50, 154; dominant caste, 21; as "Old Christians," 18

Estrada, Agustín, 97

Estrada, Juan, 242

Ethnographic state: definition of, 136

Eugenics: and postrevolutionary government, 139

Europeans, 50

Evans, Colonel Albert, 234

*Excursión al puente de Metlac*, 105

Exposición Iberoamericana de Sevilla, 102

Expropriation: failure to create propertied citizenry, 75

*Ex-voto giving thanks to the Virgin of Guadalupe for a successful medical operation*, 26

Familial idioms, 59

Felipe, Don, 272, 273, 285; Fiesta de Quetzalcoatl, 273; and national Mexican anthem, 273

Fernando VII: portrait of, 92

Fiestas, 150, 156, 161, 190; and campaign events, 162; and corruption, 162; Fiesta de Quetzalcoatl, 273, 285; and patriotism, 155; and use of sports, 155

Filipinas, 15

Films, 118, 126; distribution of, 118

Fiore, Joachim de, 15

*Five Families*: reviews of, 258

Flores Magón, Ricardo, 151

Fondo de Cultura Economica, 219, 259

Foucault, Michel, xxii, 202, 210; definition of biopower, 14; definition of governmentality, 198; governmentality, xxii; "history from the present," 213

Foreigners, 16, 134, 140–41; attraction to indigenous peoples, 135; business, 131–32, 140; challenge to nationalists, 140–42; destabilization of, 135; European, 134; investments, 140, 252; nationalist reactions to, 135; North American, 134

Franciscan missionaries, 15

Freemasonry, 29, 30, 31, 146; masons, 31; Masonic lodges as networks, 30; Masonic organizations, 31; and Mexican nationalism, 31; Joel Poinsett, 31; as political parties, 31; rite of York, 30, 31, 32; role following independence,

clergy, 86; destruction of towns, 84; emancipation of slaves, 62; end to tribute, 62; essay by Victor Turner, 109; excommunication endorsed by Archbishop of Mexico, 85; excommunication of, 84–85; level differences between castes, 62; martyred by Spaniards, 69; *Mexico: Biography of Power,* 224; response to excommunication, 85; as scientifically inclined, 202

Hippie movement, 134–35, 171, 186

Hispanicized, 174

Historians: Latin Americanists, 4; reaction to Benedict Anderson, 4

Holism: definition of, 228–29

*Hon. William Seward Traveling in Mexico,* 238

*Horse and the Zapilotes, The,* 234

Huerta, Victoriano, 98

Huitzilopochtli, 39

Human rights, 56, 57; recodification of, 56

Iberians, 46

Identity production, 128

IEPES *(Instituto de Estudios Políticos y Sociales),* 76

Illegal immigrants, 139

*Imagen de Jura con retrato de Fernando VII,* 92

*Imagined Communities:* and Anderson, 3; critique of, 3. *See also* Benedict Anderson

IMF (International Monetary Fund), 129

Immigration: as critical perspective, xiii

INAH *(Instituto Nacional de Antropología e Historia),* 231, 254

Inca, 16, 21

Independence, xiv, 5, 13, 14, 29, 33, 86, 149, 202; and American War of Independence, 27; and Bourbon reforms, 25; and Catholicism, 47; and citizenship, 62; Constitution of Cádiz, 27; Creole symbols, 47; *cuerpo unido de nación,* 25; European influences of, 4, 83–84; failure to centralize, 87; and governmentality, 198, 203; and governmental state, 198, 199; historiography of, 4; and indigenous communities, 48; lack of Creole bourgeoisie, 30; lack of stability, 233–34;

and mestizo, 50, monarchists, 87; national consciousness, xiv; nationalization of the church, 47; notions of caste, 50; practical concerns of nationalism, 46; process of, 62; and public sphere, 150; radical insurgents, 87; reliance on Spanish legal thought, 87; role of communities, 10; role of Freemasonry, 30; Spain against French invaders, 27; state power, 83; territorial consolidation of, 127; transformation of Creole patriotism, 46; view of Anderson, 4

Indian, 5, 16, 33, 36, 37, 44, 46, 48, 50, 52, 55, 63, 153, 191, 263, 267; and citizenship, 51; collective identity of, 42; communities, 267; conversion of, 153; described as *nacos,* 111–112, 114; dislocation of, 42; governors, 274–75; ladinoization, 45, 275; legal category of, 41; as less likely to commit crimes, 244; and marriage, 42; massacres of, 52; mortality of, 40; population movements, 40; in Querétaro, 243; racial category of, 41; republics, 8; rulers, 168; and theft, 244; tribute, 85; women, 17. *See also* Aztecs; Inca; *Mazahuas;* Otomi

Indianness, 112, 170, 172, 192

*Indigenismo,* 49, 51, 53, 103, 109, 231, 232; aims of, 232; as atomizing, 262; a defense against U.S. society, 103; description of, 231; distinct from liberalism, 51; against foreign aggression, 54; incorporation of the Indian, 232; maintenance of indigenous communities, 49; against neocolonial exploitation, 54; and Tepoztlán, 170, 179

*Indigenista,* 97, 134; art, 97; export of national anthropology, 254; Rodríguez Puebla, 48, 51

Indigenous communities, 40, 146; adoption of saints, 41; Christian worship, 40; as corporate structures, 204; dislocated Indians, 41–42; and Benito Juárez, 51; links with family, 40; links with gods, 40; links with land, 40; loss of legal protection, 150; organization of labor groups, 40; organized by race, 41;

constitution, 96–97; messianic image of, 98; as a spiritualist, 207; toppling of Díaz, 206–7

Madrid, Miguel de la, 55, 223; and educational system, 215; election of, 222; *Mexico: Biography of Power,* 222; nationalist reaction to, 55; reforms of, 55; subsidies to intellectual groups, 219; as well-meaning democrat, xxi

*Magníficos* ("Magnificent Seven"), 231, 232, 261

Mallon, Florencia, 65, 220–21

Maps, 3, 199

*Maquiladoras,* 139

Maroons, 45

Martyrdom, 89, 95, 109; degradation of insurgent priests, 89; images used by aspiring presidents, 109; linked to ideal of sovereignty, 94; martyred national leaders, 89; martyrs of independence, 89; Álvaro Obregón, 94; and presidential persona, 94; proof of cleanliness, 280; Guadalupe Victoria, 94; Pancho Villa, 94

Marx, Karl: and Mexican education, 140

Masses: as obstacles to progress, 65; insufficiently civilized, 65

*Más vale cabeza de ratón que cola de león,* 118

Maximilian, 87, 241; boulevards of, 133; killing of, 87–88; and Tepoztlán, 176

Mayas: sold as slaves, 235

*Mazahuas,* 37

Media, 117, 152, 157, 158, 284; and social persona, 159

Medical doctors' movement, 151–52, 214

Mendieta, Gerónimo, 15

Merchants, 146, 147, 168, 200

*Mestizaje,* 51

*Mestizo,* 16, 50, 53, 263; feminine arguments for, 53–54; as fortified version of the indigenous race, 53; and independence, 51; masculine arguments for, 53–54; nationalization of, 54; as national race, 52; protagonist of national history, 53; revaluation of, 52

Mexican Americans, xii

Mexican anthropology: challenges to foreigners, 255; contemporary crisis of, 230; final phase of, 262; and Great National Problems, 260; historical development of, 230, 233; *indigenismo,* 231; institutional infrastructure, 230; modern aesthetics, 231; and nationalism, 231; and 1968 student movement, 231, 261; process of, 230–31; romanticization of Indians, 259; Bernardino de Sahagún, 238; stabilization of national image, 242; state absorption of, 232, 260; strategies of government, 242

Mexican democrats: critique of corporate state, 77; rise of democracy

Mexican history: and public sphere, 157; theories of, 81

Mexican nationalism, 53, 86, 87; Luis Cabrera, 53; contemporary discourse of, 55; under current regime, 55; formulation of, 53; foundational strain, 86; Manuel Gamio, 53; and mestizo, 54; as modernizing, 53–54; Andrés Molina Enríquez, 53; principal ideologists, 53; as protectionist, 53–54; as revolutionary nationalism, 53

Mexican nationality: and communitarian ideologies, 35; historical product of Mexican peoples, 35; importance of *mestizaje,* 51; after independence, 46; and liberals, 51; and Mexican Revolution, 52; during pre-Hispanic period, 35

Mexicanness, 224

Mexican proverbs, 60, 78, 118, 176

Mexican Revolution, xi, xxi, 52, 75, 86, 139, 178, 183, 199, 205, 216, 218; degradation of citizenship, 79; and democracy, 216; goals of, 216; ideologues of, 86; *indigenista* anthropology, 231; *indigenistas,* 231; and indigenous world, 134; "intellectual caudillos," 218; *Mexico: Biography of Power,* 223–24; and peasant organizations, 151; popular public spheres, 279–80; project for nationality and modernity, 114; and proletarian organizations, 151; rapid modernization, 79; and role of intellectuals,

210; teachings of, 121; and Tepoztlán, 178; watershed for nationality, 52

Mexico: ambiguity of status, 127; consciousness of backward condition, xvii; desire of nationality, xiv; intellectual and artistic production, 210; labeled "developing nation," xviii; narratives of Mexican people, xvii; nationalism of, 4; source of nationality, xiv; state parties, 75; usage of symbols, 47

*México a través de los siglos*, 245–50; evolutionary scheme of, 245; interpretation of pre-Columbian past, 245; Nahoa, 246, Otomis, 245–46

*Mexico at the World's Fairs*, 241

*Mexico: Biography of Power*: absence of citations, 221; Alemán, 223; Ávila Camacho, 223; Emilio Azcárraga, 224; comparison to National Museum of Anthropology, 226; composition of, 215–16; Cosío Villegas, 221, 224; Porfirio Díaz, 223; Díaz Ordaz, 222, 223; election of de la Madrid, 222–23; Hidalgo, 224; and historical evidence, 222; intellectual production, 215; Krauzometer, 222; *Labyrinth of Solitude*, 222; de la Madrid, 223; metaphors for power, 224; Mexican history as a struggle for democracy, 216–17; Mexican Revolution, 223–24; as a mirror of presidential power, 220; nationalist myth, 226; O'Gorman, 221; opinions stated as historical facts, 222, 223; Paz, 221; readings of, 218; sources of, 220; Spanish versus English translation, 222; treatment of 1968 student movement, 221; José Vasconcelos, 224; Zapata, 224; Zedillo, 223. *See also* Enrique Krauze

Mexico City, xii, 158, 171, 175, 178; as "balcony of the republic," xii; crowds, 60; drivers, 60; earthquake of 1985, 184; freeway to Tepoztlán, 184; growth of, 152; lack of services, 60; mediated movements, 159; and national statistics, 205; periodicals, 200; politeness of, 59–60; during the Porfiriato, 206; prostitution, 137; and public opinion, xii; and pubic

sphere, 114; and role of intellectuals, 114; seat of viceroyalty, 46; and Tepoztlán, 167, 186

*Mexico: Its Social Evolution*, 241, 243, 244, 245

*México Profundo*, 263

Meyer, Lorenzo, 213

*Miamicito*, 129

Migrants, xii, 142, 143, 188, 190, 192, 193; to Canada, 187; from Guerrero, 186; migratory process, xii; nationalist backlash against, 121; to Tepoztlán, 186; to the United States, 187

*Milenio*, 212, 213

Military leaders, 146, 147

Miners, 146, 147, 149

Moctezuma, 218, 241

*Modernidad indiana: Nación y mediación en México*, xix, xx

Modernist ruins, 213, 214, 215; and Tlatelolco massacre, 214

Modernization, xv, xx, 57, 82, 111, 122, 163; and corruption of morals, 131; critical to national state, 136; indigenized, xxi; and nationalist reactions, 138; and postrevolutionary government, 214; principles of 128; relationship with the state, 82; reproduction of social classes, 118–19; threats to nation states, 82; use of nationality, 114

Molina Enríquez, Andres, xvi, 53, 54, "action" and "resistance," 53–54; argument for mestizos, 53; mestizo ideology of, 53; as pro-mestizo nationalist, 53

Monsiváis, Carlos, xi, 55, 205

Mora, José María Luis, 48, 49, 83, 84; critique of Rodríguez Puebla, 49; and *indigenismo*, 49; interpretation of the constitution, 83

Morelos, José María, 29, 47, 85, 227; abolishment of slavery, 85; accusations against Spaniards, 29; Apatzingán constitution, 64; edict of 1810, 85–86; martyred by Spaniards, 69; national ideal of, 86; persistence of political spirit, 86; "sentiments of the nation," 158, 227; servants of the nation, 225

Morelos (state), 167, 266, 267, 271, 273, 279; construction, 183; industrialization, 183; migration to the United States, 183; postrevolutionary economic organization, 183; regional space, 182; state governor, 182, tourism, 183

Morenos, 45

Morrow, Dwight, 137

Mulattos, 16, 17

*Nación*, 7, 9, 13; and Benedict Anderson, 8; distinguished from *patria*, 9; extension of national identity, 8; and panimperial identity, 8; and sovereignty, 8; usage of, 7, 8

*Naco*, 120; Art-Naqueau, 113; categorical transformation of, 114; changing connotations of, 111; closet *nacos*, 113; as colonial imagery, 112; definition of *nacos* kitsch, 112; description of, 111; foreign-sounding names, 112–13; as lack of distinction, 113; lumpenpolitics of, 113; as mark of Indian, 114; and modernization, 113; Nac-Art, 113; *naquismo*, 112, 113; as sign of provincial backwardness, 111; similar process in Latin America, 112; threat to traditional political forms, 113; as urban aesthetic, 112

NAFTA (North American Free Trade Agreement), xxi, 108; backlash of, 121

Nahoa, 246

Nahuatl, 37, 172, 173, 192, 272, 273, 274, 278, 285; national anthem, 177; speakers, 174

Nation, xiii; 48; appeals to nationhood, 11; as Christian utopia, 86; and citizenship, 48; as community, 13, 35, 146; identification with homeland, 47; importance of blood, 43; importance of land, 43; intellectuals and nation building, 212; local process of state formation, xv; myths of, xiii; nationalization of the church, 47; and race, 27; redefinition of, 46; and sacrifice, 11; symbols of, xiii; transformation of semantics, 7

National culture: as dismodernity, 114

National history, 81, 139; failure to deliver, 81

National identity, xx, xxi, 14, 128, 132; adoption of foreign techniques, 130; changing aspects of, 111; formation of, 141; formed in transnational networks, 126; frames of contact, 130; internal business, 132; narratives of identity, 125; and neoliberalism, 129; production of, 125; production of "Mexico," 126; sociology of, 127; topography of, 130; women and children, 10

National image, 143; implementation of, 126; management of, 141

Nationalism, xxiii, xv, 5, 10, 11, 13, 54, 55, 120, 122, 191; alternatives for Mexican, 56, 83; and Benedict Anderson, xx, 3, 30, 200; bonds of dependence, 12; citizenship, 10, 11; and communitarianism, xvi, xx, 3, 33, 34; connected to consumption, 121; connected to work, 121; contradictory claims of, 126; Creole nationalism, 6; crisis of, xxi, 114; definition of, 6–7, 33; development of, 27; discourse of, 13; evolution of, 27; exclusion of Spaniards, 29; failure to reformulate, 122; formation of, 30; and fraternity, 12; freemasonry, 31; ideological construction, 132; as invented nature, 4, 7; under ISI, 121; and language, 14, 229; and linguistic identification, 5; and Mexican anthropology, xxiii; mythology, 151, 279; myths of, xiii; origins (anthropological stories), 233; polemical nature of the national question, 47; politics of, 122; power of, 12–13; and racism, 14; and religion, 14; revolutionary nationalism, 56; sacrifice, 7, 11; as a sign of modernity, 128; and sovereignty, xiv; standardization of, 125; and subject-formation, 3; substitute for religious community, 7; successor to religion, 3; thick description, 32; and transnational relations, 125; unity and the intelligentsia, 209; violence of, 30; of weak nations, 126

Prieto, Guillermo, xi, 250–51
Primordialist nationalism, 265
Primordial loyalties, 36, 40
Primordial titles, 40
*Principales*, 174
Print capitalism, 3, 5, 6, 14, 22, 33
Private sphere, 268
*Progresistas*, 268, 269, 280
Progress, 54
Proletarianization, 113
*Pronunciamientos*, 209
Protochronism, xix; definition of, xix
Puebla, Rodríguez, 48, 51
Puebla (state), 155
*Pueblo, El*, 78, 79, 80; bad *pueblo* as fodder for politicians, 71; discourse of good and bad *pueblo*, 70; portrayals of, 65; positive and negative, 65; substituted by progress, 79
Public opinion, xxii, 146, 156, 157, 159, 206, 208, 210, 266; concentrated in Mexico City, xii; and intellectuals, 197; lack of, 284; mechanisms of, xxii; and social movements, 152; subsidized by the state, 233
Public rallies: as corporate organism, 76; divided by sectors, 76; increase in participation, 78; 1988 PRI campaign, 76; use of dress, 76, 77; use of television stars, 117
Public sphere, xv, xxii, 10, 25, 82, 102, 145, 147, 149, 153, 159, 233; and collective actors, 150; definition of, 265; development of, 149; geography of, 146; and independence, 150; and local intellectuals, 283; media of, 266; obstacles for creation of, 163; and popular will, 156; preference for gossip, 158; and proletariat, 151; segmented quality of, 83

Quetzalcoatl, 47, 272

Race, 27, 33, 48, 55; "Old Christians," 32
Racial identity: manipulation of, 51
Racial ideologies: during colonial period, 50; and Indians, 50; and procreation, 50; Spanish forms of, 50

Railroads: centralization of the government, 72; under Juárez, 72; and public sphere, 205
Ramos, Samuel, 53, 74, 78; on Mexican national character, 73; *pelado* as enemy of good society, 73; *pelado* as massified citizen, 76; use of the *pelado*, 73
Ranchers, 155
*Reconquista*, 14, 15; importance of blood, 42; *limpieza de sangre*, 16; nationalization of the church, 42
Recycling: definition of, 118
Redfield, Robert, 166, 175, 182, 270; *correctos*, 192, 275; and orientalize, 166; radio interview, 255–56; *tontos*, 275
Regional cultures: composed of, 116; culture of, 115; dependence on commodities, 117; and telephone, 117; and television, 117
Religious festivities: and collective actors, 147, 150; slave and black, 147
*Representante de bienes communales*, 268
*Republica de indios*, 44
*Respeto*, 270–71; when doing ethnographic work, 270–71
Restored Republic, xx
*Reto del Tepozteco, El*, 281, 282
Revolutionary nationalism, 55–57; model of, 55; reanimation of, 56
Revolutionary state: and the church, 156; creation of corporate groups, 74–75; differences between Porfirian state, 74; forms of citizenship, 80
Revolutions, 207, 208
*Reyes, Los*, 189
Ritual, 151, 153, 159; appropriation of corruption, 146; and common culture, 155; connection with politics, 145; constitution of polity, 159–60; and corruption, 155; domination and subordination, 153; expansion of state institution, 157; importance during colonial period, 153; and political discourse, 154; production of, 146; and public opinion, xxii, 160; and public sphere, 145, 160; and rumor, 154–55; and schools, 155–56

Sonora, 52
Sovereignty, xiv, 81; dynamic of cultural production, 81; and *fueros*, 9; as *pater potestas*, 9; as point of reference, xv
Spain, 14, 15; Bourbon reforms, 21, 23, 82
Spaniards: intellectual representation, 276
Spanish: concept of, 17; legal category of, 16; legal notion of, 17
Spanish America, 5; administrative colonial practices, 5; enlightened monarchs, 200; following independence, 199; *gente sensata*, 200, 202; and nationalism, xx, 4; national symbols of, xiii; presidential power, 225; revolutions, 27; upper classes, 200; and Alexander von Humboldt, 199
Spanish conquest, 250; as origin of national race, 53; as a "war of images," 153
Spanish Cortes, 64
Spanish Enlightenment: and patriotism, 23
Spanish invasion of 1829, 70
Spanish language, 21, 32, 172; language of, 18; as modern form of Latin, 32; nationalization of the church, 18
Spanish last names, 174, 274
Spanish nationalism, 18, 21; built on religious militancy, 21; development of, 27
Spanishness, 9, 18; and civilization, 18; and connection with church, 18–19; and language, 18; national construction of, 18; and religion, 18; and territory, 18
Spencer, Herbert, 50, 52
Sports: and fiestas, 156
State formation: and intellectuals, 198; and population information, 198; role in creating national citizenry, 117
Statistics, 136, 204; in Chiapas, 244; as a measure of common good, 198; and mystique of modernity, 205; in Yucatán, 244
*Statue of the Mexican Goddess of War (or of death) Teoyaomiqui*, 240
Stavenhagen, Rodolfo, 232
Stern, Alexandra, 139, 252
Student movement (1968), xi, 77, 214, 216, 221, 226, 259; and *indigenistas*, 232,

254; and Mexican anthropology, 231, 232
Superbarrio, 158

Tacubaya, 179
Taxco, 266
*Teatro Santa Anna*, 90
*Tecolotes*, 269
Telephone, 116, 117
Televisa: and high culture, 116; and Enrique Krauze, 200; links to intellectual groups, 116; and "transition to democracy," 220
Television, 116, 117, 122, 156, 219
Tenochtitlán, 37
Tenorio-Trillo, Mauricio, 241, 249
Tepoztecan mythology, 168; center-periphery mythology, 168–69; story of El Tepoztecátl, 168–69
Tepoztecátl, El, 168–69, 181
*Tepozteco, El*, 181, 282; pseudonym of El Tepoztecátl, 181
Tepoztlán, xxii, 159, 161, 188, 189, 265, 266, 279, 285; antiprogressive discourse, 184; artificial flowers strategy, 176, 181, 192; *brujos*, 270; *calpullis* of, 173; *campesinos*, 280; carnival, 188–91; and Catholic church, 169; and citizenship, 286; Colonia Tepozteca, 179; and colonization, 184; constitution of, 167; constructed as peripheral, xxii; construction of the center, 169; and corruption, 267; and cultural mediation, 283; *curanderos*, 270–71; education, 186; elites, 174, 180; employment, 186; fiestas, 188–90; 1540 census, 173; foreigners, 185; as "Indian," 170; intellectuals, 169, 272, 277, 280, 282; *The Intruder*, 169–71; lack of communal voice, 276; land prices, 184, 185; location of, 167; make-up of jurisdiction, 173; Mexican Revolution, 178; migrants, 171–72, 185, 186, 187, 190, 192–93; multiculturalism, 186; *los notables*, 276, 277; Genovevo de la O, 179; Ome Tochtli, 173; and orientalization, 166; peasants, 167; peripheral status of, 167; political

CLAUDIO LOMNITZ is professor of history and anthropology at the University of Chicago. His areas of interest include politics, culture, and history. He is author of *Exits from the Labyrinth: Culture and Ideology in the Mexican National Space*, *Evolución de una sociedad rural*, and *Modernidad indiana: nueve ensayos sobre nación y mediación en México*.